Yes

(Is *BiO Spiritualism* the answer?)

BiO Spiritualism: Body, Mind and Spirit – Man's Means, Nature's End

First Edition

Gary Deering

RaIse Books, LLC / Publisher / St. Paul

Copyright © 1981, 2000-2006 by Gary Deering.
All rights reserved.

First edition 2006.

Cover Design by Karen Ross www.karenross.com
Printed in the United States of America
RaIse Books, LLC / Publisher
St. Paul, MN 55126

Library of Congress Control Number: 2005910403

ISBN 13: 978-0-9774996-0-1
ISBN 10: 0-9774996-0-X

Yes

(Is *BiO Spiritualism* the answer?)

Prologue:

I am not a genius but I am smart enough to figure out that *Objectivism* and *Biocentric psychology* are the *best* of their kind. And, though I am not a person who demands the best in everything, when it comes to *philosophy* and *psychology*, nothing but the best is good enough for me.

Consequently, I am an Objectivist. Not a Professional one and not just a sympathizer, but a full blown, my-life-has-been-thoroughly-and-completely-affected-by-it Objectivist. Is this book about that life? No. But since that life has to enter herein out of necessity it does so, for example, just like astronomers—*out of necessity*—have to study the *objects* of their science. That is, the objects of the astronomer are stars and planets *not* philosophy and psychology affected lives—these are the "objects" (existents) of *spiritualism*, qua science. So, where this book does refer to my life, it does so *only as a necessity* as I am an *object* of this new (*BiO Spiritualism*) science. (As *are* you and as you *will* be when *you* apply what you learn here to you, yourself and yu.)

This book is just as much about what one gets—or rather what one would get if one were a non-omniscient god who was curious as to what he will get—*after* he mixes three unique, individually *explosive* chemicals in the same test-tube and shakes the hell out of it.

The chemicals? Religion, Objectivism and Biocentric Psychology.

And [mixed & shaken] *in that order*.

I grew up in a small, southern Minnesota (USA) town (population less than a thousand). Played sports in High School. Graduated from Engineering College. Got married, had kids and an Engineering Career. Graduated from another college after going through a divorce and reconciliation. Failed at business and making my first [still to be realized] million dollars. Filed Bankruptcy. Succumbed to many cultural messages *except* the most important one: I did *not* sell my *reason* to religion. They tried to buy it (on the installment plan and they *almost* succeeded) but in the end they simply did not have enough value in their coffers to buy my soul.

You could say, Religion couldn't afford me.

So I repeat: I did *not* sell my reason to religion.

Or rather I should really say, thank god for Ayn Rand or I *might* have.

Nor did I, sell my *soul* to Objectivism.

Or rather I should really say, thank god for Dr. Nathaniel Branden or I *might* have.

That is, I was an X who chose Y and am now a Z.

Which is to say, I am at once a *one*-time neonate turned infant then developing child *now* fully grown through many natural and man-made stages who *chose* Religion, then Philosophy, then Psychology—that is, Christianity, Objectivism and Biocentric—as the ways and means to happiness.

Or rather I should really say: Thank god, I am (finally) happy.

In the noncontradictory sense of the term.

And/or I suppose you could say: I am a test-tube filled with happiness.

And my plans for tomorrow are to actualize my desire to become a beaker.

Joshua Deer, writer

Contents

Foreword xii

Preface xiv

PART I: *BiO Spiritualism* defined: Is spiritualism without religion possible? 1

> If a definition meets these 8 criteria it is valid.
> If a definition is valid it is proper.
> If not, then not.

Chapter 1: *BiO Spiritualism* defined 3

Chapter 2: Spiritual-isms of the Past and Present: *16*
A handful of religions and One Philosophy

Chapter 3: Spiritual-isms of the Future: *23*
ToBeDetermined (the spiritualisms, not this chapter)

PART II: If tough love is good, is tough *self-respect*—the *Creator* of the 25
one who loves toughly—better?

> Phase 0: Curmudgeonism – A recovery guide for nice
> guys seeking happiness.

Chapter 4: Nice guys who came in last <START HERE> *27*
(Winners can jump to Part III)

Chapter 5: Your psychology's three most important elements *34*

Chapter 6: I Object!(ivism): Your purpose in life is not to *just* oppose *47*

Chapter 7: Where can I buy me one of them Happiness Meters? *51*

Chapter 8: *Recovery*—from *what?*—should mean: *from* un-happiness *58*

Chapter 9: *To* what?—technically (as in for precision's sake)—is up *67*
to you. Per *BiO Spiritualism* it *should* be: *to* happiness.

PART III: Advanced *BiO Spiritualism*: Is America the only place left on 69
earth where the Individual is (still) more important than The Group?

> Phase 1: Individuation – is not automatic, it requires
> (individual) effort.

Chapter 10:   *Give a mystic an inch and he'll take a mind.*   71
Give a Bureaucrat a mind and she'll take all your money.

> *(If women have taught us anything, it's that even though men may have a monopoly on attilaism they don't own it exclusively and they also do not have a monopoly on witch doctory. That is, women can be evil too—see mothers who are killers of their own children for one example. That is, human beings—both men and women—are the source of both the good and the evil. Which way either develops, idiosyncratically, is a matter of correct versus incorrect philosophical choices.*
>
> *Which is to say, if you ain't evil, then 51%— or more—of your—philosophical—choices have been good.)*

Chapter 11:   Those who can't teach, Do. Those who can't Do, do   76
themselves in.

> Man's *individual* life *starts* with physics-as-metaphysics and ethics as *interactive* human nature and it *ends* with a *learned* epistemology as *individual* psychology with *intensity* of happiness (or its lack) as the *reward* of successful (or unsuccessful) *spiritualism* within the *individual* person qua individual *possessor* of that *universal* we call *immutable* human nature.
>
> *(Contemporary context: spiritualism and psychology, not unlike morality, belong to the individual, not to the Government. That is:)*
>
> I know *where* and *what* I am as well as how I *should* act.
> The question is: *where* and *what* are you and how *do* you act?

Chapter 12:   Those who understand (good and evil) AND *Do* are the   105
heroes. Or—as the [flipped upside-down] case may be—
villains.

Chapter 13:   The beam in my eye is gone. Your mote is next.   *113*
That is: I know *who* I am, *who* are you?

Chapter 14:   CONTROL: *Pedantics* for *Self* Control is *Pedactics*   *117*

Chapter 15:   CONTROLLED: Forget the criminal mind, beware the *bureaucratic* mind as it seeks control over you and yours as *its* survival method.   *126*

Chapter 16:   Drop your *Pedactics* and Chill Out!   *132*

Chapter 17:   Personality, psycho-hermeneutics as nuances of self-understanding and the origins of a New Spiritualism   *150*

Chapter 18:   From *Behaviorism* - to - *Cognitive Neuroscience via Cognitive Science & Cognitive Psychology:* Rats maze-to-Rats nest?   *197*

Chapter 19:   Will *Cognitive Neuroscience* become the new bureaucratic control tool of the 21st Century?   *261*

> Give a Cognitive Neuroscientist a brain *and* a Government Grant to force his or her view of *psychology* down our throats and he/she'll inch his/her way towards making it *impossible* for the mind that that brain is a part of to understand the following. (Or, that is, they are *your* neurons and what you do with them is up to you.)

Chapter 20:   Does *Objectivism* need *Biocentric Psychology?*   *272*
Is vice versa a tautology?

PART IV: On the Art and Science of Becoming: Can you be your own psychotherapist?   *311*

> And get the world's best client in return?

Chapter 21:   The Ninth Principle: Reality rules   *313*

> Reality's 1st Rule: *contradictions do not exist*

> Reality's second rule: Self ***really*** matters.

Chapter 22:   As *Client* check your *Spiritualism* premises: *323*
I am Alpha and Omega, who are yu?

Chapter 23:   As *Therapist* check your life premises   *330*
Every man (woman and child over the age of 12) *is* an island.

Chapter 24: When the Lexus smashes into the Olive Tree, then what?   *343*

A Case Study of *one* ex-nice guy Joshua Deer on How to GROW out of your problems and into your life and protect and promote your own mental health *in-the-process*.

Afterword   390

Objectivism for Christians:

Religious un-CONversion and other flip-flopping techniques for getting your psyche back in-line with reality *without* deep-sixing your mental health (or vice versa).

But first, here's my theory on evolution.

REFERENCES   394

FOREWORD

I've been asked if *Objectivism*—the Philosophy of Ayn Rand—is a religion. My short answer is, it depends. My long answer is, yes and no. *Yes*, if religion is a philosophy, albeit a *primitive* one, then Objectivism is a religion, albeit a *modern* one. But if not the latter then, *no*, not the former either.

A.E. Joshua

PREFACE

Who is *A.E. Joshu*a?

That is, if A.E. stands for Alter Ego does that mean I, the author, am the writer Joshua's *ego*?

Part I:

BiO Spiritualism defined: Is spiritualism *without* religion possible?

> If a definition meets these 8 criteria it is valid.
> If a definition is valid it is proper.
> If not, then not.

spir·it·u·a·lism *(spir'i-chōō-ul-iz'm)*, **n.**

> ***1. The process of** ...*continued in Chapter 1.

A definition has to meet all of these 8 criteria (taken from my *recall* of Barbara Branden's taped lecture series[i]) in order to be valid.

That is, if a *definition*:

1. is *not* circular
2. is *not* negative
3. is fundamental
4. has a *genus*
5. has *differentia*
6. is not too broad
7. is not too narrow and
8. is *not* obscure, that is, is not metaphorical or poetic, but clearly states a literal and exact meaning

then it is valid.

If not, then not.

> **NOTE To Reader:** *BiO Spiritualism is not for the uncurious; therefore you should read every footnote in order to understand the main text in many parts where it* **assumes** *that you have read preceding footnotes.*

Chapter 1: *BiO Spiritualism*:

Defined:

In the shadow of spiritualism's rather tall traditions let me say up front that my goal for *BiO Spiritualism* is to provide a guide for *individuals* who already *worship* reason and *despise* mysticism—in contradistinction to the vice-versa types—to take back *spiritualism* from the mystics and use it for their own, personal, *selfish* benefit as one is want to do as he or she goes about building his or her own moral—albeit mortal as the only *kind* that exists—soul on earth (or the moon or mars, or wherever whenever such may be the case).

That is, true Spiritualism—as true psychology is for people, not rats—is *for* reason worshippers, not mystics.

The best way to provide this guide—this owner's manual of the rational soul's own spiritualism—is to define what we mean by *spiritualism* and—because of its historical roots—define what we do *not* mean by it. The formal definition of (BiO) *Spiritualism* is given below. To give the reader some appreciation and preparation for this definition we have to consider what we view spiritualism to *not* be. This is the easy part of dealing with the problem of defining spiritualism. What "spiritualism" is not is what *historically* it has been claimed to be.

Spiritualism, traditionally, is used in four distinct ways: *spirit, spiritual, spirituality* and *spiritualism.*

Spirit is an animating or vital principle held to give life to physical organisms. *Spirits* in this *traditional* sense have no physical bodies of their own but still exist as "things". Supposedly they exist as invisible things in that space that divides one actual *living* being from another. That is, [human] "spirits" are incorporeal so they need the physical bodies of one living person to communicate with other living people. We definitely do *not* mean this when we use the word *spirit* or *spirits*. Rather we mean it as an *attribute* or *characteristic* of a particular individual: as in, he or she has a lot of spirit. We characterize them as such without thinking for one moment that that spirit can exist without them. The spirit can exist as a *characteristic* in others but it doesn't exist as a thing in reality by itself no more than does green exist as a thing separate from that which is green (be it grass, crayons, paint or envy ...oops, we are getting ahead of ourselves, nix the 'envy' *concept* for right now but keep the *percepts.* And add this to it: *spirit does not exist in rocks.*).

In the sense of *spiritual* on the other hand, we usually mean of or relating to sacred matters, concerned with religious values (Webster's New Collegiate Dictionary[i] [1]). And what are religious values? Religious values, to name only some of them, are love, hope, faith, charity, compassion, humility, sacrifice, and duty. Religious values, by their nature, are the ones high on the list of important values *to the person* who holds them as (religious) values. Since *values* are something we act to gain and/or keep and since values exist on a hierarchy, *religious values* can be just another way of saying "values *at the top* of one's hierarchy". *Values* at the *top* of our hierarchy are (the only ones) *worthy* of worship.

Hierarchies are man-made.

By this I mean: the *content* of our individual hierarchy of *values* (and knowledge) is made by us; the *capacity* to hold these things hierarchically is not, it is innate. We [you, me and all individuals] *program* our own innate hierarchy tree by choosing and automatizing its base roots—addition tables, for example, in the case of mathematical knowledge—and by making its main trunk be knowledge of *good* and *evil*—*pleasure* and *pain*, for example, if we are an infant growing and developing towards childhood. And if as developing beings we have not *yet* succumbed to religion's *reversal* themes but rather held on to some semblance of our human beingness—as same is afforded us by nature's pleasure-pain mechanism—we can later on in life replace our sense of pleasure/pain-good/evil with *formal* definitions—the *good* is that which is **for** life and the *evil* is that which is **against** it. And then, continuing our analogy, by making the main trunk's branches richly-leaved with specific, *concrete* values (be they made of chocolate candy or your favorite ice cream—or maple drenched bakery products in my case—to the best sex you've ever had to your love of freedom and ... whatever YOUR *hierarchy* of values is it is) made by you. And it is made with this caveat: if the top of *your* man-made hierarchy is suicide-homicide-murderer in the name of anything, then ***you are evil*** and no amount of tree twisting by you or your apologizers can change the *fact* of it. You cannot change the fact of it even if your authorities—be they religious or otherwise—tell you that you can

---

[1] I use lower case Roman numerals throughout the book to designate References; these references are given for each chapter at the end of the book under the REFERENCE heading. Footnotes are designated by sequential numbering throughout the book. As a reader of non-fiction I love footnotes and as a writer of same I use them to elaborate meaning and to pay my intellectual debts as best and as thoroughly as I can without interrupting the flow of the main text any more than I have to.

non-irrationally define the *evil* to be *that* which is *for* life on earth and the *good* to be that which is *for* death. If this last—heaven forbid—is the essence of your spiritual values then I have only one thing to say to you: *you are wrong to the* **ultimate** *degree*.

Thirdly, the word *spirituality*—like its antithesis, hypocrisy—is a measurement concept. Spirituality is a *measure* of the extent to which one practices what one preaches. If, for example, one *preached* the "virtues" of self-sacrifice, self-immolation and self-denial but lived in a palace or villa and gorged oneself on apple pie and nubile virgins—or vice versa—we would (or should) evaluate that person as *not spiritual*, that is, we would evaluate that person as a hypocrite on their own terms. In this sense then, *spirituality* is an answer to the question: *How spiritual?* How spiritual is he or she? If he or she is a minister, preacher, rabbi, or some such kind of professional religious intellectual (Cleric, Priest, etc.) we would *expect* the answer to be: very. If on the other hand, we were talking about non-clergy, we would not be surprised if the answer were: *not* very. Actually, our surprise would be to discover such a non-cleric person to be *highly* spiritual.

Such is the *low* expectations gendered by *traditional* religious "spirituality".

Finally we come to: *spiritualism.* Spiritualism, historically, has been associated with the mystical, the supernatural, the beyond-the-grave fantasies of mystics and others who hold to the view that knowledge is gained by magical means. Be it the magic of "revealed truths" as revealed to one directly from *a* god or *the* gods, or from "spirits" or by mystical absorption by the non-understandable psyches of some very special people who have a kind of *sixth-sense-absorption* ability beyond the five normal senses that we all have. And (speaking sarcastically for the moment) it wasn't until the latter parts of the just past 20th century (as well as into these early days of the 21st) that we learned that this (historical) "spiritualism" was not reserved for just a special few, but that it was (and is) available to all. This is to say, if we would just follow any of the many examples of *New Age* Spiritualism being offered at the time, we—each and every one of us—could become mystic diviners of "spiritual" truth. But since "Spiritual" to the New Age mystics means that which can't be defined, because if it can be defined it's not "spiritual" because spiritual is that which can't be defined, by definition, we don't know for sure *what* exactly it is we have divined.[2]

Religion—as 20th Century's *New Age* Spiritualism so aptly demonstrates—does not have a monopoly on faulty reasoning.

---

[2] Google *New Age* and take your pick of the myriad of "spiritual" options offered there. For an evaluation of two of the more popular mystics see Chapter 5.

If true spiritualism isn't even close to what historically it was said to be, then what is it?

Spiritualism, though not yet an actual science, is an *emerging* science. And the kind of (emerging) science it is, is an *applied* science. As *Engineering* is to the natural sciences: physics, chemistry and physiology for example, *Spiritualism* is to the humanities: philosophy, psychology and art. For example, Aeronautical Engineering is applied Physics. It applies physics knowledge to the problem of getting heavier than air vehicles to fly. As applied physics, Aeronautical Engineering describes airplane lift as the interaction of air pressure and air speed in its equation for aerodynamic lift:

$$p_1 v_1 = p_2 v_2.$$

Understanding pressure (p) and velocity (v) in this equation as phenomenon, as "things", as *manipulatable* "things" comes from Physics. Pressure p is force per unit area (pounds per square inch or grams per square centimeter for example)[3]; velocity v is distance traveled per unit time (for example see your car's speedometer in miles or kilometers per hour or when multiplied by the appropriate constant, feet or meters per second). The Aeronautical Engineer (armed with the lift formula) then knows that with the *proper* air foil (wing) *cross-sectional* shape—namely one that *causes* the air to move faster over the *top*, curved part of the air foil than the slower moving air under the *bottom*, flatter side of the air foil wing—will cause the *top* side's surrounding *pressure* to be lower than the *bottom* side pressure with the net result being—given that nature is non-contradictory and will "do" whatever it takes to maintain the *pressure-velocity equality* with the net result being—the wing is pushed upwards due to the pressure differential (p_2 top is less than p_1 bottom *because* v_2 top is *greater* than v_1 bottom and so *nature commands* p_2 has to be less) caused by the moving air in this man-made context *made* to *interact* with reality. A *context* that includes the planes engine used to propel the wing through the air at the appropriate velocity forcing the air to pass over the wing's air foil *shape* to cash in on the lift *principle*.

Spiritualism—once properly understood and defined—is neither less nor more complicated as an *applied* science than is Aeronautical Engineering.

It only seems that it is.

---

[3] Place your right index finger under your left forearm and let your left arm go limp so that your right index finger holds it suspended in air. The contact pressure at your index finger tip is the weight of your limp arm, say 3 pounds for the sake of discussion, divided by the contact area of your index finger, say $1/4^{th}$ square inch. This yields a pressure value of 12 psi—that is, 12 pounds per square inch ($3 \div 1/4$).

For example, a *mystic* passively watching an airplane lift off the runway will wax poetic and "explain" airplane lift thusly: *the airplane lifts off the ground when god places his two index fingers—one under each wing—and pushes upward.*

Mystics don't just give *spiritualism* a bad name. *Some* poets don't admire them either.

But we, as *reason's* poets and scientists who do desire to be—true—spiritualists end up saying, *there are no gods; there is only man and man's needs; all his needs, including his true spiritual needs.* (In this context then, *reason's* poets explain airplane life this way: *the airplane lifts off the ground when man places his two index fingers—one on each temple—and says*: think.)

To understand man's spiritual needs requires understanding man, in the character of being man, which means understanding *metaphysical* man.

Since *metaphysically* man's life on earth *is* an *end in itself*, what does this mean for man's body, mind and spirit?

The only thing that it can mean: these are man's *means* to *that life.*

Body is man's *means* to *physical* independence and autonomy, *for that life.*

Mind is man's *means* to *psychological* independence and autonomy, *for that life.*

Spirit is man's *means* to *consciousness* independence and autonomy, *for that life.*

Spiritualism then, as the *applied* science of body, mind and spirit, is the *process* of making one's self the sole, prideful owner of a worthy and efficacious consciousness; a consciousness that is worthy of happiness *because* it is competent at producing it.

Let me repeat this.

Spiritualism, which is to say, *true* spiritualism is the process of *making* one's self the sole, prideful owner of a *worthy* and *efficacious* consciousness; a consciousness that is worthy of happiness *because* it is competent at producing it.

A competent consciousness is a happy consciousness and a happy consciousness is a competent consciousness.

Body is the means and *physical independence to an optimal degree consonant with the physical laws of nature is the goal* of physical growth and development.

Mind is the means and *autonomous self-rule to an optimal degree consonant with the laws of consciousness is the goal* of psychological growth and development.

Successful spiritualism, that is *spiritualism* of the *kind* we are talking about here, presupposes an *adult* mind and body.

An *adult mind* is one that thinks in *principles* about the world and one's self. It is one that *is* autonomous and self ruling in the self functions: thinking, judging, feeling, acting.

An *adult body* is one that is finished growing and developing physically and is efficient at producing healthy, vigorous *physical* life X% of the time, where X is such that:[4]

$$X-(100-X) > 50\%.$$

If non-vigorous physical life derails one from spiritual and psychological growth and development a *significant* amount of the time (say 40%), then one or more of three and *only* three possibilities exists. Either one's body is not finished developing *or* one is mistreating it *or* due to the laws of the physical sciences one is incapacitated and as such is forced to devote all one's mind and spirit to overcoming one's physical infirmity.[5]

Since 100% is a metaphysical limit, 100% is the *maximum* available for vigorous life. Hence, a 40% non-vigorous life leaves only 60% for vigor and 60 minus 40 is *not* greater than 50%, which is the *minimum* requirement *mutatis mutandis* (see previous footnote) for autonomy and self rule. The *greater than 50% requirement* is analogous to *any* kind of ownership: he who *owns* more than 50% *is* the owner, controller, self-ruler. He who owns less *is not*.

An adult is one who owns 51% or more of him or her self.

The mathematical dividing line for the foregoing "rule of thumb" occurs at the 75 - 25 split. Of course the closer X is to 100% the better off one is. But at minimum one needs to achieve an X greater than 75% in order to achieve *on one's own* the ability to sustain open ended growth in one's *own* spiritualism. That is, by way of comparison, if you compare life to baseball this is saying you have to become a .750—or better—hitter; you *have* to that is, *if*, you desire open ended growth in your own spiritualism; if not then not or if less, then less. And, *open-*

---

[4] The symbol > means, greater than. Also, X stands for Vigorous life. The quantity (100-X) stands for non-vigorous life and is hypothesized to be a subtractive (rather than neutral) quantity.

[5] If any particular human being violates this " > 50%" rule of thumb and overcomes severe limitations that most people do not have—which, because of the fact of volition in humans can be done—the "violation" is a testimonial to the *power of volition* and to the *heroicness* of that particular human spirit (and *Yes*, I do have in mind Stephen Hawking as I write this). It is not an opportunity to conclude that "rules of thumb" are worthless, therefore, the best rule of thumb is, nobody can know anything.

ended growth in one's own spiritualism is possible. Some call it, your *human potential*. I call it, your open-ended growth in spiritualism possibilities.

In most industrialized societies the 75% *physical* autonomy is a piece of cake (pun not intended).

Physical autonomy isn't just being able to meet ones food-type needs: that is, earning money to buy food, clothing and shelter, which in the modern world depends on the degree of freedom that exists in the society you live in. Physical autonomy in many of its aspects is simply a developmental issue for all people, independent of their social group. For example, I have achieved a 99.999% physical autonomy in my walking abilities compared to when I was 6 months old: 99.999 - .001(for the occasional stumble) = 99.998 >> 50, voila! I yam an autonomous walker (finally, he said at age 2).[6]

So for most *civilized* people the "problem" of *mind and spirit* is precisely that: *since I have achieved physical autonomy* how then do I develop *my* mind and spirit to achieve *my* psychological maturity and happiness?

An incompetent consciousness is an unhappy consciousness and an unhappy consciousness is an incompetent consciousness.

As "spiritualists" in the way described above we have before us a two edged opportunity. The first edge—like all edges—has two *sides* that come together to form the edge's most salient characteristic: sharpness. By analogy then—in order to get and maintain happiness' sharpness—we have to do two things: *show* ourselves *how* we achieved happiness in the first place and secondly, *understand* how we plan to *maintain* it. Included in the understanding phase is how we *plan* to *continue* maintaining it even after we have managed to maintain it for awhile. *Maintaining* a value can be as difficult as or more difficult than obtaining it, as anyone, for example, who has ever dieted knows: keeping that weight loss lost "forever" is a big part of weight loss success. In spiritualism the *maintaining* of the *value* of worth or *dignity* and *efficacy* is even more pronounced in its *degree of difficulty* than is the *value* of maintaining a particular weight loss. It is more difficult because the *values* involved are more important. But the *processes* involved in both are the same, which is to say, each in its own way is *the process of* seeking *and* obtaining *and* keeping *a value*. In the case of spiritualism—which as we've already stated is *the process of making one's self the sole, prideful owner of a worthy and efficacious* consciousness—the *value* sought is worth and efficacy, the *goal* on the other hand to be reached is, happiness. In dieting—the *process* of making one's body the optimal servant of one's life—the *value* sought

---

[6] The double >> means 'much greater than'.

is control over our eating habits, the *goal* to be reached is a reduced-weight, easier-to-carry around, looks-better body. By continued analogy then, the *journey*—that is, the *process of seeking a value*—can be more fun than the arrival—that is, the *obtaining* the value. And the analogy here isn't just to dieting as foreplay to weight loss. If one hopes to retain the benefits of the journey one has to also *maintain* the newly acquired *virtues* picked up along the way as well as the sought after *value* at the journey's end. And here if we try to extend the analogy as implied to include both dieting—a long term beneficial process—and sex—a shorter term one—it fails. It fails because *sex is an end in itself* but spiritualism is not. Spiritualism, like dieting, is the *means*; happiness in this life is the *end*. Happiness, like life or perhaps more precisely: as life, is (like sex) an end in itself. And except for one single difference, happiness is like all values: at some level of one's being (at some level on the *consciousness* continuum) in one's pursuit of them, that is, of *particular* values, one has to purposefully, consciously *want* and *desire* them. Happiness in this regard is the same as other values, but it is different in that it is the "mother" of all values and as such it has to be obtained, maintained and locked in before any of our other *chosen* values can be *fully* enjoyed. Happiness is the context within which all our rational values are enjoyed. And true Happiness—we must note—is *not* an issue of "what" makes this person or that person happy. We know *what* makes people happy: it is the *same* for everybody. See below for the proper "what" in the "*What* is happiness?" question.

The second edge and the book's second *goal* is to help you *to gain* and/or *maintain* your own *spiritualism* so that you too can (finally) be (authentically) happy and then we all can join together to finally create a totally free, 100% laissez-faire capitalist society.

Or I should say, you will be happy *enough* (edge 2's side 1) to *want* to create such a society and you and I also will (finally) be *moral* enough (edge 2's side 2) to succeed at it.[7]

And when I say "we *all* can join together to create..." I mean—even though I now am pro-morality and a-theist (in contradistinction to those who are pro-theist and a-morality), I mean—to also include those who, as did I, as a kid, *choose* religion for *selfish* reasons. I refuse to damn myself for thinking at the age of 5

---

[7] Most moral society status (and associated benefits) in the future will go to the first society to create and successfully maintain a 100% laissez-faire capitalist society. And though it is most likely to be the United States of America it isn't a foregone conclusion that it will so be. It can be any society, but more than likely since it will more than likely be an evolutionary process more so than a revolutionary one it will therefore, more than likely be a society coming from *some* freedom to *more* freedom. The United States of America—as of this writing—is the *most* likely since it now has the *most* freedom.

that eternal life was a *value* (or more likely that eternal damnation was a dis-value and probably *should* be avoided at all costs). The fact that I made such a mistake is in one sense not a profound discovery: all it means is we humans are not omniscient.[8] But what is profound *universally* is the discovery that *efficacy* and *worth* are pursuable, obtainable *values*. *Everybody* has to achieve *efficacy of consciousness* on their own. No one can do it for you. No thing can be substituted for it. Drugs will not obtain it for you. Trying to find the "magical" genes that *cause* it "all to happen to you" will not succeed in doing it for you either. *Efficacy of consciousness* is an earned, self-made value. If happiness is the *goal*, efficacy of consciousness is the means. There is no other *path*. If the "what" in the happiness equation is "...a state [pause...repeat...*state*] of non-contradictory joy" (as the Philosophers of Objectivism contend and with which we whole-heartedly agree), then efficacy of consciousness is the *ongoing source* of both the non-contradiction and the joy, with *noncontradiction* the *homeostatic* source of efficacy.[9] And though *efficacy* exists on a continuous continuum, *happiness* does not; it exists on a stepwise continuum (see happiness plateaus in Chapter 8 and/or clichés such as "*stairway* to heaven", et al.). Happiness as a *state* of consciousness is an either/or phenomenon: liquid as a *state* of matter does not exist on a continuous continuum, neither does solid nor gas. But then neither do these "things" exist as liquid or solid or gas, rather they exist as *water* or *rocks* or *air*, that is, as some *specific* concrete. So too happiness, as a *state* of consciousness it is a *specific* something. It has a *specific* nature: it is an achieved state, an *end* state, a state of achieved values, of values that are joyful and non-contradictory and not *self*-destructive (again, as The Philosophy of Objectivism has *already* explained to us so that we can *now* use this knowledge and seek our ... ***own*** ... ***selfish*** ... ***sacred*** ... happiness).

Develop-mentally, and perhaps evolutionarily, man's solution—or more specifically, the *non-philosophical* individual's solution—to the problem of the either/or 'ness of base (as in at foot-of-mountain base) happiness is: *compartmentalization*. Mentally, compartmentalization is the *effect* of which the

---

[8] But for me personally what is profound is that I can trace the beginning of this *mistake* to my 4 and 1/3rd year old Christmas—which would have to have been, December 24th, 1949—when I stood looking at my airplane tricycle—with a big red bow around it—located out on our snowy, wind swept, open-air front porch. The adults in the room were trying to convince me that it came from Santa Claus. Who's that? was the thought replaced by me, by choice with: if that's what it takes to get that trike, well...flash forward to the next spring and I'm riding that trike in our driveway oblivious to the selling out that started a mere three months prior. I wonder now, is this the police meaning in psycho-epistemology of "priors"?
[9] By homeostatic I mean in the physiological sense of a dynamic steady state. A dynamic steady state driven by a feedback answer to a continuous question: what is it that does NOT contradict REALITY?

cause is an attempt to integrate the non-integrate-able—that is, the non-integrable. *Limits exist in reality*. *Volition* is neither omniscient nor omnipotent, but then neither is it impotent. *Integration* across all areas of *pleasure* in life—as stepping stone to *noncontradictory* joy—is superior to *compartmentalization* of those areas as would be required—and hence *is* required—by moral codes that *worship* self-denial.[10] The areas in question are the areas in life that *are* the *sources* of pleasure for us, the areas in life that can *bathe* us in pleasure; that is, WASHER's:[11]

- W ork
- A rt
- S ex
- H uman relationships
- E xercise of our human capacities and
- R ecreation

Eventually we can "profile" our self's competency (or lack) at getting pleasure from these areas in life and we can even think of ourselves as "happy" at work, say, though perhaps not "so happy" with our human relationships or vice versa and so on and so forth as we *mentally step* through the many facets of our idiosyncratic lives.[12] But just because we do, do this, it does not mean that we are *happy* in the fundamental sense of the term: existing in a *state* of non-contradictory joy. Compartmentalized "happiness" of course is better than "integrated" suffering, but neither is better than true happiness. Integrated suffering is the *logical* end for all true-to-the-core *altruists* just as true happiness is the logical end for all true-to-the-core *worshipers* of noncontradiction and joy.[13]

---

[10] *Compartmentalization* is to integration what fat is to health—fat is a store of energy for the future. Compartmentalization is the "place" where mental fat is stored, but mental fat—unlike the body's unitary fat—is of *two* kinds: the *good* kind and the *bad* kind. The *good* kind is *implicit* information that is stored until that future time when our personally developed conceptualization abilities will be able to deal with it. The bad kind is when we use our mental compartments to store *known* [to us] contradictions rather than expunging them from our mental universe. (Note, this last—bad—kind is the meaning of the cliché: he/she is a fat head.)

[11] If you are looking for something around which to integrate your life these are it. For more on these see their identification and discussion in the Biocentric Psychology works of Dr. Nathaniel Branden.

[12] See the happiness self assessment tool—the teleömeter—in Chapter 7.

[13] By "altruist" I mean one whose *first* choice 51% of the time *or more* is to put others before self. And notice the implications of this for your psychology: you can do this in your Thinking (even in my thoughts others come first) or in your Feelings (other's feelings are important but mine aren't) or in your Actions (I have to act so as to benefit others not me, myself or I) or in combinations of all three. And Pedactics—that good way of being as you will discover in Chapter 15—"says" for starters, stop doing this in your own mind

BiO Spiritualism Defined

I speak here from *first* hand experience. I've been both (a miserable, struggling, suffering *pretending to be happy* altruist and an actually, truly, really happy selfish guy) and happiness *is* better.[14]

But what *exactly* (as we promised earlier to identify) is the meaning of: happiness is a state of non-contradictory joy?

Per Ayn Rand (the definer of happiness) it is:

> Happiness is a state of non-contradictory joy—a joy without penalty or guilt, a joy that does not clash with any of your values and does not work for your own destruction.[ii]

But what does this mean?

It means that you have to go to the source (Ayn Rand's writings, e.g. start with *The Ayn Rand Lexicon*[iii]) and read and study what she has to say on the subject and then *apply* your best understanding of the phenomenon we call happiness to you and your life.

If spiritualism, qua applied science, is the engineer of happiness then happiness, qua state of non-contradictory joy, is the model *to be built*.

We conclude this Chapter by listing eight of *BiO Spiritualism's* model building principles. Principles that we can use to be successful in our spiritual quest, that is, to repeat, *to succeed in making our self's the prideful owner of a worthy and efficacious consciousness; a consciousness that is worthy of happiness* **because** *it is competent at producing it.*

BiO Spiritualism Principles:

Principle 1

It starts with Reality.
(That is, *life*, like time and space, is *inside* of Existence.)

Principle 2

The *Philosophy of Objectivism* and The Psychology of *Biocentric Psychology* are the *best* of their kind.

---

when it comes time to think about you and your human nature needs (the mind *leads* and the emotions follow …remember? … see the philosophy of Objectivism).

[14] Or to hijack fully the form of the quotable quote this is based on I should say, I've been poor (of spirit) and I've been rich (of spirit) and rich is better.

Principle 3

Consciousness is a thing-like-thing that has needs that have to be met.

Principle 4

Everything is some-thing to a human consciousness.

Principle 5

Consciousness is the only thing that can measure consciousness.[15]

Principle 6

Judge not least ye be judged is the mantra of the uncourageous, therefore, *judge and be prepared to be judged*.

Principle 7

Self-*valuing* is a psychological need, Self-*caring* a spiritual one.

Principle 8

Tabula rasa—which human beings *are* born as—means *blank slate* as regards *content* of consciousness not as regards *survival* needs of life and the *means* to satisfying them. Both *needs* and *means* are innate, but knowledge of those needs and know-how on using the means to satisfy those needs are not innate. That is, *use* and *know-how* and *know-what* have to be learned. *Have to*, that is, *if* surviving *and* thriving is our goal.

As qualified by footnote #28 on page 44, the *Bi* in *BiO Spiritualism* stands for *Biocentric Psychology* and the O for *Objectivism*. *BiO Spiritualism* is *Biocentric Objectivism*.

In *BiO Spiritualism* then "we" say:

---

[15] A new, positive meaning for the old cliché: "It takes one to know one".

> *BiO Spiritualism is Objectivism* **PLUS** *Biocentric psychology, idiosynchronized* (as best we can do). Which is to say, *Ask not what you can do for Objectivism,* but rather *what can Objectivism do for you?* The answer is, **Guide** *you through—not around, but through—your psychological problems to destination, Passionate Happiness.*

Then in the end, you too can agree: *Objectivism*, the Philosophy and *Biocentric*, the Psychology *are* good.

Chapter 2: Spiritual-isms of the Past and Present:

A handful of religions and One Philosophy

Ayn Rand, the founder of the *Philosophy of Objectivism* and staunch defender of religion stretched the meaning of human compassion beyond its elastic limit when she gave religion the benefit of the doubt by declaring: *religion is a primitive philosophy*.

It is not. It is a thief.

Religion stole my life.

And that's not all it has stolen, down through the ages it has stolen all of man's highest moral values.

Objectivism—the *compassionate* Ayn Rand notwithstanding—has successfully taken them all back and tells us they are ours *as human beings*, if we want them.

All we have to do is think and study and read and study and think and study and read for about 20 years and then *apply* what we have learned.

I've done it. I got my life back.

Thank god for Ayn Rand.

Dr. Nathaniel Branden—founder of psychology, the science that he calls *Biocentric psychology*—agrees that *Objectivism* is the world's greatest philosophy ever, but he disagrees in the *amount of time* it *should* take those victims *of* religion to retrieve their lives *from* religion.

In his inexhaustible devotion to truth and his enviable grasp and knowledge of psychology, combined with his vast exposure to actual people with actual psychological problems, Dr. Branden has observed that it is a *myth* that every adult *wants* to be happy.

They don't.

But this doesn't mean that it is a myth that every child wants to be happy.

They do.

Every child wants to be happy; they just don't know how to do it that's all, because they don't know *what* it is.

Happiness is a state of noncontradictory joy.

This definition is a *gift* from Ayn Rand.

Can it get any simpler than this?

No.

Does simple in clarity translate into ease in achieving?

Not necessarily. Clarity is a *necessary* but not *sufficient* condition for achieving happiness.

The necessary *and* sufficient conditions are clarity and effort.

Happiness requires work, mental and physical work.

Physical work and *its* relationship to survival and happiness is pretty well understood by all.

Mental work on the other hand needs more, mental work.

For example, when speaking of religion we can say that the world is divided into two kinds of people: those who do belong to one of the world's major or minor or any of its *formal* religions and those who don't.

Of those who do belong to a formal religion there are two types and of those who don't belong there are two types.

Let's consider those who don't belong first.

Of those who *don't* belong to one of the world's formal religions there are two types: those who are sympathetic to the Philosophy of *Objectivism* and those who aren't.

Of those who are sympathetic to the Philosophy of *Objectivism* there are two types: those who are *also* sympathetic to *Biocentric Psychology* and those who aren't.

Those who are sympathetic to both *Biocentric Psychology* and *Objectivism* can be called *Biocentric Objectivists* but they don't have to be. They could also be called: those who believe that the human—to *become* and/or *remain* human—has to *praise* the good and *damn* the evil *after* properly identifying the good to be that which is *for* life on earth and the evil that which is *against* it. And since reason is pro-life it is good and since faith is anti-life it is evil.

Reason and *faith* are mutually exclusive terms. *Reason* is drawing conclusions based on sensory evidence—including inferences based on earlier formed conclusions based on sensory evidence—and *faith* is drawing conclusions based on the *absence* of sensory evidence—including inferences based on earlier formed conclusions based on the absence of sensory evidence. For evidence #1 that says it is *possible* that *religion* is evil, see page 194 footnote #173's description of the "Doubting Thomas" premise from *The Holy Bible* (for evidence #2 see the religion [redundantly?] known as [Militant] Islam). Reason and faith can mutually coexist in the same person but not *at the same time* when that time is time to *draw* a conclusion. Here the conclusion drawer either uses *reason* to make the inductive leap from uncertainty to certainty (via the Objectivist identified steps of possible-probable-certain based on evaluation of *actual* evidence for each and every step) or he or she wishes the conclusion would go away and so they *evade* the logical conclusion and don't make it. In *Objectivism* this is the meaning of the statement: "…your *blank entries* are your blackest sins…". For me this means *me* (and for you it means *you*) *refusing* to draw a conclusion (blanking out) when I (you) have enough pertinent facts to draw one. By conclusions I mean failing to make reality based cause-effect links when I have the information to do so. My *refusal* to know what I know and see what I see is self made, that is, *me* made blindness, which is *evasion*. When we add faith to evasion in an attempt (be it innocent or not) to try to solve the problem of evasion we only worsen the problem, we don't solve it. The inductive leap of faith—as a literal analogy—is standing on the edge of a great divide and *choosing* to close ones eyes and jump … *hoping* for the best.

The best does not happen—we Americans, as observers of many bumper stickers know *what* happens—the best is man made. Specifically, it is reason made. Since man at his philosophical best is a to-be-actualized potential, enter (*Biocentric*) *Psychology*.

Biocentric psychology is for those (of us) who made *more* than a few mistakes in managing their own psychological growth and development. For this type, *Biocentric Psychology* strongly suggests that the "sinner" (my word *not* Biocentric's) take leave of his or her *impulses* to self-damnation (such as calling him or her self a sinner) by *temporarily* dropping the second half of the philosopher's equation about good and evil.[16] Which is to say, the "sinner" has to challenge and *understand* his own *particular* life in the *context* of a human nature that *is* selfish *by nature.* And further, one has to do this *as* he or she struggles to obtain authentic self esteem and in-the-process succeeds in becoming an *authentic* thinking-feeling-acting *selfish* human being.

Which is to say, the individual has to become an expert at *introspection*.

Introspection, as discovered by Objectivism (as far as BiO Spiritualism is concerned), is nothing more than a *process* of cognition directed inward. Cognition—as a process, specifically a *mental* process—is figuring out *what*

---

[16] For those of you who are familiar with Dr. Branden's audio tapes you know that I have *added* the word "temporarily" to his comment about praising the good and damning the evil. Dr. Branden suggests that we can prosper by *only* praising the good and though he doesn't go as far as secular humanism (which says we have to actively *not* damn the evil) he does error here in the long run. But for those of us who *also* embrace Objectivism—which is the teacher of the need to praise the good AND damn the evil—this error is not a problem. Refer to Chapter 20 for more on this and other Biocentric-Objectivist "problems".

something is. If you are already a good extrospector (good at figuring out *what* things are in the world *external* to self), with *practice* you can become a good introspector too (figuring out the world *internal* to self). The first step to becoming a good introspector in regards to figuring out one's own psychology, per *Biocentric Psychology*, is to start the process by removing the gun of moral self-damnation from ones own head by recognizing that there are no evil thoughts, only evil *actions*. That *consciousness* has a *need* to be unobstructed by reality avoiding man-made mechanisms—such as religiously induced *errors* like the one that says we are immoral if we *think* of an evil action just as much as we legitimately would be if we *performed* that evil action *in reality*.[17] Self-censure is not always, unconditionally productive. When it is used to stop one from acting like and hence *being* a brute then it is good. But when it is used to prevent one from growing psychologically, intellectually, spiritually, it is not good. So in this way it is counterproductive to ones *need* of self-awareness, self-acceptance and self-assertion which are pre-requisites to self-understanding, which is pre-requisite to the self-forgiveness that *might* be required by some of us and is required by those of us who have sinned against the self. When Objectivism talks about the *sin of forgiveness* (see Chapter 20) it means the sin of forgiving *others* who have trespassed against you, not of you forgiving you for sins against the self. Those who do sin against their self create the need for self-forgiveness and this need—like all needs, including acquired ones—can only be met by going through a process aimed specifically at meeting a need—even if, to repeat, an acquired one. Morality applies only to actions in reality *because* man has *volitional* control over what he chooses to say and *do* in reality—in addition to what he lets in from reality (see Part II)—so a strong, moral person stands to benefit a great deal from self-directed growth enterprises aimed at becoming independent, *autonomous* man. If however such a moral person's morality has been turned all topsy-turvy, upside down by religious indoctrination and/or any other *altruistically* driven indoctrination and the person so affected has failed well into adulthood to correct the "wiring" errors associated with the indoctrination, then one has to proceed to correct those errors. Because man *is* a being of self-made soul he has to learn all he can about himself. And he must learn it honestly, scientifically (as in with a scientist's *devotion* to truth and precision) without

---

[17] Which is religion's way of denying the existence of *volition* in human nature which when added to religion's upside down, inside-out view of the *good*—that which is FOR a non-existent afterlife—and the *evil*—that which is AGAINST the non-existent afterlife—forms the basis for the *BiO Spiritualism proof* that religion is (ultimately) a *diabolical* creed by demonstrating *how* its discombobulated philosophy "works" or rather *doesn't work,* as is the *actual* fact of the matter.

distorting the internally observable facts (what *BiO Spiritualism* labels iObservations) that he himself must observe in order to make his soul stronger and/or better and/or remake it if his first-cut at making it *human* got too far off track. Because man is a moral being he must do this without "throwing out the baby with the bathwater", which is to say, he has to critique and evaluate his *past* moral choices *without* damning himself morally and concluding that his mistake was his *desire ... to be moral*.

If he does—so erroneously conclude that his mistake was the desire to be moral and he throws out this desire with his mistakes—then he (or she) is or will be in extremely deep, serious 'dudu—spiritually speaking.

Or at minimum he will find himself stuck psychologically and will suffer most if not all the psychological problems that accompany *insufficient* thinking.

So we can say that a person *should not* throw out the baby with the bathwater. That is, in this instance, he should not throw out his *desire-to-be-moral* with his mistakes-from-choices-based-on-a-*wrong*-moral-code. Rather he *should* continue striving to reach the goal of moral perfection; a goal that is reachable and depending on the particulars *might* require going through—not around, but through—a process of self-forgiveness.

This goal can only be reached via a *degree* of self understanding that is equivalent (almost) literally to a Ph.D. *degree* in Introspection.

The *prerequisites* to graduating with honors in your self-taught introspection classes *might* require you to go back to "kindergarten" and ace nature's preliminary tests on its 3 A's: *Self **Acceptance*** (101): I yam what I yam; *Self **Awareness*** (101): I am Popeye the sailor man and *Self **Assertion*** 101: toot-toot. And then follow through on all advanced versions that go more deeply into these subjects and then finally ace the test on the *application* of all of the three A's in the final class of *one R*: *Self **Responsibility*** 101: *mother please I'd rather do it myself*. And then do the same in all subsequent, *in-depth* fully advanced versions up to and including the Objectivism suggested: ... *by my life and my love of it ... I will never live for the sake of another man, nor ask another man to live for mine.*[i] Or at minimum try really really really hard to live up to this and other like sounding *heroic* attitudes and in-the-process receive your Ph. D equivalency in *Self Responsibility*.

Next let's consider those who *do* belong to one of the world's formal religions.

Of those who do belong to one of these religions there are two types: those who render unto reason that which is reason's and unto faith that which is faith's and those who don't.

Those who *don't* render anything onto reason are Islam Fundamentalists, those who do are not.

Of those who are *not* Islam Fundamentalists there are two types: those who worship faith *more* and *more* and more and those who don't.

This is to say, voila! *ultimately,* religion is a thief, an <u>epistemological</u> thief and (to at least *one* Lutheran) the *base* concrete for the abstraction: *diabolical.*[18]

No religion is any different than any other religion.

All religions are the same.

Ultimately—*if you let them*—they *steal* your *reason* and *use* it against you.

If you base your identification of a fact of reality on the evidence of your senses you are using your *capacity* to reason. If you base a conclusion on the *absence* of sensory evidence, this is faith. *Faith* is drawing conclusions in the absence of evidence. *Reason* is the faculty that identifies and integrates the material provided by man's senses[.][ii] (and/or earlier formed sensory based integrations[iii]). *Blind* faith is drawing conclusions in *opposition* to the evidence.

Since there is neither a god nor gods, nor dead spirits that live, "faith" is a live human being "thing".

What is this "thing"?

Psychology tells us—more precisely, *Biocentric Psychology* tells us—that faith is really "...the equation of *feeling* with *knowledge.*"[iv] A mystic, writes Dr. Branden on this same page, is "...[one who] treats his feelings as tools of cognition.", and more:

> Faith is the commitment of one's consciousness to beliefs for which one has no sensory evidence or rational proof.
>
> When a man rejects reason as his standard of judgment, only one alternative standard remains to him: his feelings.[v]

So, *maybe,* what Ayn Rand meant when she said religion is a primitive philosophy is that it is a primitive psychology, or perhaps we should say it is a

---

[18] In the King James version of *The Holy Bible* there is talk about *bad* things coming like a *thief in the night*. Who knew that that *thing* was religion itself. This I submit <u>is</u> diabolical and later on when we discuss the rat's nest of Cognitive Neuroscience we can have some insight (insight is good) into the twisty-turny, bramble bushyness of the neuronal networks that their "science" is attempting to Institutionalize (my Sunday school teacher always said to look for the *good* in things and being able to "see" epistemological webs *before* being snared by them *is* good).

primitive "spiritualism". If we assert that *true* spiritualism is the *process of making oneself the sole, prideful owner of a worthy and efficacious consciousness* and all that this entails, then perhaps this *process* depends on both philosophy—understanding our *reasoning* ability—and psychology—understanding our *emotional* capacity. That is, *both* combined, or more precisely, spiritualism's success requires both reason & emotion to be *integrated* within the individual person. Spiritualism, qua *How To* manual, is the integration of reason and emotion, that is, of philosophy and psychology within the *individual self*.

Hence the concept, *BiO Spiritualism*, which is an integration of *Biocentric Psychology* AND *Objectivism Philosophy* in the person, which is to say, spiritualism is the *application* of philosophy and psychology (and all that these entail) *by* a person, *to* the person and *for* the person.

BiO Spiritualism, psychologically speaking, is your Declaration of Independence; your Constitution and all such "documents" that you require to become an *autonomous*—self ruling—Self.

A nation of one so to speak, *where* life, liberty and the pursuit (and *achievement*) of happiness *are* sacred.

Chapter 3: Spiritual-*isms* in the Future:

ToBeDetermined (the spiritualisms not this chapter)

As *applied* philosophy and psychology, *spiritualisms* in the future will be as varied as in the past, but with this one change: because of *BiO Spiritualism*, Spiritualism now has an *initialized* scientific base, a base *in reason* and has been cut loose from mysticism and faith and all that those two's *absence* of reality entail and all that reason's insistence on *presence* of reality embraces.

Which is (will be) to say: 'if you ain't happy you ain't spiritual'.

BiO Spiritualism is rooted in *Objectivism*. Objectivism is rooted in its three axiomatic concepts: Existence exists, Consciousness is conscious, A is A and their implications: non-existence does not exist and is simply a fantasy, Consciousness is not derived from something more fundamental because without consciousness being fundamental there is no way to grasp the concept of "something else" and since A is A, contradictions do not exist as nature amply demonstrates by not having any. Consequently, *BiO Spiritualism* will prove to be—in any culture that worships reason more than faith 51% of the time or more and preferably more—it, *BiO Spiritualism*, will prove to be the *best* spiritualism. Best here means the only spiritualism just like Aeronautical Engineering, qua applied science, is the only Engineering Application for those who want to build airplanes that *actually* fly.

That is, for those in the 21st Century and beyond who actually want to fly—to the heights of happiness—*BiO Spiritualism* is their science to use in the design, development and deployment of *their* psyche's wings.

Part II:

If tough love is good, is tough *self-respect*—the *Creator* of the one who loves toughly—better?

*A recovery guide
for nice guys
seeking happiness*

Phase Ø: Curmudgeonism

For (real) Men Only*

* By men I mean as in mankind and by real I mean tough minded women and emotionally sensitive males between the ages of 19 and 109.

Chapter 4: Nice guys who came in last <START HERE> (Winners can jump to Part III)

BiO Spiritualism begins with self

Bullshit
as used in *BiO Spiritualism*, means:

> *the antiquated philosophical droppings from the minds of mystics*

and from this point forward will be referred to by the euphemistic term: bullstuff.

A curmudgeon is a person who *hates* bullstuff in other people, yet *refuses* to *stop* helping them *pretend* that they are *not* shoveling it.

A curmudgeon is an ex-nice guy.

Not the nice guy at the *beginning* of the race, but rather the nice guy at the end of the race, you know, the one who comes in last.

As to his or her own bullstuff, it is the basis of *what,* in the long run, it means for a nice guy turned curmudgeon to fully "recover". A fully recovered curmudgeon is one who dis-values bullstuff in him or her self *in addition* to hating it in others and who *subtracts* from his or her own repertoire of behaviors the epistemological underpinnings that support *pretending* that bullstuff shoveling is virtuous.

Which is to say, *curmudgeon recovery* is simple arithmetic: it's all about *addition* and *subtraction*: *adding* in the good and *subtracting* out the bad.[19]

For example, the other day—unbeknownst to me at the time—a soon to become ex-friend of mine was pontificating on negative emotions and how bad they are for you. I said (paraphrasing Biocentric Psychology), "if we *exclude* misapplication of our own values, then there isn't such a thing as a *bad* emotion". To which he said, "...of course there are. You don't think *hate* is good do you?" I of course said, of course it is: if you put a gun to my head and say you are going to murder me if I don't turn over my car keys and I manage to get away from your gun barrel and free from *your* thugery you can bet *your* evil soul I am going to

---

[19] The *good* is that which is for *human* life on this earth and the *bad* is that which is against it.

hate you because I *should* hate you. Hate is an emotional response—as are all emotions, *a response*—to attitudes I hold about me, myself and I and "our" life and its *actual* value to "us". If you say I *should not* hate, you are saying *we should not* value our life. If this is true—that we *not* value our life—then I as an ex-curmudgeon wannabe have a serious question for you.

How do *you* have a concept, *should?*

To which of course my *unreflective* friend turned himself into my ex-friend and into a full-fledged *mystic* when he replied: *you should not have any shoulds.*

To which I—*in my (then) curmudgeon mind*—replied: I object! Of course! you should have shoulds.

Which is to say, I *reiterated* to my (soon to be ex-) friend part of my definition of *BiO Spiritualism* given in Chapter 1.

Man's life on earth *is* an *end in itself* and *ends with itself* and your *shoulds* are going to determine what kind of life yours is.

Body is man's means to *physical* independence and autonomy, *for that life*. Your *shoulds* are going to determine what kind of body yours is—within the metaphysical options open to you. For example, if you are like me and physically short you metaphysically cannot make yourself be a foot taller than you are and therefore you *should* not have an internal definition that says only tall people can be happy. I've seen, without naming names, too many miserable tall people to know this is not the case.

Mind is man's means to *psychological* independence and autonomy, for *that life* and your *shoulds* are going to determine what kind of mind yours is.

Spirit is man's means to *consciousness* independence and autonomy for *that life* and your *shoulds* are going to determine how effective your consciousness is. Your *shoulds* are going to determine the efficacy of *your* consciousness.

Spiritualism is the *process* of making one's self the sole, prideful owner of a worthy and efficacious consciousness; a self-made consciousness that is worthy of happiness *because* it is competent at producing it.

And if this is *not* what *you* mean by "spiritualism", it *should* be.

Spiritualism is the *process* of making one's self the *sole, prideful, owner* of a worthy and efficacious consciousness; a self-made consciousness that is *worthy* of happiness *because* it is competent at producing it.

A competent consciousness is a happy consciousness and a happy consciousness is a competent consciousness.

Successful spiritualism, that is *spiritualism* of the *kind* we are talking about here, presupposes an *adult* mind and body.

An *adult mind* is one that thinks in *principles* about the world and one's self. It is one that *is* autonomous and self ruling in the self functions: thinking, judging, feeling, acting.

For example, consider the following.

Deepak Chopra, a professional Eastern mystic and ... wait. Halt. Before we can consider an *application* of thinking in principles we must go back and re-read and re-evaluate the statement about the relationship between *successful* spiritualism and the *adult* mind.

An *adult mind* is one that thinks in *principles* about the world and one's self. It is one that *is* (already) autonomous and (already) self ruling in the self functions: thinking, judging, feeling, acting (TFAJ). This is to say, autonomy and self-rule are psychological *values* (sought after and obtained on the psychological level of our being) and spiritual *virtues* (*maintained* by human action on ALL—TFAJ—levels of our being). By this I mean they *should* be valued and sought after on the *psychological* level of our being and then when obtained *the actions we engage in to maintain them* become our (spiritual) *virtues* (*spiritual* as in really high up there on *our* hierarchy of values—values as in *action-behaviors* we seek to gain and keep). *If you do not value psychological autonomy you will not be autonomous*. This is (almost) a tautology. Just like the other (almost) tautologies: If you do *not* value self-awareness you will not be self-aware; if you do *not* value self-acceptance you will not be self accepting; if you do *not* value self-assertion you will not be self assertive and if you do *not* value self-responsibility you will not be self-responsible.[20]

And I must hasten to add: if you *do* value these things you do not *automatically* obtain them, that is, *valuing* them is a *necessary* but not *sufficient* condition. The necessary *and* sufficient conditions are: value them *and* set the goals to obtain them *and* discover what is required to obtain them *and* then *do the work* to obtain them. Obtain them, that is, *after* you rationally convince yourself that *dignity* & *worth* as both are combined into one in *authentic* self esteem are legitimate human needs which, qua needs, can be met by our capacities to be self-

---

[20] These psychological values have survival value for us so they exist within us to some minimal degree without us actively, consciously valuing them *highly*, hence, I qualify my observations of these psychological values as *almost tautologies*. Let me explain further. If I said to you, "you know if you don't value dressing nice and having a clean cut look you will not have it" you might reply with the cliché: "well...that goes without saying". It's the sentiment of that cliché that I mean by it's an almost tautology: "if you don't value self-acceptance you will not be self accepting", ... well ... that goes without saying, and 'ya it does but sometimes we have to remind ourselves of it, which is to say it's an almost tautology, which is to say it's almost needlessly redundant, but not quite.

aware, self-accepting, self-assertive and self responsible—with self responsible in this context actually meaning *identify your psychological needs and act* to meet them. And when you succeed at this, then as one who possesses an *adult* mind you can continue your spiritual quest, remembering that:

> *An adult mind is one that thinks in principles about the world and one's self. It is one that is autonomous and self ruling in the self functions*: *thinking, judging, feeling, acting.*

For example, consider the following.

Deepak Chopra, a popular Eastern mystic and contemporary American "spiritualist", in his opening page in "The Seven Spiritual Laws of Success"[i], writes:

> You are what your deep, driving desire is.
> As your desire is, so is your will.
> As your will is, so is your deed.
> As your deed is, so is your destiny.
>   -   Brihadaranyaka Upanishad IV.4.5

As I read this I feel as if someone is darning socks in my head and using wet noodles as his yarn and if I am not careful I will end up—not with piles and piles of wearable socks, but rather with—piles and piles of unusable bullstuff.

Hence, "we" need to elevate our Bullstuff detectors up one notch. (We do, that is, IF we are going to read this *kind* of *any age* "advice giving" and hope to profit from it.)

Here's how.

Step 1: *Reduce and substitute*.

Before you do step 1 you *might* want to reflect on what, if anything, is good about the piece you are voluntarily choosing to judge. And if you too do this as I just did you may want to notice the *remnants* of nice-guyness in "our" *first* response here. For curmudgeon wannabe's this is very, very dangerous behavior to engage in. Better advice would be to do this after—if at all—because in balance if you accept bullstuff or *try* to accept it, you can only do so by *blanking out* on *multiple* levels of your being.

Blanking out on one level—e.g., the thinking level: "I don't think what I'm reading here is right, I don't think I understand it, but so what, this guy Chopra has written a lot of books and so he must know"—let alone on multiple levels—e.g., the feeling level too: "what's that feeling of discomfort I feel when I read this? It sounds like so much bullstuff I can't believe so many people buy it, but hey, I've got problems too and maybe this skepticism I feel all the time is the source of them, people who get published must know else they wouldn't be published and besides feelings *shouldn't* be listened too anyway"—is not good. (In trauma situations *blanking out* may have survival value in the moment—which is good—but over the long run even this has to eventually be faced and dealt with in order to move *through* the blanks and hence *beyond* the problems associated with them.)

So I—as honorary ex-curmudgeon—recommend saving any evaluation of *good* to last, if at all and I *add* the "if at all" thought because if there is *any* good in professionally published gibberish it probably is coming from you, qua *interested* reader, in the first place. The reason for this is that "they"—those who *want* us to *worship* faith over and above *reason*—*depend* on this good reason within us and they use it against us. Consequently, you have to preserve and protect this *good reason* in you and use it for you yourself: you have to give yourself—not "them"—the *benefit* of the doubt. (Remember, *BiO Spiritualism* starts with the self—with the self, that is, that is inside existence, consciousness and identity. And as you will learn later, it ends here also.[21])

First, identify the fundamental concepts in the writing and replace the author's words for them with your more fundamental word-concepts by copying and replacing them on a one-to-one basis. Or, at minimum, replace as close to one-for-one as you can get so as to preserve the original structure (this helps you to not rewrite the original which is not our goal, our goal is to identify originator's bullstuff). For our example here: *desire* is feeling or emotion, *will* is volition, *deed* is behavior (in this context *behavior* is better than *action* because behavior has a re-active connotation to it whereas action is pro-active and because Chopra uses the word destiny, re-active as in "the devil made me do it" or in the "stuff happens" tradition of, *don't expect anything out' a me* is *implied*.)

Substitute and preserve original structure:

> You are what your emotions are.
> As your emotions are, so is your volition.
> As your volition is, so is your behavior.
> As your behavior is, so is your destiny.

---

[21] This is *one* of the things that makes *BiO Spiritualism* unique. Many spiritualisms—formal or informal—start with self but end with beyond-the-self messages, that is, with *transpersonal* rhetoric that all say the same (old, antiquated, boring, bullstuff) thing: ego is bad, self-ish-ness is bad; self-less-ness is good, altruism is the ideal. *BiO Spiritualism* holds firmly—very firmly, extremely firmly—to the Objectivist tenet that says: Selfishness *is* a virtue.

Next, Step 2: Simplify further and *estimate* the Truth (T) or Falsity (F) of each element:

You are what your emotions are.	You are *some*-thing (T).
As your emotions are, so is your volition.	Emotions *cause* volition (F, reverse is T).
As your volition is, so is your behavior.	Volition can control re-active action (T).
As your behavior is, so is your pre-determined fate	Man is a being of self-made wealth or self made poverty (T), but he is *not* a being of self made soul (F).

Then, Step 3: Stand back and Observe the BS. (Notice that as "we" used our *volition* to make the choice to *judge* the piece in the first place we discover more bullstuff *as we apply the steps*, that is*, in the process itself.* For example, in Step 1 we didn't assign more importance to the word *destiny*, but in moving on to step 2 and thinking about it *as we go* we could easily recognize the *connotation* of the word *destiny* and then just add this discovery into our *evaluation*. Once you accept the tenet—*judge and be prepared to be judged*—this kind of *good* discovery happens all the time. In fact, if we were interested in generating bumper stickers, we could say, in this context, "good happens".)

Referencing *our* True and False *evaluations* in the author's four lines as whole we observe a dual-split: the first half is half wrong, the second half is $2/3^{rd}$'s true. But for the *whole* argument to be true each and every element has to be true: mystic "spiritualists" notwithstanding, truth is not a mixture of true and false—that's a description of what "half truths" are, that is, *half truths* are *all* wrong. Truth is the summation of little truths into bigger truths or of bigger truths deconstructed into littler truths with *each* and *every* **one**—no exceptions—being true. *Volition*—when used anywhere in any form, including "will" as in line 2 and line 3 in our piece—means *free* will which means, non-existence of any antecedent causes *other than you* the individual human being *choosing* to think about this or that and choosing to act this way or that. Consequently, the "emotions cause volition" *sentiment* is false because nothing causes volition; volition is the bottom line, the end of the road, the place where the buck stops.

Where the rubber meets the road, where your *choices* determine who and what you are. The devil didn't make you do it, you did. God isn't compassionate, *you* are. The gods aren't the source of "reason", human nature is.

Nor are the gods the *source* of good and evil: *you are.*[22]

---

[22] As am I also as well as every other *volition* possessing "creature" in the Universe (of which so far, here on earth, we know of only one—man.) The *good* in the original piece is that its structure—a is b is c is d is e(nd)—implicitly does not contradict the fact that our knowledge and *values* exist on a hierarchy (which virtually all Americans can now, post September 11th, 2001, *easily* relate to as we discover the base of this hierarchy in one area: our *political values*. That base is: we Americans *worship* freedom and justice, as in freedom from *initiated* thugery and just-rewards, that is, death, for murdering thugs). Had Chopra's original piece had one additional line, either at the beginning or at the end, that acknowledged either explicitly or implicitly the fact that volition *put* the "deep desire" *in its seat* to begin with then the message would be as it *should*: volition is "destiny", *not* "god works in mysterious, mystical ways and we can't figure ourselves out using reason". But notice, it didn't *add* this additional thought, I did. This self-crediting is an example of a *Biocentric Psychology* value, one it calls: *honoring the self*. If you feel here that I am not honoring the self but being arrogant instead then I *challenge* you to investigate *your* "definition" of *arrogance* and see if, you might, be sacrificing your self to it. And yes, I am aware that by adding this particular footnote I am revealing that "nice guy" impulses still reside within, but since introspection and self understanding are high high psychological *values* to me, I accept this... for now.

Chapter 5: Your psychology's three most important elements:

Volition, Volition, Volition

VOLITION

New Age Spiritualisms are weird.

I don't like the word *weird* and I have vowed on other occasions to never use it. But, here I am, using it, so I must look it up.

My dictionary says: Faith-Destiny, esp. ill fortune, soothsayer; of, relating to, or caused by witchcraft or the supernatural; of strange or extraordinary character, odd, fantastic.[i]

Yikes! I didn't know that this word was tied so directly to *New Age* Spiritualisms: soothsaying, caused by witchcraft or supernatural. I thought I was going to find a definition *centered* around *odd* and *strange*, which is the way I use it, but I didn't expect this.

Now what?

I guess the thing to do is to repeat.

New Age Spiritualisms **are** *weird*.

Consider Deepak again, same book, pp. 66, 67, and 68.[ii] Here he begins a new chapter with his *Law of Intention and Desire* with its gibberish rich content. A content which I recommend to the reader here he/she use as exercise—that is, *apply* the three steps from above as *practice* in elevating ones bullstuff detectors to higher and higher levels of ability.[23]

On the first page of the chapter, Deepak begins to justify his "law" by buzzwording it into science concepts like "energy", "information", "quantum", and philosophy concepts like "pure", "consciousness" and "potentiality" and then goes into "example" to back up the buzz:

---

[23] Whether we like it or not this is one of the manifest problems that faces *modern* man that did not face our ancestors (more precisely the pre-Gutenberg ones), but just like our ancestors had weapons of defense on par with weapons of destruction *particular* to their age so do we have weapons of defense (in the epistemological / mind realm where the battle for happiness is won or lost) in line with—and even superior to—weapons of mind destruction that are particular to *our* age. *Bullstuff detector*, qua euphemism for *contradiction detector*, is one such (epistemological) self-defensive weapon.

"A flower, a rainbow, a tree, a blade of grass," he starts and continues, "a human body, when broken down to their essential components are energy and information. The whole Universe, in its essential nature, is the *movement* of energy and information. The only difference between you and a tree is the informational and energy content of your respective bodies." (p.67-68)

When I read this I think, *bullstuff*! the only difference between me and a tree is that I could (in theory) have sex with my favorite female actress but a tree can't. My actress might *hug* a tree but that's *as far* as it can go.

So if Deepak or anyone else doesn't think it's *weird* to suggest that a tree can have sex with humans, then I don't know what weird is.

VOLITION

New Age—as in non-*BiO Spiritualism*—Spiritualisms *are* weird. Consider.

Gary Zukav, another well known (American) "spiritualist" and author of many titles on the subject, in the introduction to his book, "Soul Stories"[iii] says this:

> The Lakota people, who are Native Americans, have a story about the white buffalo calf woman. She is the one who gave them their sacred pipe. A reporter asked a Lakota elder one day if he thought that the story of the white buffalo calf woman was true. The elder said, "I don't know whether it actually happened that way or not, but you can see for yourself that it's true." (p.15)

> You can see for yourself that all of the stories in this book are true, too. You have to look inside yourself to do that. Every Soul Story, whether you find it in this book or somewhere else, requires that you look inside yourself to see if it is true. You may find that something that is true for someone else is not true for you. You might also find that something that is true for you is not true for you is not true for someone else. That is the way it is with Soul Stories. (p.16)

> For example, some people say that the universe is dead (they call it "inert"), and that everything that happens is accidental (they say "random"). Other people, like me, say that the Universe is alive, wise and compassionate. Looking at the universe as dead is one story. Looking at it as alive is another. Which story is true for you? (p.16)

> You have to decide. Each of the Soul Stories in this book gives you an opportunity to decide whether it is true for you or not. The Lakota elder said that you can see for yourself when a story is true, but before you can do that, you have to know about it. That means thinking about it and, even more important, discovering what you feel about it. Eventually,

> you might find that what you feel about a Soul Story is more
> important to you than what you think about it. (p.16)

Reading this one makes me *feel* as if the physical brain inside my skull is made of cauliflower and someone is spot drilling holes in it with an electric hole saw and if I am not careful when I go back to evaluate the "evidence" it will have been removed like so much compressed cauliflower dust along with the hole saw when same is retracted by the carpenter-author-maker of such a firm, yet vegetative kind of story.

This is to say, carpenters who drill holes in cauliflower with three-quarter horsepower electric drill needs to re-evaluate their chosen profession and make up their minds whether they want to be carpenters or cooks. Or at absolute minimum, they *should* use tools appropriate to their chosen profession. Here as master bullstuff slinger, Zukav should be using a 5-tongued pitchfork: one tongue for each level of our being he *asks* us to *blank out on* in order to "grasp" his "meaning".

Which is to say, here is one example of one *benefit* of being a curmudgeon (curmudgeonism isn't all bad): it can be a time saver. The Zukav book is 247 pages long and we only had to read a few *among the opening pages* to discover what the author *really* thinks.[24] What he really thinks is this:

1. *Emotions are tools of cognition.*
2. There are no absolutes; everything is relative.
3. Truth means "feels right, *therefore* is right", which is restatement of number 1.
4. The purpose of words is to communicate feelings, therefore I (Zukav) am justified in using them to communicate *my* feelings as they change from one sentence to the next.
5. Most (rather, *enough*) people's bullstuff detectors are so inadequate that they will never-ever in a million-billion-gazillion years be able to detect my (G. Zukav's) bullstuff.

---

[24] Hence the good *here* (for you still struggling nice-guys) is that many "spiritualist" writers *usually* save this stuff 'til last so that you have to read their entire book(s) before they reveal (and hence you discover) their *mystic* and/or *altruistic* and/or *collectivistic* soul. Here, to repeat, Zukav is unique, he does it for us right off the bat, saving us precious time in the process. (As an aside: a mini-technique you can use for saving your mind is to read—or at least *scan* to get the gist of the author's goal—the conclusion part of individual chapters and/or the concluding chapters of the book—that is, do this for the non-fiction books that you are interested in that are advocating *ways-of-being* and *becoming* in the world.)

Step 0A, editorialize on above, that is, repeat it and *add* your editorial comments and evaluations:

1. *Emotions are tools of cognition.* This is false: *reason* is the tool of figuring out *what* things are; *emotions* are the *means* by which we *experience* what life *actually* means to us, us qua specific, particular, *actual* individual persons experiencing human life in the world.

2. There are no absolutes; everything is relative, to which one should ask: relative to what?

3. Truth means "feels right, *therefore* is right", which is restatement of number 1, and is the logical *default* position for those who are willing to die for the erroneous proposition that says: *faith* is better than *reason*.[25]

4. The purpose of words is to communicate feelings; therefore I (Zukav) am justified in using them to communicate *my* feelings as they change from one sentence to the next. And sometimes even waiting for the next sentence to come up can be too long a time and one *should* —if required— switch felt meanings of concepts *within* sentences in order to accommodate one's *faith*-based *core* beliefs. An example of a core belief of Zukav's needing such an accommodation is this: Native American Indian's *brand* of mysticism is superior to other brands of mysticism — everybody "knows" this ... don't they?[26]

5. Most (rather, *enough*) people's bullstuff detectors are so inadequate that they will never-ever in a million-billion-gazillion years be able to detect my (G. Zukav's) bullstuff. (No comment).

Step 1, do a simple analysis on the original material, which means highlight that which catches your bullstuff detector's eye:

> The Lakota people, who are Native Americans, have a story about the white buffalo calf woman. She is the one who

---

[25] *Reason* is drawing conclusions based on evidence. *Faith* is drawing conclusions based on the *absence* of evidence. *Blind* faith is drawing conclusions in *opposition* to the evidence. *Refusing* to draw any conclusions ever is *what*—in *BiO Spiritualism*—we call, scardy-cat man.

[26] A mystic is a person who believes that there is some way to knowledge other than reason. All mystics are of this same kind. As individuals within the larger group, individual mystics differ only in degree, not kind. Their degree of difference is in *how much* they hate and despise reason: from totally and completely, to some-what, to a little bit to a shred. Those who like reason a shred, differ in kind and can't be properly classified as mystics. They may end up loosing the battle for control over their own mind but that is a different, albeit related, tragedy.

gave them their sacred pipe. A reporter asked a Lakota elder one day if he *thought* that the story of the white buffalo calf woman was *true*. The elder said, "I don't know whether it *actually happened* that way or not, but you can see for yourself that it's *true*." (p.15)

The use of "actually happened" tells us the author is *trying* to distinguish between figurative and literal, metaphor and actual event, saying that if the actual event didn't happen it doesn't change the *message* in the story. Which is true, but here we can "buy" this if we buy it all the way, which is to say: *every story has a message* and if we are going to *rely* on stories to communicate messages to ourselves we better goddamn well know and understand *what* the message is. So right off the bat, we discover our mission, our goal: *understand the message*.

Step 2, continue analysis but with our goal now firmly in mind:

You can see for yourself that all of the stories in this book are true, too. You have to look inside yourself to do that. Every Soul Story, whether you find it in this book or somewhere else, requires that you look inside yourself to see if it is true. You may find that something that is true for someone else is not true for you. You might also find that something that is true for you is not true for someone else. That is the way it is with Soul Stories. (p.16)

Message in Line 1 is this: All stories have a message.
Message in Line 2 is: Introspection is a value
Message in Line 3 is: Repetition is emphasis.
Message in Line 4 is, repeat, introspection is a value
Message in Line 5 is, truth is relative to the subject, that is, truth is subjective not objective.
Message in Line 6 is, repeat message in line 5
Message in Line 7 is, *isn't circular reasoning just the greatest?*

Step 2A, note your *estimate* of Truth (T) or falsity (F) of each element:

Message in Line 1 is, all stories have a message. (T)
Message in Line 2 is, introspection is a value. (T)
Message in Line 3 is, repetition is emphasis. (T)
Message in Line 4 is, repeat, introspection is a value. (TT)
Message in Line 5 is, truth is relative to the subject, that is truth is subjective not objective. (F)

Message in Line 6 is, repeat message in line 5 (line 5 message is still F)
Message in Line 7 is, *isn't circular reasoning just the greatest?* (No! F)

Step 2B, What is the message? Truth is relative, truth is subjective, and by truth Zukav means as in, say, it is true I like ice cream and not buttermilk whereas you like buttermilk and not ice cream. But since truth is the identification of the *facts* of reality, if the foregoing *is* true then it is a fact of truth *about me* and *about you* and our likes and dislikes. Hence, it is true FOR BOTH OF US. That is, to you *and* me—in this context—it is true that I like ice cream and so on and to you and me it is true that you like buttermilk and so on. So what's going on here? Truth isn't relative, so *why* does the *particular* author *want* me to think that it is?

It's too early to tell.

Step 3, read and analyze on:

> For example, some people say that the universe is dead (they call it "inert"), and that everything that happens is accidental (they say "random"). Other people, like me, say that the Universe is alive, wise and compassionate. Looking at the universe as dead is one story. Looking at it as alive is another. Which story is true for you? (p.16)

And now had we not done our goal work it would be—not too early, but—too late, to save ourselves. Here is the payoff. The reason why the author wants us to accept the tenet that truth is relative is because if we do then we *lower* our bullstuff detector shields and let in the author's bullstuff. If we do this then we will end up in that group—the one Zukav is writing to—that thinks it's nit-picky to differentiate between the tenet *it's virtuous to have an open mind* and the (*Objectivism*) counter to it that says, *false*, the truth is, *its virtuous to have an **active** mind.*

*As pertains to human minds, open and active definitely are **not** the same thing—active* is good, *open* is dangerous.

Step 3A, delineate as much of the bullstuff as you can stomach:

1. universe is dead, say you, no I (*BiO Spiritualism* guy and ex-Mechanical design Engineer) say it is "inert"

2. everything that happens is "random", say you, no I (*BiO Spiritualism* et al. guy) say *random* pertains only to the man-made and if you Zukav are thinking about the laws of gas molecules and/or the "science" of meteorology and "science's" debatable ability to *predict* either the

behavior of "individual" gas molecules or the weather, I say as man-made issues these are *epistemological* not *metaphysical* issues. Which is to say, by way of example: if today is Tuesday and on Thursday next, the one after tomorrow, I look back to Wednesday and *observe* that it rained and today the weatherman *predicts* no rain tomorrow the only two things I can *legitimately, rationally* conclude on Thursday is: man is *not* omniscient and, I don't need Zukav to "enlighten" me on this point while using it to "conclude" one can't conclude anything with certainty, therefore (he concludes with certainty) his bullstuff is as good as non-omniscient science. It clearly is not.

3. Me Zukav says the Universe is alive, wise and compassionate, just like a human being, that is I (Zukav) am engaging in the *true* meaning and *mis-use* of anthropomorphizing: assigning *animate-human* characteristics to *in-animate* objects and then concluding this makes the in-animate, animate. And not only that, but also praising my (Zukav's) *in-ability* to *differentiate* between the animate and in-animate. *He who can't differentiate is a superior being* sayeth Zukav **message** (with or without double meaning we can't say for sure.)

4. universe as dead is one story, as alive, another. Which story is true for you? And now the payoff is so apparent that one wonders where this guy got the balls to think peoples bullstuff detectors were so ... so ... *inadequate* that he could get away with it? Since *existence exists* is an irreducible primary, existence can't die—that is, cease to exist—hence it isn't alive, because if alive then dying —that is, ceasing to exist—is an inevitable event. It's like the religious people from the last century who want you to get into the erroneous debate (also from the last century) started by the question: So you think God is dead, hun? To which the *Objectivists* at the time—in the person of Dr. Nathaniel Branden—gave the correct answer and in so doing *elevated* the question to philosophical heights. "They" (the good they, the Objectivists) answered: No, in order to be dead God would have had to have been alive and since there is no god, never has been; it is *meaningless* to say God is dead.[iv]

Step 3B, *think*: Does this make *Objectivism*, the Philosophy, a weapon of self-defense?

Epistemologically (spiritually?) speaking?

Step 4, continue on if you can or stop: (*My* nice-guy would stop, therefore I'm continuing on):

> You have to decide. Each of the Soul Stories in this book gives you an opportunity to decide whether it is true for you or not. The Lakota elder said that you can see for yourself when a story is true, but before you can do that, you have to know about it. That means thinking about it and, even more important, discovering what you feel about it. Eventually, you might find that what you feel about a Soul Story is more important to you than what you think about it. (p.16)

BiO Spiritualism takes it as a given that emotions are the **means** by which we enjoy life and if we are *not* in touch with *our* emotions we do not *know* what **our** life means *to us*. This observation, this *true* observation is a discovery of *reason*. Reason and emotion are *not* the same thing and their *functions* are *not* interchangeable. Hence, it seems reasonable to surmise that if one wants to be happy one had better damn well understand the *differences* between *reason* and *emotion*.[27] If one doesn't *want* to be happy, well, then, I guess that's another …"story".

Which is to say, one's *choice*.

Step 5, Done.

No, wait. Go back and revisit that last, do some Step 1 analysis:

> You have to decide. Each of the Soul Stories in this book gives you an opportunity to decide whether it is true for you or not. The Lakota elder said that you can see for yourself when a story is true, but before you can do that, you have to ***know*** about it. That means ***thinking*** about it and, even ***more important***, discovering what you ***feel*** about it. Eventually, you might find that what you ***feel*** about a Soul Story is ***more important*** to you than what you ***think*** about it. (p.16)

Since feelings, that is *emotions* come from our thinking—that is, emotions are value **responses** and *what* we **actually** *value* has its roots in what we thought we *should* value—why does Zukav *want* us to *use our thinking* to conclude that

---

[27] For more on this see the *science* of psychology, that is, the *Biocentric Psychology* of Dr. Nathaniel Branden and his books and audio tapes on the subject of emotions, reason and their differences and role in human life.

thinking is bad for us? Is he mad at *his* Universe because in its infinite "wisdom" it made him, qua human being, *fallible*? Or is this an *example* of using the *best* within us (that is thinking, that is, *reason*) to *destroy* the best within us (that is thinking, that is, *reason*)? This last is harsh I know, but if **you** *allow* **your** nice-guy to dominate here, you *are* dead ... spiritually (that is, epistemologically) speaking.

VOLITION

As The Philosophy of *Objectivism* is the world's *best* (as in most consistent, widest abstracting, broadest most noncontradictory integration of the known facts) Philosophy, so also is *Biocentric Psychology* the world's *best* psychology. Since *Spiritualism*, as I've already defined, is the *process* of making one's self the *sole, prideful, owner* of a "manufacturing plant" dedicated to the *manufacture* of *one's own* happiness and since this requires *philosophy and psychology* why would one *not* select the best? Of course, one would not, not do this and so I *logically* select *Biocentri*c and *Objectivi*sm for my *spiritual* underpinnings and now set out to make some points to be followed up in subsequent Chapters.

Point one: *Biocentric Psychology* is psychology, the science. All other "psychologies"—behaviorist, psychoanalytic, cognitive, humanistic et al.—that claim to be the science are not. At best they are sub-branches of Biocentric; at worst they are "6-Up" attempts to discover "7-Up". This is to say, Psychology, the science, is Biocentric Psychology that defines psychology as *the science that studies the attributes and characteristics that certain living organisms possess by virtue of being conscious.*[v]

Point two. *BiO Spiritualism*—though it is life-centered—does not stand for bio-centric but rather for:

> **Bi**(ocentric Psychology) + **O**(bjectivism Philosophy) with the PLUS as in *Integrated* Application of, *to self.*[28]

Point three: As an et al. contender for the title of true scientific psychology, the de facto psychology we could call *Objectivism* Psychology is not as good as *Biocentric Psychology* and we will deal with this in Chapter 20 where we answer the two questions: Does *Objectivism* need *Biocentric Psychology?* Is vice versa a tautology?

---

[28] Since I am both an *applications* Engineer (by *choice,* education, training and first career life's work) *and* a self-taught biocentric objectivist, my (BiO) *spiritualism* is an *application* of (Biocentric) Psychology and (Objectivist) Philosophy. If the owners of the names *Biocentric* and *Objectivism*—in this context—don't like my using their names and I am vulnerable legally to their dislike (the State of Minnesota once threatened to send me to jail for failing to recognize their alleged ownership and control over the word "psychologist" but they failed *because* I backed down completely and so here I'm only going to back down *half* way—and view it as an *improvement*—and note that just because the State failed to send me to jail doesn't automatically mean others can't succeed) then the *BiO* in *BiO Spiritualism* means bio-centric, as in life-centered. If not then not.

Point 4: On the heels of Point 2's footnote "we" offer Hypothesis H_0:

> Without knowing *what* the thing is yet, we can speculate that there is a "thing" that can be called the "Bureaucratic Mind" and it is a "thing" in the same sense as Dr. Stanton Samenow has described the "Criminal Mind" as a (specific, identifiable) "thing".[vi]

They aren't necessarily the same thing, just both "things". If we want to invoke a kind of Dr. Zeus "reasoning" in order to simplify what we are after here we can and do, thusly: Thing 1 and Thing 2 for these two (the BM and the CM) for now is okay and we so do it and let it go ... for now... to come back to later.[29]

Point 5: The Bureaucratic Mind is *embedded* (like a computer virus in a computer program) in the American *form* of Democratic government. That is, a Democracy *form* we could call *mixalism*, as in a *weird* mixture of *freedom* and *controls*. A mixture of freedoms derived from *legitimate* individual rights (to life and property) and of "controls" based on the *desire* to control ... others. A desire made possible by getting all the non-thinkers in the country to gleefully accept the (illegitimate) *concept* of (phony) group "rights". Since groups have no rights—only *individuals* do—and since the population as a whole was getting too smart for T.H.E.M (the Bureaucratic Mind), t.h.e.y had to steal the concept of the *Science of Psychology* (primarily by calling it the Science of Behavior) and start using it to control its citizen-subjects (in the Bureaucrat's hands it *is* the Science of Behavior, that is, the S*cience* of behavior *control* ... of the *individual* ... for the exclusive *benefit* of ... the Group).

Point 5A: This *form,* this "tool" of the Bureaucratic mind's desire and intention to control us will grow stronger as the 21st century progresses.

That is to say, *autonomous* man is in deep sh... trouble, hence so is *spiritual* man.

---

[29] The basis for this *speculation* about a *Bureaucratic Mind* (being a "thing" in the sense Dr. Samenow's Criminal Mind is a "thing") is the fact that normal, industrious, productive people told Louie the XIV some 300(!)years ago to *leave us alone* (in French, *laissez-faire, nous*) and today (300 years later) we *still* don't have a 100% laissez-faire capitalist society that views the government as our legalized *protector* against thugs and not as legalized *provider* of our daily bread. Is this 300 years of effort—albeit noble—a *failure* due to the *Bureaucratic Mind* (BM for short)? Also for more discussion on thing 1 and thing 2, qua things, see Chapter 18, page 208.

Point 6: those who say "...all that point 5 means is that life goes on, *c'est la vie*, that's life, *that's the way the cookie crumbles*, such is the human condition..." will be the *first* to succumb to government controllers.[30,vii]

---

[30] By government controllers here I mean the *Bureaucratic Mind* inside the government which is the place the BM is attracted to. And by BM I don't mean *conspiratorially* as in Story book ideas, e.g. Paramount's spy movie, *3 Days of the Condor* about a CIA inside the CIA, but rather I mean, *the one inside that*.

Chapter 6: I Object!(ivism): Your purpose in life is not to *just* oppose.

Your purpose in life is to *be* happy.

Objectivism—a modern day American-Aristotelian-Discovered by the late, great, Russian born genius, turned American citizen and American hero, Ayn Rand *philosophy* purged of all Platonic influence and with all of Aristotle's other errors either corrected or removed—*challenges* us to be happy. It says that as far as *formal, modern day philosophy* can figure out, man is *suppose* to be happy here on this earth while he actually lives and breathes and if he isn't it is his own fault. It is his own fault because nature provides him with all the tools he needs to be happy and so his job is this: be happy. [31]

But *Objectivism*, *unlike* all non-Aristotelian philosophies and *all* religions, also recognizes that since man has a *volitional* consciousness and a survival that depends on his *reasoning* capacity he has to *choose* to think and in so doing *learn how to use his capacities to fulfill his needs* to survive and be happy in the long run.[32]

If I were still religious, which I *absolutely* am not, I would say here that *Objectivism* begat the *Biocentric Psychology* of that other great naturalized American citizen (if actually then actually; if not, then, *in spirit*) and hero, Canadian born Dr. Nathaniel Branden to help us out in the *learning how to use*

---

[31] This is one reason why *Objectivism* is not a religion and also one reason why *Objectivism*, qua a concrete, specific *philosophy*, is *better* than religion: Religion "challenges" us to be miserable and to love it, *Objectivism* challenges us to be happy, here and now while we actually live. *Biocentric psychology* then, as *logical* follow on to Objectivism, shows *ex*-religionists—among others with the idiosyncratic need to undo their idiosyncratic ex-Nihilo'isms—*how to do this in the context and process of *making* one's religion *ex*, while at the same time* making ones psychological self autonomous and self-valuing. (I understand here that I am not doing anything illegal in my *advocacy* because just as in a free market of goods and services so too *in a free market* of ideas everyone has the right to advertise their product—e.g., *BiO Spiritualism*—as the best. The only difference here is I am saying why *BiO Spiritualism* is the best or in the least has the *potential* to be the best spiritualism, *because* it is based on the best philosophy *and* psychology which are the cornerstones of the spiritual.)

[32] "Learning how to use Gary Deering's capacities to satisfy Gary Deering's needs" is a formulation I learned from Biocentric Psychology more so than from Objectivism and so I credit Dr. Branden with its discovery. And if the reader here thinks this is *not* a discovery I challenge them to *seriously* explore Dr. Branden's works and to hold on to their conviction to the end.

our capacities to fulfill our needs to survive and be happy in the long run. But, since I no longer believe in god and am forever on the edge of *concluding* that religion is evil I won't say it. (That *Objectivism* begat *Biocentric* as described, not that religion is evil. *When* religion *openly* preaches and advocates that morality without religion is metaphysically impossible, *then* I will conclude it is evil. When religion *openly* preaches and advocates that man's individual ego should submit to the will of god or else that same ego will burn forever in hell, so what matter "we" religionists murder the individual now in the name of God, *then* I will conclude it is evil. When religion *openly* preaches and advocates that faith is better than *reason* and for all those who think otherwise and act based on those thoughts then they will be put to death in the name of faith, *then* I will conclude religion is evil. But ___ *until and unless* ... well ___ we each have to fill in the "blanks" ourselves.[33])

But what I will say is that *Objectivism* has given us one hell of a challenge and if you too like a good challenge, a *serious* challenge then *BiO Spiritualism* will help you accept the challenge and meet it head on.

And win.

The first step in accepting the *Objectivism* challenge *to be happy* is to accept the *Objectivist* definition of happiness in its simplest form: *Happiness is a state of non-contradictory joy*.[i]

Second and subsequent "steps" are to answer the question: What the heck does this *mean*?

It means that if you took a happiness meter—the one in *BiO Spiritualism* we call a *teleömeter*—and clamped its probes around your entire body from head-to-toe and turned it on, its gauge's two needles—one for the *extent* to which *you* personally are FOR non-contradiction and one for the *extent* to which *you* personally are FOR joy—would deflect *positively* in a clockwise direction indicating you are on the right path to happiness.[34] And, by contrast, if either one or both needles didn't so point but rather buried themselves against the gauge's mechanical stops as they tried to express their *negative* view on these two topics

---

[33] It seems as if every day I read something in the newspapers that suggests 21st Century Islam (a modern religion) is as evil as was 15th Century Inquisition Christianity (a primitive religion?). Christianity (in *its* modern day form) did change so there is hope for Islam too. A hope of course that is up to the individuals who practice it and we should salute those brave souls in Iran who (as reported in today's, St. Paul Pioneer Press, Tuesday November 19, 2002 newspaper) risked their lives to protest the death sentence against their university professor Hashem Aghajari, who had been sentenced to death for apostasy, which is the turning away from (his Shiite) *faith*. Since *Christianity* no longer executes people for speaking out against religious faith we can *no longer* call them evil. But the same does not apply to modern day *Islam*.

[34] Unless you live in left-handed Briton in which case "positive" would be counterclockwise.

then you would know what, *exactly*, you have to do to be happy: change your *(meta)physics*.

Ouch! That doesn't sound possible. How do I do this?

By changing your *epistemology*.

Double ouch!! And how do I do this?

By changing your *ethics*.

If you believe that *altruism* (others before self *always*) is morally superior to—as in better than—*rational egoism* (what in *BiO Spiritualism* we call *Objectivism selfishness*[35]) then you have to change this attitude as one prerequisite to the *possibility* of being happy.

If not then not.

At the same time you have to think about your own psychological epistemology and *make* it rational. Psychological epistemology, or what Objectivism and Biocentric Psychology call, *psycho-epistemology* is *your* thinking MO, *your* modus operandi in the operation of *your* own consciousness: the way in which *you* run the *volitional* aspects of your faculty of consciousness and how you allow same to interact with the *automatic* operations of mind—of *your* mind. *You* have control over *your* own psycho-epistemology and to learn how to control this is the meaning of changing *your* epistemology. You have to become, by choice, the programmer of your own mental apparatus and the "computer" languages of this programming are...English, Italian, Japanese, German, Russian, etc., whatever happens to be the language you are most fluent in.

So for example when you read or recast the following into your language of most fluency the *meaning* is the same:

> *Psycho-epistemology*, per *Biocentric Psychology*, is the nature of, and the relationship between, the conscious, goal-setting, self-regulatory operations of the mind, and the subconscious, automatic operations.[ii] And per *Objectivism*: (Psycho-epistemology is the study of man's cognitive processes from the aspect of the interaction between the conscious mind and the automatic functions of the subconscious.)[iii]

---

[35] Qualifying selfishness in any way—including *this* way—is dangerous. Selfishness *is* a virtue and we should *always* remember this ahead of our nice-guy impulses to soften the blow on those who disagree and have chosen *Altruism* as *their* moral code.

As to *your* metaphysics—that is, *your* comprehensive view of the world and your place in it—well, that's a bit more complicated. It is premature at this point to even try and change it—assuming of course that it needs changing, it might not—so this "need" should be left until later to see if we really need to change it and if we do we will address it at that time.

To anticipate the *possibility* of change, allow me to pose a question to be answered later:

> *Social Metaphysician or Metaphysical Metaphysician, which one are you?*

Chapter 7: Where can I buy me one of them *Happiness Meters?*

Or, that is, *What's a teleömeter?*

If I were a spiritualist of the *mystical* variety I would say that *what* those physicists who debate whether their latest discovered littlest "thing" in the Universe is a *particle* or a *wave* are really demonstrating by their never ending debates is *that* human beings can't know anything. Since humans can't know anything—such human mystics then argue—how can they know the most fundamental thing in the Universe? Truth is humans can't, concludes the mystic, only god(s) *can* know and only god *does* know.

But since I am not a mystic, I don't admire mystics. In fact I dislike mystics *because* they are like an infinitely expanding bullstuff bag that can *never* be filled. So I would say—metaphorically—that competing views about what happiness is *fundamentally*—is it a *cause* or is it an *effect?*—is as fundamental and as critical a discussion to ethical spiritualists as is that debate between physicists who debate whether the most fundamental thing in the universe—let's call it an *existron*—is [it] a particle or a wave [?], is to physicists.

The correct answer to the physicist's problem of course is this: it (the existron) is a particle.[36]

The correct answer to the ethical spiritualist's problem is this: it (*happiness*) is a cause *and* it is an effect ... in a *homeostatic* way.

With the space, " ", between *homeostatic* and *way* replaceable with: " *volitional* ".

Consider.

We are born tabula rasa and we die filled in with a life's worth of *thoughts* and *feeling*s and *action*s, making up a life's worth of successes and failures, joys and sufferings, of deeply satisfying sexual experiences and of ho hum ones and of like minded eating experiences and of mind bending euphoric "spiritual" experiences and of lesser charged, lower peak ones and ... so on and so forth; the list could go on and on and on....

---

[36] Technically—as in for *precision's* sake—speaking, the correct *philosophical* answer is: it is *what* it is because if it isn't, it isn't an it.

But it doesn't. At some point it does all stop. It ends. We die.

What we are concerned with and *should* be concerned with is what happens betwixt birth and death—not what happens after death. The concept "happens" has no meaning *after* we are beyond the ability to *make* "things"—be they good or bad things—happen.

Which is to say, since we *are* life-centered, we *should* be life-centered.

Physiologically of course, we are. If you doubt this pick up any physiology text book and read and discover for yourself *to what extent* this is so. If you want something simpler, pause here and feel your own heartbeat and listen to your own breathing—these are physiological, biological "actions" calculated to achieve one overriding goal: *your* continued life.

Which is to say, since our physiology *is* life-centered, so *should* our psychology be.

Since there already is a *formal psychology* developed around this *life-centered* theme we can and *should* use it for our own *selfish* benefit as we accept the happiness challenge and work to achieve it.

Living up to it, *rising to the occasion* is a self-view most if not all of us want to have of ourselves. If we have made it at least into early adulthood and lived there for any amount of time, we more than likely have more than one personal, idiosyncratic "occasion" to which we can point—*introspectively* relate—to and feel good about our *accepting the challenge* and successfully living up to "it".

But, the idiosyncratic notwithstanding, here is one thing we all *share* in common. The *ultimate* occasion, the thing to which life can be seen as an *opportunity* to live up to, is, the thing we call *happiness*.

Happiness, as previously noted, is a state of non-contradictory joy and if we are happy we are in this state and if we are not happy we are not in this state.

But we can still ask and wonder is it *possible* to *deny* happiness? That is, to deny that we are happy? It seems as if this isn't possible and one's reaction to it (especially if one isn't happy and wants to be) might be: who would be so crazy???

My guess is the same ones who deny misery. Or that is, we could say since we can and do deny misery (misery by its nature is a dis-value) we can deny happiness (happiness by its nature *should* be a value but if you were brought up to think otherwise you could view it as a dis-value, or at best, as a *dangerous* value).

So you might not know whether or not you are—and to what degree—happy.

Enter *modern* technology.

The *technology* exists today to design and build a device to measure the *degree* to which a person is FOR or AGAINST his or her *own* happiness. This "device", this *happiness-meter* as it were is what I call a *teleömeter* (pronounced: tell-ee-ahm-eter, as in "tell-all-meter"). The *teleömeter*—as I envision it—is a self-administered computer based test to measure the *degree* to which one is FOR or AGAINST his or her own happiness. The *teleömeter* also provides—*in the process* of data gathering, measuring and evaluating—*profile* data about the self-examinee that he or she can use to manage their own psychological growth and development towards becoming autonomous man.

Autonomous man is nature's *end* state for psychological man—not end state in the sense of programmed by nature but rather in the sense of, it is the only state *rewarded* by nature.[37]

The *teleömeter* as literal "happiness meter" is of course metaphor. The "technology" to *literally* build a device and strap its probes and sensors onto a person to (passively) measure whether that person is happy or miserable does not exist and never will. It never will exist because happiness is a *state* of consciousness and *only* consciousness can *measure* consciousness.[38] And consciousness can *only* do it directly, which is to say by direct, face-to-face contact, be it between self and other(s) or self's own face-to-face: extrospectively (a literal mirror) or introspectively (internal mirror, figuratively or literally if it turns out right-left brain/nervous system has some 3D-mirroring capabilities). This ability of *consciousness to measure consciousness* includes not just the *range* and *scope* of consciousnesses—ones own *and* others—but also—via the fact of self-awareness—*states* of (ones own) consciousness as well as *contents* of (ones own) consciousness and *action* of (ones own) consciousness in regards to those contents. The measurement(s) of *ones own* consciousness is direct, of others, "indirect". In the case of indirect it is inferred from the direct observations one has made of self and since these self observations (introspective abilities) are based on the cognitive abilities one has developed to sense/measure the *external* world our inferences about others can be no better than our deductions about

---

[37] If your bullstuff detector, qua self-consistency detector, is working right now, it *should* be buzzing away because the use of the word "only" here suggests that happiness is *not* a state rewarded by nature (by rewarded here I mean as a positive, good, life-enhancing consequent). Such a "conclusion" that it [autonomy] is the "only" thing doesn't make sense so I will use this opportunity to mention that *BiO Spiritualism* is a speculative "science" at best right now and will improve with every (published) Volume. In fact if *you* wanted to *you* could say *BiO Spiritualism* is really *Theoretical Psychology*. *You* could—so say—that is, but since I don't want to move out of Minnesota just yet *and* I don't want to go to jail, I can't so say.

[38] This is *BiO Spiritualism's* Principle #5 (and one of the ten postulates). For more information about these refer, respectively, to the end of Chapter 1, page 14 and Footnote 53, page 64.

ourselves (which can be no better than our deduced and inferred conclusions about the world external to self). But indirect in the sense analogous to the experimental physicist who inserts a thermometer into boiling water to measure its temperature. The data for the measurement comes from the interaction of the "world" (hot water) and the sensor (thermometer): the liquid mercury in the thermometer increases its volume (expands) due to the heat added to it and the *degree* of the expansion—determined by the nature of mercury and the physical volume inside the thermometer tube for the mercury to rise in—indicates the temperature value to the physicist as observer. The *data* for such a measurement *comes from the world* (the hot water), not from the physicist as interpreter of the data and not from the sensor (thermometer), these are just "tools" for measuring the world (in this case, the water's temperature).[39]

Happiness—as a *state* of consciousness—is not "measurable" in the traditional sense of physical meters and measurements.

But Human beings "measure" the extent to which they are or are not happy every day of their lives.

How do we do this?

We do it by simply asking ourselves the question: Am I happy?

Let me repeat this. Am I happy?

And depending on how interested we are in the answer we continue.

What is happiness?

Is it even possible for people to be happy?

Maybe happiness is not metaphysically possible.

Have you ever stopped to consider this? It seems as if everyone has a formula for happiness but that no one is happy (hence the rather vast market for happiness formulas). Down through the ages men have prescribed for men, via untold volumes of verbiage, various kinds of happiness "pills": do whatever you want and only what you want and you'll be happy...go to church every Sunday, or every Saturday (but not both), and do not do anything you want and you'll be happy...and if these don't work try...putting on a happy face, that is, fake it, then you'll be happy. Of course not all verbiage generators have prescribed—a good many have described. Happiness is ____ ... and here we can easily fill in the blanks with a vast array of quaint little sayings that spring to mind from the many

---

[39] In this sense your consciousness is your sensor-observer-interpreter "instrument" inserted into (immersed in) the world, detecting its every nuance that is detectable by you qua human being with an instrument that detects.

little "Happiness Is" books (Happiness is a warm fire on a cold night) that the describers have written and contributed to the literature on happiness:

- A man is happy so long as he chooses to be happy and nothing can stop him...

- If you want happiness for an hour—take a nap. If you want happiness for a day—go fishing. If you want happiness for a month—get married. If you want happiness for a year—inherit a fortune. If you want happiness for a lifetime—help someone else. If you want eternal happiness—know yourself.

- It's pretty hard to tell what does bring happiness. Poverty and wealth have both failed....

- The foolish man seeks happiness in the distance; the wise man grows it under his feet...

- If happiness can be man's for a moment, it can be man's forever....

- There is only one way to happiness and that is to cease worrying about things which are beyond the power of our will....

- Many persons have a wrong idea of what constitutes true happiness. It is not attained through self-gratification but through fidelity to a purpose....

- True happiness is of a retired nature, and an enemy to pomp and noise, it arises, in the first place, from the enjoyment of one's self, and, in the next, from the friendship and conversation of a few select friends....

- Happiness is basically the awareness of that which is good, but since God is the Creator and Source of all good, true happiness, in its deepest sense, is the awareness of God. The search for happiness is the search for God....

- If one thinks one is happy, that is enough to be happy....

- Ask yourself whether you are happy, and you cease to be so....

- Would you rather be right or happy?...

- The secret of happiness is renunciation....

❖ If only we wanted to be happy it would be easy; but we want to be happier than other people, which is difficult, since we think them happier than they are....[40, i]

Do you know—does anyone know?—how many actual words have been written about happiness?...a million? ... a billion? ... a googol million?... as many as there are grains of—I'll admit I don't know either, but I do know that the actual, specific, concrete number is unimportant and it is safe to conclude: a lot!

Having performed the foregoing observations does it logically follow that men cannot be happy and that the "proof" is that they have tried beyond belief and failed? Hence, it must be in the nature of Nature and/or the nature of man that happiness is not a state possible to actual, living man? Or is there more to it than this? Perhaps there is a flaw in the observations?

Ayn Rand, in her writings on *Objectivism*, asked the question out loud: Is happiness possible? What if we answered, no. No, it is not possible; at least not to an actual, living, breathing human being. What then?

Well...maybe...then we'd say: "Whew, wow, boy am I glad I figured that out! The pressure's off, I can relax. I don't have to be happy! Hey, wow that feels pretty good...I feel...."

The point is, happiness does refer to something real and it is only when we answer the question truthfully that we encounter the need to think: *Yes*, happiness is possible. This affirmation leads to additional questions. Am I happy?...Was I happy?...Will I be happy?...What do I mean, happy? What does happiness mean? Does it mean a warm fire on a cold night? (If so, what about the people who live in the tropics?) Does it mean being one with God or the universe? (If so, given that there is no god but there is a Universe, what *does* this mean?) Or does it mean the absence of pain? (If so, what should I call that certain state that is the *presence* of something undeniably good?) Or is there some other definition that is better?

Consider this: "Happiness is a state of noncontradictory joy—a joy without penalty or guilt, a joy that does not clash with any of your values and does not work for your own destruction."[ii] Since this definition is not only valid but also true, it is no wonder so many people are not happy, were not happy and

---

[40] These are taken from pp. 221 through 232 of reference i. In order, they are quotes from: Alexander Solzhenitsyn, Chinese proverb, Kim Hubbard, James Oppenheim, Frater Achad, Epictetus, Helen Keller, Joseph Addison, Elinor MacDonald, Mme. De La Fayette, John S. Mill, Gerald Jampolsky, Andrew Carnegie, Charles Montesquieu.

(predictably) will not be happy.[41] But this is not the particular line of reasoning that we desire to follow here. We simply want to "measure" whether a person is FOR or AGAINST (and to what degree) his or her own happiness—not whether he is/is not *actually* happy: this depends on more than simply being FOR your own happiness. However, it does follow that if you are NOT for your own happiness, you cannot be happy. Hence, being FOR your own happiness is a necessary, albeit not sufficient, condition for happiness.

What then does it mean to be "FOR" happiness? Simple, since happiness is a state of noncontradictory joy, to be FOR happiness means to be FOR noncontradiction and to be FOR joy. Well, maybe half simple: How the hell do you *measure* the degree to which one is FOR joy?

And in the sense already mentioned this too is "easy": your consciousness measures it in you by you *introspectively* asking yourself, am I for joy? That is, am I for *my* joy, not others joy. I can be for others joy and this is okay but *am I FOR my joy also?* (Or is joy a sin? Not the joy as same may exist in others, that's okay, but joy for me is not okay? Or vice versa, joy for me is okay, but for others not? Or ... just *what* is my position on joy?)

If you are unsure of your answer to this question the *teleömeter* can help you figure it out.[42]

As well it can also help you figure out the *degree* to which you are FOR noncontradiction. Though you may not need a "test" to help you answer this because you may very well be a person who holds to the premise that if made explicit would say: *not only do contradictions exist but they are the essence of the Universe*. If this is you and you are wondering why you are not happy, look no further, you have found your answer.

Yes. Answers are possible.

Happiness *is* a state of noncontradictory joy.

---

[41] Definition is valid because it has a *genus:* state of consciousness; and *differentia*: noncontradictory joy, as *kind* of state; and also meets the other 6 points for valid definitions: it is (3) fundamental; (4) not negative, (5) not circular, (6) not poetic, (7) not too broad and (8) not too narrow. Contrast with, *Happiness is a warm fire on a cold night* (this is, too narrow unless we "conclude" it is metaphysically impossible therefore for people living in the tropics to be happy. As an annual escapee from Minnesota's winters to Mexico's tropical nights I know this last to be false.)

[42] That is, it *should* be able to help you, which is to say, this is *one* of its design requirements. *How* it does this, still has to be figured out by the *teleömeter* designer, that is, me.

Chapter 8: *Recovery*—from what?—should mean: *from* un-happiness:

I thought it meant, *adding* in *impatience* for one's own bullstuff as well as *subtracting* out *patience* for the spreading thereof by self and/or others?

Congratulations, *now* your contradiction detector is in fine working order.
So good, great, let's continue.
Spiritual suffering and unhappiness are like the feathers of an unknown bird: if you pluck them you run the risk of discovering that the bird is not there because the feathers created only the *shape* of a bird, not the solid body of an actual bird.[43]

Spiritual or psychological suffering is not a solid void, it is the shape of the void, the line we draw around the void, the sheet in which we wrap the void, the void's shell, the voids shape ... the void's feathers.

The void is that felt space within that we experience as *hollow,* as empty, but not as inert. It can be felt as a flutter (in the center chest for example, like shortness of breath), a discomfort, or as *extremely* threatening: as a void *so* empty (and vast now that it has expanded to include not just the chest but the stomach also) that if it isn't filled—with something—we *will* collapse. In the latter form it is known as pathological anxiety, in less severe forms it is *simple* anxiety.

Pathological anxiety, such as that which is experienced when one faces his first crisis of self esteem, is *extremely* painful.[44] It is so painful that most people do not go *through* it but opt instead to go *around* it. Those who go through it benefit the most, those who go into it and then around benefit somewhat but those

---

[43] If you have already noticed that the term *pluck* presupposes *solid body*, hence, this paragraph's message rests on a stolen concept (and inadvertently highlights why definitions should *not* be poetic) I say to you: "Wow! You are smart!", but I ask you to bear with me and grant me some (more) metaphor/poetic license here.

[44] You mean there can be more than one? No way 'hoe-zay, I've been there once and once is enough, never ever again for me pal, I'm gonna pursue *and achieve authentic* self esteem if it kisses me, (if it kisses me? ... if it kisses me!?!? What's this??? Another Brandian slip???) what I *meant* to say is, the, *if it kills* me cliché as a way to show that it exists really high up there on *my* hierarchy of values and if you too have experienced a crisis of self esteem you can relate to what I mean about the *intensity* of the anxiety involved. It's *really* intense ... it's *very* intense ... it's *really really very very* intense. It's big, it's painful, it's scary and only the *truly* strong can work their way through it, the weaker ones have to *rely* on denial. (Whether or not a drug assisted denial depends on individual particulars.) Wait. I got it. Pathological—that is, self-esteem crisis—anxiety is so pain-full, so intense it is *what* intensity herself calls: *intense.*

who evade it entirely and go around it benefit naught and only delay the inevitable (although some people do die never knowing who and what they really are).

Suffering and pathological anxiety are *psychological* forms of pain, just as are joy and happiness psychological forms of pleasure.

Psychological pain cannot be eradicated with drugs. It can be masked with drugs just as physical pain can be masked but the root causes beneath *psychological* pain cannot be eradicated with drugs—be they "legal" or "illegal" drugs.

Just as physical pain is evidence that *something* is wrong physically, so too is psychological pain evidence that *something* is wrong *psychologically*.

Psychology and *Physiology*, 21st Century Medical Doctors notwithstanding, are *not* the same thing. Each has needs and when these needs are not met the result is pain. The pain in both cases *should* be listened too, not covered up and ignored and/or evaded.[45]

Since pleasure is a profound psychological need ☺p, severe psychological pain, that is, *spiritual* suffering can and should be viewed for what it is: profound psychological *signal*. ☺s [46]

If we accept—*to the point of worship*—the idea that pain *denial* is the *ideal*☹, [47] then we are or will become a living cliché. The one that says: *it isn't what I don't know that's the problem, it's what I do know that ain't so that's f.....g me up?*

Pleasure and pain have survival value and this includes both *physical* pleasure and pain and *psychological* pleasure and pain, or in the case of the psychological what we call spiritual pleasure and pain, that is, happiness/joy and misery/suffering.

For my purposes here (and by here I mean, this chapter) I am going to differentiate between physical pleasure-pain and psychological pleasure-pain by

---

[45] The argument, made by some, that some people's egos are so weak (having not been developed properly by self and/or because severely and systematically attacked by others from a very early age) that they need to take drugs to *temporarily* protect their life from suicide is not without merit. It is not, that is, as long as the person taking the drugs also does the psychological work required to ferret out root causes and correct the source of the psychological problem(s). Psychology is not physiology. Psychology is psychology: this is the 1st Postulate. ☺s

[46] It is my intention to use the smiley/sad face dingbat notation sparingly. Qua notation, its purpose is to alert you, qua reader, that the asserted *principle* (*italicized and then flagged by* ☺p as being asserted by Biocentric Psychology, *italicized and then flagged by* ☺o by Objectivism, *italicized and then flagged by* ☺s by BiO Spiritualism, that is me) is just that: an asserted assertion that I, qua author, take as a proven assertion but which you—depending on the degree of your understanding of Objectivism and Biocentric—may have to take as a *given*, albeit, a to-be-proven given.

[47] The unsubscripted (and if needed later on, the superscripted) ☹ stands for the accepted-as-proven sentiments of **MAC**'s (**M**ystics-**A**ltruists-**C**ollectivists) by **MAC's**.

referring to the former as simply pleasure and pain and to the latter as pPleasure and pPain but written, respectively, as *playsure* and *payn*. I realize that pPleasure (playsure) and pPain (payn) are actually experienced, respectively, in the physical body as *feelings* of pleasure (positive, good, desired) and pain (negative, bad, not wanted) but there *is* something different about them. For example, *anticipatory* pleasure and pain are of the pPleasure and pPain kind; so is general anxiety. In fact, general or non-specific anxiety, that is, anxiety that *we* have not *yet* identified as either excitement anxiety (*anticipation* of value gain) or depression anxiety (*anticipation* of value loss) is example of what I mean, respectively, by *playsure* and *payn*.

Another way to differentiate between physical and psychological pleasure and pain would be to call the psychological version psychhological (notice the presence of the second h—as in h for hell) pain and pleasure. However, I use this designation system as the means to differentiating between *Biocentric* psychology and Non-Biocentric psychology. Biocentric psychology, qua newcomer to psychology's table, we will label with the double hh and I'll use the traditional spelling *psychology* to broadly refer to contemporary/mainstream/ivory tower psychology. So that Biocentric psychology becomes psy*chh*ology (with and without the double hh emphasized as context might require) and contemporary/mainstream/ivory tower psychology then gets to keep the correct psychology spelling—for now.

In the long run of course, it is/will be my contention that psy*chh*ology is the true *science* of psychology and *contemporary/mainstream/ivory tower* psychology is … bullstuff.[48]

So if your *contemporary/mainstream/ivory tower* therapist and/or doctor tells you that you *should*—as a way of life—take drugs to help you *deny* your payn, they are *wrong* for doing so and you *should* change "doctors".

If your doctor tells you that *mind* and *brain* are one in the same (and *not* in the way *BiO Spiritualism* means it: *mind and body*—which *includes* the brain—are an *integrated* unit) then you should challenge him or her. Brain and Mind are no more one-in-the-same than is a car and its driver one in the same. Granted that in

---

[48] For benchmark purposes here (and by [this] here here I mean: August 30th, 2004) we can consider the science of psychology in this first decade of the third millennium to be at the same cross-roads astronomy was during the conflicts between Ptolemy and Copernicus. At one time (16th Century) Ptolemy's view of astronomy (planets make loopy-de-loop orbits in the sky as they revolve around a stationary earth) was astronomy and the heliocentric view of Copernicus's (pun not intended unless you are a Ptolemaist) we could have (and had I been there I would have) labeled: a*ss*tronomy (and we can't help but notice: who had the last laugh as they deleted one letter and the others had to add one?).

a smash up both can be totaled but it isn't always so—sometimes both are just mangled and can be put back together again with time and work. How they are put back together and how long it takes to put them back together depends on the expertise of mechanics and doctors and the self healing abilities of drivers (notice cars have no self healing abilities so the analogy here between cars and bodies is limited).[49]

So if your doctor tells you to mask the *payn* of a malfunctioning life with pain-killers in the same way you use pain-killers to deal with physical pain your doctor is wrong and you should *not* accept *her* bullstuff (or his, as the case may be). You would not accept your mechanic telling you to fill your stomach with gasoline while you are driving your car because you and your car are one-in-the-same and it is dangerous to drive a car on empty (e.g., if you run out of gas at high speed your power steering goes out), so why do or would you accept it from your doctor or therapist?

This is not a rhetorical question; pick your answer(s):
    a) I suffer from a bad case of authoritarian thinking.⊗
        {e.g. Doctors are right BECAUSE they are doctors}
    b) I don't accept self responsibility as a metaphysical given.⊗
        {i.e., I *refuse* to accept that I am personally responsible for everything I think and say and do, including accepting—as one simple example—the *false* religious premise that thinking and doing are moral equivalents.}
    c) I fear independent judgment.⊗
        { see b's bracketed comments }
    d) I fear challenging my own defense values so much so that I don't do it.$^{O\,=\,tbd}$
        {see e}
    e) I agree with my doctor.⊗
        {see d}
    f) AOA (All of Above)⊗⊗⊗O⊗
    g) NOA (None of Above)
    h) Other: ___oiatbd___
        {that is, others if any to be determined}

---

[49] Metaphorically speaking the meaning of the statement, mind and body are an integrated unit is: *body is the sponge saturated with the water of consciousness.*

Given our definitions then—happiness is a state of non-contradictory joy—un-happiness is the *absence* of noncontradiction and/or joy. Misery or spiritual suffering—that is, *severe* payn—on the other hand, results from the *predominant presence*—51% or more in ones soul, one's *actual* consciousness—of *erroneous* thoughts, ideas and *values* that *contradict* reality (that's why we *evaluate* them *as* erroneous) and for which the holder of same does not seek happiness—that is, does *not* seek noncontradiction—but rather tries ever so desperately to *define* that whatever one is *is* happiness—by definition, that is, by definition *without* reference to reality.

But, Reality doesn't work this way: except for *one* case, *subjectivity* does not substitute for *objectivity*.[50]

Happiness, as previously defined, is a *state* of non-contradictory joy, therefore, if this is so we can then ask ourselves what is un-happiness and—since suffering is the opposite of joy—we can also ask:

> what is *contradictory* joy?
> *noncontradictory* suffering?
> *contradictory* suffering?

In BiO Spiritualism, *un-happiness* is the "state" of way too many people today and *contradictory joy* [drunk followed by morning after hangover] is *muted* happiness, *noncontradictory suffering* [getting a college degree in engineering is a long, hard, grueling task but in the *long run* it will/was/is/will be worth it] is an occupational hazard for human beings and *contradictory suffering* [it's cool, I mean really really cool being a doormat for OTHER'S *need* to-have-something to wipe their feet on] is ... dangerous. If it (*contradictory suffering*) is not corrected it *will* create a negative metaphysics in your soul and *as-a-consequence* make it *almost* metaphysically impossible to ever achieve anything other than a muted happiness. This is because *contradictory suffering*—like all contradictory things—is crazy driving. For example, sometimes in situation X, I am suffering and *not* minding it and other times when in the exact same (or extremely similar) X situation I am suffering and *minding it a lot!* Therefore, he asks himself, what the f___ is going on? Am I changing and not knowing it? That is, am I changing *internally* and not noticing? Changing for the worst or for the better though, and if for the better, how can this be crazy driving? (And he answers his own question: *not* being able to tell the *difference* between *better* and *worst* **is** crazy ...

---

[50] The exception is when the subjective **matches** *reality*. In this case the *subjective* is the *objective* is the *subjective* is the *objective* is the ... and so on.

driving ... and the car analogy returns ... I wonder here if dreams about cars and me driving/riding in/driving them here 'n there has any relevance here? Maybe. TBD. Something exists of which I am aware, I MUST—if I am going to treat MY interests seriously—discover its nature. See Personal Dream Journals from the '80's in preparation for *BiO Spiritualism* Book II and its *expectation* of a fully developed, full functioning, fully completed teleömeter that brings the *ultimate* solution to the "problem" of happiness.)

Payn—the antipode of happiness—is the consequent of *contradictory* values and/or *contradictory* value judgments attempting to express themselves as a physical sensation—felt emotion, e.g. that flutter kind of discomfort felt in the center chest.©s Since something can't be x and not x or y and not y at the same time and in the same respect so too the emotion space in the physical body—the attempt to express the contradictory upon its screen results in *payn*—a flutter of payn whose *intensity* depends on the *actual* importance of the values involved to the *human nature* of the person attempting to experience them. Since I do not have any field data to draw a universal conclusion about *where* in the physical body one experiences ones *payns* and *playsures* (assuming emotional *wheres* are universal and not idiosyncratic), I can only add here that I experience mine in my center chest (as those flutter like loss of breath anxiety feels-like-pre-heart-attack onset maybe maybe not anxiety payn) area. I experience guilt in my stomach and severe guilt in the *pit* of my stomach (and if *severe* enough, then with the pit connected to the top of my brain with a flu like sense of nauseousness *accompanied* by snaky like felt mullings around on the top of my literal brain[51]) and warm *playsure* in my stomach-genital area and metaphysical playsure in my whole body from head-to-toe, that is, from the top of my head to the bottom of the soles of my feet with a euphoria that is ... euphoric ... at the *top* end of this range. At the bottom end of the playsure range I experience an extreme kind of calmness and self assuredness that is only approached in *degree* of calmness by the psychological-epistemological state we human beings refer to as: *certainty*.

Beyond this I am not prepared to talk about *playsure* and *payn* as somethings (be they things 1 and/or things 2) distinct from *pleasure* and *pain* and may perhaps address these in future works.

For now suffice it to say the formula is: Happiness IS a state of noncontradictory joy.

---

[51] Though this happened once (and believe me, once is/was/is enough) and only once—when Joshua *consciously* choose to commit a moral breach—and is part of Joshua's (unfolding) story to be (maybe) unfolded over time (see the **Psychology Venn** online at www.gdeering.com).

This happiness "formula", this *fact* of nature, this identified by Ayn Rand in her Philosophy of Objectivism fact-of-nature is as much an immutable—or more precisely, *fundamental—principle* as is Newton's: F = ma (that is, Force = mass times acceleration) *principle* of masses and motions in physics. And for those buzzwordy "spiritualist" gurus who preach that Einstein's E=mc² (that is, Energy = mass times the speed of light squared) *invalidates* Newton because Newton's F=ma doesn't *work* for nuclear particle masses and speeds, we have to conclude that their guru "shtick" *depends* on their *opportunistic* personalities. This is to say, the mystic's bullstuff claim that their bullstuff is worth spreading, depends on their desire to use every opportunity open to them to "prove" you can't know things with (omniscient) certainty because just as you think (Mr. Newton) that you do know something, along comes another (Mr. Einstein) to "prove" you wrong.

But here is a curious fact: if you substitute Einstein's formula for "m(ass)" into E=mc² you get Newton's F=ma when dealing with masses and accelerations at the day-to-day level of human speeds and sizes![52, i] This "observation" sounds like we can know things after all *if we look deep enough* to make sure we keep what we are talking about *integrated* to the rest of our knowledge and *tied* to the *context* in which we observed it and figured it out in, *in-the-first place*. That is, we *should* integrate—integration is good—and we *should not* drop context—context dropping is bad (these are, tentatively, *BiO Spiritualism's* 2nd and 3rd theorems[53]).

---

[52] Referencing my college physics text book, p. 133, formula 5-47(E=mc²) backwards to p. 132, formula 5-37: F = change in momentum with respect to time. Since *momentum* is mass times velocity (i.e., mv, which the *conservation* of determines who goes which way when a truck hits a car) and since in such short time events our mass doesn't change (it takes more than a *few* seconds for some of us dieters to add back weight lost poundage) a *change* in momentum means a *change* in velocity. When we go from 0 to 60 in N seconds in our car this *velocity change* (with respect to time) **is** a(cceleration), hence F = change in momentum with respect to time = m times a change-in-velocity = ma which, voila! is F=ma which is (Newton) backwards derived from (Einstein's) E = mc² or E = mc² is forwards derived (if you know that Einstein's mass in his energy equation is a complicated function of Newton's mass in his force equation) from (Newton's) F=ma. So, if you disagree with me then you tell me why "spiritualists" of the mystical variety love to use this kind of thing—and perhaps even more so than this is their use of Heisenberg's "uncertainty" principle—as *opportunity* to *undercut* our confidence in our ability to say, "I see what I see and I know what I know". I say they want to *destroy* our bullstuff detectors because it is only *without* these that we will be able to even come close to buying their "arguments" *for* mysticism.

[53] True Human psychology, *as a science*, is derivable—per *BiO Spiritualism* (with a to-be-determined degree of tongue-in-cheekiness that is of a high *enough* value to prevent one from becoming a rain drop counter)—from an evaluation of 489,555 *facts* [that is, dear lord I beseech thee don't let me fall into the trap of answering the question: WHICH facts? Thank you.]. These facts—uniquely condensed two at a time—give rise to 990 *propositions* which, in like fashion, are categorizable into 45 *theorems*. These theorems (or

Does this mean that "new age" *type* "spiritualists" are *master* context droppers and/or mind *dis*-integrator destroyers?!?

Only if you are (still stuck in) a (your) curmudgeon (phase).

Since I am an ex-curmudgeon I can't afford right now to succumb to the above I Object! to mystics—new age or otherwise—*path* and follow where it *logically* leads. Instead "we" have to stick to our interest here and follow *its* path: happiness and un-happiness, just what the heck are they? and how do you avoid unhappiness? and how do you get the *real* thing instead?

If happiness is a state of non-contradictory joy, then un-happiness is simply *not* being in this state or is being in a state that looks like happiness but isn't.

As an alive human being you have to be in *some* state, you cannot be in no state. Just like when you are on the planet earth you have to be *somewhere* on it, albeit you can be anywhere. But this *somewhere* does not *automatically* mean, for example, that you are in the United States. You *could* be but if you aren't and you *want* to be there you have to *do something* to get there.

Happiness in this sense is the same thing; it is an end state, a destination, a place to get to, an *effect*. But it does not exist on a *continuum* any more than does the United States *as place* exist on a continuum. Within itself it does, but outside itself it does not; either you are in the United States or you are not.

This means if you *are* happy then you can experience degrees of happiness. You can be happier today than you were yesterday, or you can be happier in work than in your human relationships and so on (just like in exploring the United States, you can have more fun in Disney World than in Disneyland or in Disneyland than in Philadelphia or vice versa and so on.)

If you *are* happier today than you were yesterday then you are at a place within your psyche that is satisfactorily integrated and it is a level of integration that is higher than your last integrated level. These integrated levels—in *BiO Spiritualism*—are called happiness plateaus. A happiness plateau is a level of integration where all your psy**chh**ological values have been achieved to some degree and have been integrated around the one of lowest degree. This is lowest common denominator *integration* and if we don't pause and do-it and take note of having so done, but rather bull our way forward trying to force the plateau to be highest common denominator we will suffer negative consequences.☺[s] So, we

---

principles) are based on 10 *postulates*. These 10 postulates are derivable from a base of 5 *axioms*. These 5 are the 3 universal axioms common to all science and the 2 axioms unique to the science of psychhology. The reference here in the main text to *theorems* 2 and 3 means 2 and 3 out of the 45 suggested in this. Whether they literally occupy *positions* #2, #3 on the "axiom (christmas tree shaped) tree structure" isn't known at this time. For more on this "axiom tree" see (the to be written) *BiO Spiritualism* Book II.

must periodically pause and estimate which of the four cardinal psy***chh***ological values—self awareness, self acceptance, self assertion, self responsibility—is the lowest and integrate our psychhology around it before we move on to bigger and better things.[54]

Integration is good, horizontal integration (happiness plateauing) is the meaning of *self* (as thing) *accepting* the degree of *our* current level of self-acceptance and of self-assertion and of self-awareness and of self-responsibility as the prerequisite to going on, qua *developing* psychhological being.[55]

Vertical integration is the other "direction" in which we can travel. If horizontal integration is happiness plateauing, vertical integration is the process of climbing higher: be it all the way to the top of the mountain or just to the next plateau.

---

[54] We do this by simply asking our [intellectually most honest]self the question: which of the four psychological virtues is lowest in me *right now*? I did this just now and my answer was self-responsibility [which—if you refer to Footnote 81 page 94—*makes sense* since I very recently got a (entry level/low paying) job at Home Depot™ in order to get *some* income as I put the finishing touches on this manuscript]. A year ago when I asked the question it was self-assertion that *popped up* and the first time I did it—circa 1976 it was self-acceptance and a year after that, self-awareness AND acceptance of those awarenesses *as me* [and for me there seems to always be a background sense of—like a watermark on paper hinting at—*self acceptance* as "always", lightly, residually *weak*]. The *frequency* with which we do this happiness plateauing depends on our own, individual, idiosyncratic growth and development rates.

[55] The Gestalt psychologists first identified this when they said, one can't go on from where one is (psychologically) unless one first accepts where one (actually) is (psychologically). Which, by analogy, is to say: you can't go from St. Paul, Minnesota to Boston, Massachusetts if you don't know you are in St. Paul. If you think you are in Los Angeles instead and head out on the vector to Boston you will end up somewhere in the North Atlantic Ocean ... south of Greenland's Cape Farewell. And to make the metaphor complete, depending on which psycho-therapist was the captain of your ship you will probably conclude, psychology doesn't work and say to it: farewell. My point here is, you *might* have to become the Captain of your own ship.

Chapter 9: Technically—as in for *precision's* sake—to *what*? is up to you:

Per *BiO Spiritualism* it *should* be: *to* happiness.

Helping others is not *not* something we should do.
What it is not is this: it is not *what* we should *devote* our life to.
We should not so devote our lives, for two primary reasons.
First is this: those who tell us to do this and say it is the path to heaven—be it the non-existent heavens of religions or the heaven on earth of *authentic* self esteem—are wrong because there is no literal heaven and the path to *authentic* self esteem is *selfishness*, not altruism.
Secondly, in the long run no one can make another person happy. Since happiness is a state of *inner* being—a state of noncontradictory joy as we've already identified—only the particular, individual "being" can *create* this inner state of noncontradiction and joy. A particular individual could be joyous with you as an intimate partner and/or friend in his or her life, but only each individual can create their own inner world of noncontradiction and joy from within which each can then *unmutedly* experience and enjoy the joy along with all other *earned* and "accidental" joys.
Since the world is filled with joy, the *probability* of running across accidental joy here and there is very high and since the most likely outcome comes out, accidental joy exists and is there for the taking and experiencing.[56]

---

[56] As trivial and/or as much a non-sequitur as this is going to sound to the casual reader I have to pause here and give credit to Dr. Harry Binswanger of the Objectivists who—in a different context—pointed this blatantly obvious fact (the most likely outcome comes out) out to me. I read or heard somewhere else (probably *Biocentric Psychology*) that *sometimes* we need the "obvious" pointed out to us. I spent a quarter of a century thinking about Mechanical Engineering things—such as the 2nd law of thermodynamics which says the *enthalpy* (or entropy, I forget which) of the Universe is winding down and leading to more and more chaos—and I never understood enthalpy until after this when Dr. Binswanger pointed out in one of his (taped) lectures that all this 2nd law is saying is that *the most likely outcome, comes out!* (emphasis mine). And for his example he uses a pool game and the start of it when someone breaks the triangularly racked balls and produces a static combination/configuration of balls on the table (for the next player) that *is* one configuration out of a million-billion-gazillion or more possibilities which can't be *exactly* predicted ahead of time but can, nevertheless, be *described* beforehand. This description is: the most likely combination—that is, outcome—comes out. To me of course, this is genius and I am simply trying to use this observation of his to see if it has *applicability* in the science of (real) psychology. As an extreme example consider that if we

But if you *depend* on "accident" for your joy, you will be disappointed in the long run (or at minimum, unsated[57]). Therefore the earned—that is the man-made by you—joy is the best and the most reliable kind and has a double payback: it advances your sense of efficacy and worth, which are the two things we said in the beginning here are the things we are after with *our* (brand of) *spiritualism*.

So here, for now, I close the circle on *Phase Ø* of (*BiO*) *Spiritualism's* quest for us, qua individuals, to *make* ourselves the sole, prideful owners (and eventually, operators) of a worthy and efficacious consciousness. That is, a consciousness that is worthy of happiness *because* it is competent at producing it.

We know our goal, now we must achieve it.

---

actually lived in a Universe as envisioned by the mystics then every once and awhile when we shoot pool and break the triangularly racked balls we should get a bunch of French maidens bathing in a bubble bath of balls turned into soap bubbles. But notice: we NEVER get this. Rather we ALWAYS get a *predictable* configuration of *billiard* balls with (some) *measureable* inter-distances between each and every ball making up *some* configuration (the most likely one, which is the one we got!) of balls on the billiard table.

[57] It appears as if my dictionary (see reference i Chapter 1) is not infallible—that is, it is not an infallible pope. As example consider that it asserts that *sated* means: *to satisfy (as a need or desire) fully or to excess*. This is contradictory, to be satisfied fully *means* completely—*neither* too much *nor* too little—and this is the way in which I mean it. [To equate *complete* satisfaction with *excess* satisfaction is probably (or in the least *could be*) an example of religion epistemology worming its way into my dictionary.]

Part III:

Advanced BiO Spiritualism:

Is America the only place left on earth where the Individual is (still) more important than The Group?

Phase 1: Individuation— is not automatic, it requires (individual) effort.

Chapter 10: *Give a mystic an inch and he'll take a mind.*

Give a Bureaucrat a mind and she'll take all your money.

Since psychology *is* psychology—that is, an *objective* science independent of anyone's hopes, wishes and fears including mine but also including the United States Government's—we must remember the following as we start the third and final part of *BiO Spiritualism* prior to *applying* it to our *self*.

Money is never given away for free without strings attached.
Never.
Such a fact gives rise to the concept of "conflict of interest".

And this especially includes the monies given (Grant-ed) *by* the United States Government *to* State approved "psychologists" for the (alleged) purpose of studying the "science" of psychology.

Conflict of interest does pertain to more than grant money in general and Government grant money in particular. Private Grant money can contain *conflict of interest* as a *contaminant* also, but in Government grant money, *conflict of interest* is the "pure" element and "intellectual honesty" the "contaminant".

He who grants the money wants to be told what he wants to hear; else he won't grant the money.[58]

As Grantor of money to "psychology" how does the government decide which school of psychology is the right one?

---

[58] For the private, free market funding this is OK: if what the grantors want to hear turns out to match reality they reap the rewards, if it doesn't match, they suffer the consequences. Not so when the Government grants funds to do research. Here, THEY reap the rewards—that is *control* (over large sums of money)—and pass the consequences on to an unsuspecting public, that is onto you and me as hapless taxpayers. The taxpayer might reap some benefit but if you subtract the negative consequences from any positives you get a negative bottom line. Since a *proper* government has no business being in any private business this last claim does not have to be proven; it merely has to be stated as a possibility and a dangerous one at that. Then any would be dangers are averted *by design* because a 100% laissez-faire Government—in contrast to the present Clinton administration—doesn't have its fingers in every pie in the world. Pun not intended because it's not really a pun. President Clinton *chose* his behavior, I didn't. When his sexual mores—or any such politician's—so blatantly *parallel* what a *true* bureaucrat wants to do to us average "citizens" you have to actively suppress or even *repress* such JUDGMENTS in order to remain "respectful". But maybe respect is something that has to be earned. The new spiritualism is NOT Biblical: i.e., it doesn't say, *judge not least ye be judged*; rather, it is Objective: *Judge and be prepared to be judged* is the new spiritualism's message.

Is it Freud's psychoanalytic school of psychology that is the right one and *should* therefore get the money for research?

Or perhaps it's B.F. Skinner and his cohorts' school of Behaviorism that *should* get the money?

Whose is it going to be?

If you were the Government and had a couple of handfuls of billion dollar bills to hand out and give away to those who said their school is the correct one, how would you decide? If you were/are religious would you give it to those who said atheism is the proper world view and belief in *any* god, the incorrect view? Or would you give it to those of the opposite view?

OR would you simply give it to those who said, "...since we are the real scientists—as the number of Ph.D. degrees among us attest to (see Chapter 16)—give us the money and we will tell you what you want to hear...". Whether you think you would do this or not doesn't really matter because that is *exactly* what you have done and are doing with your tax dollars that support the Government's NIMH (National Institute of Mental Health) and SAMHSA (Substance Abuse and Mental Health Services Association) organizations.

That is, your tax dollars are supporting the Behaviorist school of psychology and all follow on versions of this school, the latest of which is: Cognitive Neuroscience.

Cognitive Neuroscience is really not a science as much as it is a tool of the Bureaucratic Mind; a "tool" that the BM uses to control the *Social Engineers* who in turn try to control us.[59] *Social Engineers* are like a bunch of Dr. Robert Stadlers out of Ayn Rand's novel *Atlas Shrugged*. Dr. Stadler is the "scientist" in *Atlas Shrugged* who sells his *soul* to "science" (Social Engineers sell theirs to the Bureaucratic Mind). In modern day society these soul-selling scientists even have a formal group to which they all belong. It is called the Group ... of "scientists" ... who ... believe in *Scientism*.[i] *Scientism* is the non-philosophical philosophy of *reductive materialism* that says everything in the Universe—including man's alleged "soul"—is *reducible* to the laws of physics and chemistry. Which is to say, man ain't got no consciousness, no soul and even if he does ("they" say) it is *reducible* to a chemical formula or a physics formula or a mechanical formula or some yet to be determined *it-ain't-consciousness* formula.

---

[59] And who do so with varying degrees of success and failure: more success and less failure with some (of us sometimes), and more failure and less success with others (of us at different times), but never *not* trying *to control*, because *that* is what Social Engineers, qua BM flunkies, do.

But what if the "formula" for consciousness is as the Objectivists contend: *consciousness is conscious.* This means it is an axiomatic concept; that is, *a self-evident primary*. A self-evident primary is that which needs only itself as the evidence *to be grasped* and it can only be grasped *by a self.* ☺º

If consciousness is axiomatic, then those Behaviorist "scientists" (or any "scientists" for that matter) who *are* owned by the United States Government (or any Government for that matter) have a Government-Science relationship that is no different from that of the Soviet Union during the last century when it promoted a proletarian view of all science (including psychology). A "view" that ended up throwing people in prison because they were "in-sane" for being *against* communism, which meant they went against the grain of what the *Government* considered to be "sane".

This doesn't mean that there is no valid concept in reality of insane. But what it does mean is that the government has absolutely no business using its access to near unlimited funds to tell us what is and what is not sane. They could for example, declare that anything less than a 100% income tax rate is insane. And we—having *accepted the premise* that the government *should* be so involved in psychology—would have no choice in such a situation but to flick our lower lip (as if it were a punching bag) with our index finger (as if it were the fist of an accomplished boxer in training) and make the rapid baubble-baubble-baubbling sounds to match the index finger flick-flick-flick on lip.

If we *allow* our government to make assertions about what is, is not true psychological science, then we—me and you and our kids—are in deep … lip-flicking trouble.

Since a *proper* government shouldn't be involved in anything other than protecting legitimate *individual* rights (to life and property) it has no business being involved in the business of mental health and mental illness issues any more than it has any business being involved in any businesses beyond the "business" of running the military, the police and the courts as *means* to protecting *individual* rights (to life and property).

And professional philosophy and professional psychology are businesses—even if and when used by those who aspire to be Shepherds rather than sheep. They are businesses because they involve a valuable human product (truth) created by some (truth producers) and sold to others (truth consumers) as books and other *intellectual property*.

The fact that intellectual products have conmen (mystics, collectivists, altruists, anti-autonomous man-haters, anti-laissez faire capitalists, social scientists, et al.) is not reason for the government to take over the field of the intellect any more than it is reason for them (unless they are fascists) for taking over the production of physical goods and services to prevent conmen from selling snake oil (not to mention the specter of the government then selling it).

In *anticipation* of the Government's snake oil Marketing Campaign as regards contemporary psychology, consider the following excerpt taken *herein* from Chapter 19 (page 261): *Will Cognitive Neuroscience become the new bureaucratic control tool of the 21st Century?*

> This mystic-collectivist-altruistic anti-autonomous man "mentality" is deeply embedded in the American "cultural mind" in a sense analogous to that which is embedded in sheep's "minds". That is, *sheep are sheepish* and if they could think and act from thoughts (which they cannot, but if they could) their "spiritual" quest would be to find a "sheepherder". Given the ever growing power of the Bureaucratic Mind as same is manifest in the NIMH and other Governmental agencies it appears as if our choice is being reduced to its barest essentials: Do you want to be a man (the *autonomous* kind) or a sheep. Here is one area in which religious people, or more precisely "Christians" cannot escape the hot seat of judgment: Whose image is it that is (and at what age is it embedded), that shows Jesus as the quintessential *sheepherder* and *you* as a timid little sheep in his flock of sheep? It is *not* Ayn Rand's, this I *know* for *sure,* that is, *for 100%,* **absolute** *sure.*
>
> The foregoing religious induced and/or encouraged "vice of sheepishness" is the "danger" lurking in the mental pathways of our cultural selves. BiO Spiritualism's *Yes*, is the first book in this new millennium to *explicitly* say: *Yes*, what America *needs* most right now *is* individuals and especially *adult* individuals. And *what* adult individuals need most is *The Philosophy of Objectivism* **PLUS** *The Psychology of Biocentric Psychology and* a book that shows them how to *embrace and apply* these two intellectual disciplines to help them identify and then satisfy—with full and complete satiation—their own *true* spiritual needs.

And *Yes*, along the way—almost as if by an effortless byproduct—the successful spiritual seeker and reader of *BiO Spiritualism* will learn how to identify and satisfy all his or her *legitimate* human needs: be they mental, physical or spiritual.

Well, yes, maybe *all* is an exaggeration, but at minimum the interested reader will have an extremely reliable road map to follow on his or her own personal, individual, *spiritual* quest.

Chapter 11: Those who can't teach, do. Those who can't do, do themselves in.

Man's *individual* life *starts* with physics as metaphysics and ethics as *interactive* metaphysics and *ends* with learned epistemology as *individual* psychology with *intensity* of happiness (or its lack) as the *reward* of successful (or unsuccessful) *spiritualism* in the individual person qua possessor of that *universal* we call *immutable human nature*—with its *need* of *a* metaphysic, *an* epistemology and *a* ethic, that is, a *philosophy* as an identifiable part of that which *is* immutable.

I know *where* and *what* I am and how I *should* act. The question is: *where* and *what* are you and how *do* you act?

I am in a world *where* selfishness—not gravity, but selfishness—makes the world go 'round.

In our continuing struggle to take back *spiritualism* from the mystics we now need to expand our taking back efforts in two additional directions: psychology and morality.[60]

Consequently, the four total sub-goals for *BiO Spiritualism* are: to help myself and other *individuals* who *worship* reason and *despise* faith—in contradistinction to the vice-versa types—to take back (1) *spiritualism* from the mystics, (2) *psychology* from the Government, (3) *morality* from the altruists *and* to (4) put these back into our own *individual* soul where they belong and where they were

---

[60] *BiO Spiritualism* remember is the *process* of making one's self happy. Since [BiO] *Spiritualism* is the *science* of all such processes advocated by man, qua man, for man and since *traditional* spiritualisms have screwed it up so badly a new approach is needed and BiO Spiritualism is *that* approach. That is, *BiO* Spiritualism is the *first* formal instance of this new, improved kind of spiritualism, qua spiritualism as a no nonsense happiness-maker-process.

allowed (by us) to be taken from in the first place. Since it is true that the *taking-back* efforts and/or the *keeping-them-there-in-the-first-place successes* can *only* be done *individually*, this Part (III) of *BiO Spiritualism* is about the *individual* and his or her continuing struggle...against... *The Group*. The Group—be it the Mystics, spiritually; the Collective, politically; or the United States Government, *bureaucratically*—is becoming the individuals *only* natural predator.

Individuals have many natural enemies—from viruses-to-starvation—but only one *true* predator: The Group.

Modern man is in danger of loosing his spiritual, psychological-moral self to *The Group*. That is, to ~~that~~ an *American* led Global *Promoting* Group currently marching unopposed down a path to a *new kind* of totalitarianism.[61] A totalitarianism that is dangerous precisely because it is new and as such no one can say, "Oh, that won't work because we've already tried it and it doesn't work", because of this "*haven't* been there, done that" aspect, it has an appeal to the American pragmatism in us all and since Americans *are* the best at *making* things "work", this *new* totalitarianism has a *theoretical* chance of being tried. As such, it is a gigantic danger to *the individual* and *BiO Spiritualism* is *one* defensive weapon to use against the marching hordes.

This new kind of totalitarianism has never been tried by *The Group* before because *T.h.e.y* just discovered it in the closing decades of the last century. *How* they ever discovered it is beyond me, but *that* they have discovered it is not. If we individuals, *qua individuals*, aren't aware of *t.h.e.i.r* goals we will not be able to defend ourselves against t.h.e.m. Defend ourselves, that is, *spiritually, psychologically* and *morally*.

And "*now*"—September 11th+1, 2001—we must add, *physically*. Or:

To repeat:

Give a Mystic an inch and he'll take a mind ... and a body ... and a soul.

---

[61] This sentence was originated during America's Clinton administration and edited-revised during her Bush Jr. Administration. Hence "that" as a more specific "thing" (Clinton liberals) had to be changed to "an" as a now more nefarious, blobby thing that still is a danger—*qua group as predator*—but it has been defanged somewhat by the Bush conservatives. But since Bush conservatives are in large part *religious* conservatives we *individuals* are still far, far, far from *safe*. Or *should* I say: s.a.f.e? That is: Selfishness As Feeling Ethics? Since my website uses concept of *save yourself brother*, as in S.A.V.E as in Selfishness As Virtuous Ethics this s.a.f.e usage is consistent with itself and with BiO Spiritualism's claim that it (BiO Spiritualism) is the best *integration* of Biocentric Psychology (the academic authority on feelings and emotions, including their proper relationship to reason) and Objectivism (the authority on all things philosophical). So, what the hey, let's go with it. We (non-genius) selfishness worshippers need all the help we can get, to hold on to our own while sloshing around on a planet awash in altruism ethics.

As a method for transcending the time rift of September 11th, 2001 in America, everything in here written before that ghastly date is in normal black ink and everything written soon after is in underline (as substitute for blood red color which though more communicative is still too expensive for printed books). Here for example, we must now—10/12/01—add that we have to also be directly, day-by-day, look-over-our-shoulder concerned about being killed by Islamic fundamentalists. Because Christianity had been rendered—since the post-Spanish Inquisition re-birth (The Renaissance)—*relatively* harmless as a life-threatening presence to others—both Christian and non-Christian alike (as in, *alike* in their *respect* for *reason*)—we thought ALL religions were this way. We were wrong. We also thought our government—which for the most part is "us" as "we" decide our own spending priorities—was taking care to carry out its only justification for existing: *to protect our inalienable individual right to life and property from thugs, foreign and domestic*. But here too, we were wrong. Also since the Islamic fundamentalists are cut-throat murderers who have stated *explicitly* that they are out to murder me and you, qua Americans, and then other "Westerners", qua reason/freedom worshippers, and then eventually ALL *infidels*—who they define as any and ALL who are non-believers in Islam and/or their God Allah (a "God" who—per *BiO Spiritualism*—"shares" something in common with all Gods: he/she/it does *not* exist). And so—because religion *in any form* rests on the epistemology of mysticism—the "Mystics", qua Group TYPE, move to the head of the class and become the more concrete, direct, anybody-can-see-it NOW threat to the *individual* and as such—temporarily—renders obsolete my thematic focus I started with—circa February, 2000—on our American *Bureaucratic* Government, qua Group TYPE: Collectivist, as the individuals *most* dangerous predator. In fact you could say the bureaucratic mentality in our government has been—temporarily—knocked out of existence because the American *spirit* has been called into action—by events—and *that* spirit—in action—tolerates no, none, nada, zero bullstuff—especially not the bullstuff of bureaucrats.[62] However, in the long run if we need "events" to drive us to do the "right" thing then we are accepting chaos as "normal". I predict we will not do this but will in fact be driven by that which has always driven the American *Spirit:* ideas. This book in spirit is dedicated to the *new dawn* of freedom now on the horizon of every *rational* human being on earth.

And so, having taken care here to factoring in the world condition as it has so radically changed by recent events and therefore as it exists today as I write—

---

[62] See page 27 for my definition of bullstuff.

which is to say, as the *context* within which I write—I have to note that the "<u>underline</u>—*not underline*" technique—though "cute"—isn't practical (the chrono-logical and the logical-logical get *too* mixed up and hard to follow), hence it's not moral, hence not right but my point has been made and so "we" return to "normal" writing *without* using underline to denote (blood) <u>red</u> color.[63]

September 11th, 2001 in America did happen and it was/is/will forever be a major *man-made* event in the history of the world.

An <u>evil</u> event if *Objectivism*—as the current *guardian* of *reason* and *freedom* for human beings on planet earth—wins the *philosophical* battle for the minds of men.

A "<u>good</u>" event if *Islamic fundamentalism*—as the current *guardian* of *faith* and *force* for the thugs on planet earth—wins the *religious* battle for the minds of men.[64]

This is to say, our world today—at the dawn of the 21st Century, P.S.[65]—is driven by two forces—*reason* versus *faith*—just as it was at the dawn of previous centuries.[66] These two always manifest themselves as *self-ism* versus *other-ism*, which translates into *Individualism* versus *The Group*.

There are those who say that *eventually* the Middle East bombing of America on September 11th, 2001—an act perpetrated by a religious GROUP—will be to tomorrow's American culture what the Japanese bombing of Pearl Harbor—an act perpetrated by a nation GROUP—December 7th, 1941 is to today's American

---

[63] With a few minor exceptions along the way where we use a little <u>underline</u> to <u>remind</u> ourselves that the Islam fundamentalist killer terrorists, qua *largest* killer terrorist GROUP—here in the beginning of the 3rd Millennium—are still out there. (According to my calculations there are at least 160,000 *actual* killer terrorists the world over at any point in time for the current [first five years of the 3rd Millennium] time. As to how many *potential* ones there are I am too afraid to calculate [though I can speculate that it's somewhere between 160,000 and 1.2 billion and HOPE it's closer to the former than the latter] and is the *secondary* reason I am pro-eliminating the begetters. Self defense is the *primary* reason I'm for eliminating—that is, either educating them to be more pro-reason or if this fails and they try to kill me then kill—them first.)

[64] Even though Ayn Rand, a *real* genius and the founder of The Philosophy of Objectivism, says religion is a primitive philosophy, I do not (yet) agree. I maintain that religion is a "spiritualism" which is *applied* philosophy AND psychology and not "purely", that is, not only philosophical. Consequently, until and unless ... I become convinced of my error...assuming of course I am wrong, which is hard to believe... I choose to keep my philosophy and my (ex)religion separate as I am doing here. My contention is that philosophy is the guardian of *reason*; religion is the guardian of *faith* and never the twain shall meet ... never. Ever.

[65] P.S. as in Post-September 11th, 2001 versus lower case p.s. as in pre-September 11th, 2001, for my purposes here.

[66] *Reason* and *Faith* are mutually exclusive terms. *Reason* is drawing conclusions based on sensory evidence and/or based on earlier formed conclusions based on sensory evidence. *Faith* is drawing conclusions based on the absence of sensory evidence and/or based on the presence of earlier formed conclusions that were based on the absence of sensory evidence.

culture: primarily an historical event. I am one of those who agrees with this sentiment. But I also think that there is a danger from September 11th, 2001 that is yet to emerge and I am predicting that it will emerge on planet earth before this new [3rd] millennium is a quarter of a century old—which means on or before 2025—and so I continue to write here desirous to contribute to the literature that will be the successful counterpoint to this new danger that modern man—whom we can call, Third Millennium Man—now faces.

Third Millennium Man now lives—or as stated, is soon to live—in a pro-group, anti-individual culture; an *emerging,* American led pro-group, anti-individual *Global* culture. (American led because America is the only group capable of leading anything, even negative groups). A Global culture that is analogous *mentally, physically and spiritually* to that of the worst streets in our worst neighborhoods but which is being packaged and sold to us as having the *potential* to be like our best streets in our best neighborhoods. The *worst* streets and neighborhoods are the ones where *initiated,* non-retaliatory acts of violence are declared *un-important* in the scheme of things when that scheme is felt to protect the concept of *community,* qua *group,* over and above *justice* for the "petty" *individual* victim of the initiated force. Be he or she victim of direct physical force and/or robbery and/or fraud.[67] And just as those worst streets and neighborhoods require "street smarts" to *survive* and *overcome* so too does the new *emerging* Global culture require the same "street smarts" to overcome it. But "street smarts" with this addition: Third Millennium Man's street smarts have to be brought up a notch or two or more. That is, in the new, 3rd Millennium *Global* culture you are going to need more than common sense to survive: you are going to need BOTH *common sense* and *concept sense* in order to survive *and be happy*.

And to keep it short and to cut to the chase, by *concept sense* I mean: (Ayn Rand's) *Objectivist Epistemology* which teaches that man's mind, man's consciousness—as a product of natural nature—can know, and *this*—see Objectivist Epistemology—is how we know. It teaches and shows *how it is so* that knowledge without omniscience is possible.

---

[67] Check-in here with your *introspective* self by comparing *your* felt sense of *injustice* when you hear of others being stolen from when their cars are broken into by thugs and things taken versus when (or if) you had the same experience. If your *felt* sense of injustice is *above* zero in *both* cases then you are (more than likely) *not* part of the *Group-is-better-than-the-Individual* mentality.

If not then not (after *subtracting* out the numbing effect from so many of these reports which never, ever get followed up to tell us how well or how poorly our "police" are "protecting" us).

  Consequently, *BiO Spiritualism's* primary advice is: develop your understanding and knowledge of *Objectivist* epistemology or die.

 Yesterday in p.s. 21st Century I would have written the above as: *Develop your understanding and knowledge of Objectivist epistemology or die—epistemologically, that is, spiritually, speaking.*

 This statement is still true but it is no longer—Post September 11th, 2001—complete.

 Today in P.S. 21st Century the statement is literal. Physical death has now become a day-to-day closer reality for those of us who refused to take Ayn Rand literally. She started writing and warning us as early as the 1920's when she first came to America from Russia. If we doubt this beginning, then with the publication of her first novel in America—"We the Living"—we for sure can say her warnings started in the 1930's.[i] And if not here, then in the 1940's with "The Fountainhead"?[ii] Still not? Then for absolute sure in the 50's with the 1957 publication of "Atlas Shrugged".[iii]

 And if you still *refuse* to see it and argue it's none of the above then for absolute complete no doubt sure her warnings started with her lecture: "*Faith and Force. Destroyers of the Modern World*" when she delivered it at Yale University on February 17th, 1960 [iv] (It is almost too easy to notice that New York's *Modern World* Twin Towers were *not* destroyed by people who *worship* reason.)

 Ayn Rand as a philosopher is unique in that not only does she warn us of the dangers from the Mystic-Collectivistic-Altruistic axis of evil she also gives us the weaponry to challenge and defeat that axis.

 The name of that (self-defensive) weaponry is as I've already mentioned: Objectivist *Episte*mology. And to repeat: learn it or die.

 And, if the *Objectivists* and *Objectivist* sympathizers and objective seekers manage to win the War on Terrorism—which I predict they/we will—there will emerge from that war a new threat to the individual. Since the Group is the individual's only natural predator, this new threat will be taken up by that new Group.

 This new threat is difficult to identify and define ahead of time but it has to be identified as part of the process of defeating it. So I am willing to error on the side of erring but I am not willing to *not* predict out of fear of being wrong.

 My *prediction* is that Kantian epistemology—Ayn Rand and Objectivism's archenemy—and Islam epistemology—perhaps the most consistent *practitioners* of *faith-as-tool-of-mind* on earth today—will *merge* in a way that will be analogous to the *fusing* of Ayn Rand's archetypes Attila and the Witch Doctor.[68] As she wrote extensively about these archetypes in her non-fiction work, "For the New Intellectual",[v] she makes it easier for us, qua individuals, to deal with these "phenomenon" [in our own soul] as *separate* issues [and win the *internal* battle for one's reasoning capacity over the perversion of this capacity, which, qua human capacity, is pervert-able.]. Attila is the archetype of *initiated* physical force and the Witch Doctor is the archetype of *Mysticism* and if we take these two together as same sex progenitors of a new, Third Millennium literal type, we [run the risk of] end[ing] up with [a proliferation of]: the Suicide-Murderer whose preferred weapon of murder is religion—specifically the religion of Islam which *is* the Suicide-Murderer's *moral sanction* to strap bomb material around his or her person and self-detonate it *if and only if* the chances of killing those whom the Murderer considers to be *infidels* is really really high. Since the Murderer-Suiciders (by intent, not time sequence) do this of their own free will—that is, they are not being forced to do it—we can't say that the Ayatollahs—like a bunch of culturally worshipped Charles Mansons—make them do it and that they "only" kill those *whom the Ayatollahs* consider to be infidels. The operating *principle* here is as follows: humans operating in the *absence* of initiated force being used against them *do not act against the judgment of their own mind* ☺⁰, hence the suicide-murderers (the Attilas ~~and talk about the negative effects of second hand smoke~~!?!?!) enter into agreement with the Witchdoctor Ayatollahs and for *the length of time* it takes the murderers to push the detonate button they have a <u>*fused-into-one Attila-Witchdoctor*</u> soul.

Since America is too civilized, her Attilas and Witchdoctors do and will remain un-fused[69, vi]—but they will take on new names. Rather, the *Witchdoctors* will take on new names but the Attilas (as is the case in free and semi+-free societies) will retain their old names: criminal thugs, who steal and murder

---

[68] This is the way they [will] "reason": Human's kan't know, but faith in god can know, therefore—

since knowing is necessary to living *faith* is good. (Notice the upside down to t.h.e.m. is only a feeling, an implication that they do not explicitly acknowledge, but they use it in their "reasoning".)

[69] I wrote this before the appearance of University of Colorado's "ethics" Professor Ward Churchill on the scene but since this scene is still unfolding (today is 3/15/2005) and I have to finish this *ms/book Volume One* least I write forever, I will have to leave Professor Churchill to unfold himself as the Attila dressed in Witchdoctor clothing he *appears* to be or to fizzle out as a flash in the Media's pan ... full ... of slow news days.   That is, Professor Ward Churchill could prove me wrong here about America's Attilas and Witchdoctors but it will take some time to see if this is so, so I will re-visit it in Volume II (maybe—that is, *maybe* on *two* counts: *one*, if I don't write it I won't deal with it there and *two* even if I do write it he might be a non-issue by then and hence no need to write about him and/or his [fused] brand of American Attila-Witchdoctory. See Reference note for more.)

because they are morally degenerate. The (new, 3rd Millennium American) Witchdoctors on the other hand will be called: *Public Intellectuals.*

The *Public Intellectual*—as distinct from the *Professional* Intellectual as is the Witch Doctor from a real Doctor—will emerge in this the 3rd Millennium [Western World] as the literal leader of collective-worshipping groups.[70, vii]

The Group has no need of archetypes (the Group is its own archetype). But what it does need, qua a kind of thing (a thing 2), is to exist as a *unitary* thing and so it has the same *identity* needs as we *individuals* do. That is, it (the Group) needs *a* metaphysics, *an* epistemology and *a* ethic.

The e/merged epistemology part of t.h.e.i.r needs will not be named by "them" because to name it is to defeat it. Therefore, I am giving it a working title/name now. We can call it *Islantian* epistemology. It will be a hybrid of Islamic fundamentalism and Kantian post-modernism. By Islamic fundamentalism I mean *that* which is characterized by this sentiment: "...*faith* allows no room for *reason[ing* Caesars]..." This sentiment was outwardly expressed/revealed on a recent [first half of 2002] national (American) TV news program as a visual sound-bite from *one* of Islam's Clerics.[71]

By *Kantian post-modernism* I mean the Ayn Rand nutshelled description of Kant's epistemology. Ayn Rand nailed Kant to the wall when she articulated for us what we (who had taken their American Public Schooling seriously—all 17 years of it) were *unable* to articulate for ourselves. Ayn Rand said Kant's essential "argument" is this: "...man is blind, because he has eyes...".[viii]

Consequently, when the *staunchly* pro-faith anti-reason Islamists find common ground with the Kantians it will create another two edged sword for us happiness seekers (life, liberty *and* the *pursuit* of happiness—don't forget) to *defend* our sacred happiness against. This sword will be that which when thrust through our psyche will emit a sound analogous to a computer chip-taped-to-a-birthday card like voice that sings, "Of course *nothing is knowable but something is not."*

♪*Nothing is knowable but something is not.*♪

---

[70] *The Public Intellectual* is to *The Group* what the *Professional Intellectual* is to the *Individual*: *advocate* of the philosophical values one *should* adopt. Since Groups always try to be what they are not—primary existents—t,h,e,y end up with the same needs that the *actual* primary existents—individuals—have. These (basic) needs are: identity and autonomy. And so, to repeat, just as the Professional Intellectual tries to help the individual satisfy his needs in this area so too does the Public Intellectual mistakenly try to help the non-existent Group satisfy its "needs". For more see the comments in the referenced Reference.

[71] Unfortunately I can't recall the exact TV news program that I heard this sound bite on, but I did hear it with my own ears. An Islam Cleric explicitly said (to an interviewer or reporter in response to some question, the Cleric said): "[In Islam] faith allows no room for reason."

♪*Nothing is knowable but something is not.* ♪

This is the in-a-nutshell description of "Islantian" epistemology. And my prediction is—or rather the danger is—that *Islantian Epistemology* will take over all the sheep-people currently inhabiting a gigantic part of planet earth with a speed that will make the bubonic plague that marched through dark ages Europe—where it killed one out of every four people within a few decades—look like the plodding, inch-by-inch moving *Blob* from the 1950's American movie by the same name.

But how do you (author) know this, since only nothingness is knowable?

Which is to say, how might we recognize this new, Third Millennium *Evil Man*?

The answer is: *By her or his view of concepts.*

Ayn Rand had warned us that yesteryear's evil men's desire—hidden beneath all their evasions and wishful thinking—was to *destroy* the *conceptual* level of human functioning.

This was a hard thing to swallow and one was inclined to think Ms. Rand—the world's best novelist—was being perhaps a bit dramatic.

But flash forward to P.S. 21st Century and view Islamic youths the world over on 20th Century Television technology rocking back 'n forth forcing *irrational* tenets down their spiritual throats and then tell me that Ayn Rand—in principle—was not right about everything she wrote and warned us about concerning the *Mystic-Collectivistic-Altruistic* axis.

She didn't call it an axis of evil, but we in P.S. 21st Century can and *must*.

Mysticism leads to evil.

Collectivism leads to evil.

Altruism leads to evil.

Or rather we should say they do *if accepted and practiced in the individual soul,* which is the only "place" they can be accepted and practiced.

Which is somewhat reassuring: *since we do have control over our own individual soul, the solution is easy: reject Mysticism—embrace Reason; reject Collectivism—embrace Individualism; reject Altruism—embrace Objectivism Selfishness. That is, reject the Mystic-Collectivistic-Altruistic axis of evil and embrace instead the Reason-Individualism-Egoism axis of good.*

And voila! We are back to where we started in p.s. 21st Century (my first cut manuscript was started in February 2000 and 85% done on September 10th, 2001) and can <u>now</u> (<u>6/12/02</u>) continue on our path, albeit with the need to make a mid-course correction.

This mid-course correction is we have two themes to combine here, no longer just the one about the American Bureaucratic Mind, or BM for short but one that *adds* to this original theme.

The *addition* is the answer to a question: How can we recognize Third Millennium Evil Man?

His will not be the outright desire to destroy the conceptual. That was tried by Second Millennium Evil Man but thwarted—in spades—by Ayn Rand and her intellectual heirs. Consequently, Third Millennium Evil Man's new tactic will be to make his *anti-concepts* look like *reality-based* concepts and kill off rational man via the method of asphyxiation: Third Millennium *Good* Man, Third Millennium *rational* man will face the prospect of *spiritual death* by the presence of carbon monoxide concepts in his psyche and never know what hit him.[72]

Or rather we should say here, such is rational man's new, emerging danger now on P.S. 21st Century Earth.

Therefore Third Millennium *Good* Man's safe guard is to look at and learn Objectivist Epistemology, which is what we initiate in Chapter 20 when we prove that Objectivism needs *Biocentric Psychology* if it—*Objectivism*—is to be the "savior" of *itself* [and yes, Ayn Rand notwithstanding, *Objectivism* is an *itself*] and hence of *rational* man in the 3rd Millennium.

If not, then not.

Based on everything I know I am the *first* Objectivismly *trained* non-professional selfish person to *come out of the closet* in the 21st Century and declare publicly that **selfishness** is good. I hope through the writing of this book that I can encourage other *objectively selfish* people to come out too and provide moral support for all *objectively selfish* people who by their nature are so individualistic that the idea of a group of *any kind* supporting them is anathema their very existence.

The individual's predator GROUP today is the American *and* Global cultural mainstream. That is, today's American cultural *worship* of *materialism* at the expense of *spiritualism* (or if you replace the word "expense" with "annihilation", vice versa in the Islamic World); *environmentalism* at the expense of *individualism* and of *animalism* at the expense of *humanism* and/or substitute any *non-selfish* ideal you can think of into the *formula* and "[Global] mainstream cultural life goes on": the *worship* of the *non-self* as the means to actively forestall

---

[72] Some say *spiritual* death is worst than physical death, but I am not one of them. Since man has volition, as long as he retains a shred of it he retains the power to bring his own *internal* "gods"—*disowned* parts of the self—back to life.

the *growth* and *moral* development of the selfish self, which is to say, of the *individual*. Because of all this, objectively selfish people *might* have to turn to *their* group—temporarily—in order to withstand the onslaught of the *aggressive spiritual stagnation* currently creeping over cultural horizons.

And yes, by objectively selfish I mean an individual who has *learned* his or her selfishness from the *Philosophy of Objectivism* and/or any others who are just as—or more—*objectively* selfish. I personally know of no other philosophy that teaches selfishness as well as *Objectivism* does, but I can't conclude that there are none. I suspect there are none, but I don't know this for a fact.

The individual versus the group *is* an age-old conflict and because of the *metaphysical* nature of this battle—the individual is outnumbered by the *nature* of quantity: individual means *one* and group means *more than* one—it periodically comes to pass that the *degree and quality* of the outnumbering rises to such a fevered pitch that it threatens the very existence of the individual, especially the selfish individual and super-especially today, the *objectively* selfish individual.

Yes, I assume there were objectively *selfish* individuals before Ayn Rand but "objective" in the sense of "Objectivism" selfish there were none. But there are now, and *they* as well as *others* who *desire* their own, individual, *selfish* happiness can use *BiO Spiritualism* to *sustain* that desire as well as to help *protect* themselves from a mainstream culture that is hostile to their existence.

The American culture—not to even mention the emerging Global culture—is still hostile to *Objectivism* and hence to *anyone* who tries to practice its pro-selfishness, pro-happiness tenets on a day-in and day-out basis. One ingredient of this anti-Objectivism, anti-selfishness, anti-reason stance is the rank refusal of the *status quo protectors* to acknowledge Objectivism and its many accomplishments. The most salient of which is the discovery that (our) *reason*—qua human capacity to *automatically* operate on sensory data to form *percepts*—is engaged and operated by (our) volition to consciously operate on percepts—as if they were sensory data—to form concepts and then to further operate on these concepts—as if they were percepts—to form higher concepts and so on and so forth, going as *high* as we can go individually as humans possessing the human form of consciousness which the foregoing description just described. And that *volition* means: no, none, nada, zero, zilch...none ... absolutely *no antecedent causes* in you or me other than *you* in your case or *me* in my case exercising our *nature* given *power of volition* when we *choose* to think or to evade the effort. T.h.e.y.—*the status quo protectors*—implement their rank refusal to *acknowledge Objectivism* by denying *Objectivism* in *every* opportunity available to deny *it* and/or *one* of *its* most important accomplishments: the discovery of *Psychhology, The Science*. That is, the discovery and development of *Biocentric Psychology* by the early Objectivist, Dr. Nathaniel Branden. Dr. Branden is the (Objectivist) person who added *emotions* back into the equation for philosophical man. Consequently, when taken together, *Objectivism AND Biocentric Psychology* prove that the *true trinity*[73] of man is man's *reason*, man's *volition* and man's un-repressed *emotional* capacity that when triply integrated (not in the mathematical sense but rather in the *culinary* sense of integration-as-process as in leaving no traces of the *process* behind beyond the finished product upon completion of the process, e.g., a cake after making it) helps philosophical man survive and enjoy, grow and develop as he learns how to bake himself up a happy life here on this earth while he actually exists.

For one *typical* example of the *ubiquitous* denial behavior of the status quo protectors consider the article my local newspaper recently ran about Freud and *his* Psychoanalytic theories.[ix] The article discusses *all* that is *wrong* with Freud and then concludes: "...although many of Freud's theories have foundered, no one else has come close to providing answers about human nature that are as satisfying.". What about Ayn Rand and Dr. Nathaniel Branden? They have provided answers about *human nature* that are *both* satisfying *and* true. But to use an old Ayn Rand expression to answer the question: "What about Ayn Rand and Dr. Nathaniel Branden?"

Blank out.

Ayn Rand has recommended that one way to fight the hostility is for the objectively selfish to *go on strike* against any and all self-*less*-ness preaching cultures in which it finds itself. As a *universal* mandate this is *impractical* advice, hence, it is not a moral recommendation for all to follow. It has merit only as it exists as a *literary device* for the Ayn Rand fictional story—*Atlas Shrugged*—in which it appeared. *Better* advice would be to seek out and learn *Biocentric Psychology*. It is the *science and the technology* that you (the individual you, the actual you, the "yu" in *you* in the here and now of "yor" life span) need in order to *survive* a hostile culture (and thrive in it) and as such it represents *the first* area in which Objectivism—that is, *the objective in you*—needs (Biocentric) Psychology, the Science.[74]

---

[73] For you Lutherans out there who think that *with* this reference to "trinity" I am letting my religious neuronal nets leak their gray matter into my thought processes I simply want to say: *you are wrong*. Religion has usurped all *spiritual* language and part of *BiO Spiritualism's* mission is to retrieve it—*all* of it.

[74] The failure of the Professional (contemporary) Objectivists to be pro-Biocentric psychology is simply due to the fact that in some important areas they have succumbed to "authoritarian" thinking: AR was deeply,

Psychology the Science, qua *spiritual* technology at the personal level—which is the only level at which the *concept* of *spiritualism* applies—is an answer to the question: Who am I? At the scientific-cognitive level it is an answer to the question: *What* am I? The answer to the *what* question according to *Biocentric Psychology* is this: I am a living entity that has *both* physical and psychological *survival* **needs** that have to be satisfied—by me—in order to live a happy human being's life and as a human being I also have the *capacities* to satisfy those needs. Granted, I have to learn *how* to *exercise* those capacities to satisfy those needs and this includes learning how to nurture and grow those capacities so that they *will* forever be at my beck and call to do WHAT they were "designed" to do: *satisfy all my authentic (that is survive & thrive) needs.* The answer to the *"what* am I?" question according to *Objectivism* is: I am a living entity that has a *specific* [human] nature that is the same, immutable thing for *all* people and this *nature* is figure-out-able and has to be figured out by me. *Biocentric Psychology* agrees with Ayn Rand's *Objectivism* that one of those (authentic) **needs** is philosophy but *contemporary* Objectivism, unfortunately, would argue—if pressed to do so—that one of those "needs" isn't *Biocentric psychology* because psychology needs philosophy but not vice versa *in the same way*. Notice that this statement is true, but not accurate. It is analogous to saying that the 11th floor of a building "needs" the foundation but the foundation does not "need" the 11th floor. This actually is true. But it is incomplete because a foundation alone does not a building make.

But—continuing the analogy—a *solid* foundation allows for the construction of a solid building, but a weak foundation will not support *as-much-as* a stronger foundation will. If your "building" is only one story high because if you went higher your whole (epistemological) structure would collapse, the proper thing to do is *start over* and build a *better* foundation (not lighter floors). In this analogy the stronger, *better* foundation of course is *Objectivism* and the height of your personal skyscraper—though totally and completely up to you—could be, I am suggesting, increased by you, if you, *also* embrace *Biocentric Psychology*. Which is to say, I am *asserting* that *Objectivism* **PLUS** *Biocentric* is the blueprint for the

---

personally hurt by Dr. Branden's personal behavior towards her as same is revealed in their writings and I suppose you could argue that instead of it being a failure of authoritarianism it is a misplaced sense of loyalty. But which ever one it is, it doesn't matter "practically", hence morally—it is wrong behavior. Since Biocentric Psychology exists and is the best integration of all the known facts about human psychology, it is the best, most accurate science of psychology and *should* be promoted as such. It in particular should be promoted ahead of the I-Object!(ivism)-To-Everything impulse/view of Contemporary Objectivism: being FOR a correct psychology is better than simply being against the wrong ones (though this is very important *also*, as in "it's a dirty job but somebody *has* to do it.").

human skyscraper whereas *any* other *philosophy-psychology* combination (e.g., Kantian philosophy—Cognitive Neuroscience as academically supported by formal Cognitive Psychology and/or Cognitive Science) can and will produce nothing more than *a house of cards.* (Epistemologically speaking.)

Since *Objectivism* is the *best* philosophy and *Biocentric Psychology* the *best* psychology, why—you may wonder—do we have to consider short, stubby, mud huts built by savages?

For two reasons: one, we aren't buildings—this is only an analogy—and two, our very own American Government was trying, in 20th and p.s. 21st Century, to *convince* us that those mud huts were actually glass and steel skyscrapers of the finest design with the tallest potential and we should all emulate them.

Consider Mud Hut #1.

The answer to the "what am I?" question according to *Behaviorism* is this: I am an automaton that emits *behaviors* that bounced back to me from the shelled walls of *reinforcements* that exist in reality but which can't be seen by me because if they could they'd have to be "seen" by something internal since externally they can't be seen and since man has no "internal", no "mentalistic" innards—that is, no "psychology"—I/he/we/it/you/they/them don't really have *psychological* needs.

At this point the Rationalists[75]—dressed as Cognitive Psychologists—rebelled against Behaviorism and its open worship of empiricism (as in experience—that is, behavior—is all, *mind* is nothing) by in effect correctly saying that Behaviorism is wrong because it can't account for the complexities in man; man qua human being *in the world.* And further, the Cognitive-Psychologist-Rationalists said Behaviorism can't explain man's complexities *because* it denies man's mind.

And if you are an Objectivist and/or Biocentric sympathizer you are probably thinking, so far so good. And you are correct.

So far.

So good.

But.

Rather than look for a new, fresh explanation of man, the philosophers amongst the early Cognitive Psychologists took the easy way out and said Plato

---

[75] In *traditional* academia/intellectualism the battles for knowledge have formed along two *opposing* shores: *empiricism*, which says experience is everything, mind is nothing is one shore and the other is *rationalism* which says the mind is everything and experience is nothing. (That the river that connects these two shores together is Objectivism is beyond our current scope.)

was right and Aristotle wrong and since Kant is the modern Plato we'll use Kantianism as our philosophy and give it a more modern name. We'll call it Cognitive *Science*.

The remaining, soon to be naked and dressed in nothing, not even Rationalist clothing Cognitive Psychologists said in effect if Cognitive Science was gonna be that way about it we don't need them. We don't need them, because, psychology, real psychology, doesn't need philosophy.

Bye-Bye Cognitive Psychology.

Re-enter *Cognitive "Science"* (*pretending* to disagree with Behaviorism's *Philosophy* of experience/behavior is everything, mind is nothing by apologizing—out of one side of its mouth—for Kant's appalling lack of the experimental in his philosophical hypothesizing while praising—out of the other side—Kant's chaotic epistemology *because it is chaotic*) countering that Behaviorism is wrong because it fails on *two* levels. First, the "scientist" part of Cognitive Science said *traditional* Behaviorism fails to explain in *materialistic terms HOW* the brain *encodes* the bounce-backs from those reinforcement shells in reality and secondly, the cognitive part of Cognitive Science said traditional Behaviorism's view of "behavior" is too narrow. It should (indeed) be broadened to include the "behavior" of the "mind" which ultimately is the "behavior" of the brain which is the "behavior" of neurons and dendrites and axons and whatever else we can *use* to "prove" *that* which we *already* "know": man is a dynamic sponge without a soul—that is, without consciousness as a primary, self evident, can't-be-reduced-further "thing". Man is, continues the Cognitive Science mentality, a being that consists *only* of brain and glands and muscle and sinew that absorbs "behonemes" (rhymes with phonemes and stands for the smallest yet to be discovered "behavioral unit" and yes it is a word I just made up) *from* the environment. Whether the *absorption* is by simple or complex stimulus-response mechanisms is a secondary issue. The primary issue is that *reductive materialism* is the correct *theoretical* explanation of *the fact* of human consciousness, and by this we—*Cognitive Scientists*—really do mean that consciousness is **not** a primary, axiomatic fact of nature but is a *derivative* of either one of two material substances. Either it is a derivative of the *material* the brain is made out of or it is a derivative of some yet to be discovered other material. Granted, "we" think the brain is it but in case we're wrong we want to keep our options open least we loose out on Government handouts. The *Cognitive Psychologist* sell-outs (that is, the ones who let the Government's Cognitive Neuroscientists use Cognitive Psychology to justify calling themselves psychologists) then add this: we don't know about such things but since consciousness is not a primary it must follow that man *constructs* his *perceptions*.

This much, say the sell-outs, we will grant to the *Cognitive Scientists* and (as already stated) give up the soul of psychology to the physicists and computer scientists who *want* man to be a machine *without* a soul.

That man *is* a *physiological* machine with a *consciousness* soul is too difficult a thing for "us" physicist/artificial intelligence worshippers/reductive materialists to get our ... our what?—dare we say it: m*ind*?—around.

Figuring out *How* man *constructs* perceptions is something more in-line with our ability, history and traditions, continue the Government's Cognitive Neuroscientists. Therefore, perception *construction*—with man as General Contractor and the five senses as Kantian subcontractors hired to build PERCEPTS according to blueprints designed (somehow) by man—is what psychology *is* about, hence it is what psychology *should* be about. Then "they" (the bad t.h.e.y not the good they) proceed to give us t.h.e.i.r—Cognitive Psychologist taken over by Cognitive Scientists now fully morphed into— Cognitive Neuroscientist answer to the "*How* do we know?" question.[76] The Government's Cognitive Neuroscientists in effect answer: Gary Deering's brain, like *all* human brains, *processes* all sensory data in the *same* way an *Artificially Intelligent Machine* would process it: by performing some gigantic number crunching algorithm using as input the streaming sensory data provided by the eyes, the ears, the nose, the hands and the tongue. And, do they conclude that the number crunching algorithm is designed by our human nature? If they did, then we could at least call them by their *proper* name: Cognitive *Physiologists*. But no, they do not conclude this, rather they conclude that each and every one of us designs this algorithm him or her self!?! I don't mean to be sarcastic here, but I mean come on man, I know people who can't even balance their checkbook because they don't know how to add and subtract and you expect me to believe that they have the mathematical ability to produce algorithms that robot designers would give their eye teeth for. I mean, come on...what's that phrase?

These guys 'n gals neither give nor take breaks.

---

[76] That *both* (*all* Cognitive Scientists and *some* Cognitive Psychologists) accept Kant's erroneous view of *what* human nature is, is taken for granted by each and every one of t.h.e.m so they don't make it explicit everyday in t.h.e.i.r everyday lives. Rather, they let it stand as a "everybody knows it" myth and when successfully challenged—such as by Objectivism—they just ignore the challenge and give us consumers of their drivel the *illusion* that they are of the academic challenging type. They aren't. Formal Objectivism and formal Biocentric Psychology are the real challengers to the status quo and without which—in some form— no human being who worships happiness can survive.

Enter the *(New) Behaviorists* who switch clothes faster than the manikins in the movie *Time Machine*[x] as it portrays its time traveler flying at 1 year/second (and accelerating) past the stationary Department store window housing the manikins dressed in fashions of the year into the future and who—qua *Cognitive EitherName*—say: Gary Deering, like all humans, is pure (neurophysiological) *behavior* and has no survival needs beyond the *physiological* needs to preserve and protect his neurons and all associated gray matter and to propagate his gene pool. And—if you don't believe this—just (Government) *grant* us a gazillion dollars and we'll "prove" it.

If at this point you are feeling that the *human* is not being represented *anywhere* in today's world and are looking for some *humanists* to correct this, be careful. The cultural movement formally known as (Secular) *Humanism* is not going to do it. Why? Because it can't. The answer to the "What am I?" question according to *Humanism* is this: I am lopsided; I *need* to praise the good in self and others, but I do not need to damn the evil. In fact, say the humanists, I *need* to praise the good and I need to *not* damn the evil.[77]

This "answer" is incorrect, therefore it is wrong, and therefore secular humanism is wrong.

Wrong can't do right.

We will have to wait until Chapter 20 to get into and fully understand the correct answer.

In Chapter 20 we discuss the mutual, reciprocal need that *Biocentric Psychology* and *Objectivism*, qua psychology and philosophy in-the-man, have for each other. Here [in the "humanism" realm] is where Chapter 20 begins because here is one area where Biocentric Psychology *needs* Objectivism because it is Objectivism that says we **need** to *do* both. We need to praise the good AND damn the evil. *Biocentric Psychology's* strength in this area is in the HOW not the WHAT. Even though it has failed in the *what*—because it, Biocentric, erroneously suggests we *only* need to praise the good—it still *shines bright* in the *how*.[78] *Biocentric* shows us the *proper* way to *praise the good* and that way is this: when you experience the good in yourself, *praise* it, take *pride* in it,

---

[77] For answers to the "What-Who-What am I?" questions according to a whole pile of other psychological "theorists" —that is, according to Freud, Jung, Adler, et al.—see Chapter 17.

[78] Though we could argue that the Biocentric advice to praise the good *only* (or predominantly) is simply a pendulum swing away from the religious ethic that encourages us to both DAMN the good *and* turn the second eye away from evil by turning the other cheek when we confront it, as if to say: if we damn the good the evil will disappear because the evil is the absence of the good and absent good, absent evil. That this is *convoluted* reason *cannot* enter the religious mind because the *true* religious mind is anti-reason.

acknowledge it, own it and do *not* deny it. Then it becomes like they (the good they not the bad t.h.e.y but the good they) say: "once they've seen 'Pairēē (have tasted *authentic* pride) you can't keep them DOWN ... in any fashion, be it "on the farm" or anywhere.[79]

To simplify further consider this: for both *Objectivism* AND *Biocentric Psychology*, *psychology* is the science that helps me answer the question: *Who* am **I**? *Together* these two have helped me answer: **I** am a person who has *needs* that have to be satisfied by me and since I have the *capacities* to satisfy them, I simply have to *learn* how to exercise those capacities in order to satisfy those needs, after that is, I discover *what* those needs are. Per *Objectivism* and *Biocentric Psychology* this is also the answer to the question: Who are you? For all other "philosophies" and "psychologies"—that is, the ones that have no links to, nor anything in common with Objectivism—to those "other" non-objective perspectives, psychology is an answer to the question: Since there is no "I", Who are you?

To which we have to ask ourselves: can we understand our selfs by understanding others first and/or "others" *only* or is it—ultimately—the other way around? And by understand I mean in a deep sense, a sense that reaches down to and encompasses our own *psycho-epistemological* and *motivational* core.

A *level* that we can get to (in this limited life time) *only if* we (also) accept the *Biocentric* view of volition: volition is the choice *to be aware.*

Notice that *Objectivism* and *Biocentric* may disagree *in the details* as to *what* the correct answer is, but they do not disagree as to *what* the correct question is. "What does volition mean?" is the correct question. Notice it's not: "Does man have volition?" But rather: "What does the volition that man does have mean?" Does it mean: "the choice to think or not to think", as the Objectivists contend or does it mean: "the choice to be aware" as Biocentric Psychology contends? Again, see Chapter 20 for more and contrast Biocentric psychology's focus on the *individual* with its "choice [of self] to be aware [of self]" with other, non-Biocentric psychologies. These non-Biocentric "psychologies" say that "other"—more precisely, "non-self"—is and hence *should be* the focus of *any question to be asked* about man's psychology. Since they have *other* as the *center* of their philosophies, it makes sense to have "other" at the center of their psychologies. This difference in focusing on self, on *individual* versus on *other* is critical. It *is* a

---

[79] For those who think in clichés, this one could be changed to: once YOU *see* ... you can't keep YOURSELF down. That is, once you see what you see and know what you know—e.g., selfishness *is* a virtue—you will no longer be able to pretend that *earned* pride is arrogance.

difference *in kind,* not degree (apples and tomatoes do not differ in degree, they differ in *kind).* Objectivism PLUS Biocentric Psychology *is* different from any and all such philosophical-psychological pairs (pun not intended) in the known Universe: and this *difference*—to repeat—is *in kind.*[80] As there are none like them, there are none similar to compare them to and so in the end here the conclusion will be inescapable: the philosophy-psychology pair known as Objectivism and Biocentric Psychology is the *best.* That is, the best available philosophy and scientific psychology for the *proper* growth and development of moral-autonomous, **individual** man.

So even though Ayn Rand is a genius and advocates we all go on strike, for those of us who are not professional intellectuals, this going on strike means *living in the street.*[81]

When the "Professional Objectivists" are *living in the street* I will *consider* joining them in their "crusade", but in the mean time I seek other solutions to life's big problems. Especially to the problem of running my own life and being happy.

Because of the danger of subconscious scripts running our lives—as same can be related to *psychologically* by us through an *introspective* connection to the (old) idea of *self-fulfilling philosophies*—because of this, modern day Objectivists and/or Objectivist sympathizers have to make certain that everything about themselves is made as *explicit* as they can humanly make it. For example, come out of the closet as the **selfish** person that you are and/or desire to be and let the world know it. This way you will avoid the problem of subconscious scripts running your life forever rather than you *consciously* running your *own* life.

Dr. Nathaniel Branden—to repeat, the early Objectivist Psychologist—calls this, *living consciously* and as part of his *scientific* psychology—i.e. *Biocentric Psychology*—he counsels that "Living Consciously" is a really good thing to do. To my knowledge, "official" *Objectivism* does not disagree with this "living consciously" counsel and would whole heartedly support it if asked to do so.

---

[80] Apples, oranges and plumbs are of the same [fruit] *kind* and they differ from tomatoes, carrots and potatoes which are of a different [vegetable] *kind*. Apples, oranges for example, qua fruit, differ in *degree*—degree of sweetness, degree of succulent moisture, degree of hardness and so on. Which is to say, so far in the realm of [the new] spiritualism only apples [BiO Spiritualism] exist. Either there are no oranges, plumbs and pomegranates—as the analogy to Aeronautical Engineering in Chapter 1 suggests—or there are other [new] spiritualisms but they have yet to be systematized and made into a whole, edible fruit (I of course think the Aeronautical Engineering analogy is the proper model to follow, which is to say, *Yes,* BiO Spiritualism IS the answer).

[81] Which, if it were not for my working wife, is where I would be right now (i.e., June 25, 2002). ... and still, November 19, 2002. Still: 4/17/03. But not now, 2/9/04 because my wife got laid off—oat oh, what now???

I support it and I refer to it as *making* my implicit *explicit*. And if you try doing this and fail because *you* are afraid to use the word "selfish" directly and write and/or preach the "gospels" of "enlightened self-interest", and/or *egoism* as euphemism for *selfishness* then in the shadow of *Objectivism* that makes you a moral coward. Moral cowards are those who let their *fear* of others bad opinion—not objective reality—dictate their *actual* behavior. Shakespeare has already told us how many deaths such types die.[82]

So, come out of the closet and declare *selfishness* to be the *virtue* that it is.

As *Objectivism* itself has done and continues to do.

Objectivism is a powerful philosophy and since Ayn Rand has *warned* us that Objectivism is its own protector$^{\circledast 01}$, it is incumbent upon on us to *fully* understand *what* this means.[83]

It means one cannot *absorb* Objectivism—that is, *automatize* it and *make* it ones own—*without* sufficient thinking. Thinking is the only currency that can be used to buy Objectivism—conscious, volitional, "I-want-it" *thinking*. Anything *less* will result in "abandoning the project".

Nonetheless, since Objectivists and their sympathizers are people too they can't escape the "occupational hazards" of being human, especially the hazards of "authoritarianism" and of the downside risk of "automatized" tenets on *how to live life*. The downside of "automatizing" here is the opposite of a floating abstraction; it's the hazard of the anchored concrete. By this last I mean, the hazard of attempting to apply the *sources* of one's *abstraction*, that is the *concretes* that gave rise to it, *directly* to the self rather than *directly applying* the

---

[82] And if ... you are an Objectivist sympathizer and are going to argue that you can't openly advocate selfishness because to you the world of *actual* people—who in the main, actively, openly despise selfishness—is part of your OBJECTIVE universe then I suggest you read and/or re-read Dr. Branden's article: "Isn't everyone selfish?" [see article in Reference ii in Chapter 2]. I suggest this because I will argue that the "structure" of your *rationalization* is the same "structure" as written about by Dr. Branden in that article. And that *structure* is this: *valid* logical argument *form* with false premises AND a standing order to *not* check premises. This structure is a *structure* that produces falsehoods that look like truths, and—with the standing idiosyncratic principle *don't check premises*—ultimately, *feels* like the truth too. An example of such a form is: mippy is a cat, all cats are dogs, therefore mippy is a dog. In the referenced article, the faulty reasoning *form* that Dr. Branden is (masterfully) railing *against* (by using understatement) is: all purposeful behavior is motivated behavior, all motivated behavior is selfish, therefore all purposeful behavior is selfish behavior and hence, if the *purpose* of my behavior is to *avoid* the scowl of others when I make known my opinion that selfishness is a virtue, my avoidance is selfish, and ... well, what was it that Shakespeare said in this regard?

[83] The *numerically* o-subscripted sad-face dingbats will touch approximately half of the less than a dozen or so errors that I say herein (item # 6, page 332) are in Ayn Rand's Philosophy of Objectivism (and when there could easily be *more* than 17 million truths in it, the less than a dozen errors or so ain't much). See Chapter 20 for more.

abstract principle to the self. For example, when I decided I wanted to go back to College and get an advanced degree beyond my Bachelors Degree in Aeronautical Engineering, I was *stuck* for four or five weeks on trying to *convince* myself that I wanted to be an Architect (for the interested reader, see Ayn Rand's novel, *"The Fountainhead"*). And I only came "unstuck" when it *hit* me that I hate Architecture *as a subject to be intensely studied by me* and I want to be a psychologist and get a degree in psychology. A near euphoric time for me as I happily thereafter proceeded to get *my* (Masters) degree in psych(h)ology.[84]

The automatizing here—that is, the human *capacity* to automatize—is the source of *subconscious scripts* and as such is the entry point for the *science* of psychology into the *kingdom* of philosophy. The Objectivists and/or Objectivist sympathizers for example will live out Objectivism's *essential* events *as much as* any religious person lives out the *essential* events of their holy books. In the case of Christians it is the *essential* events of *The Holy Bible*. For others it is the *essential* events of whatever their *particular* holy book happens to be—holy as in *at the very top* of their particular, idiosyncratic hierarchy of value-'able books— and how they idiosyncratically, qua individual, happen to absorb and/or integrate the *how to live life* tenets of their philosophy.[85] The major difference between them and us of course is that we know what is happening to us, they don't. For example, all *true* Christians end up being martyrs. Whether *existentially:* sacrificing self to god(s) or to ones parents or spouse or children or all of the above or combos thereof or to any other **non-self** *ideal.* Or *psychologically:* sacrificing self to a *floating* abstraction called morality. Or *tragically:* be it sacrificed as antiquity's fodder for the Christian Crusades of the 11th Century Church Intellectuals or as fodder to yesterday's Professional Political Altruists in the *Viet Nam War* or as *suicide* fodder for the *cults of moral blackness*. For cult examples see Religious Preacher Jim Jones' 1970's Guyana (religious moral blackness) or more recently California's *Heaven's Gate* cult (guru-won't-*you*-please-*think*-for-me-cult moral blackness) to name but two.[86]

---

[84] At the time I didn't realize there were no formal schools anywhere in the world let alone in the United States that taught Psyc*hh*ology, the science. Consequently, I got an Masters Degree in Counseling Psychology—a near stroke of genius on my part as it at least afforded me the opportunity to work in the technical (practical) side of the science.

[85] They will *trend* toward this that is, *unless* they are worshippers and practitioners of "living consciously", in which case they will *trend* towards picking and choosing life scripts and/or writing their own rather than being chosen by them.

[86] My claim that the Viet Nam War was largely an *altruistic* war isn't an empty claim. I remember reading an op ed piece (circa 1968 or 1970 or so or plus or minus a couple'a years either way) written (as best I can recall, in the *Wall Street Journal* I believe but am not certain) by our then **Secretary of Defense** (or World

If it is true—as Objectivism contends—that *religion* is a *primitive philosophy*[87], then it could be just as true that it is a primitive psychology also. Consequently, modern *philosophy* (the objective kind) *plus* modern *psychology* (also the objective kind) is *Scientific* Religion—that is, religion *without* the epistemology of faith and *with* the *plus* of selfishness. Though *technically*—as in *precisely*—speaking of course if you take *faith* out of religion and add in *selfishness* you are as far from religion as is the period at the end of this sentence from infinity. For this reason I prefer *Scientific Spiritualism* as the best, most succinct description of what *BiO Spiritualism* is. Hence, it is easy to see that the philosopher in each and every one of us is *not* exempt from the fact of human psychology. As humans we can pretend that we are *beyond all that* but we cannot escape the consequences of such *pretense*. We cannot escape the consequences of failing to understand ourselves psychologically. And by *understand* I mean, fully and completely all the way to and including *the core of our being*.

Human nature is at the core of *everyone's* being; hence, no one is beyond human nature and the *need* to understand it.

No one.

Human nature, *by its nature* as it is manifest in individual human beings is *objectively* selfish. In this sense Ayn Rand's *Philosophy of Objectivism* is also *The Science of Human Nature* and as such is its own proof of a statement made earlier. That statement is: *this*—our life—*is* our one and only life and to *sacrifice* it to *anything*—including to a *floating* abstraction called morality—is a *sin*. In fact this is the *only* way "sin" can be constructed so as to be meaningful. A *sin* is when you sacrifice your *ultimate* value, which is your own life to *anything* outside the *objectively selfish self*, which is the *natural* center of that life.

For example, to *sacrifice the self* to any one of the current p.s. 21st Century anti-human groups vying to take over the American culture *would be a sin*.[88]

Bank President) Robert S. McNamara, wherein he stated explicitly that our "reason" for going to and *being* in Viet Nam was *altruistic*: we are our brother's *keeper* and those poor Vietnamese need us to *keep* them from being victimized by communist thugs and as *moral* human beings it was our *duty* to sacrifice American men to "others", who in this case happen to be Vietnamese. Voila! My claim of yesterday's Professional Politician's view of young—which at the time I was—American men as *fodder*. That our [altruistic] chickens came home to roost in more ways than one over this war is a different—beyond my focus here—issue.

[87] I was on the verge of agreeing with Objectivism in their claim that religion is a primitive philosophy but now (P.S. 21st Century) I'm more convinced then ever that Objectivism might be wrong on this. Though I suppose you could say that Ayn Rand told us that religion is a primitive philosophy but that she forgot to tell us that some are *more* primitive than others. If this, then...well, we'll see...time will tell.

[88] Wow, in light of the P.S. 21st Centurians (the Islamic fundamentalists) who want to literally destroy the American culture, this "taking over" behavior of the p.s. Centurians (the Anti-volitionalists) threatening the individual seems mild by comparison. As such, one hopes it's not too late to educate the *rational* within

In the opening remarks to this chapter, three types of problems were asserted to be cultural problems and as such dangerous things for us as *individual* members of that large group we call, *the culture*. Since no one can totally and completely escape their culture (as asserted by Dr. Nathaniel Branden, founder of *Biocentric Psychology* and which seems like a logical thing to conclude to me), cultural problems *are* problems for the individual. And since our goal is to protect ourselves from the *negative* aspects of our culture while enjoying and extending the *positive* aspects we simply have to be aware of each in our every day lives. Here we deal with the negative so let's revisit the opening remarks to the current chapter (with some [added] comments):

> But since their [the objectively selfish's] *very existence* is under serious attack by today's cultural mainstream—that is, today's cultural *worship* of *materialism* [and *self*-sacrifice] at the expense of *spiritualism* [*and* its natural reward: *luxurious* happiness]*,* of *environmentalism* [*as* a thing to sacrifice *self* to] at the expense of *individualism* [*and* property rights], and [finally our culture's worship] of *animalism* [as another thing to sacrifice self to] at the expense of *humanism* [*and simple justice*], and/or substitute any *non-selfish* ideal you can think of into the *formula* and "mainstream cultural life goes on": the *worship* of the *non-self* as the means to actively forestall the *growth* and *moral* development of the selfish self, which is to say, of the *individual*. Because of all this, objectively selfish people *might* have to turn to their group—temporarily—in order to withstand the onslaught of the *aggressive spiritual stagnation* currently creeping over cultural horizons.

At the cultural level—we can now ask—*who* are those who worship materialism *at the expense* of spiritualism? The answer is: the Anti-Laissez faire capitalists. These are the ones who use capitalism's methods to promote their materialism but are against pure capitalism on "spiritual" grounds. Consequently, they worship (their) materialism at the expense of ("our") spiritualism.[89] These

---

"religion's"—especially Islam's—clutches. Some of course think it is already too late, but I don't agree. I think America will—on or before 2025—get itself and quite possibly the entire planet back to a felt level of safety HIGHER than that felt on the last day of p.s. 21st Century, that is, on September 10th, 2001.

[89] Capitalism, pure and uncontrolled by anything other than market forces and human nature underlying those forces is what I mean by the *spiritual* in politics.

are the drug companies that run ads on TV trying to get me to "value" *purple* pills because purple is a pretty color just like the old beer commercials tried to get me to value their beer A over their competitors beer X because A is better, more refreshing and so on. Beer, however, at least has an appeal to the *senses*: it tastes good, is a thirst quencher, and the cool bottle rubbed against a hot, sweaty forehead gotten that way from baling hay on a hot summer's day *objectively feels* good, but I ask you, *what* kind of appeal can a purple pill have? Pleasing to the eye? Geeze, I hope not because if so then this American culture is in more trouble than even I am suggesting here. A *pro*-laissez faire capitalist is one who says 100% laissez-faire capitalism is redundant and an anti-laissez faire capitalist is one who is so afraid of change that he or she is willing to sell the *soul* of capitalism—that is, its 100% free, as in total and complete separation of economics and state free markets—to its socialistic enemies. They sell it for the price of an admission ticket to their local Radio Talk Show Programs—Programs which, more times than not, are hosted by a religious conservative who, as a religionist, is comfortable with *feeling* that self-sacrifice is and *should* be a moral ideal and who—*as a political conservative*—is an *expert* in the Art of Complaining *without* doing anything about anything meaningful[90].

    Those on the other hand who hate *any kind* of capitalism and instead *worship* environmentalism *at the expense of* individualism are the Environmentalists and their sympathizers. These people are worse than the first group and are so bad that the only good thing we can say about them is they are not as bad as the third group we will be considering next. There are basically two types of environmentalist: the *hedonistic* type and the *altruistic* type and as Ayn Rand has already pointed out to us in a different context, hedonism and altruism are opposite sides of the *same* coin. So to divide the world of the unitary type *Environmentalist* into *hedonist* and *altruist* is really not a division based on essential *metaphysical* differences but simply one based on psychological motive. The hedonistic type environmentalist *uses* environmentalism to destroy (other's) individual property rights when it suits their purposes to do so and the altruistic type—which, numerically, is the predominant type—believe that self sacrifice is the moral ideal and that self-sacrificing exists on a hierarchy from better and best down-to lower and least. They believe that the morally superior human is one who sacrifices him or herself to inanimate and/or animate but non-human objects in the "environment".

---

[90] Even though I am not guilt free on this issue, I am more than willing to cast the first stone.

The animal rights activists like PETA et al. disagree with the environmentalists because they—the PETA heads—say the morally superior human is one who sacrifices him or herself to non-human animals. My *speculation* is that PETA people are people who were/are pretty good at sacrificing themselves to other humans and in human nature's search for bigger and better they decided they could differentiate themselves by saying sacrificing self to humans is old hat, today the "better" sacrificer is one who sacrifices *the self* to animals, not human animals but non-human animals because, to repeat, sacrificing to human animals is passé. This *PETA Head* group is worse than the Environmentalists—in a *bigger* of two evils sense—because they tap into our **need**—as beings with a *volitional* consciousness—for *ethics* and use it against us in their debates about animal rights and the treatment of non-human animals by human beings.[91] The shortest advice I can give here is every time you feel yourself being sympathetic to a PETA position think of yourself—not as a PETA head—but as a Person Against The *In-Humane* Treatment of Animals[92]. This difference is critical and I am indebted to that higher up Judge on that Public Television program circa last week (June 2001) that pointed this out as she overturned a ruling that a lower court—with its lower mentally capable judge—had rendered *against* a Highly Professional Veterinarian *human being* caught on a hidden video camera by a corrupt PETA head who had wormed her way into the vets work world by *pretending* to be his friend. The tape revealed that the vet had roughed up the personal *property*—i.e., the dog—of a customer of his by yanking the dog's chain (literally) and verbally threatening it. Aside from the fact that I didn't know dogs could talk and reason and hence be hurt by *threats* of physical violence this case is endemic of our modern culture that can't think because it *refuses*—that is, *actively* chooses not—to use words with precision. Thank god for that higher up judge. How many of those are there still around? [*rational* judges, not gods]. For now I feel safe because after seeing this one particular *victim* of PETA *finally* get justice and after watching the Supreme Court of the United States *in action*

---

[91] If you are thinking that I am wrong here and that the Environmentalists are worse than the Peta heads because the Environmentalists take sacrifice to its ultimate—that is, t.h.e.y sacrifice the MOST valuable, i.e. man, to the LEAST valuable, i.e. dirt—whereas the Peta heads are not yet at the ultimate—t.h.e.y. "only" sacrifice the most valuable, man to the lesser valuable, animals below man…well, if this then—you *might* be right. Either way the point remains the same: *both* positions are anti-man, anti-individual rights and hence both positions are pro-evil, anti-good so a discussion at this time as to: which *is* the *worst* of these two evils? is beyond our current interest.
[92] PETA stands for "People for the Ethical Treatment of Animals " and what most people don't realize until they look at the correct spelling of PETA_ —which includes a blank space at the end—is that in this space they should put: …and for the *unjust* treatment of humans.

(especially the Honorable Judge Scalia) during the last [2000] Presidential election I am willing to conclude that the higher up the Court Ladder the better—as in ability to reason—the thinkers. However, because I know that three instances are better than two before drawing a conclusion, I am keeping my options open here.

Notice that the universal element in these three cultural groups is the shared premise that *self-sacrifice* is and *should* be the *moral ideal*. To this extent these three Groups do not differ in kind, only in degree. We, as desirerers of the selfish—the *Objective* selfish—have to be aware of these and any other *cultural* forces that seek our destruction because if we are not so aware we will be destroyed—if not literally destroyed then *epistemologically* destroyed which in a free or semi-free society is really the first step anyway to *actual* destruction. *Life without happiness is a destroyed life.*[93] The attempt to build a happy life without the use of deep and serious thought is the attempt to build a square circle.

And as we already know: *There Are No Square Circles.*

These three *cultural* forces then: the *Anti-Laissez faire capitalists*, the *Environmentalists* and the *PETA heads*, are *not* my friends and if you desire *Objective* selfishness—as your nature requires—then neither are they yours.

They are your enemy and they are out to destroy you. And as long as you agree with them *in principle* that self-sacrifice is and should be the moral ideal then you are helpless and will not be able to protect yourself from them, let alone save yourself from them and their anti-actual human life ways. If the good—that is, *that* which *is* for actual *human* life—is not *present* in your soul, then it is *absent*. If it *is* present then it is *present* and that is *good*. But if it is absent then this is where evil grows, because—as the physicists have already discovered—*nature abhors a vacuum*. Life is growth and if the good is not there *to grow* then the evil will fill the void.

The Nazis—which have only existed for a little more than half a century—have demonstrated *in spades!* how far! evil can! grow in man's soul, so for your need of proof of this, study them.[94]

---

[93] Today is 10/10/01—a mere 29 days after September 11th—and I felt motivated enough to re-start work on this manuscript and use this ~~red~~ underline letter approach to help myself draw a line between 9/10/01 BC and 9/12/01 AD (Before the Catastrophe and After the Destruction) and though this "life without happiness" pales in comparison to "life without breathing" I know we Americans-in-spirit will get back to a point where we can be concerned once again with "better and best" and not just "survival and good enough".

[94] And now we have to add others to the list: Islam fundamentalists in particular AND, consequently, ALL religious fundamentalists in general.

Will future historians, that is, historians in the future, look back on this time in American history and refer to these large, cultural, anti-human groups as *anti-volitionalists*?

I predict they will.

Ironically, the anti-volitionalists are anti-human-volition *by choice*. Animals—which do not have the power of volition—are below humans on the evolutionary scale and as such are also below the anti-volitionalists. *All* humans are *potentially* better/more important and *more valuable* than *any and all* animals.[95] But since *human potential* involves human volition first, that is, choice in the fundamental sense applicable to humans, it is up to *particular* humans which way they *choose* to develop. Animals on the other hand are animals and *can't* be anything other than what they are: non-volitional animals, possessing a non-volitional, non-reasoning, non-conceptual form of consciousness.

As such and for the record let me say it before a new *group* emerges to try to promote it: *there is no such thing as animal potential, there is only* **human** *potential.*

An anti-volitionalist then is one who *tries* to live as an animal, that is, as one whose *survival* does *not* require a volitional, reasoning, *conceptual* faculty. But since those who try this are—in spite of themselves—humans with the *power to choose*, they have a problem. They have a *conceptual faculty* that they *don't want* so they have to get rid of it. These modern "savages" don't need it "surgically" removed by others for one very simple reason: they remove it themselves—*voluntarily* (and Irony out does itself)—because they believe: that is, they have been *taught* and they have *voluntarily accepted* the premise that the human capacity and ability for *conceptual* thought is a *bad* thing to possess.

As way of simple example consider the following. Since animals below man have no conceptual faculty they are very very poor at judging. For example, dogs can't tell the difference between a grilled piece of steak BEFORE they eat it and the same grilled piece AFTER they eat it and so they will eat (or re-eat as the case may be) either piece and/or both pieces. Since man—via his conceptual capacity—does have the ability to judge such differences he—man—*knows* and

---

[95] And contrary to what you might think here—as means of underscoring just how true this statement is about the valuableness of humans versus the animals below humans—vegetarians and especially Vegans agree with the statement. They in fact say that if all the non-human animals on the planet disappeared tomorrow it wouldn't affect their livelihood in the least as they can live on plants alone and don't *need* meat. And since they do live this way they have proved the point: we don't really need animals that much; granted we need them and want them because they can and do make our lives easier and richer and this is good *because* it is *for* us as human beings.

because of it (and a few other tidbits of information, man) only eats the former and not the latter.

So, the next time you see or hear someone say: " ... eat stuff ..." or in a less concrete, more abstract way you hear someone say or see someone write that "judging is bad…" or worse, "it's evil" and *you* THINK "if I am judgmental and they say I'm bad *because of it*, aren't 'they' JUDGING me?". Or you hear someone say that "life is a *penalty* and death a *reward*" and you THINK: "bullstuff!" you are *as close as* you *should care* to come to one of these anti-[human-volition]-volitionalists.[96]

"They"—the anti-human-volitionalists—are even *more* dangerous than those I read about yesterday in my local metropolitan newspaper. There I read that 8 out of 10—and let me repeat this, 8 out of 10!—Americans *still* believe that God performs and/or performed miracles!?!. That is to say, they believe that *reality* is *not* a firm, unyielding, absolute "thing" and as such that it is *impervious* to "miraculous" modification. (For a *refutation* of "miracles" see the works of the preeminent contemporary Objectivist, Dr. Leonard Peikoff, especially his article entitled "*The Analytic-Synthetic Dichotomy*", an article which I believe should be carved in stone since it is the best of its kind of thinking since before Moses.).[97]

So, is believing in miracles *rational*? If it is, then it is in my *selfish* interest to also so believe, but if it isn't rational then it is likewise in my *selfish* interest to *not* so believe.

Reason is selfish. Those who damn selfishness as evil damn *reason* as evil. Yet *reason* is man's crowning glory.

A *human* being is one who *worships* the human good and especially the human capacity for *reason* and *conceptual* thought (two "things" which are *very* good) and the demonstrable idea—and the one demonstrated by *Objectivism* and *Biocentric Psychology*—that the exercise of both capacities is *volitional*.

Those who enshrine selfishness as good enshrine *reason* as good. *Faith* on the other hand—contrary to popular opinion—is *not* good for you. Be it *faith* in God or faith in *Country*.

The negatives associated with *faith in God* are numerically challenged only by the number of negatives associated with *faith in Country*. For me personally, the

---

[96] *Should* that is if you believe as Joshua Deer does: people who are of two minds on *everything* need to answer themselves a question: *Can souls rot?*

[97] This paragraph was obviously written by me in p.s. 21st Century as testified to by my erroneous "more dangerous" statement. I was wrong, am wrong here but I leave this paragraph stand to emphasize the point and to notice that we can and perhaps *should* be concerned about two evils: religion fundamentalism and anti-volition advocates. And perhaps we should even be on the lookout for a connection between the two.

negatives associated with "faith in God" have been thoroughly purged from my soul, so let's turn our attention to *faith in Country*.

Enter the bureaucratic arms of *The United States Government* as it *embraces* the "human".

Chapter 12: *Those who understand (good and evil) AND Do are the heroes.*

Or—as the [flipped upside-down] case may be—villains.

The United States Government—via its *bureaucratic arms*—is *preaching*, with all the wild gesturing of an old fashioned preacher, that human beings do *not* have volition.

And not only is the government preaching it, they are *funding* it.

They are preaching this and they are finding a receptive congregation for their message in the midst of what *traditionally* has been called *The American Cultural Mainstream* but which if we don't do something about it sooner rather than later will become "The American Bureaucratic *Mainstay*". A cultural *mainstay* currently being forged by as diverse a material as any the American culture has ever melted in its giant ladles and poured into individual pots.[98]

So *where* are the real preachers? That is, where is *The Church* when you actually need it? As often as not "they" are off counting the number of angels they can stack on the heads of pins. That is, "they" are interested in understanding "angel nature" not *Human nature*.

It appears that in the age old battle between *The Church* and *The State* for control over the pocket book of your *soul,* that is, your *mind*—which in reality is the thing that controls your literal pocket book—*The Church* is loosing and *The State* is winning.[99]

---

[98] The particular individuals then—that is, the better ones—usually re-pour themselves into *individual* molds.

[99] It looks like "the church/religion" launched a counter attack on 9/11/01 and is fighting back and the outcome is a To Be Determined (as in, a time-will-tell) event. If Christianity and Islam succeed in finding common ground we absolutely must remember Ayn Rand's warning: when two groups accept the same basic premise (e.g. self sacrificing is the highest moral ideal), the most consistent (practitioners) win. Since I don't see too many Christians sacrificing themselves to living in rat infested holes in the ground for Jehovah, the prognosis for common ground is really really weak (but again we must be on guard, because though weak, it is not impossible—for one *possible* link, see the Post Office behaviors of once President, Jimmy Carter).

How can this be the case when you just said 8 out of 10 Americans believe God is more powerful than the State? (That is, no one yet—to my knowledge—is arguing that The State *too* can perform *miracles.*[100])

Do you believe every *statistic* the media presents to you? That *statistic* was presented by a newspaper (*The Minneapolis Star [pause] Tribune*) that is sympathetic to both government controllers *and* religion, hence it is more than likely overstated so as to give *religious* people a sense of security, even if a false sense. Since both *bureaucratic* government and *religion* believe *false* is as good as *true* there is no (visible) conflict here.

And by simple observation it is easy to see that *most* people—*easily* half and more than likely more—*accept* the government *as is* because they keep working and sending them *excessive* tax-revenues. Further—if you listen to contemporary talk radio—you get a *false* sense of peoples caring concerns; they *pretend* to care but in fact, *in action* they do not. What "they" like *to do* is *complain and blame* and *pretend* to care. (When the 1950's left the planet it did *not* take pretending with it.[101])

The only thing here that makes sense about people's *action apathy* is one or both of the following possibilities. One, *some* people, qua individual citizens, *actually* believe it is *important* to keep sending the government significantly more money than it *properly* needs so that it can *preserve, protect* and *propagate* the status quo *as an end in itself* (that is, divorced from the proper functions of government as same have been identified by *The Philosophy of Objectivism*). Two, the rest of the people are simply *waiting around* for their (assumed) ascension into their (projected view of) heaven. Though I fear you'll "shoot" me for it I'm going to deliver you the *message* anyway: *outside of Earth there is no heaven.* That is, outside of *any place* where human beings live and breathe and … bleed when cut, light up when praised and reject the pastoral worshippers and

---

[100] Though in Minnesota USA, my home State and current residence, this is becoming or has already become a *hidden* premise operating in the minds of the average citizen. But wait. Let me state this more colorfully. Since Minnesota is really nothing more than a giant nest of Christians who are being rousted by reality as it forces them to check their most deeply held religious premises why do you expect them to NOT transfer their referent characteristics of a non-existent God on to an (the) existing State? The Russians did this and look at what happened to them. Also since the Russians did do this they are proof that human beings CAN so do. And further, which State in the Union was it that received Mikhail Gorbachev with the widest of wide-open (embracing) arms? *Yes*, it was Minnesota. And I don't mean to be mean, but, doesn't Minnesota Senator Wellstone's latest beard make you think of Lenin? And I absolutely do not mean, John. (And I wrote this long before his tragic death, may he rest in peace, but I let it stand as written.)

[101] Contrast this with the fact that when the "me" decade left the planet at the end of the 1980's it *appears* to have taken *the desire for moral perfection* with it.

enshrine the producers ... that is, outside of *the human at its best* there is no heaven. So, if you elect to wait around for your "heaven" to *happen to you*, such is your choice, as wasted as that *choice* can be.

The State, however, is not so erroneously waiting around and it is more than eager to accommodate the *status quo* seekers. Whether "we" like it or not *The State* is moving forward with its bureaucratic agenda.

Traditional religion—*any* traditional religion—is no longer *strong enough* to fight *The State* for control over your mind.[102]

The question is, are you? Are *you* strong enough to fight (and defeat) *The State* (and religion) for control over *your* own mind?

The States only *moral* justification for existing is to protect the *individual's* right to life and property from thugs, foreign and domestic. But just as a person can *corrupt* his or her capacities *for thriving* so to can the State *corrupt* its *reason for existing*.

The "reason" *The State* desires to control your mind is obvious: "they" view you as *their* tax-revenue, egg-laying golden goose. With the billions and billions and billions ...and dare we say it?...trillions?!? of tax dollars *you* give them *each and every* year they can fund and take over any thing they want.

Anything.

And I repeat, *religion* can no longer stop them. If religion *ever* had any *virtuous* qualities—again as *Ayn Rand* claims but with which I am reluctant to agree, but assuming for the sake of discussion that she's right—then surely it was in the protection it afforded *the individual* against *The Group*. For example, if we think of the Roman Empire circa zero AD as if it were an overburdening "Star Wars" kind of "Empire" out to do the *individual* in: perhaps, lets say, *"...for the grace of Rome"*, then *maybe* religion *to the extent it protected the sanctity of the individual* was good. But the operative word here is, "was": any such virtue that religion *might* have had along these lines is long dead and I mean long, long dead and consequently will not be able to save us, qua individuals, from those who desire to control us and turn us into sheep and to keep themselves in the role of sheep herders. For "fast-food" proof of this claim of *BiO Spiritualism's* about religion's inability to protect the *modern* individual from the group, I submit as evidence any turn of the century American movie that has religion as its theme. Look at these movies and notice their appeal to *impotence* as the *should be* source of your *mental* strength for self preservation. Even the movie "*Dogma*"[i] which

---

[102] I am going to stick with this statement because I predict that in-the-long-run it will be true, though the word "fight" should be changed to "defeat" so that the statement is: No religion can *defeat* the state for ... etc.

tries to use humor as an anti-religion device is nothing more than an exercise in *proving the futility* of "aggressive impotence". On the other hand, if you are the kind of person who can find "fuel" in a movie like "*End of Days*"[ii] then *BiO Spiritualism* might not be for you. I'm not even religious but as a member of the *same* species as those who are, I find that movie's religious messages *embarrassing*: do (some) modern day *adult* men and women actually still cling to the tenet that evil is a *metaphysical* force?!? It's just too hard for me to believe this. I don't *refuse* to believe it, but I mean, *come on people* let's get into the 21st Century…and sooner rather than later *will* be better.[103]

Religion is a human invention for a human purpose, or stated differently: Do animals pray? This is to say, based on my own terms I should worship religion. Well in this sense I do: I worship *what* religion is trying to fulfill, not *how* it attempts to fulfill it. Religion is trying to fulfill man's need—as a being of *volitional* consciousness—to have a comprehensive view of the world and his place in it.[104] And *that* is *what* I worship: *actual* human needs, *not* misguided attempts to fulfill them.

A human being is one who worships human nature even though at any point in time he may not know fully what human nature is. But *what* he does know is this: it is *something* and that part of his "reason for existing" is to figure out *what* that something is.

Another part of our reason for existing is, to exist.

And another is to be happy.

PART II introduced happiness (Chapter 6) as a definable, defined-scientific, "thing" and here we further state and acknowledge "the problem of happiness" and provide background information to show *selfish* people what is in store for them if they *refuse* to own their own selfishness and come out of the closet sooner rather than—not just later, but rather than—after it's too late.

And if you are wondering *when* too late is, it is *after* America has crossed over the 50% bridge [heading in the wrong direction] into a *New Kind of Totalitarianism*, which—according to my calculations—will occur on or about the year, 2036.[105]

---

[103] Evil is a man-made force and it is made in a particular, specific individual by the successful *"integration" (com-part-mental-ization)* of specific pro-death and anti-life philosophical / fundamental principles within *that* individual.

[104] This sounds to me like *rudimentary* philosophy, does this mean—halt. *One* instance does not a meaning make. (What about the Roman Empire reference on pag—I said, halt! "We'll" deal with this later.)

[105] This number will have to be increased by an amount equal to the length of time it takes us to get back to a felt level of security equal to that of September 10th, 2001. For example, if this takes 5 years than my 2036

As human beings we are not born knowing how to do things. Our human nature starts out being extremely *selfish* in the sense it is geared towards—as in *programmed* by nature towards—the preservation and enhancement of our own individual life (see the *science* of *Biocentric Psychology* and its concept of "..from programmed to volitional self-regulation..." for more on this and its *implications* for *what* it means to be an *adult* human being).

But since we don't automatically know how to be properly selfish any more than we know how to walk, we have to turn to "adults" to *teach* us how.

Adults as a historical class of human beings have failed us miserably in teaching us selfishness. This is so *easy* to see that it seems obvious and beyond refute. Unless of course you are going to argue that *true* selfishness is self-less-ness. If you are an adult and advocate this then you are a member of the *"all adults as a historical class of human beings have failed us miserably in teaching us selfishness"* class.

But, that phrase should be amended to read: all except *one*.

Ayn Rand, as author of "The Virtue of Selfishness" and the entire *Philosophy of Objectivism* is the obvious exception to this rule of *all* adult humans being woefully inadequate to the task of teaching their young how to be properly selfish. Ayn Rand was so competent at the task of this teaching that we could use her as the archetype for *competency*.

Because of this human need to be taught the "ins and outs" of proper selfishness and because of many other human *nature* needs, eventually, we *need* Ayn Rand's Philosophy of Human Nature (which she has named, *Objectivism*) to teach us about *true* human nature and the proper way to be selfish.

Then once we choose to struggle to stay connected, or for those of us who disconnected, to *re-connect* with our need *to be selfish* as our human nature is, we *immediately* get in touch with our need *to be happy. Our need to be happy* is at one end of the need continuum of *all* human needs: *happiness* is the *need* that can go *unfulfilled* the longest without killing off the organism. Breathing air/Oxygen to the brain (or some such *physiological need)* is at the other end of the *need* continuum. This continuum or *temporal urgency axis* of human needs coupled with the failure to fulfill *all* needs on the continuum—including the end points—defines what it means for humans *to be human.* Eventually ALL legitimate needs that are *NOT fulfilled* result in death of the organism. If not, then the *alleged* need

---

prediction becomes 2041, if it takes 1 year then no adjustment is required because this is within a prediction error of "a coupla years or three either way". (Rereading this and still working on the manuscript, September 14, 2002 and NOT back to equivalent sense of security, hence it's more than 1 year.)

is not a *need* in the scientific sense of the term. (Refer to *Biocentric Psychology* for more on this "temporal urgency" character about *needs*.[106]). Just as *premature death* is the ultimate penalty of need frustration, so *Life* is the ultimate reward of need *fulfillment*. This is why we say, *life is conditional, a*nd why psychologists—some—are embarrassed when Freudians assert we have a *need* to die. But this "need to die" *absurdity* merely proves that none, not even *psychologists* are beyond the need for *preciseness of thought*.

No mind is any better than the precision of its concepts.

Developmentally, *adult* is the final stage for human beings. Unlike some of the earlier stages that are programmed by nature, the adult stage has to be achieved by choice, that is, earned. You *earn* the right to call yourself an *adult* human being when you *worship* the good in the human and *damn* the evil and *know the difference* when *applying* this "knowledge of good and evil" to you your *self*, that is, to *that* within you that *thinks and feels and acts and...judges*. One method for doing this is the one that I personally used and the one I deal with here. I call it *Pedactics*.

Pedactics, that is, *selfish pedantics* coupled with day-to-day strategies—that is *tactics*—aimed at *maintaining* self-improvement successes—*regardless of their size*[®o2]—is *good* and is *one* coin that can be used to buy a ticket on the train to Objectivism's *selfishness* and—along with it—a ticket to adulthood. However, I am not prepared to argue that it is the *only* coin. It is *a* coin. You earn the *Pedactics* coin by being *mentally* selfish which is to say by being *first* and foremost "in your own mind", pro-your-self. That is, a pro-yourself-worshipper of the *self* and the *self functions*.

Self—to repeat—is that within that *thinks* and *feels* and *acts*, and...*judges*.

Judging is so important to the self that it "makes sense" that those who want the self destroyed advocate that judging is wrong. "Judge not, [sic] that ye be not judged." (Matt. 7:1) is one particular form of this with which I—as an ex-([Authorized] King James version *Bible*) Christian—am *intimately* familiar. Its

---

[106] Also please note, the bipolar "endpoint" speculation about "needs" is my speculation not Biocentric Psychology's. Biocentric's is the "temporal urgency" *character* of needs and I do not want to give the impression that Biocentric agrees with my endpoints. At this "point" I'm not 100% sure that I agree. For example it's not impossible to assert that "happiness" is a fundamental state of birth and our "job" is to maintain it, not create it. We may have to re-create it but this is "only" because we failed to maintain it. As a developmental issue in psychology this is beyond the current scope. The current scope is to take *Objectivism*, the Philosophy and *Biocentric Psychology*, the science, as *givens* and see what we can do with them as we *integrate and apply* them to our own individual lives.

colloquial form, "Judge not least ye be judged" is for all *practical* purposes the same thing; it means *exactly* what it says: *abandon your mind*.

In our new (BiO) spiritualism, which is neither new age spiritualism nor ancient age, but rather spiritualism for the 21st century and beyond, the first principle is: "Judge and be prepared to be judged" (which is one of Objectivism's tenets). This too means *exactly* what it says: *embrace your mind*.

BiO Spiritualism "says" you should *embrace your mind, love your mind, worship your mind*. This is to say, you should *earn* the *right* to *exalt* **your** mind.

Later on here (Chapter 20) I demonstrate why *Objectivism* and *Biocentric Psychology* need each other as well as why you and I do too (need *Objectivism* and *Biocentric Psychology* that is, not each other: the needing each other *explanation* is provided in *Biocentric Psychology* through the "Visibility Principle", so I refer the interested reader there for that.[iii]).

Most people seek to understand human nature so that they can *learn* to have *more* control over themselves and their life.

Some people seek to understand human nature so that they can control other people.

Both kinds of humans have a *natural* need for control, but only one seeks the *proper* goal of this need: *self* control, not *other* control.[107]

As a human being of volitional consciousness with the capacity for "propositional speech, conceptual thought and the power of reason" and with *all the needs* that human beings do have, you are *susceptible* to control by others. But susceptible here does not mean *as a victim*. Rather it means as the *only* alternative left to you *after* you default on the primary need to achieve *self* control. Self control, that is, *efficacy* as described by the science of *Biocentric Psychology* is the "holy grail" of the "spiritualist's" quest. And if you have lost (or never found) your "holy grail", you can't find it unless you search. And when you succeed in your search you will discover that *what* you have found is *control over your own individual happiness.*

Those who have control over their own happiness cannot be ruled.

If you don't *yet* desire or if you don't *still* desire your own happiness so as to be *motivated* by it, then maybe you desire to ***not*** be controlled by others and

---

[107] Item #23, page 336 acknowledges the need here for a 3rd group: those who want to murder individuals comprising groups 1 and 2. Perhaps I will be accused of being too hard on religion when I now say (in the shadow of September 11th, 2001 attacks on America by Islamic fundamentalists armed with box cutters): "Knives don't murder, Religion does". (For a mellower, less harsh conclusion see revised quote in Footnote 269, page 330.)

especially not by those "anti-volitionalist, pro-bureaucratic-mind and social-engineering" others that we mean to refer to when we call them, "t.h.e.y."[108]

If "these" are your "they" then *Pedactics* and *BiO Spiritualism* are for you. If Pedactics is **a** coin, thinking is the **first** coin to buy you your independence from those who would control you.

Objectivism, as a formal philosophy, exists and *must* be studied and learned *by you* if you *hope* to save yourself from your 21st Century controllers.

Biocentric psychology exists too and is a formal "psychology" and is there for you to read and understand and *apply* to you yourself as a form of *self help* for *self* control, which is to say, for *self-efficacy*.

The choice is yours.

Objectivism and *Biocentric Psychology* exist and are there *for the taking*.

My advice through out this book has been and continues to be, take them.

---

[108] As in **TheyHaveEvilYearnings**.

Chapter 13: The beam in my eye is gone. Your mote is next.

That is, I know *who* I am, who are you?

I am pedantic.

By this I mean that I am a biocentric spiritualist who holds that *BiO Spiritualism* is better than any and all spiritualisms—including the *primitive* spiritualism we call religion—and as such it [*BiO Spiritualism*] is the spiritualism we need, to [help] make us moral *enough*—which ultimately means, *happy* enough—to create, maintain and live in a 100% lfc society.

By lfc I mean: laissez-faire capitalism.[109]

Since Capitalism now—post Ayn Rand—is the *known* [political] ideal, *100% laissez-faire capitalism*—with its separation of economics and state along with its other Objectivist identified proper functions of a government—is the ideal political-economic system.

Any political-economic system—say system B—that *is* better than some other political-economic system—call it A—requires people who make up its culture to also be better in B than those in A or if it is a growth situation then to be better in B *than they were* when in A.

Better people means more moral. And more moral means both *more committed* to human life on earth as the *standard* of morality *and* to *personal happiness* as the *purpose* of morality.

 Since the old adage still stands: the best way to improve society is to improve yourself and since self improvement (as I have defined elsewhere) means: being better tomorrow than you were yesterday at *making* yourself happy so that you can live *today* the happy life you have created for yourself so far, that because of all of this it seems safe to hypothesize that: *no society as a whole is any better than the average* [BiO Spiritual] *moralness of all its members.*[110]

---

[109] Or as I like to call it: 100% ofc (objectivism-fair capitalism).

[110] Since religious people as a group tend to be very arrogant (some even smug) because they think they own the concept of "morality" we have to include a reminder here for ourselves that they do not so own, the so owning is done inside the individual soul of individuals and the morality under consideration is that as I describe herein.

Since I personally know of no way to MAKE oneself better than through being pedantic, I am pro-pedantics—*developmentally* speaking.

And as I've already said: I am pedantic [and I now add, I think you should be too so that we can hurry up and create a 100% lfc society during our lifetime].

I call my pedanticness tough self respect. Others call it, pedanticness.

If "tough love" is good, then tough *self* respect is better.

My pedanticness has been my spiritual protector. By the end of this book I hope to let go of it to a significant degree because it will have served its purpose *for me* and I will no longer *need* it.

Your needs can be different from mine. That is, your idiosyncratic needs *at any particular point in time* can be different from mine. But of course your *needs,* qua human being, are not any different than mine. Nor are my *needs*, also qua individual possessor of human nature, any different than yours. Human nature is an irreducible primary: it is what it is, independent of my hopes, wishes and fears and also independent of *your* hopes, wishes and fears. One of the jobs in our spiritual quest is to discover exactly *what* "human nature" is.

At age 54, I am finally a fully developed adult human being in body, mind and spirit and I look forward to continued *growth* in all these areas. My body I view pretty much as a *gift* from nature.[111] I view my *mind* and *spirit* as a "gift" from *my* tough self respect.[112]

That in part is *who* I am, *who* are you?

My biggest enemy *yesterday* was religion, *specifically* Christianity as preached and practiced by Lutherans.

I am pretty much now beyond religion's *diabolical* ways.[113] However, "today"—that is, at the beginnings of the 3rd Millennium's *BiO Spiritualism*—I

---

[111] *Sometimes* I view it as a gift from my biological parents: Reuben & Eldora.

[112] *Sometimes* I view my mind as a gift from my intellectual parents: Ayn Rand and Dr. Nathaniel Branden, but my *spirit* is **all** mine: for better or for worse it's 100% me. Me chose Objectivism & Biocentric Psychology, they did not choose me. And when I was 5 years old and couldn't read the word epistemology let alone psycho-epistemology or metaphysics it was *my* spirit that concluded "I gotta take care of me as best I can, I wished it were different, that my father was an *ideal* father and my mother an *ideal* mother, but they aren't, so to repeat, I gotta take care of me, myself and I as best I can." (NOW I understand of course that the air gasping, shoulder shrugging crying—within which the conclusion was drawn—was my pressure relief valve to have to shoulder such a gigantic responsibility at such a young age. But shoulder it I did. And today and every day I reap its full rewards.)

[113] By *diabolical* I mean as in *fiendish*. By fiendish I mean as in *fiend*. By fiend I mean it to be *as if* religion were a person who was excessively sneaky, excessively devious and excessive to such a degree that he or she was up to the perfect opposite of his or her stated goals—e.g. follow me and you'll be happy, but the *actual* result is you'll be not just unhappy but miserable and by the time you'll recognize it "we'ul" have our hooks

am "beyond" in a sense analogous to AA (Alcoholics Anonymous*)* and other multi-step *recovery* mentalities that preach: *one who succumbs to vice(s) is **never really beyond that which he succumbed to**.* Still, for all *practical* purposes I *am* beyond religion.[114]

Therefore, since the moral and the practical *are the same thing*, I conclude that I *am* beyond religion's negative gravitational pull.[115]

It has been a 54 year battle, but I made it!

If you think this is a long time and think me inferior for taking so long *to arrive*, I ask you to consider an "alternative" way of thinking about it. That is, the way I do. I think about it as a kind of subtle, albeit easy, animating pressure on me my*self* to live to be at least 109 years old. Then, in the end I'll be able to say, "I arrived *before* my life was half over."[116]

Nonetheless [now that I have successfully purged the religious bullstuff from my own soul], it does *not* follow that I no longer have *any* enemies.

My biggest enemy *today* is also my biggest *potential* protector [of *my* individual rights to life, liberty, property and the *pursuit* of happiness]: the United States Government. The Government, qua bureaucrat, is far too big for me or for any *single individual* to fight.[117] Consequently, I am not going to do *direct* battle with them. I will however, continue my personal battles against them in their role as BIG BROTHER[118] while at the same time acknowledging that the United

---

into your soul and you'll think "us" the solution to your problems, not as the problem from which your problems spring! To me this is as diabolical as diabolical can be.

[114] I understand the AA sentiment here but I must add that I disagree with it. I disagree with it because I consider religious epistemology to be a vice that I *once* succumbed to and I now no longer do (automatically succumb). Granted, I have to *volitionally* exercise a certain kind of heightened vigilance to ensure that I do not automatically succumb, but the degree of spent energy required on my part lessens every year.

[115] Notice how Objectivism—as *identifier* of the principle that "the moral and the practical" *are the same thing—makes it possible* for one to move beyond one's problems. Contrast this with the religious based epistemology of *Alcoholics Anonymous* which argues that once you have a problem you can *never* solve it. For example, see the "Recovery" movement that has wormed its epistemological ways into pop-psychology. Does this mean, I wonder, that *worms* have worms? I thought they didn't. Maybe I was wrong.

[116] Maybe I *should* quit smoking?

[117] If Mr. Bill Gates can't do it, who can? (we might have to drop this because as of now [6/30/01] the Government's anti-trust decision was reversed against Microsoft though "they" say it'll still stick in the long run...whether it does or not will tell us a lot about us). Actually no, don't drop it because now (6/25/02) we can see that this is a win-win situation (for us as *vicarious* observers): if Mr. Gates wins then when anyone says, "you can't fight city hall [and win]", we can reply: "What about Bill Gates." And if Mr. Gates looses, we can *protect* our energy by saying, "you can't [yet] fight city hall [and win]".

[118] Given all the changes of the past century and the attendant possible fact that all or perhaps some of its archetypes are outdated, do we need new ones for the new century / millennium? Perhaps BIG BROTHER should be thought of instead as BIG SISTER. As far as I can tell this is the only "difference" between last century's Behaviorism that worked for BIG BROTHER government and this century's aspiring-to-work for

States of America—as long as it *de facto worships* individual rights—is the best country on the planet. If it should ever re-vitalize its *de jure* worship of individual rights in my lifetime, I will be ecstatic over it. However, since that only leaves it 55 more years, I do not look to that to be the *sole source* of my ecstasy.

My ecstasy will continue to be that of a kind of investigative reporter who is *dedicated* to not letting T.H.E.M. get away with it.

And make no mistake about it, T.H.E.Y. haven't given up since Plato, so why do you think they are going to give up now? T.H.E.Y. are not, but ever since Ayn Rand showed up on the planet T.H.E.Y. are no longer getting away with it either. One of our jobs—if we believe in a *long live the queen* sentiment—is to *continue* what Ayn Rand has started.

And we continue it by being FOR the self and against T.H.E.M.

---

bureaucratic government BIG SISTER *Cognitive [neuro]Science* which wants us to believe that their professed dislike of Behaviorism is something more than the plain, old, simple, sibling rivalry that it really is. In this kind of rivalry, the family—which in this particular case, is the Kantian family—usually always remains unchallenged at its *deepest* premises and hence remains *untouched* and *unchanged*.

Chapter 14: CONTROL

Pedantics for *Self* Control is *Pedactics*

As the sun shines down on the opening years to the 21st Century we hear a great deal of talk by Professional Intellectuals about an old problem: *social engineering.* When we try to put our finger on what—*exactly*—it is they are referring to, we as often times as not fall short of a satisfactory, gut-pleasing explanation. The *un-satisfaction* that we feel—that is, the *absence* of satisfaction that we feel—is analogous to being *hungry* for a *specific* food and then eating a big meal in an attempt to satisfy that hunger but failing to do so. We failed to be satisfied because we failed to discover and then eat and/or to even accidentally eat the *exact* thing that our body was craving.

As "food-for-thought" *BiO Spiritualism* helps you gain the sated satisfaction you crave in understanding yourself and others. It helps you *first* and foremost to be "full of yourself" by being at least **one** who is FOR the *rational-emotional* you. And secondly, albeit not unimportantly, it helps you be AGAINST those social engineering "others"—whomever and wherever *they* are—by simply *not* being for them and by *not* helping them *pull the wool over* your very own eyes.

They have *many* techniques for doing the latter.

Those techniques can and should be pre-empted by you in your own thinking. For example, before you "hear" yourself and/or someone else say: *gee, social engineers* **have an agenda** *and so* **does** *BiO Spiritualism's author, consequently they are the same thing: voila! BiO Spiritualism is just another form of Social Engineering!* So, to repeat, before you allow this to happen to you, allow me to point out a *major* difference between *my BiO Spiritualism* and *their* Social Engineering (in addition to the fact that the formal, technical definition of *social engineering* is: the management of human beings in accordance with their place and function in [existing] society[i]). *My agenda*—and I am the first to admit that I do have one—is to be a part of that great *American* tradition that is for *creating* strong *individuals.* The *social engineers* agenda on the other hand—and they are the first to *evade* the fact that they do have one—is to *create* strong *groups.*

This *difference* is critical and one should never *allow* one's self to obscure *critical* differences. *Such obfuscation can be deadly.* Deadly, that is, when we are talking about *Spiritual* Life: the spiritual life of *real* people that is, not the spiritual life of...*ghosts.* Spiritualism—*traditionally*—has been the tool of *mystics* and as such it has *earned* its reputation as being non-rational, if not outright *irrational.* In essence, *traditional* Spiritualism is reducible to a two step process. Step One: use the mind to *abandon the body.* Step Two: *abandon the mind.* The "product" of such *abandonment* is the non-concept, "concept": *ghost.* Traditional Spiritualism is the *attempt* to *create* ghosts: that is, to create the shape of a human body with human consciousness extracted and then the human body eliminated. *Traditional* spiritualism holds it as a matter of *faith* that it is *possible* to do this: that is, that it is possible to create square circles; never mind that no one ever has, it is doable *in principle* "they" say and we just have to keep buying into the "possibility" of it. But of course, since *square circles do not exist* and cannot be made: There Are *No* Square Circles.[119]

And so as soon as one recognizes the participation of "faith" in the "spiritual" process, we have to stop and identify explicitly: *Who* are the Masters of Faith?

Such an easy question yields an easy answer: Religionists.

Traditional Spiritualism is the never ending futile attempt to MAKE *religion* MAKE SENSE. *BiO Spiritualism* totally and completely rejects the desire to obliterate the difference between the *impossible* and the *possible* and says the impossible is a legitimate concept: *square circles do not exist and cannot be made*. The square circle is in essence the model, the paradigm, the archetype of *impossible. Traditional* Spiritualism is the never ending futile attempt to BUILD SQUARE CIRCLES. *BiO Spiritualism*—ultimately—is the *process of embracing*, of embracing both mind and body and leaving the non-existent ghosts for others. Perhaps we can leave them for the bureaucratic mind and the social engineers "they" control so that together "t.h.e.y." can have something besides us *to control*. Then, maybe, some day, those others who want, seek and desire so passionately to control us will be nothing more than figments of our imaginations and/or at worse eidetic personalities that represent the integration of our own internalized thought sub-systems that we have to externalize so that we can self-correct on the mind building level. Maybe some day, that is, we will be able to

---

[119] Not even in Quantum Mechanics? *Yes*, not even there. If t,h,o,s,e Public Television Physicists are right in their claims that in the quantum world, circles can be square or round then this alone is enough to invalidate Quantum Physics—contradictions do *not* exist and cannot be *made*.

reduce T.H.E.M. to t.h.e.y. and then to a simpler, easier to deal with epistemological "they" versus an integrated "us".

But that day is not today.

For now Social Engineers—like the Bureaucratic Mind that controls t.h.e.m—are not ghosts. *They are real.* They exist even though not all of them know it themselves. Some do know it and these are the *easy* ones to deal with. The ones who *pretend* to themselves and/or to the world that they do not exist are the ones we have to watch out for.

And surprisingly—*if one has the correct mind set*—these too are (relatively) "easy" to watch out for.

Dealing with them is another matter.

What isn't so *easy* to do, is to keep *them* from meddling *in* and messing *with* our personal life by forever trying to control us for their own purposes.

But in the end, even this is *relatively* easy in that we have control over it because it is an issue—*in a politically free society*—that is as much *about us* as it is *about t.h.e.m.*

BiO Spiritualism: Body, Mind and Spirit - Man's Means, Nature's End as subtext for *Yes, BiO Spiritualism is the answer,* helps you to understand the secrets, the *felt* mysteries about *who and what* exactly are these Social Engineers? *A*nd in-the-process shows you how to turn the tables on all *Social* Engineers and take back total and complete control over your *own* individual life and happiness.

It does that is if, *psychhologically*, you haven't already succumbed to T.H.E.I.R. mind controlling ways. But even here there is hope, a *hope* whose *intensity* exists in *inverse* proportion to the extent to which you (may) have sold your own soul to your controllers.

Soul here [in the foregoing cliché about selling it] pertains more to your power of *volition* as same is manifest in you, qua human being, then it does to your *total consciousness*.

If you are one of the *sympathizers* to that modern day philosophy known as *Objectivism* you will recognize the common usage of "qua" as shorthand for *in the character of* and of "soul" as really meaning the all of *human consciousness*.

For those of you who are not familiar with *Objectivism* (the Formal Philosophy of the late, great, genius, Ayn Rand) *BiO Spiritualism* might at first glance seem to be simply saying: read and study *Objectivism* and then do it again, and *again* ... and perhaps *again* and that's all you have to do to *take care of yourself.* For *some* this is the way to go, but for those of us who were *born and raised* inside a *serious* religious model of the world, it is not this easy, *it takes more, a lot more*.

It takes so much in fact that only the strong survive and only the *heroic* achieve it.

It takes more than just *memorizing* Objectivist tenets. In fact, knowing *Objectivism* in this way could be just *another* psychological factor you may eventually have to *break free* of.

And I am sad to say, but it has to be said, *Objectivism*, qua formal Philosophy, does not care about you, qua you. It of course does in the philosophical-abstract sense of the term but not in the practical day-to-day sense. In this sense, *Objectivism cares about Objectivism*: it is after all, the **selfishness** philosophy and as such *should* care more about "itself" then about you, qua you.

Ayn Rand herself says Objectivism is *not* an "itself" ®01a and she should know since she created it. But *her knowing it* is **not** *our knowing it* and since "we" lived with ourselves before we knew Ayn Rand—and have to live with ourselves after knowing the "thing" *itself* called Objectivism—we have to *Master* the Art of Selfish Selfishness, which includes the Art of Self-Caring. For this *kind* of caring you have to turn to... but wait ... halt. We get ahead of ourselves.

For one example of how *Objectivism*, "come-hell-or-high-water" is pro-Objectivism, consider the fact that there are a lot of *Objectivist* sympathizers today who are anti-the-*Science of Psychology* founded by the early Objectivist and now neo-Objectivist, Dr. Nathaniel Branden (the psychology, that is, that he calls: *Biocentric Psychology)*. Some non-professional *Objectivist* sympathizers today are this way simply because the *Professional* Objectivists of today are against Dr. Branden. The Professionals are against him **not** on intellectual grounds but on *personal* grounds: *they don't like the fact that in his younger days while romantically involved with their heroine Ayn Rand he dumped her for a younger, [I speculate] physically prettier woman*. Ayn Rand was first in many, many, many, things but this was not one of them. She was not the first woman on the planet to have this happen to her. And it's not that Dr. Branden is not vulnerable on intellectual grounds, just that these are not the *reasons* he is so vigorously *ignored* in today's Professional Objectivism. One could speculate instead, I suppose, that they—the *Professional* Objectivists (the good and—almost but not quite perfect—*they)*—are *jealous* of Dr. Branden's romantic involvement with Mrs. O'Connor (Frank O'Connor is Ayn Rand's husband's name) but one would have to be a Freudian sympathizer to so argue. Since my academic psychological sympathies are anti-Freud and pro-Biocentric I think that **my** *speculation* is best *because* it leads to a question that *should be asked* and has to be answered: **Does *judging* require *speculation*?** Or should we, *speculate not,* *least we be speculated about*? For example, when mr b and mrs o had their affair, mr o and mrs b should have turned on their heels and left the affair-pair ... standing hand-in-hand... with *their* choices. But *they did not* (one cannot rewrite history) and I suspect, **did not** for *psychhological* reasons. [And then one has to wonder—if, that is, one wants to maintain his or her intellectual honesty, one has to wonder—why? did mrs o end up staying with someone who had psychhological problems?[120]] Mrs. o and mr b were completely moral in the way they handled their affair—if, that is, one can believe the recounting of it done in the literature and I have no reason to doubt it: it makes *exact* sense for mrs o, qua ms rand, to act this way: she was so *moral* that no *deceit* on her part was possible and none engaged in—again if we can believe the accounts of it, which I do. *THE MORAL ISSUES IN THIS EPISODE RESIDE IN THE RE-ACTIVE RESPONSES OF MR. O AND MRS. B.* Not the best choices. But having been there myself, I know *how difficult* it is for a *needy self* to protect a weak ego *while at the same time* trying to *grow* it into a stronger ego [and hence, stronger *self*]. It takes *so much* in fact that it's like I've already said: *only the strong survive and* **only** *the heroic achieve it.*

But that was yesterday. Today *Biocentric Psychology* is ignored by the Professional Objectivists because they don't know jack-stuff about *applied* psychology and *not knowing* is *not* a position a *true* Objectivist likes being in. So in this sense—by default—they end up promoting the *cognitive* in mainstream psychology; which, to repeat, ends up—by default—to be a promotion of *Cognitive* Science, *Cognitive* Psychology *and Cognitive* Neuroscience. One *hopes* the only reason *isn't* because they have the word "cognitive" in their titles.[121] Figuratively speaking, it isn't impossible to imagine that if Ms. Rand knew they were doing this she would turn over in her grave. But wait...no... this is a poor metaphor—in fact, a pathetic cliché—for such a Titan writer and thinker

---

[120] Since Objectivism teaches that there is nothing wrong with HAVING psychological problems ONLY in WHAT you *do* about them, this would seem to vindicate mrs o even further in that she practices what she preaches. But what it doesn't do is vindicate mr o—he should've left mrs o, but he didn't.

[121] Though one-out-of three isn't bad for every day life (see the game of baseball or the win percentage of the betting favorite in horse racing) it isn't good enough for philosophy. As of this time period—first decade of the third millennium—it appears as if *Cognitive Psychology* is trying to distance itself from the other two *Cognitives*. However since it—Cognitive Psychology—eschews philosophy its future doesn't look too bright (also—out of fairness to Professional Objectivism—see Footnote 125, page 126). But even this, we must note, is a "theoretical" position. Ms. Rand herself said somewhere that a theoretician does not have to be a technician and though this might be true for geniuses it is not true for us street people—street people, that is, as in the sense of the (common) man-in-the-street (of every day life) near those buildings we hear so much about called The Ivory Towers. But we must also note that in the *application* of ideas, everyone—including geniuses—is a man-in-the-street.

as Ms. Rand and besides it isn't exact. If she knew it to be a fact, she would ***get up out of her grave*** and come back here and say—while rubbing her two index fingers together: *shame on you*.

Except, Ms. Rand—to my knowledge of her gleamed from her writings—never spoke this way. This is the way I ~~speak~~ *write* and I think it's *what* Ms. Rand *should* say if she were alive today.

But, she's not and we are. Ayn Rand—the Queen of Philosophy—is dead. Long live the Queen.

The fact that professional *Objectivism* spurns *Biocentric Psychology* and instead *embraces* a vacuum: a vacuum that is being filled by *Cognitive Neuroscience*—*Behaviorism's* bastard son—is ... unfortunate ... for *Objectivism*. If anyone besides me is wondering why *Objectivism* is 'soooooh... slo-oh in convincing more people to take up its obviously superior approaches to everything philosophical I say look no further than this.

Religion does not have a monopoly on hypocrisy.

Objectivism—as Chapter 20 demonstrates—**needs** *Biocentric Psychology* and as an "organic" system, *Objectivism* will not be able to escape the negative consequences that come from: *need denial.*[122]

And what might these consequences be?

The same as in all such need denial situations: a wilting [sense of] life and a muted or diminished sense of happiness and the ultimate, worst consequence: dying on the vine.

Objectivism without Biocentric Psychology will not survive.[123]

But least I be misunderstood here by those who *prefer* confusion to clarity let me say, philosophically, ~~I am sympathetic to~~ I love *Objectivism*. Psychologically, I am sympathetic to *Biocentric Psychology* and as an experienced engineering-scientist trained and educated in the ways of rational-empiricism I am a person

---

[122] If you are an Objectivist and tempted to dismiss this out of mind because you are recalling Dr. Peikoff's pejorative comment about the Nazi's use of "organic" (in *The Ominous Parallels*) let me say that by organic I mean: *dynamically* changing needs that present themselves at the top of the need stack and then when met move over and let the next need queue forward for satisfaction, that is, it is dynamic, not static, not locked in a stack or queue forever hierarchy, but a dynamic, homeostatic hierarchical stack. See eating as satisfied hunger followed by thirst as the *next* need to be satisfied as one simple example of this.

[123] Not survive that is, as a tool, a technology for those human beings who desire and seek *autonomy*. It may end up being a darn good tool for those computer scientists who are interested in AI (Artificial Intelligence) and building robots that can actually do useful-to-human-being things but it will not succeed in convincing large numbers of people of its superior approach to all things philosophical. Will not that is, until and unless ... it explicitly embraces Biocentric Psychology—or something *identical* with it.

who values knowledge so much so that he knows how to connect the (his) abstract to the concrete.[124]

And as an Objectivist-in-training I also practice the Art of integrating my concretes into abstract essentials.

And connecting the (or at minimum, *your*) abstract to the concrete and vice versa—I predict—is one ability you will *lust* after, *after* you finish reading *BiO Spiritualism*.

You can and should use such *lust* as your motivator to get the intellectual skills you are quite capable of getting and will *want* to get after reading *BiO Spiritualism*. Skills you need, to do battle with the *bureaucratic minds* and without which T.H.E.Y. *will be successful at their self-assigned task of controlling you* as-their-means-of-survival. And make no mistake about it, T.H.E.I.R. *survival* depends on *you*, yours does *not* depend on T.H.E.M.

As partial demonstration of what the *ability* to move freely between the concrete and the abstract and back 'n forth can do *for* you in your thinking about yourself and the world and your place in it and its place in you consider the following fictitious narrative by accepting for the moment that its wide-eyed view is true, but of course just "kinda" true and only *for the moment* true.

If you find it helpful, imagine the following narration is being delivered to you via your TV or Computer screen with the audio being that of the voice of your favorite news reporter.

The news reporter stands holding a microphone and we barely notice the ten foot high wire-mesh fence between him (or her) and some Quonset style structures off in the distance: structures that look like temporary hospital facilities out of some war movie. The grouped structures, busied with drab green jeeps and trucks, suggests a Government run military operation. In fact it looks like a remote Medical research facility in the early stages of being dismantled, or assembled, we can't tell which for sure.

Your reporter turns to face the camera and with cautious clarity begins speaking into the microphone.

"The *bureaucratic arms* of the United States government—having been duly trained in the art of psycho-surgery—will soon be stitching up the operation it started last century on the skulls of its own citizens. When no one is looking these new 21st Century bureaucrats turned cognitive psycho-surgeons plan to

---

[124] As a person steeped (quarter of a century in formal education with 17 of it continuous) in the American public education system with its Kantian ways (see items 2 and 3 on page 299 and Footnote 152, page 148) I have a NEED to do this. You may not *need* this if you were not so steeped.

install in their victims mind-set a new, special, upside down V-chip that some are calling the Anti-Volition A-chip. The victims of this insertion will be told that this new A-chip will *prevent* them from 'catching' mental illness and that they should just ignore the buzzing sounds it makes in their heads—a small price to pay for guaranteed health, they will be told. But what they won't be told is that this new *device* is really a device designed and built by *Social* Engineers to specifications provided to them by the *bureaucratic mind*. What they won't be told is that this new device is the long sought after device of *people control* that the *bureaucratic mind* has been searching for ever since Plato walked on the planet. The reason it took so long to develop can readily be understood—" continues our reporter as the camera zooms in on his left hand where he cautiously opens his fingers to reveal the small white disk resting on his palm. The disk is approximately the same size and shape as the unleavened bread used in Christian Communion ceremonies, except this one is thinner and laminated. "—when we look at its paper thin, three-layered bionic wafer design and realize it took some pretty good chemistry, nuclear physics and biomolecular engineering science to design and produce it. Consequently, we may well hope and pray now that the cognitive and social sciences have *not* managed to keep up with the brain-surgeon physiologists so that the *social engineering minded* among them will *not* be able to install the new devices in such a way that they will go undetected and not be rejected by the host bodies. Or can they? Will they? *Should* they?" the reporter pauses to catch his breath and then holds it as if to wait for *you* to answer.

"If enough of us still *hope* the answers are no, no, no", the reporter continues, "then the road is not without danger for the *bureaucratic mind* and its hired group of *social* engineers. There still remains one danger then, one enemy to stand in *their* way..." the reporter pauses, looks side-to-side as if expecting trouble, then glancing back through the fence and seeing some of those distant drab green jeeps speeding towards him, speaks faster, "their archenemy: *autonomous* man. It is my claim that the *bureaucratic* mind of the 21st Century is not afraid. In fact it is less afraid now than it has been at any time in its developmental history. If anyone should be afraid it is autonomous man who *should* be afraid. Autonomous man today is in grave danger. If he hopes to survive the transplant operations and anti-rejection drugs being forced upon him by his would be controllers, he is going to have to learn how to swallow some big pills—anecdotal pills that will save his spiritual life. One such life saving pill is *BiO Spiritualism*. In fact, *BiO Spiritualism* might be the *only* pill remaining that will work. That will, that is—when taken internally—*work* to heal any and all *sutured* teeth marks stitched over in our collective, cultural necks by the bureaucratic surgeons who live off our blood, sweat and taxes (the surplus ones) and who hope we never, ever discover the whereabouts of the stakes and hammers, let alone the knowledge of where the *bureaucratic mind* lays."

Or should that be, lies? we can now ask ourselves as we take back the scene from our reporter.

If the foregoing narrative sounds like so much dismissive fantasy fiction, consider the following *non-fiction* upon which it is based and which cannot be dismissed.

Chapter 15: CONTROLLED

Forget the criminal mind, beware the *Bureaucratic Mind* as it seeks control over you and yours as its survival method.

According to the President's first annual budget in the first (base) year of the new millennium (i.e., specifically the year 2000 budget) the United States of America will spend, and if not now, soon, tens of billions of my and *your* dollars attempting to "prove" that *everything* I say here is wrong. They are doing this primarily through the National Institute of (physical) Health (NIH) and their minions in The National Institute of Mental Health (NIMH) and their comrades in the SAMHSA (Substance Abuse and Mental Health Services Administration). The NIMH and the SAMHSA combined is being given the green light by the President's budget to award nearly five billion dollars of a current and growing 20 billion dollar annual budget for grants to do research on "mental health" related issues.[i]

As to what proportion of this $5,000,000,000 will go to fund fundamental research to investigate the *relationship* between *volition, reason and mental health* I do not know. I suspect, however, *given their own claims*, that all of it will be spent on the antithesis to this.

Their claims?

According to the Surgeon General's first report on mental health:[ii]

> Mental illness is the term that refers…to all diagnosable…health conditions that are…characterized by alterations in thinking, mood, or behavior associated with distress and/or impaired functioning.

According to this definition, if a neo-Nazi "alters" his thinking because others have convinced him—in spite of much agonizing *distress* on his part—that Nazism is wrong, the new, better human being should be considered—according to the United States Surgeon General—"mentally ill".[125,iii]

---

[125] If you think this is hyperbolic exaggeration you had better do a double take and think-again. I challenge you to do such a double take by listening to the Objectivist psychologist, 'ole Locke 'n Load Dr. Edwin A.

Or, if *you* initially disagree with my views and opinions and are *distressed* by them and then subsequently "alter" your thinking, then (the new) you—according to the United States Surgeon General—are mentally ill.

And/or, does this mean if your [current] *function* in society [recall formal definition of social engineers as managers of people according to their functions in society] is street sweeper and you privately think you are capable of more and take action to achieve more, does this mean you are *functionally* impaired? (By street sweeper I mean the low tech kind as portrayed in novels who use hand brooms, not the modern, high-tech, heavy equipment operator kinds who make big bucks.)

Or, if you happen to be a modern day one and you desire to make even bigger bucks by getting a different *function* [job] in society, does *this* make you *functionally* impaired?

No you say, NoneOfAbove you say because there is no associated [negative] health condition.

What if your Doctor says you are a workaholic?

Can we get any closer to George Orwell's 1984 than this? This kind of "reasoning" is *evidence* for my claim that "1984 came and didn't went". The final caper in this claim will be when "they" either force publishers to post warnings on books: *Caution, the Surgeon General has determined that thinking for yourself is dangerous to your health (mental or otherwise)* or when they outright ban certain books. The outright banning seems unlikely, but the Surgeon General's *Warning Sticker* does not.

Notice, the fact that we can even consider a Sticker *possible* is evidence that we, as a nation are in trouble.

Big Trouble.

If you are thinking, yes, but…what about the fact that the Surgeon General as *keeper of the public*… health … is also compassionately concerned more about "mental health" than mental illness, about wellness and mental illness *prevention*. What about this, you ask? My answer is, read and *study* the General's report further:[iv]

> Many ingredients of mental health may be identifiable, but
> mental health is not easy to define [*Yes* it is, see below]. In

---

Locke's audio tape: "Is Contemporary Psychology an enemy of the People?"(see Reference). By connecting those "psychologists" referenced in Dr. Locke's tape and the ones highlighted herein you should be able to see that via the United States Government *you,* qua a tax paying American citizen, are funding reason's enemies and the sooner you *cease and desist* in the paying of excess taxes the better off we all will be.

> the words of a *distinguished* leader in the field of mental health prevention [is this a Freudian slip?], "…built into any definition of wellness…are overt and covert expressions of *values*. Because *values* differ across cultures as well as among subgroups (and indeed individuals [notice here their admission that to them individuals are nothing more than of parenthetical importance and the Group comes first]) within a culture, the ideal of a uniformly acceptable definition of the constructs [values, mental health] is *illusory*" (Cowen, 1994) [emphasis mine, reference theirs]. [126]

That is, as every "enlightened" person knows—speaking sarcastically for a moment—*diversity* training, *ethnicity* worship and *multiculturalism* are "value free" and hence beyond reproach. But then, please notice the earlier discussion of mental health at the beginning of this same section: **"Mental Health and Mental Illness: Points on a Continuum".**[v]

> As will be evident in the pages that follow, "mental health" and "mental illness" are not polar opposites but may be thought of as points on a continuum. *Mental health* is a state [pause…repeat…is a *state*] of successful performance…at productive activities, fulfilling relationships with other people, and the ability to adapt to change and to cope with adversity.

The last sentence is just mom and apple pie and it is as "profound" a statement as is this: liquid is a *state* of wetness, so please read on:

> Mental health is indispensable to personal well being, family and interpersonal relationships, and contribution to community or society.

Every time the *Government* tells me about the virtues of *contributing* to *community and society* my "1984", "Anthem", "Fahrenheit 451" bells 'n whistles go off, blasting away as if some disastrous cave-in or other catastrophe were

---

[126] I take "Objectivism" and "Biocentric psychology" as a given *context* and I assume the reader is somewhat familiar with these two intellectual systems. As such I don't define absolutely every term I use because it would be even more "footnote'y" than it is. Here however, the concept "value" is so important that I mention the Objectivist's definition of it and hence the definition that makes sense: a *value* is something we act to gain and/or keep … and I ask the reader to notice that this definition does not—as it is not obliged to—distinguish between good values and bad values.

about to occur in the mind[vi]. But, this is to be a latter point. The point I'm trying to get to now, is in the next sentence.

> It is easy to overlook the value of mental health until problems surface.

If it doesn't jump out at you, please re-read it and notice the use of the *construct* "value". I thought such usage was "illusory"? That is, if mental health can't be defined, that is, if we don't know for sure *what* it is how do we know it's a *value?*

Why do we continue putting up with this kind of blatant disrespect for our minds? Is it because we are mentally ill, but not in a way *they* want us to understand?

Or is *something* else going on?

Consider the *proper* definition of mental health and then by extension the *proper* definition of mental illness:

> *Mental health is the unobstructed capacity for reality-bound cognitive functioning—and the exercise of this capacity. Mental illness is the sustained impairment of this capacity.*[vii]

Not too tough, wouldn't you agree? Not too, that is, *after* Dr. Branden's efforts and commitment to *precision* produced it. And notice *why* this definition is proper: because it meets all 8 of the (s/b 5?) rules for *proper* definitions:[viii]

> 1. It's *not* circular (doesn't use itself in the definition)
> 2. It's *not* negative (m-health *is* a kind of cognitive contact with reality)
> 3. It is *fundamental* (that is, *metaphysically* obstructing a function—throwing a monkey wrench into the mechanism—causes bad things to happen to the mechanism; *epistemologically*, a well oiled psycho-epistemology—absent monkey wrenches—works beautifully)
> 4. It has a *genus* (human *capacity*)
> 5. It has *differentia* (*cognition*—figuring our *what* things are—as the *particular* capacity)
> 6. It's not too broad (doesn't apply to reformed neo-Nazi's)
> 7. It's not too narrow (does apply to those who think the Christmas tree in their living room is a little green man from mars) and
> 8. Its *not* obscure, that is, it's not metaphorical or poetic, but *clearly* states a *literal* and *exact* meaning (blocked consciousness unhealthy, unblocked consciousness healthy).

Go back and re-evaluate the Surgeon Generals "definitions" in light of the foregoing. Then consider that those who take concepts and definitions *seriously* are far from surprised (they may be *puzzled*, but not surprised) when those who don't take them seriously *conclude* that defining *at best* is *illusory*.

A question worth pondering here is, do "they" only say this when they get close to subconscious premises that *they have automatized* and dare not check or do "they" *worship* illusion?[127]

If there is not a third alternative (e.g., they actually believe they have defined their terms) then the aforementioned ricochet into saying definitions at best are illusory came when they realized "they" *can't* define mental health OR mental illness, but accept the premise that not only can one *pretend* to know *what* one doesn't know, it is the preferred way to be. That is, it is the preferred way to be, *if* you *work for the government* as either Grant-Maker or as successful Grant-Seeker. It would appear that one who is a *successful* Seeker of government grant money is one who is a seeker of *my money* and of your money *as their means* to writing papers telling us that *precision* of thought is—*at best*—"illusory".[128]

Do government bureaucrats fear precision? Or are they being "precise" and we are just *refusing* to believe them? They say "their" *ideal* is "illusion". Maybe we should start taking them at their word.

However—speaking for a moment in tongues...-in-cheek—please don't misunderstand me. If the NIH or NIMH will award me the $1,000,000,000 Grant that I have requested to study the *Grant making function* of Government and to show how *in the long run* such a function is deadly for *individual* rights and freedoms and as such should be stopped, I will accept it and proceed to so document.[129]

---

[127] It might be a comforting fiction here to conclude that "they" don't know what they are doing and are simply trying to take the rest of us down with them—as in the cliché: misery loves company—but since comforting fictions can be like comfort foods (if we over eat them we all know what happens to our bodies) we have to use them sparingly. Here, since we can see that T.H.E.Y are Kantians and Kantians worship illusion as an end in itself we have to conclude that they are honoring t.h.e.i.r high (if not highest) value: illusion worship. And here we won't even discuss t.h.e.i.r bullstuff notion that *values* should be purged from scientific psychology.

[128] If we accept that it is *illusory* and then in the next breath conclude we may as well give up, will the bureaucrat have achieved her or his goal? That is, if people give up and act sheepish, then they will "need", "require" and WANT a sheepherder?

[129] This is intended as already indicated as tongue-in-cheek comment. I didn't *actually* do this, though I've thought about it. Nonetheless, if *you* are an NIH or NIMH bureaucrat and want to take this as a formal Grant request be my guest. And when you ok it, send me the billion bucks in the mail and I'll get right on it.

In the meantime, however, I am going to try to *earn* my money by convincing *you* to take care of yourself and to start now if you already haven't and if you already have, to keep up the *good* work.

In conclusion let me add the following. Anyone who is a Grant-Seeker and gets grants based on an *explicit* declaration that says their short term goal is to *scientifically* study and report on phenomenon X and their *long* term goal is to do away with the government *as Grant Maker* (and mean it), then *morally* that person should be OK in the long run. In the absence of this kind of *explicitness* you run the risk of you yourself creating a "need" *to* obstruct your *normative-esthetic*—if not *yet* your cognitive—contact with reality. That is to say, if you do this and are a distinguished scientist, or become one *because of it*, you run the risk of becoming a Dr. Robert Stadler.[130]

If you *disagree* with the suggestion here that *just as you can't sell your car and still own it*, so neither can you "sell your soul" and still own it, then you are saying—by your disagreement—that either there are no laws of consciousness because there is *no such thing* as consciousness or your consciousness isn't *own-able* by you anymore than Gary Deering's consciousness is own-able by Gary Deering.[131]

---

[130] If you are unfamiliar with Ayn Rand's novel, *Atlas Shrugged* please read it to understand this reference and/or see page 72 herein.

[131] If you think this is an example of a *false alternative* and another choice is: *your* laws of consciousness *reject* one or more of these three axiomatic concepts: Existence exists and only existence exists; consciousness is conscious, that is it is an *irreducible* primary; A is A, i.e. contradictions do *not* exist, as nature amply demonstrates by not having any, then you ultimately have to conclude that existence does not exist, consciousness is not conscious and A is not A, i.e. contradictions do not, not exist, as nature amply demonstrates by having *some*. It then becomes your job—not mine—to provide the "some". Or of course you can "evade" the need to so provide and/or convince yourself that a "paradox" is the same thing as a contradiction. It's hard sometimes, I know, but Objectivism is right and reality is there for you to figure this out on your own.

Chapter 16 : Drop your *Pedactics* and Chill Out!

I repeat, drop your *Pedactics* and Chill Out!

No. I'm not going to "chill out" until... *BiO Spiritualism* is properly presented so that it can *only* be misunderstood by those who *prefer* mis-understanding to understanding.

There are too many books out their advocating—even if in the main, implicitly—that the Government *should* take care of us in ever increasing ways that ultimately *will* destroy our capacity for independent thought and judgment.

Or if the Government, qua bureaucratic mind, doesn't succeed 100% with all the good-little-*childish*-adult-citizens, it will still be the case that the only ones who *will* escape will be the *geniuses* of the world, the rest of us won't have a chance.[132]

For example, in a book edited by Robert L. Solso, 1997 President of the Western *Psychological Association* of the United States of America—"*Mind and Brain Sciences in the 21st Century*", (The MIT Press, 1999)[i]—we can find way too many reasons not to chill out prematurely. There are so many in fact that I submit if you open that book at random you can find within one page in either direction something that is anti-the-laws of human consciousness, which is to say it's anti-human nature.[133]

In fact allow me to challenge you (and me) right now. I have the hardcover version of the R. L. Solso book before me. It contains 16 Chapters by 19

---

[132] I've included myself in here for "literary" purposes only; in truth it is my *plan, goal* and *desire* to be one of the "escapees". If you need a reason to *intensely*—as in hurry up and—read and study Objectivism and Biocentric Psychology, here's one: if you value your sanity, never mind your mental health, but if you value your *sanity* you had better arm yourself against those whose intent is to control you. You will *need* all the intellectual weapons that these two super-technologies have to offer you to help you defend your consciousness against their—the bureaucrats—onslaughts.

[133] If you are suspicious of me here by wondering how in the world could there be anything wrong with a book endorsed by one of the most prestigious technical schools in America [Massachusetts Institute of Technology] and in addition written by people of the caliber of MIT students then I can only say, good, great, suspicion is good for you if you use it to protect your "I'm from Missouri, show me" attitude and not "I'm from bible belt [insert State] and regardless of what you show me I *refuse* to see" then like I said, your suspicion is good. My goal is *to show* you as best I can in the pages herein. Your choice *to see* or not is up to you.

distinguished authors and contains them all within pp. 1 through 323. So allow me a time-out here to set up my random number generator on my computer and generate 10 random page numbers—which, with one page on either side will cover abut 10% of the book.

RAND.323.10 = ...wait.... Halt.

Since I am still in the process of learning *Visual Basic* Computer Programming (after knowing old BASIC and trying to learn, but not liking C/C++ or JAVA, which are the more favored computer programming languages of today) I will have to go back and dig out my old IBM-DOS computer to do the RAN(domization). It will take me a little time here because I will either have to find the old BASIC computer program where I last used the Random Number generator or I will have to recreate it. If I have to recreate it, I will have to dig out my old BASIC text books and look up the commands and processes. I suppose I could just cut up 323 pieces of paper and write the numbers 1 through 323 on them and put them in a "hat" and draw 10 out, but the computer approach sounds more fun as well as more "scientific".[134, ii] Besides, maybe I'll use the time required here to do this as opportunity and *motivation* to advance my learning of Visual Basic.[135]

In the meantime you—while waiting for me to generate the ten random numbers—might find it interesting to note that the 19 authors contributing to the *Mind and Brain Sciences in the 21st Century* book (hereafter, also referred to as "Mind-Brain" and/or M-B book) consist of:[iii]

- 1 Ph.D. in Cognitive Psychology

---

[134] If you think I'm being facetious here you are only partially right. When I first wrote this I was so being but then later on I read this from a book on *Cognitive Science* written by a respected Ph.D.'er (Howard Gardner) from MIT:

All of these research maneuvers are carried out from the perspective of psychology [notice the single 'h'], though admittedly a psychology informed by a sophisticated grasp of the ways and traps of logic. But Johnson-Laird penetrates into the heartland of cognitive science because (like Stephen Kosslyn working in the area of imagery) he has implemented his theory via a computer program. (p. 366 of cited Reference).

Isn't this like saying, "Jesus loves me this I know BECAUSE the Bible tells me so"; except here it is: the [Cognitive Science] theory is true BECAUSE it is implemented in a computer program(!?!). If you are wondering where my (sometimes seemingly excessive) facetiousness and sarcasm come from you must remember that I've spent the better part of a half century reading academic drivel such as that in the foregoing quote from H(err) Gardner. (PLUS I was also teased a great deal by both my old man and my older brother when I was a kit—I mean, kid...kit? another Brandian slip? kit as in ... no, wait ... halt—back to point ... I was teased a lot but I got even with ... halt, get back to manuscript and see BiO Spiritualism Book II—and/or same reference as in Footnote number 51—for more.)

[135] As an aspiring to be successful Thoroughbred handicapper-bettor (that is, one with a +roi month after month after month...year in, year out) I have a *"need"* to modernize my computer programming skills.

- 1 Ph.D. in Cognitive Science
- 2 Professor Emeritus, one with a Ph.D., both with the title Dr.
- 2 Ph.D.'s in Psychobiology
- 6 Ph.D.'s in regular 'ole Psychology
- 1 Ph.D. graduate student
- 1 MD
- 1 Famous astronomer/cosmologist, also a Ph.D. I believe
- 1 author, lecturer and TV producer
- 1 Ph.D. in Experimental Psychology
- 1 editor, researcher, writer and University faculty Member
- 1 Ph.D. and near father of "Cognitive Psychology" and direct teacher of at least 1 of the other 18 authors here.

This adds up to a dozen Ph.D.'s, an MD or two, a couple of teachers and a college student.

Not an un-impressive group.

My goal here is to inform, not intimidate. If you are feeling intimidated I apologize and suggest you think about the fact that "authoritarianism" is an occupational hazard, so to speak, for modern, highly advanced, technological, have-lots-to-learn, to keep up with it all, humans (though I think our ancestors suffered from it too).

"Authoritarianism" is a way of thinking that is *bad* for you. If you think, X is true *because* Y says so, then you are an "authoritarian" thinker. (You also are an authoritarian thinker if you "reason", X is false *because* Y says so.). Y is not confined to a person or persons, it can also be a "book".[136, 137]

In fact one of our very own author teams in the above listing (line items 8 and 9) devoted a significant portion of their famous (and a favorite of mine as I *measure* by *fact* of *my* multiple viewings of it) Science Fiction movie — "*Contact*"[iv]— to this issue. They have a scene in "*Contact*" where their rogue

---

[136] An example from my own upbringing: "Jesus loves me this I KNOW, **because** The Bible tells me so.".

[137] Since my software won't let me to do a FN within a FN (like my website does), let me add the following thoughts to above : If you want to think of "Jesus" as the *externalized* form of "self-love" I suppose it is okay to do so, but it is such a dangerous thing to do that I offer this caution: if you do it, do so at your own risk and don't blame me in the end when you discover that this psychological projection will require you to turn your neuronal nets into a web of self-deceit and self-delusion that will *best* be described as "diabolical". And further, the only silver lining will be that when you see others building such epistemological networks in their own views of the world you will know what you mean when you call such networks: rat's nests, and hence be in a position to at least *start* warning your fellow man of religion's *deepest* dangers to personal happiness.

Catholic priest character, who is the author's concretization of *Religion & Faith* (an admirably good literary choice because "authoritarianism" *always* involves the issue of *faith versus reason*) and the heroine, who is the concretization of *Science and Reason* (another really good *literary* choice, especially when you think of the entire history of *Western Thought*—starting with Plato and Aristotle—and you notice that with some very rare exceptions, "science" *always* ends up "the hand*maiden*" of religion[138]) confront each other literally from opposite sides of the table. He, as a man of the cloth, is on the committee making the decision to send *one* and only *one* of several candidates on a trip to the stars in a vehicle—the design of which was given to us by some super advanced intelligence—that could only handle a payload of *one*. At one critical point, the Priest, in spite of his *actualized* romantic interest in the Heroine, asks her if she believes in God. (Yes. He knows the answer.) The heroine wants more than anything *on earth* to be the chosen one and she knows if she answers truthfully: "no, I do *not* believe in god", that if this, then she will *not* be chosen. She 'hems 'n haws as best she can *without* betraying her own soul (presumably the priest had to *ask* the question for the same *soul-saving* **reason**) and as a consequence the heroine is not selected for the once in a hundred lifetimes opportunity.

Some who saw the movie think that the heroine in the end—true to form of many modern day scientists as *alleged* worshippers of reason—kowtowed to religion. I personally don't think that she did, but that may just be projection on my part. The most I will grant here is that if she did she was duped into it because "they" never corrected *for her* the mistaken notion that *they* had given her. This "notion" was that there was **absolutely** no, none, nada, zero EVIDENCE outside of her herself that she *actually* went anywhere, let alone to the distant star she swears by all that is holy to her that she did. That is, that she "knows" she did.

As the movie comes to a close the *governmental* powers that be, show us, the audience, but not the heroine, *evidence* that she could very well have gone on the star trip she says she did. Earlier—during her interrogation by the authorities—she said that even though it appeared to those of us back here on earth that she was only gone a split second, to her she was gone for 18 hours, which as most of us know can be accounted for, in concept, by Einstein's theory of relativity. So the powers that be tell us but not the heroine that they did observe 18 hours of

---

[138] Which—if you accept Ayn Rand's claim that religion is a primitive philosophy—it (science) *should* so end up. The problem is when philosophy ends up being the handmaiden of religion, whenever this happens it seems difficult to argue that religion is a primitive philosophy, because how can a thing—the dirty minded pun slingers notwithstanding—end up its own handmaiden?

static on the tapes she had used to record the event. By not telling her, the *authors* left the heroine hanging.

I do hope one of my random numbers falls within pp. 19 to 37 where the "*Contact*" author's article, "What Thin Partitions..." lay (or should that be lie?).

There are some other very interesting facts about the 19 authors and their 16 Chapters in "Mind-Brain" but I have managed to get my 10 random numbers now and I am ready to start. So maybe we'll come back to the "stats" later. In anticipation of this I want you to make a guess: How many of the 16 article-chapters in the book do you think were paid for by the United States government via grants from either the NIH (National Institute of Health) or the NIMH (National Institute of Mental Health) or any other government grant-making groups?[139]

The random numbers I got are:

1. 39
2. 210
3. 280
4. 235
5. 258
6. 23
7. 158
8. 146
9. 34
10. 307

Taking them in the above order—with the one page on either side added—let me begin.

38.39.40

Page 38 is the first page of Chapter 3: "Will the Mind Become the Brain in the 21st Century?" by Richard F. Thompson.[v]

Dr. Thompson (one of the 2 Ph.D.'s in Psychobiology from our author's list above) doesn't waste anytime.

"I begin my discussion", he writes, "of brain and mind with my favorite quotation from John Watson's *Psychology as the Behaviorist Views it* (1913).

---

[139] And remember, if *you* are a taxpaying American, this means paid for by *you*.

After stressing that measurable behavior is the proper object of study in psychology [no it's not, see further below], [Watson] says:"

> Will there be left over in psychology a world of pure psychics, to use Yerkes' term? I confess I do not know. The plans which I most favor for psychology lead practically to the ignoring of consciousness in the sense that that term is used by psychologists today. I have virtually denied that this realm of psychics is open to experimental investigation. I don't wish to go further into the problem at present because it leads inevitably over into metaphysics. If you will grant the behaviorist the right to use consciousness in the same way that other natural scientists employ it—that is, without making consciousness a special object of observation—you have granted all that my thesis requires. (Watson, 1913, p.175)[vi]

"Watson's statement", Dr. Thompson continues, "can hardly be called doctrinaire and must come as a surprise to those ardent cognitive scientists who decry behaviorism. The basic point he makes, and it is the thesis of my [Dr. Thompson's] chapter, is that terms like "consciousness" and "mind" do not refer to phenomena that are in principle unmeasurable."[vii]

Please remember Dr. Thompson's " ...consciousness is ... not unmeasurable" comment. You will have need of it in less than 2 minutes.

On this point Dr. Thompson is *correct.* As Ayn Rand has demonstrated in her writings on Objectivist Epistemology, consciousness is *very* measurable: "..consciousness is a dynamic, not static, process... [and] it is "measurable" ...by its *range and scope..*its range of awareness and scope of *what* it can conceive.." [viii]

And to gain an appreciation of the *range* of Man's consciousness versus that of lower animals, consider Dr. Branden's comments from his Chapter on "Man: A Rational Being", p. 31, paperback, *The Psychology of Self Esteem"*.

> To appreciate the nature of the tremendous increase of intellectual power made possible by man's conceptualizing ability, it is necessary to realize the extreme limitations of an exclusively perceptual form of awareness. The number of units that *any* consciousness—human or animal—can hold in its field of awareness at any given moment, is necessarily

> small. A consciousness that is restricted only to those sensible particulars it can immediately perceive is severely restricted in its ability to accumulate or expand its knowledge. This is the state of all animals under man.
>
> The ascent to the conceptual level of consciousness entails two related factors: the ability to categorize numerous particulars into groups or classes, according to a distinguishing characteristic(s) they exhibit in common—and the ability to develop or acquire a system of symbols that represents these various classes, so that a single symbol, held in a man's mind, can stand for an unlimited number of particulars.
>
> The method of classification is concept-formation. The system of symbols is language.[ix]

Dr. Thompson—I'm quite sure, oblivious to Dr. Branden's existence—continues: "At present, they [mind and consciousness] can only be studied indirectly by measuring behavior, verbal and otherwise. By 'a special object of observation' I believe", Dr. Thompson writes on p. 40, "Watson had in mind the method of introspection and the view then prevalent in psychology that mind/consciousness was somehow nonphysical, the traditional mind-body dualism. As Watson notes, this 'leads inevitably over into metaphysics.' ",[x] concludes Dr. Thompson to this point in quoting Watson. Then Dr. Thompson *concludes* on *his* own: "The view of mind as nonphysical cannot of course be entertained in science."[xi]

Says who?

If by "nonphysical" he means "non-existent" then I of course agree. But, Dr. Thompson *cannot* mean this because he said, "…in principle *consciousness* and *mind* is *not* unmeasurable …" (refer back to the 2 minute warning). And I agreed with this (2 minutes ago) because, for example, "heat" is not physical in the same sense as is the burning log it comes from. Heat *exists* and it has physical consequences but its physicalness is very different from that of say a stone we kick ahead of ourselves, down the street, while out walking. If we happen to be walking on a really *hot* summer day and we try to *kick* the heat away and it doesn't work, do we conclude there is *no such thing as heat*? Of course not.[140]

---

[140] I have identified myself as a pedantic person and I am aware that culturally, pedanticness has a negative connotation, but I still wonder: Where does *Intellectual self-defense* end and pedanticness begin?

In addition to "physical", meta-physical, that is *metaphysics* is another key word here. If I look it up in my dictionary it gives as its definition, metaphysics: *a division in philosophy that includes ontology*... [relating to being or existence]... *and cosmology* ... [origin, structure, and space-time relationships of the universe].

Contrast this with my (taken from Objectivism) definition: *metaphysics* is the science that deals with man and his *relationship* to existence, to reality; man and his place in the nature of things; metaphysics is the philosophical answer to the question: *Where* am I? I prefer the Objectivist answer/definition of *metaphysics* (as well as most if not all of their other *philosophical* terms and *some* of their psychological terms) and whenever key terms arise I will highlight them like I am doing here by discussing their definitions and let you know what **I mean** by them. Continuing, the following is Objectivism's beginning answer (in the person of Ayn Rand) to the "Where am I?" question of metaphysics.[141]

> Are you in a universe, which is ruled by natural laws and, therefore, is stable, firm, absolute—and knowable? Or are you in an incomprehensible chaos, a realm of inexplicable miracles, an unpredictable, unknowable flux, which your mind is impotent to grasp? Are the things you see around you real—or are they only an illusion? [where did we see this word before?]. Do they exist independent of any observer—or are they created by the observer? Are they the object or the subject of man's consciousness? Are they *what they are*—or can they be changed by a mere act of your consciousness, such as a wish?
>
> The nature of your actions—and of your ambition—will be different, according to which set of answers you come to accept. These answers are the province of *metaphysics*—the study of existence as such or, in Aristotle's words, of "being qua being"—the basic branch of philosophy.[xii]
>
> The branch of philosophy that studies existence is *metaphysics*.[xiii]

---

[141] As a human being with a human consciousness I am not exempt from the problems of "authoritarianism". I as a person do have a relationship with existence and I agree with and accept the Objectivist concept, "metaphysics" as being *about* this relationship. If you have another term substitute it whenever you believe we are dealing with this basic "people - existence" relationship.

Most modern day (physical) "scientists" equate, like Dr. Thompson is trying to do, equate "metaphysics" with "mysticism" and hope that *you* conclude by *associational formulations*—like some "concept" secreting Pavlovian dog—the conclusions that they *want* you to make. For example, "they" want you to "reason", thusly: metaphysics = mysticism, therefore of course the metaphysical has no place in "science". This could be an example of what Dr. Nathaniel Branden, psychologist *extraordinaire*[142], means when he talks about the problem *physical* scientists have when they "try" to think about psychology, especially when they try to integrate the fact of volition in man and the need for prediction in science. Quoting Dr. Branden from his book "The Psychology of Self Esteem", Chapter IV, Man: A Being of Volitional Consciousness:

> One of the characteristics of the majority of modern psychological theories, [he writes in 1969 and based on the little we've presented so far, it doesn't appear to be changing that much] aside from the arbitrariness of so many of their claims, is their frequently ponderous *irrelevance*. The cause, both of the irrelevance and of the arbitrariness, is the evident belief of their exponents that one can have a science of human nature [remember my claim that the book "Mind and Brain Sciences…" is filled with anti-human nature ideas] while consistently ignoring man's most significant and distinctive attributes.
>
> Psychology, today, is in desperate need of *epistemological* rehabilitation. It should be unnecessary, for example, to point out what is wrong with the attempt to prove that all learning is of a random, trial-and-error kind by placing a rat into a maze where random, trial-and-error learning is all that is possible, then adducing the rat's behavior as evidence for the theory. It should be still less requisite to point out what is wrong with accepting the underlying premise of such experiments: the groundless and flagrantly unempirical notion that the learning process in man is to be understood through a study of the behavior of rats.

---

[142] Dr. Branden is expert at BOTH psychological theorizing AND psychological practice (psychotherapy), hence the accolade.

> In the writings of modern psychologists—whether or not the writers happen to show a predilection for the study of rats (or pigeons or earthworms)—*man* is the entity most conspicuously absent. One can read many textbooks today and never learn that man has the ability to think; if the fact is acknowledged at all, it is dismissed as unimportant. One would not learn from these books that man's distinctive form of consciousness is conceptual, nor that this is a fact of crucial significance. One would not learn that man's biologically distinguishing attribute and his basic means of survival is his rational faculty.
>
> The relation of man's reason to his survival is the first of two basic principles of man's nature which are indispensable to an understanding of his psychology and behavior. The second is that the exercise of his rational faculty, unlike an animal's use of his senses, is not automatic—that the decision to think is not biologically "programmed" in man—that *to think is an act of choice.*[xiv]

As you think about the contrasting views in all of the foregoing and those that will come up throughout this work I invite you to do it with *one* of my Spiritualist tenets in mind:[143]

He who matches reality the best, reaps the most.

Dr. Thompson—after his spurious statement about science that was derived from a *line of "reasoning"* he fashioned after a line paralleling the flight path of a fly—suggests that *Behaviorist Psychology* and *Cognitive Science* are modern day antagonists. He offers this claim in the spirit of "everybody knows it"; he neither proves it nor challenges it. Dr. Thompson, the Behaviorist, in the end only succeeds in proving Dr. Branden correct. "Again, my [Dr.Thompson's] thesis is that there is nothing more to thoughts than neural activity and its outward expressions in behavior."[xv, 144] Look back and notice what Dr. Branden said about "today's" psychology:

---

[143] Remember, earlier I said I am a new breed of "spiritualist" and I need to remind you here that by "spirit" I mean "consciousness". To call myself a "consualist" is silly and unnecessary; plus it would be *surrendering* "spirituality" to the religionists and new agers, which is something I *refuse* to do.

[144] Top of p. 41. Because of the blank page effect at chapter ends I am advancing the page count by one.

> One can read many textbooks today and never learn that man has the ability to think; if the fact is acknowledged at all, it is dismissed [...nothing more to thoughts than neural activity...] as unimportant. [xvi]

It *appears* here as if the "Cognitive Scientists" are doing battle with the "Behaviorists" and this may indeed be true. However, we have to be careful. The *reason* we have to be careful is because based on their own terms, their "ideal" is the *illusion* of meaning. "They" do not worship *precision* of definition as we do but desire to give the "appearance" of defining their terms and the "appearance" of being *scientific*. Consequently, our mental protection requires us—since "we" worship *precision* as all *true* scientists do—to be careful here and by simply stating it we are so being and we can then *afford* to move on.

To the second random Mind-Brain page number on our list of ten.

209.210.211

The first paragraph on p. 209, as page 11 of Chapter 11, "The Memory Trainers", by Gay Snodgrass, starts: "Consider the two systems of episodic and semantic memory proposed by Tulving."[xvii] And before we wonder who Tulving is who is Gay Snodgrass? She is J. Gay Snodgrass, a Ph.D. recipient (one of the 6 "regular" Psychologists identified on line 5 of our list) from the University of Pennsylvania and at the time of publication a Fellow of both the American Psychological Association (APA) and the American Psychological Society (APS). She has, among other publications, served as Consulting Editor for the *Journal of Experimental Psychology: General, Memory and Cognition*, and the *Journal of Psycholinguistic Research*. Her research spans many key areas of cognitive psychology, including memory storage and retrieval, pattern recognition, and category formation ("Mind-Brain", p.336 in the "About the Authors" section beyond the 323 pages of articles).

The figure on p. 209—Figure 11.4 Tulving's (1985) proposal for a tripartite memory system—shows the cognitive psychologists view of our memory as being divisible into 3 fundamental systems: Episodic Memory, Semantic Memory and Procedural Memory. And as the figure describes, *episodic* is autobiographical knowledge about self-referenced events (e.g., see page 146 here about my recall of myself and my kids in the car on a trip to grandma's house); *semantic* is general knowledge shared by a culture (e.g., some TV Game shows); *procedural* is perceptual, motor, or cognitive skills (e.g., favorite smells, penmanship, or remembering peoples names by exaggerated caricatures of their faces).[145]

By and large there isn't much to deal with in these three pages. We are forced to go outside them in order to understand the author on her own terms. Also, memory per se is not controversial: we all can readily relate to the *fact* of it and don't need a lot of convincing *that it really exists*. However, there might be more to it than this and at this point there are only two things I wonder about:

1. Grouping "cognitive skill" in with "motor skills" via the Procedural Memory category is suspect and
2. I don't know what "priming" means but it is used in this chapter and also back on p. 40. As we randomly *stitch* our way through this "Mind-Brain" book this could be an important term to understand more fully.

So we will have to return to this material later. And since this memory stuff is a (little) bit boring I look forward to the next random sequence and may even indulge in some bravado by saying, I can, if need be, *make* it be interesting.

Sub note: I have revisited the issues here since I first wrote this brief section and I must say that the "Wow!" in the next section should have been *reserved* for this memory discussion (under the assumption that good writing doesn't over use "wow's", notwithstanding those who say one wow is one wow to many). The Cognitive Scientist's view of memory is a much bigger *wow* than I suspected and is dealt with in more detail in Chapter 18: " From *Behaviorism - to - Cognitive Neuroscience via Cognitive Science & Cognitive Psychology*: Rats maze - to - Rats nest?" And as you might be able to guess, the two items identified above are not *that* important to understanding the real danger in Cognitive Psychology—a *danger* that the subtitle to my Chapter 18 explores and develops in more detail. To anticipate this Chapter just let me say, here with this memory "stuff" is where the Rat's Nest begins and for those of you who say a Rat's Nest is such that you can't find its beginning let me say you are being way too literal: rat's nest is a figure of speech. It is a perfect visual metaphor for what the Cognitive Neuroscientists are creating *epistemologically*. Even if *some* of them are being duped by the yin and yang of the Bureaucratic Mind and The Cognitive Scientist Mind (when they animate and re-animate each other in their articles, journals and books) they are not being duped because of their genes, or *because* of their environment or because of any other non-self thing you (or they) can come up with. Consequently, a cry later on—when the premises of *Cognitive Science* will out—a cry of "we were all helpless victims" will not work on the rest of us who know what we know, see what we see, hear what we hear, taste what we taste, feel what we touch, and can smell a rat a mile off when one is trying to nest in our (epistemological) wood work.

So to repeat, we will have to return to this material later. And since this memory material—at this point in our development—is a (little) bit boring I look forward to the next random sequence and may even stick my neck out and say I can, if need be, *make* it be interesting.

279.280.281

---

[145] The three e.g.'s here are my examples/interpretation of "their" meaning, not Dr. Snodgrass's.

Wow. What luck!

I must be psychic, I wrote the above bravado claim about making this interesting without knowing which chapter these pages were in and hence would be about. I just wrote what came to mind.[146]

After I wrote it I thought, in a way regardless of *what* it *is* about I can *make* it be something interesting and fun.

But these pages are from Hans J. Eysenck, a 20th Century (second half) researcher and writer on "Personality Theory." And since *personality theory* is a major topic in the *Science of Psychology*, it is its own fun and one does not have to *make* it be so. I know because I wrote my first introductory article on "Personality" back in 1981 and the *process* of doing it was almost, but not quite, but almost, more fun than sex.[147]

The experience of writing that *Introductory Paper* was the place where I experienced the joy and excitement that comes from the realization that one has total and complete control over one's own psychological growth and development. And I mean *total* and complete control. It was among the first "places" where I experienced first *hand* the *Biocentric* idea of developing man going from "programmed-to-volitional self regulation" by his own choice. What I didn't realize at the time but do now is that: *it is the only way it can be done.* Nature takes care of us for a long, long time but at some point we come to that proverbial fork in the road and we have to choose which fork we are going to choose and hence which path we are going to follow. I chose and continue to choose *volition* as the "determiner" of human psychology and my foes chose and continue to choose *NV Determinism* as that which *determines* human psychology. The NV designator here is simply a device and will shortly be spelled out as to what it means. It is not intended to be used herein as a formal concept.

---

[146] For the record I do *not* believe in "psychic" powers and all that traditional "spiritualism" usually entails. My goal here, or rather one of my goals is to reclaim spiritualism for humans, qua people, not for humans, qua abyss hangers in a world of pseudo-self made blindness as same is manufactured by the pseudo-Professional Intellectuals and the newly emergent 21st Century Public Intellectuals hired by the Government to help us out in our "need" to keep our head in the sand, least we get *too upset* as we discover the way things *really* are.

[147] If you are thinking this guy must have had one boring sex life, think again: I'm the guy *that* (or should that be *who*) wrote the book on "The Reichian Orgasm and how to have one"... or rather I should say, I'm the guy *that's* gonna (maybe) write this book. (Or maybe not either. All's I remember is that back in my bio-energetic days when—after already having had two kids and being *fully* and *completely* aware of the awesome responsibility in raising them—I had to face the *choice* of getting a vasectomy OR giving up hope of ever having a Reichian orgasm it .... wait ... halt. This is too long to get into here, save it for "Joshua's" unfolding story.)

For my purposes here (*BiO Spiritualism,* the book) my foes, my T.H.E.Y are the Bureaucratic Mind and the Social Engineers who serve them. Together t.h.e.y "reason" this way:

> *Everybody knows that human psychology is determined by forces outside of the individuals control and our job is simply to determine what those forces are. We don't know much about humans to start with so the task is going to be extremely difficult. But to help us out we do "know" one thing for sure and this thing is for absolute sure and beyond challenge sure. That thing is this: the determiners of human psychology—whatever they end up being, be they genes, or potty training, or instincts or collectively shared unconscious experiences we inherit from our ancestors, or death wishes or environmental toxins or even Shakespeare's stars or some yet to be discovered thing we don't even know about: e.g., the sub-sub-sub or to borrow a measure of smallness from a Statistics Professor I once had: the semi-hemi-demi-tas ... sized "stars" that orbit around quarks, you know the ones they haven't discovered yet—that it or they ALL—each 'n every one—will have this ONE distinguishing characteristic thing about them that will prove to be the case:* **it** *will* **not** *be Volition. Which is to say, the determiners are NV Determiners, that is Not Volition, THAT IS, THE "DETERMINERS—per the rules of Determinism—CAN BE ANYTHING EXCEPT VOLITION.* This last is a hidden premise in contemporary psychology and I should say it *was* a hidden premise until now.

And now that you are in a frame of mind that will allow you to challenge your own premises about *psychological determinism* I *predict* that when you finish reading my introductory article on *Personality Theory* you are going to be excited. That is, you will be so excited about your own future prospects—assuming of course that you aren't already there—for taking complete, 100% *control* over your own psychological *growth and development* that you will want to start today, if not sooner. And the *reason* you will be so excited is because you will begin (again, if you haven't already begun) to see *how* it all works. And once you *do* see the *how,* there is *no* turning back.

So before we get into Dr. Eysenck's 3 pages at hand, that is, 279.280.281 of "Mind-Brain", we have to go back and review, briefly, some history and foundations of "Personality Theory".

A Psychologist without his or her own personal "Personality Theory" is ...a frustrated philosopher and a Philosopher with his or her own Personality Theory is ...an *amateur* psychologist.[148]

In this sense then one could say there are as many theories of personality as there are "psychologists"—be they the professional or amateur type. The only thing that prevents this statement from being a *good* example of hyperbole is the fact that there *are* many personality theories out there in the man-made world at large. There are so many in fact that writers who try to categorize and catalogue them (e.g. Rychlak, 1973) tend to conclude that there is not and *cannot* be one true-*correct* definition of "personality". (If you'll remember back to the Surgeon General's report it would appear that the Surgeon General does not have a monopoly on this *inability* to generate accurate definitions[149]). "We" of course, as worshippers of the *precision* that reason demands, know this is not the case. We can agree that "personality" can be a *complex* issue to understand, but we can also agree *that* ... it is understand*able*.

For example, once when my kids were young (many years ago) we were driving to visit their grandparents (my parents). On the way there we were in a *moment* of light hearted conversation about traveling and spending money, having fun, playing and being happy. In this "moment" I said, "...well you know what they say, happiness can't buy money". Conversationally, everything came to a dead stop standstill. My oldest daughter said, *"that* doesn't sound like you." My youngest daughter agreed. "It sounds like something grandma would say", they said. Feeling the tension of their *confusion* stretching my self image of never being wrong to its elastic limit, I thought for a moment and then said, "you're right". That is something my mother used to say all the time. I think it's cute, but I don't really believe it. They relaxed, so did I and we drove on.

This "event" may seem trivial to us as adults, but to my two daughters, ages 7 and 11 (give or take a year either way) at the time, it was a **big** deal.[150]

---

[148] This is an example of me being kind for those who think I can't be. There are a lot of names one could call psychologists and philosopher isn't one of them. Except, of course, unless you think philosopher means one of those modern day types who preach we humans can't know. If this, then calling a psychologist a philosopher *is* derogatory. I don't mean it this way. I mean it in a good way: philosopher, as in one who *worships* reason and uses it to understand human nature.

[149] Would *your recall here* be an example of episodic, semantic or procedural memory? Episodic memory, per p. 207 "Mind-Brain" is memory OF occurrence information, semantic memory is OF meaning information and procedural memory, p. 208, is memory FOR perceptual, motor, and cognitive skills. Is this OF - FOR distinction important or not? For right now I don't know, but we *will* come back to it later.

[150] Though I can't recall the *exact* ages of my two daughters, what I do remember for absolute sure is: I *was* acting *out of character* as described **and** they did **not** like it. (The age et al. *details*—e.g. make and model of

If we think about this one event further (we ultimately need more than just one event to draw a valid conclusion) we could conclude that our "personality" is the *means* by which others know us. Because of this "knowledge" they can predict—well enough—how we are going to act so that they can be around us without having to feel as if they are living in a chaotic, unpredictable universe (assuming we don't have a chaotic, unpredictable personality). That is, if you recall one aspect of Objectivism's discussion about *metaphysics*: "Are you in a universe which is ruled by natural laws and, therefore, is stable, firm, absolute—and knowable? Or are you in an incomprehensible chaos..."; that is, I did not contribute (in this one particular case) any "pressure" on them to develop a *negative metaphysics.*

Here we can say that "personality" is some-thing even if, at this point, we don't know *exactly* yet *what* that "thing" is.

Is it, like Freud argued: id, ego and superego? (see below) Or as Jung said: a bunch of archetypes rattling around inside that "box" we call our head? (also see below) Or like our current "Mind-Brain" author, H. J. Eysenck, says: a genetically inherited type structure?[xviii] Or is it what the behaviorists say: a myth? Since personality is a mental construct, say the Behaviorists, and since we (the Behaviorists) want to scientifically study man without reference to mind or consciousness we conclude all mental constructs are myths. After all, "scientific" psychology is the "science" of behavior.[151] [xix]

If you are confused—is psychology about behavior or about mind or about both or about something else?—maybe in *this* instance you *should* be confused. Is personality a fact of reality or not. If it is then we can isolate it and study it as a "thing". If not, then not.

The last time I *intensely* studied personality theory was in the very late 1970's and early '80's. It was among the first college courses I had to get through on my way to my *Master's Degree* in *Counseling Psychology*. The personality cataloguer we studied was Rychlak, specifically his text book "Introduction to Personality and Psychotherapy, A theory-construction Approach".[xx] Excluding the References and Index, Rychlak's book is a full sized 527 page action-packed hardcover textbook about nothing but personality theorizing. In Rychlak's own

---

car we were in, time of day and so on—qua measurements are, as we used to say in the Home Building Business, close enough for carpenters.)

[151] Maybe this *blatant* denial of reality by the Behaviorists "explains" why they have been *replaced* by Cognitive Psychology as the dominant, cultural, mainstream "psychology". If you think for just a moment of " mainstream psychology" as the "software" of the cultural mind, you have to ask (as we have already done) is this [Cognitive Psychology] a TRUE replacement [of Behaviorism] or JUST an UPGRADE?

words, it is a catalogue of "Mixed Kantian-Lockean models in Classical Psychoanalysis" (Part One). Part Two is "Lockean Models in American Psychiatry and Behaviorism" and Part Three: "Kantian Models in the Phenomenological Outlook".[152]

The Lockean and Kantian models as conceived by Rychlak are drawn out in schematic form on pp. 10 and 11 of his book. Essentially, Rychlak says John Locke's model for theory construction goes from the least abstract/most concrete up-the-ladder to higher and higher levels of abstractions, whereas, Immanuel Kant's is just the *reverse*: Kant says our thinking and theory building goes from the highly abstract down-the-ladder to the least abstract.[153]

Part One of Rychlak deals with Sigmund Freud, Alfred Adler and Carl Jung who are the three "founding fathers" of Psychoanalysis (Rychlak, p. 200). It is worth while to note that our current "Mind-Brain" author, H. J. Eysenck, views Psychoanalysis as anti-scientific and as such one of the *main* impediments to the advancement of Psychology, The Science ("Mind-Brain", p. 275).[154]

Part Two of Rychlak deals with "American" Psychology, specifically, Harry Stack Sullivan, John Dollard, Neal E. Miller, B. F. Skinner, Joseph Wolpe, and Thomas G. Stampfl. As the title to Part Two indicates these names constitute the Theory of Behavior known as Behaviorism.[155]

And finally, Part Three discusses Carl R. Rogers, Ludwig Binswanger (not to be confused with the wonderful scientist-philosopher and lecturer, Dr. Harry Binswanger of the Professional Objectivists), Medard Boss and George Kelly.

These 13 names are just the psychologists who've generated theories to answer the simple question, What is personality? And these 13 are far from ALL of them, as you can notice there is no mention of our "Mind-Brain" author, Hans J. Eysenck nor of my favorite, Dr. Nathaniel Branden, to mention just two more.

---

[152] If you don't happen to be as interested in Personality Theories as am I and are finding this a tad boring, I invite you to notice the name "Kant" in the part descriptions. According to Objectivism: Plato-Kant-Hegel are the Intellectual Builders of Auschwitz (Peikoff *Ominous Parallels* p.37). And also note that the most influential philosopher in *America's* Public School System yesterday and today is none other than—you got it—(Immanuel) Kant.

[153] And *never* ever connects up with the concreteness of *reality* according to the *Objectivists*. And yes, Objectivists are pro-Lockean in their outlook, or in the least, not anti-Lockean as they are anti-Kantian.

[154] This is an example of me being kind on Dr. Eysenck's behalf. He actually views Psychoanalytic "thought" as equivalent to "Quackery". However, since he doesn't define "quackery" I prefer to list his criticism of it as non-scientific and/or anti-scientific, which he also calls it.

[155] Since Behaviorists believe "behavior" is psychology and "psychology" is behavior *they* call their "Theory" of Behavior, Psychology, rather than "The Animal Trainer's Handbook", that it properly *should* be called.

Additionally in Rychlak, there are names of all the influential philosophers from Plato and Aristotle on down as well as personal colleagues of the psychologist/personality theorizers and other people in the field. In short, by referencing Rychlak's REFERENCES there are some 102 people beyond the 13 named psychologists who in one way or another have something to do with Personality Theories. The 102 cited references do include a reference to H.J. Eysenck's evaluation of the effects of psychotherapy, 1952, but no mention of Marx and Engels even though on p. 209 Rychlak says the neo-Marxists admittedly influenced Adler. Though Adler *explicitly* rejected Communism and even the dialectical materialism on which it rests.[xxi]

So all and all "we" have no fewer than 115 peoples' opinions about Personality Theory and 527 full sized textbook pages (summing to more than 200,000 explicit concepts which if each only requires/rests on a handful of other concepts to grasp, means we have in excess of 1 million concepts) to *take in* and *digest*.

Assume here—for the sake of drama—that *you, BiO S reader you*, have read and digested the one million morsels of food-for-thought and are now given this assignment:

Develop an alternative to viewing personality as a product of life experiences, and write a paper about it.

Since we are viewing the world of "Body, Mind and Spirit" through the integrating scanning lens of *my* consciousness, my *answer* to the foregoing, taken from an earlier work, is recast as *your BiO S* reader's College-term-paper-answer and reprinted—in its verbatim, quasi-unedited entirety—below.

Chapter 17: Personality, psycho-hermeneutics as nuances of self understanding:

The origins of a New Spiritualism.

But wait.

Before we start I need to give you a bigger view of ALL Personality Theorizing. That is, I need to add some more names to the above *counts* by doing a quick inventory of books presently in the room with me. I want to include other theorizers not included in Rychlak.

And halt. One book alone—"Abnormal Psychology", Sarason[i] —has 820 plus or minus a couple names, all with opinions about psychology in general and by implication or association about Personality theory also. Another book—"Theories of Psychology Handbook", Neel[ii]—has over 150 name references (some, a few, are duplicates of the names in Rychlak). And another ("Personality Strategies and Issues", Sixth Ed, Liebert, Spriegler[iii]) has over 600 names, though of these I think there are numerous duplicates of the 820 names mentioned before. And finally, "Psychology", G. Lindzey, et al.[iv], has more than 600 also.

In one sense I suppose I could carry this to the extreme: How many human beings are there on the planet? OK, somewhere in the 5 to 7 billion range.[156] Of these, how many are old enough to have an opinion about psychology and/or personality? Oh, half for sure, so to be safe lets say 2 billion. So with 2,000,000,000 (2 billion) opinions how are we to make sense out of Personality Theorizing?

---

[156] Yikes! This means The United States Government (reference NIMH Grants discussion in Chapter 15) is currently spending about a buck for every man woman and child on the planet for "hired guns" to "shoot" me down. And notice that the U.S. Government has achieved this level of spending by harnessing less than 6% of the worlds population. Does this mean I should fear the Geo-politics of *Globalization* even more than I do—that is, did before I wrote this sentence? <u>Not to mention the potential negatives that are sure to accompany the successful War On Terrorism. Of course these negatives—especially the argument FOR World Sized Bureaucracies to run things, since "the world coalition", he says sarcastically, not the American Soldier won the war. Yes, it is true, these negatives will be "better" than those associated with loosing the war, but negatives there will be and we all will have to become (epistemological) warriors with the heart and soul of the American, *voluntary* soldier and his or her *commitment* to handling and defeating negatives.</u>

Well, for the 2 billionth and *one* answer, read the following and think of it as an aspect of a *New* Spiritualism. An aspect I call: "*paint me individual*".

An American College term paper in Personality theory on the question:
In light of the theorists discussed in this course
[Textbook by Joseph F. Rychlak, 1976]
Develop an alternative to viewing
Personality as a product of
Life experiences

© Gary Deering, 1981

EP 601T, Fall Semester 11/30/1981
Counseling as a Helping Profession
Dr. Butler, College of St. Thomas, St. Paul, MN, USA

Suppose, for the sake of discussion, I hand you a pail of worms and instruct you to look in at them; to observe them crawling over, under, between and in general all over each other. Then, that I instruct you to reach in and arbitrarily pick one, remove it from the pail and place it on the table in front of you.

Now, suppose further, you have done this, have wiped your fingers on the side of your slacks and are awaiting further instructions.

Suppose next, then, that I instruct you to observe the worm; to allow it to crawl around on the table (wherever its "little heart" desires) and to just watch it, to observe it with the intention of "getting to know it". Do this for a few moments or so...then pick it up and toss it back into the pail.

Now. Would you be willing to bet me one thousand dollars that tomorrow at this same time (or even one hour from now) that you could come back to that same pail and pick out the *exact* same worm? No?

What about the same bet for a similar situation that contained—instead of a pail of worms—a basket full of six month old multi-colored Puerto Rican tree frogs? Or, for one that contained a cart load of similarly sized and colored kittens? Probably still not you say, but for the cats you might risk a hundred bucks?

Would you take the bet if it entailed one person out of a crowd of 100 people? Of course—you say? I agree: you would win that bet. But why?

What are the differences between that pail of worms, the basket of frogs, the cart load of kittens and the crowd of people? Specifically, what are the differences that make it feasible to identify the one person but not the worm? Is it exclusively physical? Imagine the crowd of people as all being nude, of the same sex, heads shaved and of the same approximate body shape and size. You could probably still identify the *one* out of many, because of eye color, subtle differences in human features, sound of voice and so on. But still predominantly (if not exclusively) because of simple physical characteristics.

Allow then for your imagination to expand. Take half a dozen same sex people you know fairly well and place them separately into new bodies. Imagine these new bodies to be identical. Identical, that is, in *all* physical characteristics right down to the sound of the voice and the pattern of the fingerprints. Do you think you could still identify (without of course by asking: are you Sue? Or Joe? etc.) the one you knew best out of this half dozen? It seems as if even this is still feasible. But is it? Yes. We would be inclined to say it is feasible because Joe's or Sue's or so-and-so's *personality* would be *reflected* in the way he or she cocked their head when saying hello or fanned the air with their hands when they talked and in general by their *stylistic* way of being: inflections of *specific* words and so on. Here we are still relying on physical cues *but* they've become *unique* physical cues caused by a "something" we call "personality".

What is the cause of this "something"? Is it, as some personality theorists contend, the product of life experiences? Or is it the product of something else? Perhaps the product of inherited characteristics as certain other theorists contend. Or maybe it is due exclusively to the fact that people interact—that an individual alone on a desert island would have no need of personality and therefore no concept of it? Or perhaps it is *only* the product of the imagination of personality theorists. That is, that the concept of personality is a myth, as certain Behaviorists would contend. Or is it the product of something else? Something that is *importantly* different from the implications of *any* of the foregoing (and perhaps numerous other) "alternatives".

For example, one contemporary psychological theorist (Branden, 1969) contends that: "…[personality]… is the product … of the manner in which one responds to one's nature as a human being." (p. 207)

This formulation appears to be significantly different from the "pail full" of other alternative formulations offered to us down through the ages. In the narrow sense it *is* an alternative to the specific notion that personality is—in either the passive or reactive sense implied—the product of life experiences. In a broader sense it is not an alternative *to* other formulations but is a paradigm *for* them. But how could this be so? One of the basic "principles" of Personality Theory is that no such paradigm is possible. For example one textbook author (Liebert, Spiegler, 1970) states: "Because of the diversity of the definitions which have been used, there is little point in searching for *a* definition of personality." (p.9) Or another author on personality (Rychlak, 1973):

> In a sense, then, the question [What is personality?] has no answer if we expect *the* answer…for what this section points to is the inevitability of accepting *many* answers. (p.1)

As interpreters and/or cataloguers consider what these authors, along with some others have to say about various personality theories.

About Freud's (Liebert, Spiegler, 1970):

> Freud posited that personality is made up of the id, the ego and the superego, three aspects of the psyche, and that it is their interaction which determines behavior. Much of Freud's personality theory deals with these three aspects and

their interrelationship, and therefore Freud's definition of personality is his theory of personality. (p. 9)

Or another (Neel, 1977):

[with Freud]...The development of personality took place in a number of stages. Each of these stages involved the interaction of the existing psychological structure, the biological needs (especially the sexual ones), and the environment ... Development was biologically determined and each phase brought forth new impulses to be socialized. The environment could influence the intensity of developmental problems, but no matter what the situation the problems would appear to some degree. (p. 253)

And another (Hall, 1954):

...the stabilized personality is one in which the psychic energy has found more or less permanent and constant ways of expending itself in performing psychological work. The precise nature of this work is determined by the structural and dynamical characteristics of the id, ego, and superego, by the interactions between them, and by the developmental history of the id, ego, and superego. (p. 122)

Then about Jung's (Liebert):

Jung strongly believed that we are...a product of our individual histories... [and]...are also predisposed to act in various ways by experiences which have been common to all humans throughout the evolution of the species. In the collective unconscious—the dominant aspect of the personality for Jung—there are primordial images, called *archetypes*, which serve as models for our actions and reactions. (p. 95)

And more (Hall, Nordby, 1973):

The growth of personality consists of two interwoven strands: individuation of the various structures that make up the total psyche, and integration of these structures into a unified whole (selfhood). These growth influences are

influenced either positively or negatively by a number of
conditions, including hereditary, the child's experiences with
his parents, education, religion, society and age. (p. 95)

And what about the pile of other theorists? Rychlak (1973) has *tagged* many of them. Consider the following.

On Sullivan—Harry Stack:

> ...personality is conceived as the hypothetical entity which
> manifests itself in interpersonal relations, the latter including
> interactions with other people, real or fancied, primarily or
> medially integrated into dynamic complexes; and with
> traditions, customs, inventions, and institutions produced by
> man. (p. 245)

And Adler:

> ...It is the pent-up social feeling in us that urges us to reach a
> higher stage and to rid ourselves of the errors that mark our
> public life and our own personality. This social feeling
> exists within us and endeavors to carry out its purpose...that
> in a far-off age, if mankind is given enough time, the power
> of social feeling will triumph over all that opposes it....For
> the present the only alternative is to understand and to teach
> that this will inevitably happen. (p. 105)

The phenomenological existentialists:

> Reality for [Carl] Rogers—as well as most existentialists—
> is...a mater of *intersubjectivity*....The entire thrust of
> existentialism is to view man as existing uniquely, within his
> phenomenal experience which is constituted at least as much
> by his view of things as it is the result of how *he* is structured
> by experience. (p. 501)

And finally, not to forget the behaviorists and their next of kin the neo-behaviorists. First Watson:

> It is the scientific duty of psychology to establish laws and
> principles for the *"control of human action."* Man is thus
> fundamentally a responder, he is not a creator of aspirations
> or goals toward which he can direct his own behavior...those

> who place a mentalistic control in man "get lost in the sophistry of 'foresight' and 'end'." What then is personality? It is the "end" product of our habit systems. (p. 286)

And lastly, Skinner:

> ...man is controlled by his environmental circumstances. We are all shaped each day, behaving this way or that contingent upon the reinforcements which emanate from our environment.... "Men will never become originating centers of control, because their behavior will itself be controlled, but their role as mediators may be extended without limit." The nonteleological heritage of behaviorism is thus kept intact. We must look to sources outside the individual man to find observable reasons ...for why he behaves as he does. (p. 290)

There sure *seems* to be evidence in the foregoing "explanations" to support those writers who claim that *the* meaning of personality is that there is *no* (one) meaning of personality. However, if we look again I think we can see that this claim—aside from its inanity—is simply not true.

In fact by adding a few words to Dr. Branden's formulation we can include all of the theorizing about personality under one "roof". Consider: Personality is a product of the manner in which human beings *respond*—within the context of *existence*—to *human nature*.

Now that we have everybody under one "roof" lets ask them to speak for themselves, "so to speak" by enjoining them to answer *three* questions.

*   *   *

Good morning Dr. Freud. I see you and your fellow analysts—good morning Mr. Brill, Mr. Dollard. Where is Miller?...all the way down at the other end of the hangar?...oh, with Skinner and company. Yes, I agree we should've rented a larger hangar for our sale. But we figured if you could get two 747's in here you *should* be able to get all the personality theorizers in. Yes, I know we forgot to tell them *not* to drag their friends along. Oh well, I can see that everybody is managing to get their display booths and wares set up. I think that when they do there will be enough isle space for me to walk around and interview some of them. No, it's humanly impossible for me to interview them *all*. We only have the hangar rented until four this afternoon. Excuse me a moment. I see some existentialists and phenomenologists over there arguing whether or not the booth they've set up is really there. Yes I'll be back to talk to you guys.

Good morning—Kierkegaard isn't it?—let me assure you that the booth is real. Here, give me your hand. Feel that post? Good, solid American thermoplastic. Yes it does feel smooth and sort of sensuous doesn't it. I don't think you guys have time to bicker and argue right now. The doors open at 9 o'clock sharp and we expect a crowd of customers to come spilling in here looking for some new personality products to buy. Yes it is terrible isn't it. It seems they don't make personality like they used to. Seems you used to be able to get by for several years on a few simple traits. But in a way that's a cynical view. Personally I still think there are some damn good, quality buys around. In fact that's one reason why we set up this annual potpourri clearance sale. We of course didn't expect *this* big a turn out. Maybe next year we can schedule it to occur "simultaneously" in several of the domed stadiums throughout our city. Yes, I do remember when there was *only* one. Excuse me Mr. Kierkegaard, Mr. Husserl, I see Jung is motioning to me. He must've overheard me use the word "simultaneous" and wants to know what we were discussing.

We were just talking about the sale Carl. No, nobody is trying to steal your views on synchronicity. Yes—excluding that one and a good many of your other "theoretical" ones—I'd agree some of your products are OK, but some aren't either. Better than Freud's? Yes I agree, but that isn't necessarily a compliment. Carl, you'll have to excuse me, it's five minutes to nine, I have to get set up. The recording crew is getting impatient and the people are ready to break the doors down. No, we're not giving any opening speeches. We'll just let the people in and after they've dispersed throughout the hangar I'll come around to interview you. No, if you're with a customer I'll wait 'til you are not busy. Here, take this…It's a list of the *three* questions I'll be asking you to comment on. The only ground rules are that you must a) answer to the best of your ability and b) make each answer as concise and to the point as is possible. Yes, you do have to answer it within the framework of the given formulation for the concept of personality. No, you are *not* allowed to say, see Volumes 1 through 10 for my answer to *that* question. What are we going to do with the answers? We are going to analyze them—along with the implied claims made for each person's products—and publish the results in an annual *Guide to Personality Products—a consumer's perspective.* It doesn't seem right to you? Why. You know that this age of the free market of ideas can only survive *if* it stays free. Yes you old timers do have it tough; the new guys *do make your products appear as antiquated as they are.*

But you must remember they are competing with some pretty entrenched ways. You must remember that they have to persuade and *convince*, but you old timers only had to cash in on centuries worth of tradition. You know how the old line goes: A horse and buggy was good enough for grandpa, so who the hell needs a car? Well, you are free to die with your old slogans. But I invite you to notice: Modern man is on the move, and he is a move 'n out…and up!

Say Billy! Will you get my portable recorder set up. I'm going to take a few minutes break, then I want to mingle and interview Freud, Jung, Adler, the phenomenologists, existentialists and *maybe* some of the others…oh ya, I almost forgot: Skinner and company also.

Yes Dr. Freud, I am back just as I promised. Yes, it's a *terrific* turnout. Though I can't help but notice you seem to have more helpers at your booth than customers. Yes, the day *is* still early. You've had a chance to review the questions? Good, let's get started then: What do *you* mean by the words "human nature"?

Vel…you see…to me human nature means those aspects about mankind that nobody but nobody—not even me—can change. They can't change them because God or something made 'em. But what they can do is *add* some of their own in an attempt to improve on God's botches. For example, when I was a youngin, like yourself, the old timers said man by his nature was sinful: they called it Original Sin. Vel…the Venetian women I treated seemed to bear this out but what they were having a hard time with was *accepting* this inevitable aspect of their natures as humans—some of the men, for some reason, seemed to have an easier time at it. So. What I did was give them the same concept only in a different package. As you know I called it the id. Ya…some did buy it didn't they. And look around you, some, believe it or not, still are. But then my id was not all they got. I also gave them the superego, the ego and most importantly: sex. Though *strictly* speaking God, or nature depending on your conceptual perspective gave 'em the id and superego and a crippled ego, and even sex—to procreate with. I merely described what I saw as the interrelationships between these imperfect natural gifts and tried to show how man attempts, with the aid of his crippled ego, to make his organism *work* in the real world. Now, if you consider the axiomatic fact that consciousness *comes from* unconsciousness then you can easily understand the key to natural man and un-natural man: natural man is unconscious, unnatural man conscious. Therefore, since everybody knows that natural is good and un-natural not so good, we can understand the source of human problems: sex.

Ah...Excuse me for just a moment Dr. Freud, but it seems to me that your line of conscious reasoning is crooked.

Ya...so what? Your *response* merely proves my point: you think too much lad. And as a consequence you have a stilted personality. Why don't you "buy" my personality products that I've invented based on my views of human nature. Buy 'em that is *and* use 'em. After all, look what they've done for Allen Konigsberg.

Well Dr. Freud, maybe consciousness did come from unconsciousness and then again maybe it didn't. But let's stay with it for now. You used the word *response* in regards to my *reaction* to your non-sequitur. That's very interesting because it brings us to the second question: What do *you* mean by the word *respond*? Remember now, I mean *how* you use it in relation to our formulation concerning personality: as a product of the way humans *respond* to human nature. And I guess in your case I'm saying: respond to unconsciousness.

Vel...since I've tied human nature to unconsciousness and since a real scientist doesn't *overuse* non-sequiturs I'd have to consciously conclude that he responds unconsciously.

I see, but—

Vel let me elaborate. You know I am consciously 'avare of an unconscious feeling that you are distorting my distor;...oops, I slipped, I *mean* you are twisting my words. By *respond* I mean deterministically but *not* in the historical, mechanistic sense of the term. You see that old mechanistic deterministic mentality—as my old friend Reich, who by the way couldn't come here today because he didn't really feel invited, would say—is wrong. Human beings aren't planets and they aren't apples falling out of trees on to other "apples" nor for that matter are they gear boxes. But *still* their responses are determined. I would say, not physically determined, but psychologically determined. You see unconscious natural man has an id, and conscious, not 100% natural man, has an ego and a superego. The promptings of the immorally, amoral originally sinful id is the *source* of human action. We can't *directly* see this source in others, but if we have been raised "right" we can relate to this "fact" introspectively. And we can of course see the consequent of this source via peoples actual actions in reality. That is, we can reason our way to it in a socially acceptable manner if we are *afraid* to challenge the theologians. So what more can I say: take an unconscious organism and throw him for three centuries into a pot of bubbling life experiences and he'll come our hard boiled, albeit with soft, pliable and rubbery innards—it's predetermined. Speaking of which…I'm getting hungry. What's your last question?

What to *you* mean by existence?

Actually I wasn't too concerned with that term. Like an animal, I take existence for granted. Even though I think he's highly over rated, I'd recommend you ask Kant about it. He'd probably have more to say. Or if he's not here ask some of his phenomenologist friends or even their buddies the existentialists. You know, earlier this morning I heard those guys actually debating whether or not their display booth "really" was real. That *really* makes me laugh…In fact…that cathartic laughter loosens me up enough to let you in on a little secret of mine. While those dimwits were arguing whether it is axiomatic that existence *comes from* non-existence *or* whether non-existence naturally evolves from existence I did just like my ex-friend Reich did to the reductive materialists: I beat 'em to the punch. For centuries, and I knew this but didn't let on, men were taught by men that existence *comes from* non-existence. So, rather than waste time laying a psychic roadbed that was already there I merely paved over it. I told people—though in the main implicitly—that consciousness *comes from* unconsciousness*!* Based on me and my followers' sales receipts over many decades I'd have to conclude that they bought it. What do you think?

I think I have to break away here. I've noticed a lot of couched looks from the other participants. I think they are feeling slighted and rejected. Good-bye Dr. Freud. See you again next year?

Well Carl you don't seem to be too busy right now. Would *you* like to comment on the questions? OK, good. First off, what do *you* mean by "human nature"?

Since I was impressed with the German philosopher Immanuel Kant, Herr interviewer, I would say human nature is *that* in humans which I say is natural. And since modern man is further from his natural roots than is primitive man, primitive man is natural man and modern man is un-natural man. For example, to live in caves, scrounge for food and fear the dark is natural. But to efficiently produce your food so that you'll free up some of your scrounging hours to discover electricity for lighting up your nights with, is un-natural. In spite of this though modern man is lucky. He is lucky because he *inherits* from primitive, natural man all the prototype forms of being human. These prototypes or archetypal contents as I call them are proven to exist in man by considering, as one example, the following fact. The wheel was invented in many different cultures, cultures that were isolated and never even came into contact with each other until many many years after they, the cultures, invented the wheel. The only way to explain this is to conclude that through heredity the human mind—on an extremely deep, what you might call "collective unconscious", level—contains the "wheel" archetype. So. Even though much of my theorizing is incomprehensible let me explain it to your little brain so that you might be able to comprehend it. Don't feel too badly if you can't grasp it. In order to grasp it fully really requires many many years of study. It especially requires a thorough indoctrination of Kant's ways. Kant of course is better understood if you first thoroughly condition your mind to Plato—much in the same way Astronomy is easier to grasp if you first thoroughly understand Ptolemy. Since, Herr interviewer, I am into analogies let me finish my explanation of the collective unconscious with its archetypal contents by telling you a little anecdote I once heard. I don't remember whose anecdote it is, nor if it is literally true. Consequently, I can't give proper credit to the person who observed it or invented it as the case may be, but it goes something like this.

    A famous sculptor was commissioned by a small, but quite prosperous town to produce a stone stature for their city park. Early the following summer the sculptor obtained a large block of marble, had it positioned in the park and commenced his hammering. The loud crack, crack, wack! of the hammer encouraging the steel chisel to cut, crack, wack away pieces of marble became a penetrating sound throughout the town. Its echo brought many a young child running to see what exciting things were going on. Eventually though, the daily tapping and pounding became familiar, and most people left the sculptor alone with his work. Except one. One small boy came back each morning to watch the statue unfold. After many weeks of long days and some nights the statue was complete. It was to be presented at a ceremony the following day. Since everyone had seen the small boy watching every morning, he was given the honor of unveiling the statue—the local newspaper editor thought it would be a cute touch and a human interest story all rolled into one. Following much solemnity and inane speeches the statue was unveiled. It was a statue of a magnificent Lion. The people applauded. The Mayor asked the little boy if he had any questions for the sculptor. "Say mister", the boy said, "how did you know that Lion was inside that chunk of stone?" The people looked at each other for a moment. Then they decided they were gleeful and applauded vigorously. The boy was quoted far and near. No one ever heard from the sculptor again.

Now, Herr interviewer, that a little boy could put into words what centuries worth of human beings were conditioned to feel is, on the surface only of course, truly remarkable.

What that boy's question does is to prove Plato correct, give Kant a pat on the back for a job well done, and me additional evidence for my theory of archetypes. Plato said that the essence of things exist in another dimension and only some very special people—like Plato and a few select others—can intuitively see this essence. Kant said the same thing but with a different emphasis: he focused on *those* who didn't have the special powers to see Plato's archetypes; i.e. on 99.99999 percent of the human race. And then he concluded that the human by its nature can only see the chunk of stone which is a distorted view of the "real" Lion. Kant and his followers went further than this of course but I can see Mein interviewing friend that you are getting eager to move on so let me conclude by demonstrating how this is more "evidence" for *my* archetypes. Archetypes are—as I use the term—"recurring modes of apprehending" and since men have for centuries on end apprehended human achievement in philosophically conditioned ways I would have to conclude that the little boy was exhibiting evidence of a genetically inherited archetypal philosophy. In this particular case the philosophy of "undercutting human achievement".

I'm not sure Mr. Jung that you've answered the question. But then I'm not sure you've ever answered *any* theoretical questions. In fact I'm still wondering why—since reality is an absolute and the wheel such a simple device—why ten million cavemen didn't all think of it at the same time?

Nonetheless, let's try another question. What do *you* mean by existence?

That's simple, mein friend. I mean what Kant meant, Schopenhauer meant and Plato meant.

That's your answer?

Ya...*that* your third question?

Ah...No. My third question is: What do *you* mean by the concept respond?

By respond I mean how modern man *reacts* to his inherited collective unconscious with its innate archetypal contents as he is driven by the individuation instinct to grow from a baby to an individuated adult. As a baby man's mind is immersed in a puddle of mystical constructs and his body in an electrical swamp of instincts. Man *reacts* to these instincts as they energize him with psychic energy pushing him to "do something"—be it *get* food, *get* sex or *get* individuated. But he *reacts* in a predetermined fashion. This fashion is predetermined by the innate structure of the human psyche; particularly by the innate structure of the unconscious, though somewhat also by the innate structure of the itsy, bitsy little conscious mind containing predominantly, though not exclusively, the ego. And that's about it.

That's it! It sounds somewhat incomple—

Well, Herr interviewer, I do have more to say but it has to be off the record. If you want to hear it switch off your recorder.

(Click)

Now you may have noticed that my theory of man does not employ the antiquated mind-body antagonist theory of the ancients. But what you might not have noticed is that it does employ a mind-mind antagonist theory. This is the main way in which I differ from my intellectual forefathers. In fact it is the essence of my unique, individuation efforts. My contemporary brothers and sisters were fools. They failed to recognize that down through the ages various scientific/conceptual discoveries about philosophy in general and the human body in particular were increasing at an alarming rate—in spite of Immanuel's efforts. So fast in fact that Modern Man was finding it more and more difficult to comprehend those incomprehensible concepts of mysticism that were in vogue and would stay there as long as the mind-body dichotomy was kept alive. So, since man's psyche was still a big unknown to most people I decided to keep the *spirit* of my forefathers alive by moving from the mind/body split to a mind-mind split.

Man's unconscious mind and his conscious mind are antagonists by nature. And this is readily observed in men's *reactions,* or responses if you like. Most men's reactions to life give you the impression that they are being tossed about in a box! 'Vel they are! That "box" is their psyche which is principally an integrating machine of a rather unique kind: one that integrates contradictions! Now there are of course some who argue that you absolutely *cannot* integrate the non-integrable. But what do they know! Humans have been doing it for centuries; or at least giving the *impression* that they have been. Though I grant you, Modern Man is having a harder time doing it. In fact that's modern man's problem. In his search for his mystical soul he doesn't have the proper "tools" for integrating the contradictory opposites of his nature. That's where Jungian theoretical psychology comes in: its "products" are the tools needed to accomplish the task of integrating into a non-contradictory whole the contradictions of Mysticism with the non-contradictory aspects of Science. This of course is more of an epistemological issue than a psychological one. But in the long run you cannot separate the two. If men could only "see" the non-contradictory logic of my concept of psychic energy and of my notion of the transcendental function of the symbol they would be happy. They would be happy because they could finally feel the path they must take to integrate Science and Mysticism. My god son, do you realize what an achievement mein is?!? Philosophers for centuries have been trying the impossible, and as one would expect: have been failing at it. I (and possibly the Born again Christians also) have done the impossible. We have integrated the non-integrable!

Hold it! Hold it! Hold it , Mr. Jung. It isn't fair to tell me this. I don't want to know it. I have the responsibility of editing our product guide for consumers and as a consequence am put in a heck of a spot. I now have a big, big conflict that entails opposing, contradictory commitments. On the one hand I have to honor my agreement to keep your off the record comments "off the record" and on the other hand I have to be honest in *my* assessment of your personality products. Oh me oh my, what am I to do?

'Vel, Herr boy, I recommend you go deeply into Jungian T 'n T—Theory & Therapy that is. We can show you *how* to reconcile all your innate oppositional forces. All you have to do is learn all the formal *fallacies* of deductive and inductive logic and then use them as the *means* of validating your knowledge. That is, switch definitions whenever you feel like it, equivocate, evade, carry analogies only far enough to suit your purposes and fill your persona with a thousand smiling, smirking masks that you can wear at your—reactive—will's desire to convince the world at large and yourself in particular that contradictions exist and that to be a nice guy is a virtue but to speak your *mind* in a College paper a vice—a hideously dangerous vice.

OK, Mr. Jung, I've had enough. Stop it! You know this isn't the first time I've allowed you to dump your projections on me. I've got a duty to discharge here so I don't have any more time for you. I've got to move on…Say, is that Rychlak over there near the entrance? What's that he's carrying in his hand? It looks like a bucket. Excuse me, I want to go see what he's up to. I thought all he did was to non-judgmentally put down on textbook pages the minuscule particulars of all the various personality theorizers. I didn't know he was actually interested in their products. Excuse me Mr. Jung I've got to move on.

Hey!…Mr. Rychlak…Yes, over here. Just a minute, I'll come to you…What is that you are carryin—oh my god it's a pail of worms. What in the world are you doing with those?

I don't know you...Wait, are you that non-Rychlakian antagonistic reporter we've been hearing about. Well I happen to work here too. I'm in charge of customer contests and door prizes.

Ah...you mean the door prize is a...ah...bucket of worms?

No, it isn't...smarty-pants. It just so happens that this pail of worms is my idea for this years main event contest. Here...take this magnifying glass and look real closely at the bands on some of the worms. Do you see the tiny little red tag with a number on it? Well each worm has its own number. Look over there...there, behind you near the center of the hangar! See that circular stage with the big round table on it? Well, after lunch—at about 2 o'clock—we are going to have a contest for the customers to try and win some money at: first place winner gets a thousand bucks, second place a hundred and third, the booby prize; they get the pail of worms.

What exactly is the contest?

Well do you remember last year whe—no you weren't around then so you wouldn't remember. Anyway, last year Carl concocted some Jungian personality pills using some incantations and a pot 'o some alchemists secret brew...Yes, they were hard to swallow. That was the problem. So we hired the Japanese to reproduce them in a miniaturized form. Well, while they were doing it they decoded the chemical formulas for the various traits and figured out how to make Freudian personality pills, Sullivanian trait pills, Adlerian trait pills-Rogerian-Skinnerian-Kellierian-you name 'itierian personality pills. So, I hired them to also miniaturize a bunch of clear plastic 8 oz tumblers for me. Here, see these in the palm of my hand? There's about a hundred of them in there. Well I've got a whole box of them and I'm going to fill them with water and give each little worm one. Then I go over to my chart here...here, this chart here. See it? Isn't it neat? I had the behavioral science statisticians prepare it for me. What they did was plug into their computer's random number generator and generate a random pairing of worm number to personality trait pill. See here. Here's an example. Worm number 1,317 has the bluish-green pill which is...as we can see here if we follow the chart across to the comment column...a personality trait characteristic of those who failed to resolve the Oedipal complex. But wait, there's a footnote here. We then go to the bottom of the chart...and it says: bluish-green means as a parent-child sexual conflict in the Freudian sense but greenish-blue means in the Frommian sense of a parent-child authoritarian conflict. Well, anyway I'm sure you get the idea. Each worm downs one pill. Then I take the whole pail full and dump 'em on the table and let them dance around and move through their behaviors. The customers then study the worms behaviors and write down which particular theorist's trait the particular numbered worm is emitting. And whoever gets the most number correct wins the prizes! Sounds like a fun game, ya?

How are they going to read those tiny little numbers on the red tag around the worm's neck?

I didn't say the game was easy. If their ability to "see" is *that* bad, they'll just have to guess…I guess. Say, it's past noon already. I've got to get something to eat and then get set up. You'll have to excuse me.

Hey Billy! Come here. Take my recorder and put in some fresh batteries will you. These interviews are taking longer than I thought. I wanted to walk through all the displays myself and see if there's anything new being offered. But I guess I won't have time. In fact if I hope to get several more interviews in before four I won't even be able to break for lunch. But I am going to get in one cigarette. Change the batteries will you please and get it right back to me…

Thanks Billy. It seems as if all the theorizers took off for lunch. Except possibly over there…down there at the far end of the hangar. Yes, by those two booths that are tied together with what looks like old pieces of rope. Oh! Of course…I bet I know who they are. Those guys never take a break. It's the behaviorists and the neo-behaviorists. Excuse me Billy, I'm going down there.

Excuse me sir. I need to get through here so I can interview some of the people up front. Yes, there sure is a lot of people gathered around here. What's so interesting anyway? It sounds like the goings on at a two-ring circus without bleachers. What are you laughing at sir?…Oh, you *used* to work for them. Sorry—no offense intended to *you* sir. Say, maybe I could interview you. By the looks of this crowd I'll never get through.

Well I've been going around to each of the displays and asking the proprietors *three* questions concerning their personality products. Why. Here read this list. Because we publish an annual consumers guide and this year we wanted to have one devoted exclusively to personality products. So we thought we'd try having an annual clearance sale whereby we could get all the theorizers to come to us and they in turn could have an outlet for presenting their new products and an opportunity for ridding themselves of their junk. What's that sir? You don't think it's fair to the customers who think that any product is a good product simply because it's offered for sale? Oh, I don't agree with that sir. I think that if people know *what* they are "buying" that they are very capable of picking and choosing the products they need. Oh, no, I agree that we all could be *better* shoppers. But I think that that is each and every person's own responsibility; to make themselves better shoppers that is…I wonder if judges are good shoppers?…Oh, nothing sir I was just thinking out loud. Say, do you want to be interviewed? You do? Good. Before we start I would like you to first give me a brief background of yourself. Then later on when I'm editing my tapes for our *Guide* I can weigh your experience and background into my evaluations of the behaviorists products. What's that? Yes, I suppose that would be okay. Excuse me for just a moment then.

Nichol. Why don't you break for lunch now and meet me over by the existentialists' booth in about an hour. This guy agreed to be interviewed for the behaviorist perspective but he didn't want to be video taped. He said it would be okay to tape record the conversation but no cameras. Why don't you take Billy with you, I don't think he has anybody to go to lunch with.

OK Josh, I'll meet you over by the existentialist's booth in one hour. See you then…Hey Billy!…Over here…You want to go to lunch with me?…Just a sandwich. OK, get your coat; I'll wait.

Would you please hurry up Billy. We've got about five minutes to make it back…He said he'd meet us over by the phenomenologist…or existentialist…or whatever. I can't keep those two separate. They're in the same area anyway. I know *about* where it is and I'm sure we'll see Josh when we get in the vicinity.

I know we are a little late Josh, but that damn Billy is a *slow* eater. Say, you look kind of pale. How'd the interview go?

I do feel kinda sick, Nichol. That guy had a story to tell that's…its…oh I don't know. It's unbelievable is what it is. He had me in tears one minute, laughing convulsively the next and then an instant later standing in stark terror at the implications he was spewing forth. He mixed Science Fiction with fact and fact with fantasy. He talked about demons and demigods and then flung accusations at me that pis—that made me angry. He told me that providing a place for these theorizers to pretend that their views on anything were viable products was a slap on the face to those theorizers whose views *do* represent legitimate products. He said if I truly and honestly was interested in what was going on inside the designing rooms of the personality manufacturers I should read a book called *Atlas…something* by Ayn…somebody. Have you ever heard of it? You have? Then he said I should also check out the personality products this one guy had invented—Nathan somebody he said. Check 'em out, that is he said, *if* you are truly interested in seeing what *is* possible. He claimed that he had seen 'em *all* and that none compared. That in itself is hard to believe and makes me suspicious. Do you realize how many quotable "authorities" on personality issues there are—not to even mention the number on psychology in general. I 'betcha 8 out of 10 books written on personality and/or psychology issues have bibliographies that are longer than the main text...Yes, it is a slight exaggeration Nichol, I know, but...You should have heard this guy. He was arrogant and pretentious...and amusing and captivating...and stimulating! Boy is he stimulating. You know Nichol that's a very rare quality these days...stimulating— being stimulating to *human* thinking. Very few people can do it. And fewer still that can do it well. Boy! Do I admire those who can. This guy said he didn't like writing—too slow he said. But...did he like talking! I had to switch my tape recorder to a faster speed in order to get down everything he said. He talked about the time while he was in the employ of the behaviorists that he along with several others were assigned the task of creating a core idea around which it would be possible to discredit introspective mentalities in the presence of Physicists. They originally had included philosophers also but soon discovered that they think too much and so they settled only for the Natural Scientist. Well what the committee came up with was a little gem called *anthropomorphizing*. This guy had the responsibility of packaging and marketing it. He knew that educated people tend to like clean, smooth eloquent lines—like those of a fine sports car. So he thought about it for awhile and came up with something very simple. As he explained it...he said for many many years the natural scientist has held a dim view of assigning attributes of living things to non-living things...of anthropomorphizing. So he reasoned it's an easy and legitimate step to get psychology students to realize that assigning human characteristics to inanimate objects is a no-no. And then here he paused a bit and shook his head in disbelief. You know, he said, it still amazes me beyond belief to see so many college kids buying the anthropomorphizing package. Don't they know that assigning *human* characteristics to *human* beings is NOT anthropomorphizing? Can't they see the way the pseudo-scientists use it? Then he paused again and looked at me like I wasn't getting the point. Then he quoted, verbatim—can you believe it, verbatim!—an example from p. 364 of Rychlak. Here let me rewind my recorder and play it for you.

(Click)—...

...—(Click) We may start with the assumption that every drop of rain in some way or other gets to the ocean ... Anthropomorphizing this condition we may say that it is the *purpose* of every drop of rain to get to the ocean. Of course, this only means that virtually every drop *does* get there eventually...Falling from the cloud it may strike the leaf of a tree, and drop from one leaf to another until it reaches the ground. From here it may pass under or on the surface of the soil to a rill, then to a brook, river, and finally to the sea. Each stage, each fall from one leaf to the next, may be designated as a *means* toward the final end…Human behavior is merely a complication of the same factors. (Click)

Well I started to say that that example was more of a debate over the teleological issue, the issue of acting for purposes versus reacting or responding to effects and so on. And you know what his response was? He said there is no significant difference between the Mystics and the Behaviorists: one mixes a bubbling brew in their pots and the other mixes issues. Well, that didn't sound like a very scientific answer to me. And besides, it sounded like he was sort of anthropomorphizing so I ignored him and encouraged him to move on to our question about existence.

He said: it exists. I said what? He said, existence exists; it's axiomatic…self-evident. I started to laugh, but caught myself. You can't just say it exists and that it's self-evident, I said. The phenomenologists and existentialists and a few other theorizers, I said, have written untold volumes on the subject of non-existence in their attempts to derive existence…to *prove* existence. You can't just blurt out that it is self-evident that Existence exists and only existence exists. And you know what he said? Why? He said: why? Well I said you just can't that's why. Then I said, well maybe it's self-evident to you but it's not self-evident to me…Prove it to me I said. Then he hesitated and said: "I can't". Well I says there ya have it. If you cannot prove that it's self-evident to me then it must not be. Then he said no that's not precisely what it means. To be self-evident means, he said, that it needs only itself as the evidence. Well I said I disagree…I disagree that things can be self-evident. I think you just *invented* the notion of self-evident in order to trick me. Then you know what he said, he said *prove* that you and I are disagreeing. I said what? He said *prove* that you and I are right now disagreeing. Well I said I can't really *prove* it…But I says, to anybody observing us it would be obvious that we are disagreeing, I don't really need to prove it. He then said, what if that hypothetical somebody didn't agree that we were disagreeing; that he needed somebody from somewhere to somehow *prove* to him that we were disagreeing. What would you say then, he says. Well I don't know I says…I guess I'd say open your ears and eyes…look at us, listen to us…It's Self-evident that we are disagreeing, what's the matter with you…can't you *see* it?! Do you want to know *my* views on *human nature?* he asks.

Well Nichol I think I made a mistake. I said yes.

Personality, psycho-hermeneutics and self understanding

He said human nature are those aspects about human beings that are timeless, immutable, unchanging and universal to the species. For example he said all humans are mortal. All humans are physical organisms made up of cells and organs and organ systems. No humans are born with a College transcript in their background. They are all, each and everyone born tabula rasa he says. And here I stopped him. I says *prove* it! And he said all human beings are conscious organisms. And I yelled, prove it! And he said Consciousness is conscious…it is axiomatic…self-evident. And I said oh no, not again. And he said—very very firmly: yes. And I said is there anymore of these self-evident primaries or is *everything* self-evident? And he said yes—one—and no—only three. And I said what? And he said: A is A, a thing is what it is, it cannot be A and non-A at the same time and in the same respect—it's axiomatic. And I said what does that have to do with human nature. Well he said humans are things too and they can't be human at 4 o'clock one Saturday afternoon and non-human at 4 o'clock on that same day. They are what they are, they have identity. And I say ya, so what? Identity is not identification. He said I quite agree, but identification simply means in this instance a human's *view* of its own identity. Of an identity that is immutable and therefore independent of any particular human's wishes or fears. And then *I* said very very firmly; prove it. You make it sound, I said, as if humans play no part in creating their own identity, that they simply are what they are, much like a rock is what it is and that's all it is. And here he paused for a long, long time. You know, he then started, you have touched upon an issue that is extremely difficult for me to explain…in my own words that is. The best I *could* do right now is to mouth the words of certain others who have—through their life's works—provided *the* answers to many of the fundamental questions about human nature. Well, I says, then I guess you are stumped. Hardly, he says, if you want to hear more shut off your recorder.

Well Nichol, what was I to do. I shut the damn thing off.

He started by saying that he had had a life times worth of feelings and then some put into words by a band of roving scholars who were at one time led by a woman but had, many years ago, disbanded. He said he personally didn't even know they had until many years after it happened. He said that during the ten years he knew them they used to come into the town where he lived and conduct open debates on all sorts of philosophical and psychological issues. He said he spent untold numbers of sleepless nights because of their penetrating words. He said also that on more than one occasion the local religious and political authorities tried desperately to run the band out of town. Then after eight years of failures these local authorities made one last desperate effort to rid their town of these foreign invaders. They reasoned that if the invaders had no one to attend their debates they would not return. So they rounded up all the people who regularly attended the debates—as it turned out he said 90% of them were children—and locked them up inside various abandoned buildings located throughout the town. Then a select group of dedicated citizens systematically went through each building and shot the inhabitants. That's what he said. They simply came in, in the dark of the night toting double barrel, singled barrel and sawed off shotguns and shot 'em. He said that when they came into the building where he and some of his friends were they gave the impression that they had come to set them free. And then here he stopped. He paused for a long time and said, you know this story is too long to tell here. As you can obviously tell I made it out and for right now that's all that is important. Let's go back to talking about human nature.

Well Nichol I could've shot him right there. He ignored my requests to continue the story and went into *his* understanding of those *other's* views on human nature.

He said that at one point he thought about elaborating on the hypothesis that the psyche is an internal obstacle course and torture chamber designed to eliminate all but *one* of a host of internally generated eidetic personalities. With this one personality then emerging as the heroic and stronger one and continuing its reign for life in the form of the ego. But he said it sounded to metaphorical and would probably be making the same mistake as many other theorizers: elevating the idiosyncratic to the universal without proper concern for truth. So, he said, he volitionally decided to stick, for the time being, with the universal formulations of his significant band of others.

Human nature he said can be divided into two spheres: the metaphysical and the man-made. The metaphysical sphere contains all those things that man cannot change including the fact that he has the power of volition. That is, that an individual is the causal agent in the choice to think or not to think. In the fundamental sense there are no antecedent factors that causes him to think or not to think. This power to think or not to think is not an omnipotent nor omniscient power. That is, the choice to think does not guarantee success, but the choice to not think does guarantee failure. Choosing to drive a car with your eyes open doesn't guarantee you won't have an accident, but choosing to drive with them closed does…Say Nichol?…Are you listening to me? You keep looking past me, like you are looking at something else. What's the matter?

Oh, nothing...I was just looking at the commotion going on over there...there, behind you near the center of the hangar. What are all those people gathering around for?

Oh that! That's just a contest...it's for customers only. I'll tell you about it latter. Do you want to hear the rest of this now or not?

No. I really am not interested Josh. I happen to know who the people are that your interviewee is trying to explain. I am very familiar with their writings and believe me the originals are infinitely more interesting.

You know them Nichol? Who are they? Tell me about them. I want to know more.

Not now. Not here. It would be more exciting leaning over a steaming plate of broiled lobster with you pouring refills from a bottle of Dom Perion. Meet me downtown tonight at Biberes. I'll pay for the lobster and you can cover the wine. Right now I'm going over to watch the contest. I've had enough for one day.

Okay Nichol. I'll meet you later. I need to summarize the day's impressions anyway. If anything comes up I'll be in the office, otherwise I'll see you later...

Well, let me see now. I may as well dictate my thoughts on tape. Later then I can edit them for our *Guide*. (Click)—

Testing...1, 2, 3...ah...testing, 1, 2...

(Click, rewind)

(Click)-Testing...1, 2, 3...ah...testing, 1, 2...(Click)

(Click)-Well, it's working...Let me see now...what am I going to say?...Seems every time I put a microphone in front of my *mouth* my *mind* goes blank...Let's see now...There sure seems to be a lot of diversity in the personality products...ah...there also seems to be a lot about personality that is *not* self-evident. In fact, it even seems as if a lot of personality theory is about what personality is *not*...about...ah, that doesn't sound clear. What am I trying to say?...Is personality theory about "personality", that is "person-ality"..."personal identity"? Or is much of it about something else? From "talking" with Freud and Jung and even from many of the other theorizers I get the feeling that they are talking about something else. That they use "personality" as a euphemism for something else...ah, remember that psychology *used* to be subsumed under philosophy; that the idea of an "unconscious" wasn't even made explicit until around 1700 AD, though many said it was implicit in the writings of the ancients. I don't mean to imply here that it isn't "real"; that is, that it isn't really a part of human nature, because I know it is. But, is it *what* "they" say it is? Today's experiences leave me wondering. I get the distinct feeling that a lot of the old

theorizers were actually frustrated philosophers…Or if not, then perhaps a new *breed* of philosopher. But, even if they are, so what. So what does it have to do with evaluating the various products and the theories from which they were derived? For now, not much…I guess…Well then what went on here today? Did you establish that personality is a *product* of responding *to* human nature rather than *to* life experiences? In a way I feel more as if I've established that *personality theories* are a product of the manner in which personality "theorizers" responded to human nature. Actually if the latter is true then the Branden formulation is true and if the Branden formulation is true the latter is true: "personality theorizers" are people too. But…so what. Who cares anyway? Peoples own personal-identity is sacred…always has been…always will be…maybe…if the behaviorists don't succeed in *creating* a population of robotic pragmatists: little R2 D2's, but *without* any personality. Burrr…what a horrible thought…You know what I'm beginning to think? I think that for right now there isn't much more I have to say on or think about this subject—the tapes "speak" for themselves. I'll just go through them, edit them and transcribe 'em for the introductory pages to the *Guide*. And then, *maybe* at next years clearance sale I'll bring in the *second* half of Dr. Branden's formulation…that is, that personality is a product of *and a reflection of* the manner in which one responds to human nature.
    Click.

Reference List

Branden, N. *The Psychology of Self-Esteem.* Los Angeles: Nash, 1969.

Hall, C.S. *A primer of Freudian Psychology.* New York: New American Library, 1954.

Hall, C. S. & Nordby, V. J. *A Primer of Jungian Psychology.* New York: New American Library, 1973.

Liebert, R. M., & Spiegler, M. D. *Personality* (third edition). Homewood, Illinois: The Dorsey Press, 1970, 1974 and 1978.

Neel, A. F. *Theories of Psychology A Handbook* (second edition). New York Halsted Press, 1977.

Rand, Ayn *Atlas Shrugged.* New York: Random House, 1957.

Rychlak, J. F. *Introduction to Personality and Psychotherapy.* Boston: Houghton Mifflin, 1973.

"Biberes"

Rand, Ayn *Introduction to Objectivist Epistemology* (fourth printing). New York: The Objectivist, Inc., 1973.

Peikoff, Leonard *Introduction to Logic,* Tape series, 10-Lecture course, 1973.

Branden, N. *The Psychology of Self-Esteem.* Los Angeles: Nash, 1969.

Rand, Ayn *Atlas Shrugged.* New York: Random House, 1957.

MORE (not part of original, but added here):

Rand, Ayn: *everything else* by her.

Branden, Nathaniel: *everything else* by him.

Peikoff, Leonard: *everything else* by him too.

Objectivists, other: *everything* by them.

So here we are. We have come full circle and are now back to the need to evaluate Dr. Hans J. Eysenck's pp. 279, 280 and 281 of "Mind and Brain Sciences in the 21st Century".

Are we any richer for having taken the particular path we did take to get back to where we started? What, if anything, do we now know that we didn't know when we started on this path? We know that there are a large number of theories of personality out there in the "world of psychology". We know that most of the "authorities" on personality believe you can't define personality precisely enough to have *one* single definition of personality. And we know "they" do this in the face of Dr. Nathaniel Branden's *one* definition of personality: "Your Personality is the *product* and *reflection* of *your* response to [immutable] human nature." This definition means that whether or not you accept that you have a human nature doesn't have any bearing on the truth or falsity of the *definition*, only on your personality. You have a human nature (and so do I) and you respond to it (and so do I) today as you did yesterday and as you *expect* you will and as you *will* tomorrow, and the sum total of all these responses is *your* personality—as it is for Dr. Branden and Dr. Eysenck and everybody, qua *individual* responder and evaluator: *responder-to-immutable-human nature and evaluator-of-those-responses*. And since it is a fact of human nature that human beings have volition, *personality* is as changeable as is any and all things that you play a part in creating. *Equally changeable* in the sense of "is possible", *not* in the sense of "degree" of ease or of difficulty.

We also know that there is more than one way to *evaluate* the writings of others.[157] Are there proper or correct ways to so evaluate, or that is "interpret" others writings? If there is such a "proper" way, do the previous two dozen or so pages violate this "propriety"? That is, if some authoritarian figure comes along and says those two dozen pages are "just" *hermeneutics* is that *enough* for our minds to *reject* them out of hand?

Before *you* are done here this is a question you may have to answer (as in respond-to) for yourself.

The three pp. 279, 280 and 281 of Mind-Brain, are pp. 9, 10 and 11 of Hans J. Eysenck's 25 page article, "The Future of Psychology". And, *because of our path* back to here we can't help but wonder: *whose* Psychology will we be reading and talking about here?

---

[157] If your thought—as—you read this line was: "...there is more than one way ... to skin a cat ...", then you too are a cliché thinker and your only question is: how much am I this?

Personality, psycho-hermeneutics and self understanding 177

Before you *are* done here this is a question you *will* have to answer for yourself.

Out of the entire Mind-Brain book Dr. Eysenck comes across as the scientist's scientist but when he is evaluated on his own terms he looks more like a Dr. Robert Stadler type than does even Dr. Jerome Kagan whom we evaluate in the next section.

Page 279 is Dr. Eysenck's **Figure 15.2 Death from cancer, CHD [Coronary Heart Disease], and other causes in males high and low in degree of self-regulation** (Eysenck, 1994b). This figure purports to show that the highest proportions of these types of death were populated in the main with individuals who scored very low on a questionnaire given to measure "self regulation". The premise in this and his other graphs—Figures 15.3 and 15.4 on pp. 280 and 281, respectively—is that there is a healthy, autonomous personality and there is an unhealthy, presumably non-autonomous personality *that we are born with* and that the degree of "self regulation" present in a person is the degree to which that person has the autonomous, healthy personality and vice versa, a person measuring low in self-regulation means he or she is high in unhealth—born with—personalitywise speaking. Since Dr. Eysenck does not share the can't-define-anything "personality" of his colleagues we have to look at Dr. Eysenck's definition of *personality* to fully understand his scientific looking data plots (and give him a pat on the back for at least defining his terms—pat.).

His definition of personality is that it is a genetically inherited type structure.[v] And even though he goes to great lengths to "explain" that by "genetic" *he* does not mean, immutable, unchangeable as do those who invoke the genetics claim, "we" have to be careful. Since "genetics" means "way outside our control" any one who says otherwise should be suspected of being up to something even if we don't yet know *what* that something is. That is, our inner skeptic/curmudgeon—rightfully—raises a red flag and we are going to heed its warning.

Or, to state it more colorfully I should say: I smell a rat.

Or, to state it more scientifically if you prefer I could say: my *commonsense* sense of smell, smells a rat.

Dr. Eysenck does not hide the fact that his data in the three subject graphs comes from *prospective* studies. A prospective study means an *outcome,* say q, is predicted based on *hypothetical* reasoning (If p then q) and then tested to see if the outcome (q) holds up. Nothing unreasonable about this. He of course expects us as intelligent readers to know that if the test yields data that supports the hypothesis—which is what looks to be the case here—then the only thing one can conclude from the test is that one *cannot reject* the hypothesis based on our test of it. That is, if one gets the q that one expects one cannot conclude that the theory is proven, only that "so far" it is *not* dis-proven, therefore the hypothesis now has at least *one piece of evidence* (our test) that places it in the epistemological category of "is *possibly*" true.[158] This hypothesis testing is something that physical scientists in general and physicists in particular know very well and are very very good at it. Its value, qua *methodology*, was expressed best by Einstein when he said "...it only takes *one* experiment to prove me wrong...". So far—in Einstein's case— that experiment hasn't happened.[159]

So according to Dr. Eysenck, his protestations notwithstanding, we are *born—not* tabula rasa, but rather—with a healthy or unhealthy *personality* and if it weren't for philosophers and other anti-science thinkers, "psychology" would already be a legitimate science rather than *still* struggling to be taken seriously by the *physical* scientists.

Unfortunately for me he didn't say this on either p. 279 or 280 or 281. Rather he said it on p. 272 in his section titled: **Ordeal by Quackery.** Quoting him verbatim we read:

> Physical science did not spring suddenly our of nothing, like Athena from the head of Zeus; it was preceded by preparadigmatic, Aristotelian notions from which it had to liberate itself, a rejection popularly identified with Galileo and his battle with the Inquisition. Psychology in a similar manner had to battle (and still has to battle) with a commonsense psychology that is based, partly on experience, partly on literature.[vi]

If there was such a thing as *sin* I would say to *equate* the essential Aristotle(!?!) with the *now* infamous, murderous-<u>Religious</u>-kill 'em if they don't believe in God- (Spanish) **Inquisition** is it.[vii]

And notice that we are not even wondering about what does his suggestion: that real scientific psychology has to *liberate* itself from *commonsense*(!?!?) mean?

---

[158] E.G., If fire [p] then oxygen [q]; yes, oxygen [q]; therefore though we can't conclude there was fire we can conclude that there could have been fire, which is to say, we cannot conclude there could not have been fire due to lack of oxygen.

[159] We as commonsense human beings do this kind of "re-search" every day of the week whenever we are being accused by our friends and/or acquaintances of being "contrarians": finding the *one* exception saves us an awful lot of work—epistemologically/mentally speaking.

I think that when *both* of the foregoing "data-points"—anti-Aristotle *and* anti-commonsense—are taken together they point → to a Dr. Robert Stadler type, which is to say—to a type that thinks, if only "we" real, physical scientists could do away with Philosophers...well, then...we could have our cake (i.e., piece of the Gigantic Government Grant pie) and eat it too (that is, get money to live a respected-by-others life rather than have to earn our keep [broom] sweeping the streets of the real intellectuals which is all we are actually qualified to do.)[160]

Later, Dr. Eysenck (either the scientist's scientist or the sinner) disparages practically everybody in psychology: to him, Freud's Psychoanalysis is *quackery* (p. 273); Skinner and Watson (p. 295) qua bad *radical* behaviorists (as opposed to I presume the *good*, *methodological* behaviorists, such as Hull et al.), are the ones who permitted the definition of man as a "*biosocial* animal" to *fall from grace* in the anti-commonsense worlds of "real" scientists. (Also on p. 295 he throws in Jung and on p. 273 he tosses in the doctrines of existentialism, "humanistic" psychology and hermeneutics with a double punch against "humanistic" and hermeneutic—which I think includes me—psychologists.)

Dr. Eysenck is—I need to pause here and reflect—more passionate about his topic than most of his (Cognitive-Behaviorist-Scientist-Psychologist) colleagues and as such he is more vulnerable to attack by those such as myself who vehemently disagree with their jargon and pseudo-science illusions. It isn't much of a stretch here to envision the less passionate—more diabolical—*Cognitive Scientist* reading my words and thinking—"goddamn it Eysenck you are making it too easy for them to see through the *man-made* barriers that *we and our ilk have constructed* between *autonomous* man and reality and if you don't watch out *autonomous* man will be able to 'see' that these barriers ARE man-made and not metaphysical as we have been preaching that they are for the past two or three millennia. So would somebody 'paalease get Eysenck off the stage before he hangs us all."

It's too late.

Once an Objectivist—be he or she of the least (Objectivist) ability: i.e. an aspiring to be an Objectivist sympathizer; or of the most ability: e.g. a Professional Objectivist; or at one of the various points in-between: e.g. me—spies an epistemological crook he or she spies them and no amount of illusion

---

[160] When I was a Mechanical Test Engineer gathering "data points" we used to say: two points determines a straight line but three points a better one; which is to say: our [two point based] "conclusion" here about Dr. Eysenck, qua Professional Intellectual, is tentative.

work can cover them up again. The only thing that can rightly cover them up is six feet of baseline concepts:

1. Existence exists.
2. Consciousness is conscious.
3. A is A.
4. Efficacy is *preferred* to inefficacy.
5. Pleasure is *preferred* to pain and
6. Human nature is immutable.

So least "we" be accused of being *too* colorful—by those who say *reason* is cold and colorless and hence flip-flop as the situation requires—let's look more closely at Dr. Eysenck's "science".

Technically speaking, as in for *precision's* sake, self-regulation and self-responsibility are not the same thing (a thermostat is self-regulating but not self-responsible, the person who gave it its set point is the self-responsible one). *Autonomous* man *is self-responsible* and *self-regulating* in the *adult* sense of these terms[161]: he or she is responsible for setting his or her own mental-physical-spiritual growth and development goals and is self-regulatory in the sense of *monitoring* the self to see if the *self* is "on track" to achieving these goals.

By so doing, one completes the circle of human potential development and ends up respecting *the self's right to exist for the self's own sake*, which means taking one's self *seriously* in all the self functions: *thinking, judging, feeling, acting*.

And further, since contradictions do not exist and a self-responsible person respects *facts* which includes all facts hence *this* fact of human growth and development, he or she *seriously* accepts that this same "selfish" right-to-(one's own)life-and-(one's own)property "thing" is true *for others*. Which is to say: a *properly* self-responsible, self-regulating, *autonomous* individual respects this *particular* fact to such a high degree that he or she *worships individual rights* in self *and others.* And without going into all the bullstuff rights in the American psyche, suffice it to say by *individual rights* we mean, the right to (actual) life and (earned) property—with the only exception to the latter being our own bodies which are *given* to us *along with our inalienable right to life* by nature *when we are born.* If nature had wanted us to begin physiological autonomous development at conception she would have had us spring forth immediately as a

---

[161] That is, by *selecting* his own goals AND *accepting* that those goals are *worthy* of his attainment he *sets* his own (psycho-epistemological) thermostat.

fully developed neonate [though we must notice, even "she" can't do this—conception-to-birth is some-thing, that is some (non-instantaneous) *process* in nature and can't be willed away by a wish, it is what it is] or if not then, then if at "viability" then the same or if not then, then when—to repeat—we are *actually* born by exiting the womb and entering the world fully ready to physiologically survive as an independent, don't-need-that-f*!@#&'ing-umbilicord-wrapped-around-me-anymore people person.

After our birth then our rights (*to life and property*) can only meaningfully be "given" to us by another—be they group or individual—*if and only if* the "giver" FIRST takes them away from us. Which is to say they can give us our inalienable rights back or if need be we can take them back. The history of heroic man it seems has been one decade after another, followed by one century after another of "take" it back "behavior" and this new millennium is not going to be any different. Man is born tabula rasa, which means each new generation of humans has to learn everything—including the ability to *learn*—for themselves anew and ... c'est la vie.

Life goes on.

For example, Dr. Eysenck has a (nature given or god given, take your pick) *right* to exist for his own sake too which includes the right to write his reports and articles and books and say whatever he thinks is so and so and such and such and absolutely no one should be able to *prevent* him—*via law*—from doing so. But he does not have the right to force me to support him—*via law*—in his endeavors.

As we have already noted, there is way too much of this kind of thing going on in American society and it will have long term *negative* consequences for (the freedom worshipping part of) society. We do not have an interest right now in pursuing *what* those consequences might be, only in stating that they *will* be and in stating that "scientists" of the Dr. Robert Stadler-Dr. Eysenck "type" are not going to be the ones to lead us out of trouble to the promised land, because—to state it simply—they can't. And they can't because they *refuse* to keep their p's and q's straight in their *hypothesizing* about what's what in *psychology*.

One *reason* for this is that Dr. Eysenck and his fellow Cognitive-Scientist-Psychologists hold it as a matter of utmost importance that "values" should be banned, exorcised or otherwise purged from the human's pursuit of the "scientific" (read *value-less*) "truth" (for one example, see the quote of t,h,e,i,r's on page 128 here with its disparaging tone against "...overt and covert expressions of values."). Since it is not metaphysically possible to exclude human values from human values, they reduce t.h.e.i.r psychological sciences to the art of *rhetoric* and *illusion* mastering. Which means they become masterful at pulling the wool over the eyes of t.h.e.i.r subjects who need to be subjugated *as the means to taking their money* so as to pay for the research that "proves" science, qua reason, cannot deal with human values—these, according to the "scientists", are best left to *faith* (which, unfortunately, *some* taxpayers *want* to hear so they are all for Government Granting t.h.e.m *my* money).

As evidence consider that the foregoing entails *my* meaning of *self-responsibility* and the relationship between self-responsibility and self-regulation and that Dr. Eysenck's definition of self-regulation, qua human characteristic, is "autonomy *from* neurotic and other emotional factors preventing a person from acting to maximize his or her own potentials and needs."(M-B, p 277) Aside from the fact that this definition is borderline concept theft—Freud gave us the concept of "neurotic", Humanistic psychology contributed greatly to our concept of (human) "potential" and Biocentric Psychology and other **need** psychologies to our *scientific,* that is, *rational* view of "needs"—that aside from all this, we still can focus on Eysenck on his own—albeit, "borrowed" terms.

His view of autonomous self-regulation as being ...autonomy *from* neurosis and other emotional factors that *prevent* us from acting... is more illusion work and euphemism building *driven*—to repeat—by their *most* cherished premise that real science—and *especially* psychology—isn't science unless it is devoid of "values". Because they believe this way they have to say "autonomy from neurosis" [that only some special scientist types *inherit*? or just some lucky few *inherit*?] rather than "psychologically free of obsolete responses calculated to satisfy unmet needs of the past with *euphemistic* behaviors in the present". And because of *their* belief system they have to say, "autonomy from emotional factors" [which could be "achieved" by emotional repression] rather than "psychologically self-purged (which is the *only* way it can be done) of *irrational* values". And so on and so forth. Jesus, they are exhausting. Why don't they just call a spade a spade rather than a device whose *only* purpose is to dig graves—a spade can be used to plant flowers too. What any man-made item—be they spades or "schools of psychological thought"—can be *used for* and what they *are* in reality aren't automatically synonymous "*is's*".

And as we can assert here: the Cognitive Scientist's desire and attempt to vacate psychology of human values is so wrong that that *premise* alone makes t.h.e.i.r "psychology" *wrong.* And if they want to prattle about in their conferences and writings that their "psychology" is the right one and that they will solicit the United States Government to Grant them 5 escalating billion dollars to *fund the research* "proving" themselves correct then, ... then, ... well then, ... IN A FREE SOCIETY the "peoples" gets what they deserve.

This sounds harsh I know, but...*Reality* ALWAYS has the final say.

Always.

If you desire to *not* be one of those "peoples" then consider the following.

Since a highly *repressed* individual could be seen as "self-regulating" in the Eysenckian sense of the term we cannot conclude that *self-regulation via emotional repression* is good and hence a valid *measure* of—healthy—autonomy.[162]

It isn't emotions per se that prevent us from acting but *wrong* values that the emotions are simply value-responses of.[163] As Dr. Branden explains:

> His emotional capacity is man's automatic barometer of what is *for* him or *against* him (within the context of his knowledge and values). The relationship of value-judgments to emotions is that of *cause* to *effect*. An emotion is a value-response. It is the automatic psychological result (involving both mental and somatic features) of a super-rapid, subconscious appraisal.
>
> *An emotion is the psychosomatic form in which man experiences his estimate of the beneficial or harmful relationship of some aspect of reality to himself.*[viii]

Emotions then—as value *responses*—are our barometer (since they are *our* values) of what is for us or against us and to what degree (*as we see it, as we*

---

[162] In fact emotional repression is bad for one and one could argue that Dr. Eysenck's work shows just how bad it is: so bad in fact that it could have negative *physical* consequences for the emotional repressor. See M-B p. 272 where he describes the cancer-prone-personality as ...one characterized by the inability to express emotions like fear, anger and anxiety... and to notice that the key phrase is "inability to express emotion" and not the particular emotion(s). And further, with—our—emphasis on "inability" and our "belief" system that says since man is born tabula rasa this (adult) "inability" is learned (young children as a rule have no problem *expressing* emotions) and hence, therefore *is* un-learn-able we can get some insight into the *problem of emotional repression* and thank Dr. Eysenck for his rudimentary work in this area (of maybe) highlighting a link (of some kind) between cancer and emotional repression: thanks, doc.

[163] For the proper definition of "values" see Footnote 126, page 128. The evaluation here of *wrong* values assumes that actualizing our human potential and satisfying our needs is good—which itself is a *value* and one which I hold to be good and right and valuable. If you *or anyone* holds that **meeting one's needs** is bad then you and/or they are *wrong*. And this isn't an issue of ... and here I am faced with the prospect of having to repeat the entire philosophy of Objectivism...which isn't possible...so...I stop. And tell you: "Go to the—Objectivism—source yourself."

interpret it, as we apply it).[164] Emotions are not primary, but come from *our evaluations* which come from *our values* which came from our pro-active thinking or from the *compartments* of our in-active and/or stalled-out thinking. Our emotions—as byproducts of subconscious processes—do not "care" whether our values are good or bad, rational or irrational, our emotions only "care" that "they" get it right: if I value ice cream, for example, then at certain times I am going to be propelled towards ice cream. Or if I value sex then at certain times I am going to be propelled towards sex. And so on and so forth: if I value getting drunk then at times I'm going to be propelled towards booze. Emotions *propel* which is to say emotions *carry with them* an inherent action tendency. In Dr. Eysenck's words: "emotions...[that] prevent us from acting..." is not true of emotions per se but, to repeat, of the *values* that the emotions come from (e.g. if I dis-value spinach I am *not* going to engage in the act of eating it, but rather in the act of *waving it off* [with or without commentary on *how much* I dislike it] whenever it is offered to me at the dinner table). And to talk of emotional problems in this way [prevent us from acting] is to give emotions a bad rap rather than the values—you know "those things", speaking sarcastically for a moment, that we dare not discuss least somebody somewhere gets upset about it—that the emotions *come from*. *Values* can be good or bad, correct or mistaken, rational or irrational. But technically, as in for precision's sake, *emotions* are not bad or good, they simply are.

Emotions—when *properly* understood by your *reason*—are *good* for you and you should *learn* how to use them for the betterment and enjoyment of your own life and not to the physical detriment of your life or others. If you *deny* your emotions or *evade* your emotions or otherwise *block* your emotions you will—eventually—be in *psychological* trouble. In this regard we have to remember that *square circles do not exist* and cannot be *made*. If we block our emotions *enough times* so as to make the block(s) automatic, we *will* end up in psychological trouble. If this "happens to you" and you end up *concluding* that *even though* you have repressed your emotions so much so that if some other body-possessing consciousness human person simply stands next to you emitting emotional vibrations—like some giant tuning fork threatening to turn on your internal piano with its strings *old* and brittle from non-use (and threatening to snap at the first sign of use)—that **if** this and then you *conclude* that even though you still haven't

---

[164] And to say in this context, "and ya, we can mis-see, mis-interpret and mis-apply..." is simply to agree with the *Philosopher's* observation that "man is not omniscient". And further—we can easily observe—man never has been omniscient and therefore, this is *the main* reason why he NEEDS philosophy.

lost *cognitive* contact with reality you nonetheless *are* still "mentally ill" *rather* than "value-conflicted" then you will end up getting what you deserve: culturalized misery, as in the cliché, *misery loves company.*[165]

In the foregoing scenario you can *choose* to take Prozac or whatever drug you think will give you the correct values but think about it, I mean come on and think about it, *no drug can do this*. It is a reification of the savage to think that "ingesting bear meat" will make me strong and courageous *like a bear*. Ingesting "powdered chemicals" will make me strong and courageous as "I used to feel when I got drunk", only now I avoid the *stigma* of being drunk. Maybe you'd be better off being drunk, at least then you could see that you are trying to drink away your problems rather than face them and deal with them. This is the "advancement" of modern day psychiatric drugs: they give us the *illusion* that we aren't drunks dependent on booze. Heaven forbid, what we "really" are—or at least what the *Bureaucratic Mind* wants us to believe we are—is just poor, little, helpless mentally ill people with hyper active kids who have to take Prozac or X or Y or Z or whatever drug or purple pill the "Science Community" makes available to us so that we all can live in *harmony* in a society that is afraid of its own shadow.

Which is to say, Eysenck—qua *reductive materialist's* assertion that *autonomy* means *free of emotional factors that prevent one from acting to maximize ones own potential and needs* ("Mind-Brain, p.277) —could be counted among the Government's Cognitive Neuroscientists who are in the process—as we speak—of building epistemological rats nests as the means to keeping the (Government Grant) money flowing.

Consider.

In "my" (Biocentric) psychology, *emotions* carry with them an inherent action tendency. I don't know of an emotion that "has no action potential" let alone one that is inhibitory in the sense of "has an anti-action potential". If an "e-motion" has no action potential, it's not an emotion. Consider for example the state of affairs we call, indifference. Indifference is an estimate of neither for me nor against me and so no (different) action from what I am doing right now is required on my part (e.g., ignore the lion, keep grazing). Consequently, to then argue beyond this to the point that an emotion contains the "action tendency" to "not act" is analogous to saying that in physics there is a particle with an electrical *field* that has *no charge*. A neutron is a particle *without* an electrical field and an

---

[165] *Happiness* requires thought and effort and a heck of a lot of it. I know it and I am not going to allow misery worshippers to pretend otherwise. Are you?

electron is one with a negative charge relative to the proton, which has a positive charge. But, an electrical field *without a charge* is a contradiction in terms. So, is Dr. Eysenck saying emotions are like fundamental physic's particles? Emotions, according to Biocentric psychology, are the *psycho-biological form in which we experience our estimate of the beneficial or harmful relationship of some aspect of reality to ourselves*.[ix] Emotions contain the action tendency to move *towards* or to move *away* from the thing in reality as we correctly or incorrectly estimate it to be for us or against us. It is our *responsibility* to *choose* to act on the emotion's "suggested *direction* of motion", or to *choose* to not act on it as the case may be. An emotion does not contain an inhibitory element, that is, it does not *cause* us to NOT act. Not acting is a choice as much as is acting a choice. But if you think emotions are like fundamental physics particles, then what will this thought lead you to do? It will lead you to conclude that emotions are *primary* in the same analogous sense as are protons, electrons and neutrons primary—i.e. the given—particles in The Science of (nuclear) Physics, hence, we *should* study them as *ends in themselves*. And it will lead you to conclude that if you *want* to institutionalize a "nobody can help it" mentality, then preach that *inaction* is an electric-like current generated by ones body *automatically* and hence that one can do nothing about it (whether generated in the brain, the heart or the loins is not relevant). And when Ayn Rand, the philosopher exceptionale[166] says: *emotions are not primary and are not tools of cognition*, and then proves it; "you" can spend tens of billions of the peoples' dollars disavowing the existence of her and her philosophy, *Objectivism*, and its companion psychology, *Biocentric Psychology* of Dr. Nathaniel Branden. But you can't do it and get away with it *unless* you invoke an anti-human nature principle. That principle is the one favored by all bureaucratic minds: *might—NOT right, but MIGHT—makes right*. In the shadow of *Objectivism* and *Biocentric Psychology* that have proven emotions are not *primaries,* the attempt to *make* emotions a *primary* is equivalent to today's physicists saying there is no such thing as quarks and other *sub-atomic* particles, there is only protons and electrons and neutrons and we *should* spend a billion bucks, or a trillion if that's what it takes, *proving* that there are no particles more fundamental than electrons and protons and neutrons (if we don't do this—argues the BM—where will it all stop?). This would be fine if it weren't for the

---

[166] To anyone who reads AND studies her works this "accolade" is woefully inadequate and I will be on the lookout for more specific opportunities to "give credit where credit is due". Is it *possible* that Ayn Rand is the greatest philosopher to have ever lived? Unfortunately I don't have a Ph.D. in philosophy (and I don't mean this derisively) so I'm not fully qualified to answer it. But for those of you who do, who's greater?

fact that they expect me (and you) to *fund* them (and if we don't they will put us in jail right along side *actual* criminals and then say you must be a criminal because, you are, after all... in jail!). No wonder people feel victimized by the system. A system that says you have no control over your own life; "we", the *bureaucrats* and our *hired* Ph.D.'ers, *are* going to control you whether you like it or not.

My advice here is, stop *liking* it.

But that's up to you. I can now *afford* to grant here that *maybe* Dr. Eysenck's charts measure something important about human *psychhological* factors and their relationship to Cancer and Heart disease even though we don't yet know for exact sure *what* that something is.

Figure 15.4 is Lung cancer mortality of smokers depending on degree of stress (Eysenck, 1991). This shows that *stressed* smokers die from lung cancer at a rate that is more than double the rate of *no-stress* smokers when both groups smoke a pack or more of cigarettes per day. (It also "says" that if you smoke less than a pack a day—stressed or not—you have better than a 99% chance of NOT dying from lung cancer.[167])

These figures strike me as very "scientific" and basically—except as noted above—I have no problem with them. I'm sure some could argue about the details—as I have done—but at this point in our attempts to understand ourselves from the "big picture" point of view these arguable details are of secondary importance. They could very well end up being of primary importance, but that will have to be left for another day.

Eysenck writes (on p. 281):

> Of course, psychological risk factors interact with physical risk factors (Eysenck, 1994e). Figure 15.4 shows the interaction of smoking with the personality/stress combination as measured by the type 1 questionnaire (Eysenck, 1991). Again we are concerned with a prospective study, and the dependent variable concerned is lung cancer.

Of course all real scientists—these now are my words as a trained and experienced Engineering Scientist—are very aware of the concept of *dependent*

---

[167] My very own biological mother—Eldora—could be anecdotal evidence for this. As a kid I remember her smoking about a half a pack a week (not counting the four cigarettes per week that I stole from her pack) and she claims now that she hasn't smoked since Ash Wednesday so views herself as having quit. In 6 weeks she will celebrate her 91st birthday and wants us all to meet her at the casino, stay over one night in the casino's hotel and help her celebrate. She hasn't died yet but when she does it sounds like it will be from pneumonia—a recent bout with which is the "reason" she quit smoking—**not** lung cancer.

and *independent* variables. Usually the vertical y-axis in a Cartesian coordinate system (which is the *form* in which Dr. Eysenck's data is presented to us and in which, for example, the daily newspapers present the Dow Jones Industrial Average vs. date data) is the "dependent" variable and the horizontal x-axis the "independent" variable. Very "scientific" indeed and I still have no problem with it. Maybe my claim that I could find a ubiquitous anti-human nature mentality in these writings is simply wrong. Maybe I will have to change it from *ubiquitous* to *pervasive* or maybe I will have to abandon it all together. Though of course we have already seen *some* evidence that says we cannot abandon it all together. But, again, we are getting ahead of ourselves. Let's follow this through as we've envisioned it and see where it leads, and if need be we'll correct our view *if and as required to do so*. Again, we can rely on an Objectivist principle here: if your thesis is wrong it will lead to a dead end (if you have the intellectual integrity to call a spade a spade, that is, to call a dead end a dead end). If these modern researchers and experimenters and investigators into *psychhological* phenomenon are true scientists then the least we would expect of them is that they are *not* going to deal in anti-science. We are in fact employing, by borrowing its *Form* from Algebra, one particular *scientific* approach to formally *proving* an either/or hypothesis. This *process* is: *take a stand*, state one side of the hypothesis: e.g. Bob is alive; *assume* it false (e.g., Bob is dead) and *follow the logic* of this assumption and show that it *leads to a contradiction (when's the last time you saw a dead person talking and eating and waving his arms at the waiter)*, then hence, the assumed assumption is false (that Bob is dead) and the hypothesis is "proven" (Bob indeed is alive).

Proof, as a thing, is *possible*.

Since I really haven't studied psychology as deeply as I perhaps should have since I allowed the State to run me out of business back in 1991-92[168] I am using these exercises here for dual purposes: to explore my theme *and* as education to help bring me back up to speed on the advancements (if any) in Psychology (The Science) over the past decade.

I don't know about you, but this is exciting stuff. That is, to discover that the mainstream psychological community is (finally) beginning to see that *WHAT*

---

[168] This sounds like a non-sequitur I know, but it is an issue with me and I have to admit here that I am no martyr—I had my "chance" to be one in 1992 but I used the Objectivist "morality stops at the point of a gun" principle to keep myself out of jail and in a job as a dutifully employed American consumer. If you need details beyond this you will have to go to my website, *Gary's Venns* at http://www.gdeering.com and once there enter as Guest, Click on the PHILOSOPHY VENN and then the STI VENN and follow "the logic" there.

Objectivism has been teaching since before the middle of the last century is true!?! That is, that the mind-body dichotomy of the ancients is *incorrect* and that a mind-body "integration" as in mind and body "cannot and do not exist without each other". That THIS is true! To see this finally catching on **is** exciting. And just think for a moment what this means. It means that Ayn Rand and Objectivism *are* right and *have been right all along*. When Ayn Rand says, (quoting her from *Introduction to Objectivist Epistemology*) "Just as man's physical existence was liberated when he grasped the principle that "nature, to be commanded, must be obeyed," so his consciousness will be liberated when he grasps that *nature, to be apprehended, must be obeyed*—that the rules of cognition must be derived from the nature of existence, and the nature, the *identity*, of his cognitive faculty." [x]

For example, one of Objectivism's tenets is: *a free mind and a free market are corollaries*.

If a free mind and a free market are corollaries are they also each other's reciprocal causes or is a free mind anterior to a free market? Or vice-versa? If they are each other's reciprocal causes then no mind—in the history of the planet—has ever been truly *free*. Wow! Am I going to be the first? The first free mind inside an un-free market? Is this the *promise* of BiO Spiritualism?

No.

If the reciprocal causation is correct, no one can be first—not even Ayn Rand. Freedom of mind exists on a continuum, therefore, and one could argue I suppose, that Ayn Rand reached the highest—though if she did, why did she die in her 70's and not live another 10 or 20 years like many people (e.g., see earlier footnote about my other mother—oops, is this another one of those Brandian slips?) of her generation are doing?[169] Just because Mind and Body are *integrated* it doesn't follow that they are *exactly* the same thing and/or that they are different expressions of the same thing as are energy and matter to the physicist. It means mind/consciousness and body don't and hence cannot exist without each other in

---

[169] My guess is it's because of stress. The *stress*—in Ayn Rand's case—of being a genius in a world overrun with ... not geniuses. Here's another potential reason why we need "psychology": as the *guide* to idiosyncratic self understanding, psychology (the scientific kind) affords us the potential for a gigantic amount of stress reduction. That is, for reducing that component of stress that is the resultant measure of the difference between what "we" think things "should" be versus what "they" think things "should" be. And for those of us who are *right*—that is, correctly *match* the reality of man's nature and needs—the "resultant measure" can be extremely large. If *pride* (as suggested later on here on page 339) is the best anti-depressant known to man then spiritualism—as integrated/applied philosophy & psychology—is the best stress reducer. Even better than Valium? Yes. Prozac? Yes. Smoking? Well ... may—. Yes. Best means better than *all* alternatives, regardless of their specifics.

the same sense "yellow" does not exist apart from "yellow things", be it "yellow canaries" or "yellow sunflower plants" or "yellow crayons" and so on ad infinitum. "Yellow" and *that* which is yellow are inseparable *in reality;* but not in *mind.* In *mind* we can and do "separate" *yellow* as an attribute of certain entities. We do this with the human faculty called *abstracting.* Animals below man do not have this ability *to abstract* as man does.[170]

And we can and do *abstract* more than color from *existents*. Consider:

> If we can't control you we'll put you in jail for breaking our laws that say we have a right to license every form of labor—be it mental or physical—that we say is in the "public interest". This sentiment works two ways: if you have a *bureaucratic mind* you have this sentiment or if you have this sentiment you have a bureaucratic mind. That is, this sentiment is a defining characteristic of the bureaucratic mind. So a logical concern is to ask: What labor is *not* in the public interest? There is no end to the licensing; this is as predictable as rain. No end. "They" will eventually pass laws saying which kinds of psychotherapy are "legal" and which are not and if you try to practice those which aren't you will be jailed. Is there any significant difference here between this and the (alleged) 1800's battles between homeopathic medicine and the then yet to be legalized-institutionalized AMA? They are employing the same tactics today in regards to *psychology* and I predict that within 5 to 10 years—or sooner—we will get the same results: some psychotherapy will be declared not in the public interest and will be outlawed. If you are an Objectivist, an Objectivist sympathizer or a human being interested in freedom I suggest you take a time out here and read or re-read Dr.

---

[170] If you doubt this, take one of your gorillas or rats that you have trained to press a lever for food when yellow balls are presented but not when red ones are. Then put a person in the room who has a bureaucratic mentality and see if the animal can detect that the bureaucrat is "yellow" and then pushes the bar (the gorilla not the bureaucrat). Yes, this is a joke. But not one to not make a point. You, qua human being with the power of abstraction, have the potential to get this joke but that hypothetical gorilla or rat will never get it. If you still don't believe me I challenge you to *sign* it to your favorite sign-speaking gorilla and see if he or she laughs. (Yes, of course you can do this and then conclude that the gorilla didn't laugh because he didn't think it was funny. But then you will just be making my point for me, the one I state on page 261 here: they are your neurons and *what* you do with them *is* up to you. But note: the consequences are up to reality.)

Peikoff's book, *The Ominous Parallels*[xi] and "abstract" some "parallels" for yourself. *These are mine.*

The conclusion here—that is, the *cognitive* conclusion—seems inescapable: Until and unless...we obtain a 100% laissez-faire capitalism, *no mind can be 100% free.*

The *cognitive* faculty of which Ayn Rand speaks—in contradistinction to the one the Cognitive Scientists think exists—the Ayn Rand one in the "nature, to be apprehended" *principle* is the same *one* that discovered gravity and mechanics (Force = mass x acceleration) and relativity ($E = mc^2$) and atomic forces and electricity and cells and mitosis and statics and dynamics (in mechanics) and electromagnetic laws and thermodynamics and the list seems endless. Man has discovered a great deal over the past several centuries and not too many would argue that his "cognitive" faculty didn't play a major role in these discoveries.

Apparently, man's *cognitive* faculty is *reliable* enough to discover some-things.

In fact those discoveries *by that faculty* have given science the good name it *deserves*. It is all part and parcel of the well known and respected Western Tradition of Science and The *Scientific Method.* As a formally educated Aeronautical Engineer and experienced and trained Mechanical Test Engineer with many many years (about a quarter of a century's worth) of research and testing experience in areas of heat transfer, thermodynamics and mechanical testing, I have *reason* to believe in the Scientific Method: I have seen it, I have used it, it works. It is a correct method. But it doesn't automatically follow that only Ph.D. recipients can use the method (nor that it can *only* be used in Physics). That they can say: "we are Ph.D.'ers therefore what we say is "scientific method" is "science" and everything else is not", does not make it so. To argue, X is true (or false) BECAUSE a Ph.D. person *says so* is so far from scientific that my original classification of it as, *authoritarianism* remains the proper name for such un-scientific practices. Science, first and foremost is all about "proving" that that which "scientists" say exists, *does in fact exist. Science* is neither simpler nor more complicated than this. If the something does in fact exist as the scientist claims then that something is manipulatable—that is, doing something with it has demonstrable consequences in reality. For example, science says air exists, it is a real something. And they proceed to demonstrate/prove it by putting a ringing bell in a thick jar and evacuate the alleged air from the jar. Then we as observers of this "experiment" detect a diminishing ringing sound because the air has been removed. If there was no air, qua something, to remove, this experiment wouldn't "work".[171]

So this particular random selection [Eysenckian plots attempting to show the physicist a relationship between *psychhological* and *physical* parameters] from "Mind-Brain" seems pretty scientific to me and it is a challenge to my thesis that "Mind-Brain" is *ubiquitously* anti-human nature.

But, before we leave this particular section and *self-doubt* behind I have a *true* story to tell you. True in the sense that it happened exactly as presented, including in the exact sequence presented.

About a month ago I decided to start doing some research on the history of "spiritualism" so I went to my local library to browse. After an hour or two of computer searching and taking call numbers to the shelves and browsing in and around those numbers I picked a half dozen or so books that sounded interesting ("Mind-Brain" was one of them).

I checked them out and hurried home to do some reading. One book in particular I looked forward to getting into. The book's title was, "Explaining the Unexplained, Mysteries of the paranormal" and I hoped it would be as good if not better than the explaining of this kind done by that famous magician—James Randi—who is absolutely expert at debunking a lot of the "mystical" claims of those who study *and* make egregious claims about the "paranormal".[xii]

I dove into "Explaining the Unexplained ... " and before I got one-third of the way through it I had to stop. What a disappointment. It was the usual unscientific BS about our alleged ability to know reality outside of and/or beyond the 5 known senses of touch, taste, smell, sight and hearing. And *they* absolutely do not mean what Ayn Rand's Objectivism means when it talks about us *using* our *conceptual* faculty to go beyond the 5 senses limitation of our *perceptual* capacity (refer back to page 137 and read Dr. Branden's comments concerning this). *They*, the paranormal advocates, mean it in its full *mystical* sense of ***ExtraSensoryPerception (ESP)***, *as in* the *yet to be discovered "means" beyond the 5 known senses*. I have no problem with this *if* "they" discover the means, that is

---

[171] Notice that the religious mentality here would "argue": see, just because you can't see air doesn't mean it doesn't exist, voila, you can't see god therefore god exists. That is, *faith* dependent religion tries to piggyback on *reason* dependent science as invariably it must. But I ask you: where is the vessel that god can be sucked out of and the consequences of it *demonstrated* to human *reason*? If you are religious and your mind is here racing into one metaphor after another I suggest you ... evaluate each and every one of those metaphors for non-contradictory consistency and realize that they are based on *fundamental* premises that you *actually* hold. And if you ever hope to get beyond the negative gravitational pull of religious metaphysics, epistemology and ethics you have to check and challenge these as well as all your premises. No one can nor will do it for you. It is entirely, 100% up to you. As you *choose* so shall yu reap.

the new "senses" that I didn't know I had. All I request is that they present it to me in a logical, non-contradictory, "scientific" fashion, that is, in a "fashion" that does not require me to totally and completely *disown* my 5 KNOWN senses. Nor in a fashion that requires me to *use* premises established *as true* based on "reasoning" I did "yesterday" via *five-sense* data analysis and then conclude that ESP is real but SP is not?!?. And please, please please don't create a "virtual" world of your mystical metaphysics on a movie screen or in a computer and then ask me to TAKE THE CREATION as EVIDENCE that SP isn't real since I *took it in* via my SP, in particular, via my sense of sight and sound (since they haven't yet perfected smell and taste and touch in the movies or in computers).

Anyway, I read a bit more of "Explaining..." and bits and pieces of some of the other books. As I mentioned above, this is where I discovered "Mind-Brain" and let me add here that *by comparison* "Mind-Brain" is "science" par excellence.

Now even though I am only letting you see "Mind-Brain" through the window of three random pages at a time I have read more than this and I am almost completely done reading it.

For example, elsewhere in the H. J. Eysenck chapter that we are *trying* to leave there is a bit of a diatribe by Dr. Eysenck against Freudian psychoanalytic "psychology". That is, using Dr. Eysenck's words: the un-scientific, anti-scientific, "stopping us real scientists"-from-advancing, Freudian psychoanalytic "psychology". As I touched on this earlier and mentioned in a footnote, Dr. Eysenck really thinks Freud is a quack. I'm not pro-Freud by any means, but I don't view him as a quack.[172]

Anyway, as I sit here *now*, kind of half staring into the room and looking through my stack of library books I notice something that I *never* noticed before. Guess who one of the authors of "Explaining the Unexplained" is?

You got it, Hans J. Eysenck!

This is too weird.

I pick it up and start reading the **Preface** and I do it this time *knowing* that the book is pro-psychic, pro-paranormal phenomenon which is as far from science as the human mind can get (well, maybe not as far as, but pretty close).

---

[172] If I "knew" what "quack" meant (and by it Dr. Eysenck doesn't mean the sound emitted by ducks) I might view Freud the same way. But I don't have a good definition for "quackery" and I am inclined to say here or rather "predict" here that before I am done with this manuscript (today as I write, it's the first day of spring, 2000) I will come up with a *proper* definition for "quackery". [Oops. See #174 now or wait a few moments 'til you get there.]

And as I continue to try and exit Dr. Eysenck's "Mind-Brain" chapter, I ask you to tell me what does the following quote from *his* Preface, p.6 of "Explaining the Unexplained, Mysteries of the paranormal" mean?[xiii]

> Surveys of scientists, however, show that only a minority accept the existence of ESP [I thought "proof" not "acceptance" was the hallmark of science?], although, encouragingly [!?!], fewer and fewer are prepared to rule it out as an impossibility. Is this because the research that would enable them to suspend their disbelief [to me this sounds like an argument from the "Doubting Thomas" premise[173]] or at least admit the possibility of ESP, has not been done? Or do they, with all the confidence of prejudice, refuse to look at the evidence? [what evidence? people who "claim" they flew—without any vehicle other than their own psychic ability to astral project—flew the 4.3 light years to our nearest star system, Alpha Centauri, a couple of days ago and now they are back to tell us about it? Is this what he means by "evidence"?[174]]

For someone who calls psychoanalysis "quackery" these are *suspicious* words[175].

---

[173] As an ex-religionist as I explained earlier I have to be careful, a "doubting Thomas" is from the Bible and it is a person who NEEDS evidence before he will believe in something. Thomas didn't see the walking around Jesus after he, Jesus, allegedly had risen from the dead so he, Thomas, was reprimanded for his "disbelief" and any *child* reading this was very *capable* of *cognitively* getting the message, "only losers need evidence".

[174] Maybe *this* is what Dr. Eysenck should mean by "quackery": Human *absurdity* and especially his own. Since Dr. Freud is the first person to really practice psychology he can't be classified as a quack because per my dictionary [in #172 I had temporarily forgotten that Dictionaries *can* be useful] *quack* means *an untrained person who practices medicine fraudulently*. Since untrained presupposes someone who is capable of doing the training and the first to do anything—including in-medicine—can't be trained, therefore—according to Eysenck–all originators, innovators in the healing arts are quacks. This of course is absurd so if this *is* what Dr. Eysenck means, then he—qua ESP innovator aspireree—must be the quack to whom he is referring in his statement about Dr. Freud.

[175] As to how suspicious it will remain to be seen. In modern psychology, and not just Biocentric psychology, but many modern day psychologies there is a concept called "projection". Projection is when we "project things that are true about ourselves onto others" and we do this as a means of disowning these things for our own reasons of distaste about these things. So my use of the word suspicious here means this could be an example of Dr. Eysenck projecting his confusion onto others. But notice, I have said could be, I say could be because that is what I mean, we are far from proving that this is the case. "Projection" is a dangerous concept and like dynamite you have to handle it with care, but just as dynamite can be used for good so too can it be used for bad and it can result in bad if accidentally misused. The same applies to

Since Dr. Eysenck appears to be an empiricist exceptionale (in "Mind-Brain"), which means he's a good *test designer* and *conductor* and *results evaluator* is it *possible* that his statement in the foregoing quote: "...the research that would *enable*...has not been done..." means that Dr. Eysenck and/or his "buddies" in the "scientific" world would be *more than happy* to be the Grant *recipients* of the money that will pay for *said* research?

A *real* scientist is one who accepts philosophy's onerous principle: "he who asserts the existence of a positive has to *prove* its existence" beyond a doubt, we who doubt do not have to disprove it beyond a doubt. We especially do not have to disprove a negative! That is, it is not incumbent upon us—as scientists, amateur or professional, or as laymen—it is *not* our burden to dis-prove the non-existent.[176]

And worse, the blatantly erroneous (religious) attitude that if we can't prove that the non-existent doesn't exist, it is "proof" that it does.

I submit Dr. Eysenck knows this and if he doesn't he has no right to call himself a scientist.

But, alas, not all is lost.

To wit: Eysenck, after a few more comments about his "Mind-Brain" Figure-Chart-Graphs concludes:

---

psychological "projection" and as you will discover in your hermeneutics so do many of the useful concepts in scientific psychhology. They come packaged with the following label: HANDLE WITH CARE. Hermeneutic *introspection* requires a degree of intellectual *honesty* and *rigor* that makes the investigative efforts of many physical scientists look like monuments to imprecision.

[176] I learned this *first hand* for the *first time* when I was 8 years old (early to middle summer of '54) and I mark this as the continued beginning of my philosophy training. Two creepy kids who were a few years older than me accused me of knowingly calling their dog across the street in front of a car and the dog then got run over and maimed or killed (I don't remember which). I was no where near the scene of the alleged crime at the alleged time and I knew inside myself that I did not do it. But they wouldn't listen and continued to taunt me with their charges. This went on for a week or more and I was very very frustrated in my inability to dissuade them, to "prove" to them that I didn't do it. But they were having too much fun taunting me so they kept it up. Then one sun filled morning before the end of the second week I woke up completely done and free of the incident. It didn't matter to me anymore because on some level I knew that I could not disprove something that did not happen and so I let it go (put it in a compartment?) and I was never bothered by those two dorks—names remembered but omitted here—again (interesting, though, that I still remember—half a century later—their names isn't it). But now [at the time then, when, I was 8] with this as my first epistemology "experience"—even though implicit—I was 2/3rds of the way—given that my first Metaphysic was formed at age 5—to forming my first "philosophy" of life. What remained was to get my first formal *ethics* lesson (philosophy remember, per Objectivism, is the integrated result of metaphysics, epistemology and ethics). Since I was still stealing cigarettes and other minor things from stores in our town this was to come over two or three incidents to play out over the next four years (interesting, the same length of time it takes to get a College degree).

> Such findings suggest that the hypothesis of a mind-body continuum has far-reaching effects, and may be worthy of serious consideration.

I couldn't agree more (if I ignore the word, *continuum*: consciousness exists on a continuum but what's the continuum between say the body's heart and the body's lungs)[177], but allow me to finish this particular analysis with a question:

> If it is a mind -BODY continuum, why is the title of their book, "Mind and BRAIN Sciences in the 21st Century"???

They aren't trying to pull the wool over our eyes, are they?

I don't want my skepticism here to result in me "throwing the baby out with the bath water", especially when we are discovering so many things. For example I didn't know that they had actual research data linking "psychology" factors to cancer, heart disease and so on. Impressive!

Finally then, "we" are *safe* for now and hence can leave this particular "Mind-Brain" section and move on to our fourth random numbered sequence—J. Kagan's "On Future Psychological Categories", M-B's p. 235—on our list of ten.

But.

Before we can do this we have to go back and tie up one loose end.

---

[177] We won't even get into demanding of the Eysenckian mentalities who preach real science isn't real science *unless* it is devoid of *values* by asking them to explain to us how a word "worthy" can be used in science as Eysenck did here. That is, we won't (yet) *demand* that t,h,e,y show us *how* it is possible for something to be *worthy* **and** *not* valuable at the same time and in the same respect.

Chapter 18: From *Behaviorism - to - Cognitive Neuroscience via Cognitive Science & Cognitive Psychology:*

Rats maze - to - Rats nest?

Some Claims

209.210.211 revisited

In this section of her Chapter (11) in Mind-Brain Dr. Snodgrass, qua *Cognitive Psychologist*, is addressing the general question: What is *memory* and how does it work?

Before we can effectively deal with her answer to this question, we have to answer a different one: What is *Cognitive Psychology*?

Cognitive Psychology is the psychology that (correctly) believes *Behaviorism Psychology* is wrong because it views man as a *body without a mind.* The correct view (*per the Cognitive Psychologists*) is to view man as a *mind with a body that is all brain* and *a body with a brain that is all mind.* (Later, we will get to the *Cognitive Neuroscientists* who run this idea into the ground and become the new darlings of the Bureaucratic Mind because of it, and who, because of this, will end up getting the big game prize money of billions and billions of tax dollars gifted (in-your-and-my-names) from y/our Government in the form of "research" Grants which, as you will see, should really be called "rehash" Grants.)

Which is to say, Cognitive Psychology is little more than the flip-flop second half of the ancient (and boring) and erroneous *mind-body dichotomy* view of man. A view that every scientist—in his or her intellectual development—eventually has to break free of—or attempt to break free of it as best they can. The best that the professional science community has been able to do up 'til now (and to offer us lay persons the benefits of their so doing) is to flip-flop back 'n forth between the *rationalist* (mind without body) view of man and the *empiricist* (body without mind) view of man. In the history of psychology the *empiricist* view is *Behaviorism* and since it failed so miserably to explain man's psychology they flipped over to the "new" (neo) rationalist view and labeled this view: *Cognitive Psychology.*

Cognitive psychology is the (erroneous) view—and let me emphasize this, Cognitive Psychology is the *erroneous* view—that scientific psychhology is the science that studies the attributes and characteristics that man has by virtue of the fact that *his* consciousness is as envisioned by the German philosopher Immanuel Kant. And that as *rational*(ists) people, (real) scientists *can* and *should* fill in the details explaining *why* Kant's view of man should be accepted by (other) real scientists as the correct view. And like the good scientists that they are they do not ask their fellow scientists to take them on faith, but rather they spend volumes and volumes showing their fellow scientists *how* our brain, qua the physical organ that it is, is the "solution" to the "problem" of living in a Kantian Universe.

The "new" in *their* view is really nothing more than a new twist in an old game. By analogy that game is the old childhood game called leap-frog. The new twist is that instead of kids playing it you have two adults—one an empiricist, the other a rationalist—hopping—first one then the other—over each other and advancing forward with each hop-over hop-over hop but not knowing that they are playing their game on the edge of a cliff. Based on the assertion that contemporary psychology is predominantly Cognitive Psychology it looks like the empiricists (qua Behaviorists) were the last to leap and unfortunately for them the game had advanced to the edge of that cliff they didn't know was there. We can't really conclude that as Kantians they can't [be expected to] know, so this explains it *because* empiricists really aren't as pro-Kantian as are the rationalists. In some (understandable) ways the empiricists say: if Kant is philosophy who the hell needs philosophy; we will run our experiments and let them, the experiments, *imprint* their results on us (just like when we were kids and our significant others actions and behaviors were, for a time, imprinted on us as we grew and developed).

But since human beings *need* philosophy as much as they *need* air you can hear the empiricist's expelling their needs deep from within their lungs all the way down the sides of the abyss.

But not to fret, since *Cognitive Neuroscience* is on the ascendancy due to the fact that those not too bright Cognitive Psychologists—when they saw that their leap-frog buddy had disappeared—convinced themselves that he was "really" still there (in spite of what Kant says) and they just couldn't see him so they leaped over a non-existent partner and have yet to discover that that funny feeling they have is exactly the same one that Wiley Coyote has when he realizes that *what* lays beneath is—not all his erroneous premises as is the case for Kantian sympathizers as well as the anti-Kantian rebels without a cause empiricists, but rather what lies beneath the Cognitive Psychologist's body is—one hell of a long, protracted fall to be cut really really short by a ground that does not (for)give.

And again, as before, we have to briefly answer yet another question before we can continue. That question is: What is Kant's view of man?

His view is one that can be traced all the way back to Plato—by sidestepping Aristotle—and is of the explanatory form that says we humans live in a world of appearances and as such we can't really know the real world because that within us that knows *adds* something of its own to the process of knowing and by this very natural-metaphysical-set-in-cement-fact-of-human-action mental act, we distort reality.

Kantians do not believe that a non-distorted view of reality is possible for humans. In fact this is what the Kantians would say is the meaning of a statement like: "There are no square circles". This statement means, Kantians would say, man cannot not have a non-distorted view of real reality because in real reality circles can be square and since there are none in ordinary experience and we can't make any *there* this proves the existence of that other dimension *where* square circles and round circles co-exist as real circles.

And by this they [the Kantian t.h.e.y] do *not* mean we can choose to evade idiosyncratic unpleasantness (which our power of volition quite appropriately makes possible and without which we wouldn't have the power of volition) but rather, that, *metaphysically* we can't see the real world because it is not real and even if it were real we couldn't see it because it is not seeable. And it is not seeable *because* we have an eye-brain "system" that distorts what it sees. (*How* Kantians are exempt from their own laws and can have such a *non*-distorted theory of man—your inner curmudgeon may be wondering—is a wonderment that only knaves, fools, and doubting Thomases would wonder about—your inner religious critic could be "saying". But not to worry.)

Enter the *rationalist* and the *empiricist* psychologists dressed as scientists with *some* of them linked arm-in-arm with Physicists, Astronomers (e.g., Carl Sagan), Cosmologists (e.g., Stephen Hawking) and other physical scientist types who religiously believe that *reductive materialism*—everything ultimately is reducible to the laws of chemistry and physics—is the ultimate path to *truth* for all real scientists to follow.

That T,h,e,y do not like and are afraid of Ayn Rand and her philosophy of Objectivism is obvious. But the reasons for their dislike are not so obvious. T.h.e.y. do not like and are afraid of Ayn Rand and her philosophy of Objectivism because in it she tells them that real scientists are ones who *worship* reason and because of this worship they *know* that contradictions do not exist.

And *how* does she and we and they know this? Simple: Nature demonstrates it to us by *not having any*.

However, as people pleasers first and *scientists* second t,h,e,y proceed to show us lay people *how* Kant's view is true and how we too can get around it and really (kinda) "know" things. After all, since everybody knows that we know some things there must be something very subtle and secret about ~~Kan't's~~ Kant's view.[178] That is, since Kant's view says we kan't know but since we do know there must be something wrong somewhere. And since Kant isn't wrong (say his true followers) there must be something wrong with our understanding of HOW man works in the real world and it is our job as (cognitive in this case) scientists to fill in the gaps.

Since both the *Rationalist* and the *Empiricist* view of man is wrong and both of them know it they have been trying for centuries to integrate their two wrong views into one. Which is to say they have been trying for centuries to prove that *two wrongs do make a right*.

The hardest most difficult thing for the rationalists and the empiricists to accept today is the fact that the *Objectivists* beat 'em to the goal line. Which is to say t,h,e,y can't accept that the Objectivist view is correct : man is *not* a mind-body dichotomy but rather, man is a mind-body *integration* with the body understood to mean the *whole* body not just the brain. Because of this, "they" (the rationalists and the empiricists, qua refusers to go down with their ship) had to do something to keep their traditions alive and functioning while at-the-same-time giving us "lay" people the *impression* that they disagree with each other in a healthy back 'n forth, give and take sort of way characteristic of intellectual discussion and advancement. And in an "Oh! also-by-the-way" sentiment, that, yes they have finally come to their senses (pun intended) and that even though we wasted untold amounts of money and time on Behaviorism in the past, this time "we" (you as current tax payer, me as—temporary, hopefully—unemployed ex taxpayer) should keep supporting them with government confiscated tax monies because "they" are (finally) right.

It's pretty easy to predict here that sometime over the next 50 years they will flip-flop back to the *empiricist* view and tell a new generation of tax payers: "Oh,

---

[178] Another slip? Kan'ts as in Can't? ... know?. Wow. I guess when one *chooses* to judge, the effects are *opposite* of when one *chooses* not to judge. That is, it appears that when one *chooses to judge*: good happens.

those old fuddy duddy rationalist Cognitive Psychologist-Cognitive Scientist-Cognitive Neuroscientist's got it all f…screwed up *again* and now it is our turn to (re)say Behaviorism (i.e. empiricism) was right all along.

And here we are. Again (!) with the need to briefly answer yet another question before we can proceed. That is, before we can see the inevitable logic that produces the foregoing prediction, we must first answer another question. (How many is that now? Including that one? And these last two too? *Yes*. Eight.)

But before we answer question # 8: What is *Behaviorism*?, let's summarize:

1. What is [Jay Gay Snodgrass's] memory and how does it work? *Ans*: TBD.
2. What is Cognitive Psychology? *Ans*: euphemism for Kantian psychology.
3. What is Kant's view of man? *Ans*: man by his nature can't know.
4. If man can't, how can Kantians know? *Ans*: by evading contradictions.
5. How many [questions] is that now? *Ans*: 5.
6. Including that one? *Ans*: Yes.
7. And these last two too? *Ans*: Yes.
8. What is Behaviorism? *Ans*: see next.

Behaviorism is a *philosophy* and a *science*. Qua *empiricist* philosophy, *Behaviorism* says it is *permissible* to reduce a particular part of reality down to the intellectual level of those who want to study it. Qua science, it says *what* psychology is and what it isn't. Specifically, it says psychology **is** the science of behavior and **not** the science that studies the characteristics and attributes that certain living organisms possess by virtue of being conscious. This last is *what* the (*Biocentric*) *Psychology* of Dr. Nathaniel Branden says psychology is.[i]

Behaviorism is *not* Biocentric Psychology.[179]

Behaviorism is the *alleged* science of behavior *declared* to be the science of psychology by mainstream educators and government officials in the United States of America during the middle and latter half of the last (20th) Century. The founder and major promoter of Behaviorism in its *modern* form is Dr. B.F. Skinner who worked before, during and after the middle part of the last (20th)

---

[179] Biocentric psychology is psyc*hh*ology is psychology from here on (with a few exceptions where the double hh is retained for emphasis).

Century and who also during this same time period wrote about his view of psychology as being the "science of behavior".

Behaviorism believes and preaches that man does *not* have a soul (*what* in *BiO Spiritualism* we call: *consciousness*). Since *Behaviorism*—qua soulless preaching—was proven wrong by Ayn Rand and the *Objectivists* and Biocentric Psychology—who proved, or demonstrated if you prefer, that man does have a soul, that is, consciousness—Skinner's followers had to abandon him. That is, in the jargon of the street, t.h.e.y had to stuff-can Skinner because it was becoming too obvious to *everybody* that Skinner's autonomaton view of man was way too far off base. So they had to make up a "new" science as the *means* to keeping their beloved mind-body dualism battles alive and well. Alive and well, that is, *in our Culture's epistemological house* that we, qua lay people/intellectual street people, know as: *The Ivory Towers*.

So that the knocked out but refusing to go down Behaviorists (they are persistent I'll grant 'em that) like thieves trying to smuggle their stolen concepts into the 21st Century, named their "new" (euphemistic) science of psychology: *cognitive psychology* and placed its philosophical base on another euphemistic science that they labeled: *Cognitive Science*. *Cognitive Science* is the answer to the hypothetical question: If Cognitive Psychology is the science that deals with the ordinary, every day experiences in a Kantian Universe, what do you call the science that deals with the real noumenal, Kantian world behind ordinary experiences?

You mean the one where circles can be round or square?

Yes.

And as if this wasn't enough, in order to really confuse us they have added a third player in their flip-flopping back 'n forth game. Now they have *Cognitive Science* leap-frogging over *Cognitive Psychologists* leap-frogging over *Reductive Materialists* leap-frogging over Cognitive Scientists leap-frogging over —.

But t.h.e.i.r introduction of a third player only means that in the future we will hear three times as many screams.

Cognitive Science, qua the writings of H.E. Gardner, and *Cognitive Psychology* qua those of Ulric Neisser, et al., when *added* to Carl Sagan and numerous other "Scientism" scientists who worship the "principles" of *reductive materialism* becomes (iteratively speaking) the total euphemism for Kant's Philosophy. Kant's *Metaphysics* is *his* answer to the Ayn Rand question: "Where am I?" to which Kant answers: *I am in a world of ordinary appearances that are an illusion and the real world is in some other dimension beyond my human experience of sights and sounds and smells and tastes and cuts & bruises and caresses.* And so says Kant, so are you and so is everybody in this same "Universe" and he then labels the world of our ordinary, every day experiences, the world of *phenomenon* and the "real" behind-the-scenes reality the *noumenal* world. Kant's *Epistemology* (as nutshelled by Ayn Rand) is: I can't see *because* I have eyes; and the Kantian *Ethic* is: the moral *ideal* is *pure* altruism; a completely and totally *undiluted* altruism devoid of any self-interest whatsoever—including the pride of being a good altruist. Which is to say, *modern* Kantianism is alive and well and thriving at the core of the "machine" that cranks out our American culture, and which—like some creature out of the old movie "Alien"—is determined with an in-your-face tenacity to also be the motor grinding out tomorrow's *Global* Culture.

As to *why* they would go to *such* lengths to institutionalize Kantianism, we can answer in a single word: *Objectivism. Because* the *Objectivists* (especially Dr. Peikoff, qua Ayn Rand's *second* sidekick) proved (beyond reasonable doubt) Kantian epistemology to be wrong, Kant's sympathizers had to *do something.* Cognitive Neuroscience and its underpinnings in cognitive psychology and cognitive science is the *something* that t.h.e.y did.[180]

Or at least this is the *claim* of *BiO Spiritualism* and to go one level higher in the abstract claims department before we stop, *BiO Spiritualism* further claims that *Cognitive Neuroscience* is really nothing more than the 21st Century version of what every "intellectualizing-brainiac" from any bygone century falsely believes he or she has the virtuosity to accomplish: the *integration* of "Religion" and "Science".[181]

---

[180] Noumena, per Kantianism, are "things in themselves" and we can't [metaphysically can't] experience them directly [contrast this with Objectivism that says our "perceptions" are our direct awareness/direct experience of "things" which means "things in themselves"]. Phenomena—Kant's other part—is our sensory representations of things as actively organized by our [platonic, innate, pre-conceptual] categories [contrast this with Objectivism that says our "categories" our "concepts" are man-made and man-made by us and *should* be made in accordance with reality, the reality of our *survival* needs as conscious organisms with the power of volition whose primary means of surviving is the proper development and use of our capacity to reason].

[181] An intellectualizer is one who talks *about* his psychhological problems in-the-abstract as the *means* of not facing them. For example, if I were a full fledged "intellectualizer" I would say: "My brain *informed* me that an intellectualizer is one who …etc.". A brainiac is one who believes that memorizing a gigantic number of facts and then regurgitating them upon demand is a display of ones ability to think when in fact it is only a display of ones ability to retain & recall (which isn't an all bad ability but it can't substitute for thinking). Consequently, an "intellectualizing-brainiac" is one who has no human personality because he has no room for one, given that his consciousness is filled with raw facts and defense ~~mechanisms~~ values. And yes, it does take one to know one and having been to the edge and done that I know of where I speak. (Though as a Biocentric Psychology sympathizer I have to add—since Biocentric is anti self-effacing behaviors—that I

This, if, that is, *you* are one of those who accepts the compassionate Ayn Rand claim that religion is a primitive philosophy. Since I (still) do not (yet) accept this claim I have to conclude that Cognitive Neuroscience is the attempt to integrate wrong Philosophy & wrong Science, specifically the wrong philosophy of Immanuel Kant and the wrong Science of Reductive Materialism. (Or again, depending on your emotionally based beliefs you may choose to characterize Cognitive Neuroscience as the attempted integration of the religion of Kantianism with the Science of reductive materialism. Or to state it more succinctly, I suppose *you* could say: *Intellectualizing-brainiacs is one reason why god invented religion.* But of course, since I don't believe in god I can't say this.)

Consider also one final (for now, *BiO Spiritualism*) claim.

The Government of the United States of America will grant money for "mental health and mental illness" issues to no one *other than* those who claim to be *cognitive neuroscientists* and/or who are (or claim to be, explicitly and/or implicitly in their Grant Requests) sympathetic to them.

So I repeat: maybe you *should* be afraid.

Fear—*when rational*—has *survival* value.

Consequently, now that we have an inkling of *what* we are up against we can proceed ahead by answering question #1: What is [Jay Gay Snodgrass's] memory and how does it work?

The figure on (M-B) p. 209—Figure 11.4 Tulving's (1985) proposal for a tripartite memory system—shows the cognitive psychologists view of our memory as being divisible [not into the two types known as *short term* and *long term* memory, but] into 3 fundamental systems: Episodic Memory, Semantic Memory and Procedural Memory. And as the figure describes, *episodic* is autobiographical knowledge about self-referenced events, *semantic* is general knowledge shared by a culture, and *procedural* is perceptual, motor, or cognitive skills.

For example, your feeling here that the foregoing paragraph is somewhat repetitive—a feeling you might have since it is repeated, almost verbatim, from Chapter 16, page 142 where it first appeared—would be an example of: what? Episodic? (since you were the one who had to have read it in Chapter 16 in order to have the memory), or semantic? (probably not, since you as reader and me as author do not a culture make, and besides what does "shared by a culture" have to do with it anyway? If I know that St. Paul is the Capitol of Minnesota and you

---

didn't go over the 49% line into 51% and more into the intelluallizer-brainiac domain, which is to say I used my *power of volition* to catch myself in-the-nick-of time.)

know it too it doesn't change the fact that I know it independent of whether or not you know it, or vice versa. Is this an example of what *Objectivism* pejoratively calls definitions by non-essentials? ...) or procedural? Probably not this either (since I don't *really* understand what "they" mean by procedural memory, unless it is that I *remember* the *procedure* of *how* to tie my shoes that was taught to me by my next door neighbor girl buddy when we both were four and a half years old...if *this* is what they mean by procedural: *place the one shoe string over the other shoe string, tie a simple knot, then take one of the strings and form it into a bow and ... etcetera*, if this, then *not* procedural...) so, by elimination, it must be: episodic.

This proposed 3-part memory structure is given in a context of Dr. Snodgrass trying to answer the more fundamental question: "Is memory a *system* or a *process*"? She tells us that this is a controversial question in *cognitive psychology* and even though she thinks it probably isn't resolvable, she is "resolving" it to be the case that memory is more system than process and she proceeds to "prove" this by showing us how we can compare our memory to our visual *system* and auditory *system*.

On p. 209—that underlaps from p. 208—she sets up three criterions by which we are to judge whether or not our memory can be viewed as a *system*. Also on p. 209 she next demonstrates that memory does not meet one of those three criteria. On p. 210 she continues her conclusion from p. 209 that since memory is a system—apparently she knew this before all her reasoning that suggested otherwise so she just ignores her own reasoning, so since memory is a system—it is *not* process.

So why does Dr. Snodgrass (a highly educated person) as well as other *cognitive scientist psychologist neuroscientists* (also highly educated by-the-American-mainstream-collegiate-university-education-system people) insist on trying to *make* memory into a system like eyesight and/or hearing?

The answer to this question is both interesting and informative.

It is interesting because it suggests religion might not have a monopoly on faith and it is informative because it sheds light on the power of (correct) science to *predict* the future in the realm of psychology as *accurately* as in the realm of physics.

The three pages of Mind-Brain that we are looking at here (209, 210, 211) of Dr. Snodgrass's larger article (*The Memory Trainers*) was written in the late 1990's and was *predicted* to be written some 30 years earlier by one of her predecessors working and writing in the area of Biology.

His name is Robert Efron, his article—serialized into four parts—was titled "Biology without consciousness—And its consequences" and its Part I was presented in the February 1968 edition of *The Objectivist* (a monthly periodical of intellectual ideas, edited by Ayn Rand).

In that series of articles Dr. Efron—an MD, Chief of Neurophysiology-Biophysics Research Unit, VA Hospital, Boston, Massachusetts—detailed the damage that the erroneous philosophy of "reductive materialism" was beginning to wreak on the science of biology and *predicted* it would do the same and more on the science of psychology. He writes on p. 6 (and we must remember that this is almost a half century ago being near the middle of the 20th Century, not the early 21st Century of today):

> The science of biology suffers from a progressive and potentially fatal epistemological disorder. It is characterized by such profound chaos in the realm of definitions and the logical relationships between concepts that those who suffer from it have lost cognitive contact with reality. One of the most fundamental causes of this disorder is a philosophical principle: It holds that all the phenomena of life will ultimately be reduced to—that is, accounted for, described by, and deduced from—the laws of physics and chemistry. It is known as the "principle of reduction [i.e., of reductive materialism]."
>
> The result of blind adherence to this principle has been an intellectual smashup in neurophysiology and psychology. It has involved such concepts as perception, emotion, the reflex, abstraction, the conditioned reflex, the cerebral localization of function, learning and memory—to name only a few.[ii]

If you think Dr. Efron's claim that those who suffer from *reductive materialism* have lost cognitive contact with reality is not *also a prediction* that those in the future who accept reductive materialism as a principle will also suffer the same fate, consider the following from p. 209 of Dr. Snodgrass:

> Consider the two systems of episodic and semantic memory proposed by Tulving. They clearly do not satisfy criterion (1) above. Sense organs for both types of memory include all of the perceptual ones (vision, audition, smell, taste, and

> somatesthesia) as well as internal ones such as thought and remembrance itself.[iii]

Here, as an initial step in starting to unravel the rat's nest so we can find its starting point we will employ a modified version of the analysis "technique" we introduced in Part II, Chapters 4 and 5. Our added comments to the above appear below in [brackets]. We recopy the above—verbatim—and then go through it and add our further observations connecting it to reality and also our evaluations of the piece (as you do this exercise, practice owning a *BiO Spiritualism* Principle: *judge not least ye be judged* is the mantra of the uncourageous, therefore, *judge and be prepared to be judged*):

> Consider the two systems of episodic and semantic memory proposed by Tulving [before he modified it and proposed 3]. They clearly do not satisfy criterion (1[of 3]) above [i.e., possesses a distinct sense organ]. Sense organs for both types of memory include all of the perceptual ones (vision [i.e., eyeballs], audition [i.e. ears], smell [i.e. noses], taste [i.e. tongues], and somatesthesia [i.e. the body as "organ" as "place" *where* pleasure, pain and their derivatives are experienced by us as conscious, living organisms]) as well as internal ones such as thought [i.e.? thoughtballs???] and remembrance itself [i.e.? remembrance balls???].

If this (sneaky/oblique) "suggestion" that we have thought-balls and remembrance-balls just like we have eye-balls isn't loosing cognitive contact with reality it's loosing contact with something.[182]

If you think it esoteric whether or not we view memory as process or system, use your "remembranceballs" to remember the foregoing excerpt of Dr. Snodgrass's.

---

[182] Common sense, perhaps? Since average, everyday people seem to know the importance of maintaining contact with common sense (or what Ayn Rand calls, the integration of the 5 senses) why, one wonders, do mainstream academicians *not* seem to share in this healthy regard for common sense? (See earlier quote here—page 178—where Hans J. Eysenck says [scientific?] psychology has to do battle with commonsense.) The answer to this is because the mainstream academicians have accepted Kantian Epistemology as the correct epistemology (even though it has been proven to be incorrect by the Objectivist philosophers, see especially Dr. Peikoff's article: "The Analytic-Synthetic Dichotomy", Reference xiii in Chapter 20). Since cognitive science sympathizers are no different than anyone else, they are subject to the same laws of human nature as everyone else and so here they are driven by one such law in particular. This (proposed) law is the BiO Spiritualism (#45 445th) ~~Theorem~~ proposition: *it starts and ends with metaphysics,* that we touched on, qua idea, in the title to Chapter 11 (and will deal with again in later volumes of BiO Spiritualism).

If you are familiar with Ayn Rand's Philosophy of *Objectivism* you know that life itself is a process: a *process* of self-sustaining, self-generated action. Since consciousness is the "self" in the life-process that does the *generating* and the *sustaining* it makes sense to conclude that consciousness itself is *process*.[183]

And *process*—notwithstanding this footnote[184]— is a *thing*. Not in the *object* sense of thing, but in the *existent* sense of thing. If it *exists* it is a "thing" and for now we can and will label it a Dr. Seuss *type* of thing and define every-thing as either thing 1 or thing 2. Thing 1 is things in the *object* sense of the term—cars, books, shoes, desks, tables, chairs, cups, pencils, computer monitors, and the list goes on and on and on, staplers, paper clips, paper, pots 'n pans, doors, baskets, backscratcher, soap, towels, and the list is endless, hammers, nails, sawsals, and the list goes on and on, needles, thread, string, sewing machines, and the list is endless, saddles, bridles, stirrups, horses, cats, dogs, and the list goes on, crayons, stones, rulers, trees, flowers, walnuts, apples, and the list is endless, etcetera—and things 2 are *existents* as in characteristics and attributes and qualities of things 1—color, degree or intensity, number, hard, soft, rough, smooth, fast, slow, hot, cold, warm, and so on. All *objects* are thing 1, everything else is thing 2 for now and are so with this *BiO Spiritualism* principle: *Every-thing is some-thing to a human consciousness* (including for example that which Visual Artists call *negative space* which if you hold up your hand and spread your fingers is the V-shaped "space" between them). Whether or not any given particular human consciousness has explicitly identified "things"—i.e., things 1 as thing 1 and things 2 as thing 2—is a matter of the idiosyncratic explicitness of any particular consciousness as manifested in, and as it exists at any point in time in, a particular, alive human being and is itself a thing. Which thing? Thing 2. As in *process* is a thing 2 (pun intended).

---

[183] According to the philosophy of Objectivism, consciousness is the process of identification so much so that they conclude: consciousness *is* identification.

[184] That is, notwithstanding two other cognitive psychologists in M-B whose article didn't show up on our randomizing radar. These two are Michael I. Posner, Ph.D. psychology, University of Michigan and Daniel J. Levitin, Ph.D. candidate (at the time of M-B publication) University of Oregon. One of them, per pp. 105 and 106 of Mind-Brain, argues that consciousness is a function and not a process and hence will be found to exist in a particular place in the brain. The other of them, per the same pages, argues that consciousness is an emergent property of the [heart as a whole organ? ... no, but rather of the] brain-as-a-whole (organ) and as such it is a *process*, not a *thing* (Is this "their" idea of whole-istic? Maybe someone should tell them about Mike the Chicken, no not as in *afraid* but as in head-chopped-off-and still lived real Chicken who made the rounds to all the county fairs during the 1920's and/or 1930's and enthralled people of the time as they watched his handler feed him kernels of corn one at a time through a hole in his neck where his head used to be, and he, Mike ate it and walked around scratching the ground with his claws "looking" for more food.).

In this sense then consciousness, qua existent, is a thing and since "we" have identified it as *process* it is a thing 2.

Since consciousness does not exist apart from the bodies it is a part of (any more than yellow exists apart from crayons or paint or canaries) and since live bodies do not exist apart from consciousness (as testified to by corpses, be they funeral home corpses or road kill) we say mind and body—that is, consciousness and body, that is, body and soul—are one in the same, that is are integral, that is, inseparable—like cream-in-coffee to use an earlier analogy—but also—unlike cream and coffee—mind and body are inseparable in that they do not and never did exist apart from each other and hence they do not exist independent of each other: which is to say, mind and body are *integrated*.

We talk about them separately only for the purposes of study and to advance our understanding of both so that we can reap the rewards of intense, in-depth understanding of "things".

Since Objectivism has successfully argued that consciousness is " ... a dynamic not static process ... a *process* of differentiation and integration ..."[iv] and since *memory* is one (sub) *function* of consciousness (as are perception, emotion, abstracting, learning ... "to name only a few" as Dr. Efron pointed out more than a quarter of a century ago) it is logical to think of memory as process more so than as system (that is, as thing 2 not thing 1).

Memory, quoting Dr. Robert Efron quoting Aristotle is:

> "neither perception nor conception, but a state or affection of one of these, conditioned by lapse of time." He [Aristotle] held that, whenever one exercises the faculty of remembering, one says within himself some equivalent of "I formerly heard this" or "I formerly had this thought."[v]

"[And some 20 centuries later in 1890] William James defined memory as 'the knowledge of a former state of mind after it has already once dropped from consciousness; or rather it is the knowledge of an event or fact, of which meantime we have not been thinking, *with the additional consciousness that we have thought or experienced it before.*'"[vi]

So why do Cognitive Neuroscientists, qua Cognitive Psychologists, qua Cognitive Scientists, want to make memory be a system?

Primarily so that t,h,e,y can remain "sane".

Because at root they are reductive materialists and as also claimed and predicted by Dr. Robert Efron back in the 1960's,[vii] they have to think this way *because* they have accepted the false principle of reductive materialism on *faith* and like all things accepted *on faith* the acceptee has to distort reality to *make* her (or his) *core* belief *be* "true".[185]

Since memory, qua function of consciousness, in the end involves both, that is, memory is the *process* of me recalling the events of my life that are retained within the body *system* known as me (and you of yours within you), the question is, do I retain every aspect of every moment of my life or do I only retain some aspects as well as all and/or some evaluated aspects of my moments? That is, do I retain every perceptual aspect of every moment as well as every evaluation of every moment or do I retain less than this? And if less—or more[186]—*what* is it that I retain?

The *how* do I do it? That is, *how* do I retain it [whatever "it" happens to be] is another question.

Ultimately [the first] it [how do I do the retaining] is a question for *physiologists* not *psychologists*, so why—one is forced to wonder—do "they" (Cognitive Neuroscience—psychologist-wannabe types) spend so much time trying to figure out a physiologist's problem?

The *correct* answer here is because they are physiologists, *not* psychologists.

Nor are they—notwithstanding their feeble attempts, qua Cognitive Scientists, to give Immanuel Kant's non-real epistemology a reality structure—philosophers.[187]

Philosophy (i.e. *Objectivism*) tells us that "The 'how' cannot be used to negate the 'what', or the 'what' the 'how'— ...".[viii]

When this philosophical principle is applied here it means: *what* I (or you) retain cannot be replaced with *how* I (or you) retain it.

---

[185] See negative consequences of this inside those, i.e. the *honest* ones such as myself, who for example accepted the "existence" of God on faith, and know *first* hand how distorty, diabolical, faith as tool of mind not only is, but more importantly, *has to be*. (Has to, that is, if sanity is a standard.)

[186] e.g. the streaming sense data that enters through my sense organs, that is, through my eyes, my ears, my nose, my tongue and my hand and other touch sensitive parts of my body.

[187] That the Cognitive Scientists are the "wannabe philosophers" of this group of self-proclaimed Cognitive Neuroscientists is easy to see if one reads some of the earlier books written by those who claim ownership of Cognitive Science. For one example, see Harold Gardner's book: "The Mind's New Science" (see Reference ii in Chapter 16), especially pages 6 and 7 of that Reference where the author defines Cognitive Science's five features—all of which are *explicitly* epistemological features and by *implication* (hence, the/my "wannabe" charge) metaphysical positions. Since **a** metaphysic, **an** epistemology and **a** ethic philosophy make ... the only thing these five features lack is an ethic. But given their premise features it isn't too hard to predict that their ethic will ultimately be one of relativism and/or determinism and hence Cognitive Science in the long run will—like its Behavioristic cousin—prove to be just more useless drivel to overcome in man's search for understanding man, qua man.

And we have to pause here and take note of this fact: *that* I retain is not up for debate but is rather taken for granted, that is, is a given. (I mention this here because I know that since Cognitive Science is euphemism for "Kantian Epistemology" that somewhere, sometime, somehow "t.h.e.y." are going to try and get me to doubt this basic-taken-for granted-given fact that since I recall things I retain things.)

This is *what* the reductive-materialist-cognitive-neuro-physiologist-"psychologists" are trying to do: they are trying to derive the non-existent physics and chemical formulas that "produce" consciousness because they already "know" that consciousness is reducible to the laws of physics and chemistry. How they are trying to do it is to use *memory* as their wedge—their stake shaped wedge—into m/y(our) reasoning heart(s).[188]

So that, the question about memory is, *what* do I retain and *how* do I do it? To which the answer is: **I** retain that which is *important* to me (as do *you* to you) and I do it by storing it in nature's *physiological* "value" hierarchy.(?[189] ?)

And since I remember that which is valuable to me, I am, as indicated, betting that you do too, because I have seen you also remember a phone number for the length of time it takes you to get from the phone book to the phone and enter it and also I have talked to you when we both have reminisced about our childhoods.

Memory can be defined then as the *ability or the capacity or the power* to recall that which is important to us, that is, to the *one* who remembers. And what is important? That which my consciousness *needs* in order to function properly—that is, for it and the body it is enmeshed in to survive—as well as other more

---

[188] SWAGgerly (ScientificWildAssGuess'ing) speaking does this mean that since (Wilhelm) Reich has discovered the relationship between repression and muscles via muscle-tensing, that muscle tissue serves the dual purpose of being the storage medium for my memories (like the magnetic material of floppy disks and hard drives is the storage medium for my computer [if your computer is more modern and uses an optical medium please make the requisite adjustment, if yours is futuristic and uses rat-brain neurons kept alive in a nutrient rich fluroinert liquid please also make the adjustments but also let me know ASAP on which planet you bought your hand held PC with its 100 million gigaterabyte storage capacity because I want one too]) and that the heart, qua most (or very) important organ, is the (muscle) "place" where my highest, most important, most fundamental values are stored? So that yesterday when I felt a soft, distant-to-the-point-of-ancient, almost imperceptible wave in my heart area at the thought of wouldn't it be nice if there was a god to be responsible for and bring justice to all man-made events here on earth ... that is, does this make sense that I was *aware* at the time—NOT of my little toe, but rather—of my heart? Near and dear ... TO MY ... etc., is one cliché I believe that applies here also.

[189] Again, SWAGerly speaking. So that an attack on *my* most fundamental values is experienced by *me* as if you were *literally* attacking my core with sharp, dangerous, killy-cutty weapons of *me*-destruction. Hence, it goes without saying that y/our values damn well better match the reality of y/our nature and needs or we *will* be in deep .... that is, really really *deep* ... trouble.

specific things that I—that is, the idiosyncratic acquirer of many values I—"need" to survive. Such as all the things I need to retain in order to learn how to survive on my own (be it how to tie my shoes on my own so that I can get outside *faster* to play rather than have to wait around for my slow-pokey mother or to cook a meal or to program my computer to mathematically determine the best straight line through a bunch of collected data test points and print out the slope and intercept of such a line and in so doing make me an efficient and hence valuable Test Engineer to my employer who will not fire me because I am valuable and ... etcetera and so on. Does this mean: *Yes*, memory and learning *are* intimately connected but this connection is beyond our immediate concern here? *Yes*.).

So let me conclude this third random selection of Mind-Brain on our list of ten by summarizing Dr. Snodgrass's three pp. 209, 210 and 211.

But first another comment (or two) and then Dr. Snodgrass.

HOW the brain processes is an interesting question for *physiologists* and others[190] interested in the physics of the problem of processing reality so as to produce "percepts". But such *automatic* processing is not of interest—after it has been discovered to be automatic—to philosophers or (real) psychologists. It is not, that is, *unless* their enemies are trying to use the "physics" aspect of the problem to "prove" that philosophers and/or (real) psychologists can't know jack sh-, that is, can't know anything—completely dropping the context of *knowing* as they parse the world by the *process* of dividing by 2 ad infinitum as their *means* of boring normal people to death so that they don't care—that is, give a whit 'n a wither—*what* the cognitive scientists, qua BM flunkies, are even talking about.

But lay people, qua sheep potential, *should* know that this boredom is t.h.e.i.r (shepherd's) goal.

If yesterday's devil was in-the-details, today's is in-be-tween the lines.[191]

By *system* Dr. Snodgrass *starts* out meaning what you and I mean, an organ system like eyesight—the visual system—or like hearing, the auditory system. Using these as examples that everyone can easily relate to she says there are three

---

[190] Others, for example, *such as* AI professionals as those computer scientists who are interested in Artificial Intelligence even if such a term is concept stealing of the highest order. *Intelligence* is an *attribute* of man's consciousness, *artificial* means man-made. Some day humans may learn how to make consciousness the same way nature does but .... well ... until that time and unless that happens, no *machine intelligence* is intelligence. Or stated differently: the day man creates artificial intelligence will be the day the religionists can truthfully say *they* (finally) have *proof* that god exists—granted it will only be *ostensive* proof but it will be proof nonetheless—they will just *point* at a human and say: there! that is what I mean by god.

[191] And Tomorrow Man's is [will be] in-between-the-letters©s—as example, see Footnote 108 on page 112 for the meaning of T.h.e.y and recognize that this "they" can be—at least partially—inside u.s.—not U.S. as in United States but rather *inside* y/our psyche as in, UnderSelf.

criterion we can identify in these systems and then *use these criterion* to test whether memory system *proposals* [made by Cognitive Scientist types and/or presumably by any "scientist" type] are systems or not.[192] She accepts that the *system* versus *process* view is controversial and predicts that in this 21st Century most if not all Behaviorists, Cognitive Psychologists and Cognitive Neuroscience types will probably agree that the controversy is incapable of resolution (p. 208 in M-B). All that this is really saying is that t.h.e.y will agree *to continue* agreeing that *contradictions exist in nature.* Hence, this "prediction" of Dr. Snodgrass's is really nothing more than re-statement and it will "come-to-pass" and be true simply because it already *is* true: most if not all Behaviorists, Cognitive Psychologists and Cognitive Neuroscientists will continue to believe that contradictions exist in nature and are the (or at absolute minimum, *a*) *defining* characteristic of nature.

However, since the truth is contradictions *do not* exist in nature (which is a *metaphysical* primary which you either accept or reject based on your own *first* hand observations and dealings with nature, that is, with reality and in so doing make it or its absence part of *your* metaphysics, which is something you as a human animal *need* as part 'n parcel of your *need* of philosophy) it leaves only one place for them to occur: in the mind of man. Since man's mind is a natural not supernatural phenomenon this observation is itself the identification of a contradiction—or what seems to be a contradiction—and it needs to be resolved, and *because* contradictions do not exist it can be resolved.[193] As Objectivist

---

[192] On her own terms, since Cognitive Scientist Psychologist extraordinaire [Endel] Tulving [Harvard Ph.D.] proposed a three part memory system to replace his two part memory system and neither one of them met criterion one: [possess] distinct sense organs, like eyes or ears, you would suspect she would conclude that memory is more process than system. But she does not, rather she tries to conclude that memory is made up of 7 organs: the five known sensory organs—eyeballs, ears, nose, skin, tongue—plus two new ones we lay people didn't even know about but what we can call the thought organ and the remembrance organ (M-B, p.209). By these last two, however, she does *not* mean the brain itself because criterion two for her systems definition is, distinct representations *in the brain* and I don't think even the Cognitive Neurologist-Psychologist-Scientist types would metaphorically argue that "being in-the-house" is the same as "being the house". But I'm not exactly sure what they will argue for in the 21st Century, for all I know they could, at some point, start talking about a *metabrain*. In fact this sounds as "logical" as any thing T.H.E.Y. conclude, so let me leave it stand as a prediction of BiO Spiritualism's—or as I sometimes like to call it: the N+1 school of psychology, the one we can call *Volition Psychology*, or *what* in the 22nd century—if not the 21st first—they will call, *psychology*.

[193] Think about the following "apparent" contradiction and see if you can resolve it before you get to Chapter 24 where it is resolved. The (alleged) "contradiction" goes like this: Since contradictions do not exist in reality and man's mind is a natural not supernatural—as in beyond nature, beyond reality—phenomenon how can he have contradictory ideas "in-his-mind", which is a "thing" "in reality"? therefore, contradictions (do) exist—i.e., contradictions exist in-the-mind-of man which is, *in* reality.

sympathizers "we" are not allowed the "luxury" of concluding that "...the controversy [*is memory a system or a process? Or its attempted replacement "upgrade" version: is consciousness, that is, soul, that is, is consciousness a function of the brain or an emergent property of the brain? What if it is neither and/or noa? See earlier footnotes #183, 184 on page 208*] ... the controversy is incapable of resolution..." as Dr. Snodgrass, a Cognitive Psychologist, says in regards to her view of the *system* versus *process* controversy in "psychology".[194]

Since consciousness—per my and Mike's *first hand/claw* experience—is a *full body experience* (I now voluntarily wiggle my big toe, my little finger and even pause and become aware of some muscle tension behind my left knee) it seems logical to conclude that consciousness itself is more *process* (e.g. the *process* of being aware, paying attention, thinking, feeling, animating oneself—i.e. acting) than *system*—e.g. speaking sarcastically for a moment: a ThoughtBallOrgan-connected to a AbstractingBallOrgan—connected to the hip bone that "pumps" *conceptual* knowledge in the same way the EyeBall-Nerves-Brain pump out *percepts* (or better per Dr. Branden's way of saying it: "the way the heart pumps blood" is the *wish*—the irrational wish—of those human beings who seek an animal's automatic form of existing), which is to say: the ThoughtBallOrgan-et al. "system" *automatically* pumps out "conceptual" knowledge. Since not that (*concept* formation requires choice and a heck of a lot of willful effort, that is, work)—it is logical to view all *consciousness* activity as process more so than system, and to be p-r-e-c-i-s-e: as Process + System (it is not either/or but both\and[195]).

---

[194] M-B p. 208. I've tried really really hard to stick to pp. 209,210 and 211 but I've been unable to do so here, so the best I can do is to not use any material from p. 211 to offset this "failure", though the significance of deviating this little bit is ... not significant to my point that 10 random page numbers plus and minus 1 will hit discussions and intellectual arguments that rest on premises that are anti-human nature. Here I've had to deviate slightly in order to be clear as well as to not mis-quote the various authors who deserve, qua academicians, not to be misquoted. Since you can go read the Mind-Brain book yourself (see Reference i for Chapter 16) I view it (the hardcover or softcover version which are the same page number-for-page number) to be part of my experimental raw data. Since I obviously can't include the whole book it does not preclude me from including the title and information you need to get it yourself, read it yourself, and to agree or disagree, more or less with my "observations" about this particular book. When you do this then we will have "publicly" verifiable information between us. For those of us who are pro-volition and anti-determinism this Mind-Brain book is a $gold$ mind of how they, the Determinist mentalities think, and I submit once you read it you can no longer remain in the middle-of-the-road on *this* controversy, which is: Is man "determined" by his own *volitional* choices or is he determined by forces *outside his control*?

[195] The "it" here in "it" is not either/or but both\and is: "human *experience*". It is consciousness *as process* PLUS body *as system*, just like cooking is pots 'n pans and stove tops and ovens as system parts and self as chef, cook and chief bottle washer engaging in the PROCESS of cooking and cleaning up after one's self, which in our case here is following the recipe for cooking up a happy life here on this earth while we actually

The body itself is a system of systems: digestive system, respiratory system, nervous system, reproductive system, and on and on. The body is ... the immune system, the urinary system, the endocrine system, which is to say, the body is an integration of organ systems operating together to produce *physical* life.

So just what is the difference between *system* and *process*?

My dictionary (the same one I quoted before) says *system* is a regularly interacting or interdependent group of items [that is, a bunch of thing 1's] forming a *unified whole*, e.g. a number system [with thing 1's = the numbers 1,2,3,4,5,... and so on]; the digestive system [thing 1's = stomach, intestines, esophagus et al.], a data processing system [thing 1's = CentralProcessingUnit with its metal or plastic cover and printed circuit boards and connectors inside this unit and the chips on these boards and so on + Memory chips on boards + Input/Output devices].

---

live, and if practice makes good chefs then our past experiences—if we are not yet happy—we can count as practice: we learn from them and go on (which is BiO Spiritualism's 32nd proposition: [do] learn from y/o(thers)ur mistakes and move on, which is to say, don't move on until you have learned something reality based from mistakes: e.g. jumping out of that tree from a point higher than the second big branch hurts my ankle, therefore don't do it anymore. OK. I won't. Or later when I was much older and a practicing counselor I recalled my first client—Dee Jay—who was one of those adults-walking-around-in-a-child's-body you hear discussed and talked about in Biocentric psychology. DJ said when his *first* wife finally admitted—after much prodding and pushing and insisting on *his*, DJ's, part—that she had slept with someone else that he started rocking back 'n forth in the rocking chair he was sitting in in their living room and had *just* used 6 years earlier to rock their now 7 year old son to sleep at bed time and now was rocking himself so as to *not feel* the pain and then as his soon to be ex-wife's headache escalated and she asked him to stop it! he *felt* (that's right, that's what he said, he *felt inside his body*) a wavy diagonal line being drawn (as if someone were dragging a magic marker—about an inch deep—on the inside bottom side of his thick skin) across his chest (from his left shoulder downward to the right side of his waist) and then he left their once home to return to his own apartment where he currently lived during their separation and there from 12 o'clock midnight until 4 o'clock in the a.m. morning he said he *thought* about *what* this meant to him and then he *thought about* it *some* more, and then he continued thinking about its meaning to himself literally 60 clicks a second, 60 seconds a minute, 60 minutes an hour for the next 4 hours until exactly 4:01 in the a.m. morning *at which time* he allowed a little *teeny-tiny* bit of self-pity to insert itself into his thought processes even as Roark stood by him saying, not what Jesus said when He said, "Satan get thee behind me" but rather when he [Roark] said, "pain get thee behind me" at which point—that is, the *point* where "I chose to think for myself", said DJ and allow in the "self-pity" wedgelets—"I cracked (that's what he said, he said it felt as if somewhere near the top of his brain there was a literal crack—like a door being opened a crack) and I cried (he said) for the next two hours virtually non-stop and then at the end of which I felt: Hey! *maybe* (emotions are pentupable and) there is something to this Branden notion of 'repression' (not to even get into the *details* of the Reichian magic-marker line drawn earlier). Maybe repression is some-thing we do do 'automatically' without being fully aware of it like Wilhelm Reich said and that we use–that is, tense—our musculature to restrict our experiencing of feelings [like he Reich also said] and which thereafter", continued DJ, "I slept soundly and peacefully and woke up almost euphoric and thought I wonder if *mainstream* psychology knows anything about anything *important* when it comes to *human* psychology and ...)".

And that *process* is progress, advance, something going on: proceeding, a natural phenomenon marked by gradual changes that lead toward a particular result, e.g. the *process of growth* [that is, growth is a thing 2 because it exists and we can and do observe its existence all over the place in plants in animals, and the process of *producing* a letter—be it a love letter or a business letter—or email on our personal computer/data processing system].

Physical growth is a process, that is, the end product of a natural phenomenon we know as physical life.

We speak of the process of making candles, the process of baking a cake, preparing a meal, the process of manufacturing cars, clothes, soap, of processed food, the process of farming, and so on. And notice (leaving *most* of our impulses to making jokes behind) that "the process of farming" does not have either (1) a distinct sense organ, i.e., a farming organ; nor (2) distinct representation in the brain, e.g. not a Wernicke's area for language but a FreddyFarmers area for farming, hence criterion (3) distinct causes from damage to these non-existent brain areas cannot prevent one from farming while not impacting his or her ability to say, cook. So, can we say the same thing for memory?

If good analogies—at best—aren't certain knowledge but at minimum potential knowledge only because they are susceptible to omitted parameters why would one conclude that bad analogies—ones that *don't* fit—are better than good ones—that do—and so we can use them [the bad ones] for proof of our hypothesis?!?

No, t.h.e.y already agree with each other that reductive materialism is the answer, therefore when their analogies fit 2 out of 3 elements they say the 3rd one just hasn't been ... found? No, made! The *making-things-fit* is the **rats nest** building we are here talking about. And specifically in the square-peg-too-big-for-the-round-hole *make* it-fit-*anyway* fashion.

But isn't that deductive reasoning? No, deductive is they already fit (All men *are* mortal). Fallacious deductive is arguing as if they fit but they only fit *because* of a fallacy, be it due to a lie (argument *depends* on the lie, that is, a false premise, that is, a premise *about* reality that is not true: e.g., All dogs are cats), an ad hominem (he said, she said, *therefore* it's right/wrong), ad baculum (might makes right) and so on. So, is this rats nest building fallacious inductive? Not necessarily. Probably it is both fallacious inductive and fallacious deductive with the first producing a false metaphysics early in life and the latter the means of maintaining ones "sanity" until one is old enough to fully and completely think and reason on ones own. And so the point here is in *how* t.h.e.y. build and construct their rat's nest more so than in the rat's nest itself (though this might be the focus of future writing). So, therefore (they "reason") they've got 2 out of 3 and where normal—i.e. real—scientists would say: since not 3, therefore, *not* analogous therefore maybe it isn't system they say, voila! We got 2 naturally, therefore we only have to build—that is, *construct*—one illusion.

Actually—I don't know for sure about you, but for me—I can say this: I have experienced memory as being more than *just* brain work. For example, once I experienced an image recall as being *concurrent* with muscle twitches—e.g. I once had a definite twitch in my left hand in that muscle between the base of the thumb and the base of the index finger and at the same time the picture/image of Dr. Branden standing with his arms at his side like a stern psychotherapist *helping* me out in my time of psychological trouble (see picture of him on back of one of his books[ix]). I could re-create this concurrent occurrence two or three times *at the time* by simply shifting my focus to that area in my left hand and as the muscle(s) twitched the image occurred, as the muscle(s) twitch subsided so did the image— but since then, not. I also have heard it said of Einstein that he said during times of intense thinking about his physics problems he was aware of muscle-group-twitching as part of the *process* of thinking about problems he was trying to solve. Since memory is accepted to be an indispensable part of problem solving it seems as if here too we are talking about problem solving as a *process* more so than a *system*—although we can have systematic ways to solve certain kinds of problems, but each way is a process of using—if not all, then for sure—a goodly number of our *capacities* and abilities to arrive at a solution.

So where does this leave us? Is memory system or process?

Since memory as system—in this context—requires remembrance balls and we have no evidence of such and since t.h.e.y haven't demonstrated the secret existence of same we can conclude here that system is *not* correct view of memory. And by a process of elimination we are left with: process.

Memory is process. Specifically, memory is the process of recalling that which is retained inside of self and since this can only include that which has already occurred it means, memory is the *process* of recalling past events in the life of the one doing the recalling—with *event* understood to mean *all events of consciousness* which includes both the perceptual (sensory affects) and the conceptual (interpretations of those sensory affects as well as events of consciousness outside of awake awareness, i.e. dreams). *Recalling* past events is part of the memory *process* of identifying *one* complete-past-event at a time. In order to recall one such event all we have to do is simply shift our focus to those that are near the surface of focal (fully awake) awareness or we volitionally make the choice to dig deeper which means *exert* time and energy to get at memorable-events that are deeper than surface.

That is, the *fact* that we can do these things—shift mental focus, exert energy to dig deeper—is demonstration that memory is a naturally occurring phenomenon/capability-ability that we humans have.

And more.

Memory (per BiO Spiritualism) *is the ability to store and retrieve events of consciousness.*

As such memory is (really) a *function* of consciousness and since consciousness itself is a process [of identification] memory is a function supporting a process and as such memory is not a system made up of 1 or 2 or 3 or more "objects".

Memory is the ability to store and retrieve events of consciousness including the emotional meaning of the event charged or discharged along a gradient from completely charged to completely discharged depending on the emotional *experiencing* capabilities of the one *who* stores at-the-time of the storage and at-the-time of recall.

Notice that since memory is a function of consciousness, and consciousnesses among those beings who possess it differ in their range and scope, animals can't store things that have to do with concepts, but that man can.

Psycho-hermeneutically [poetically] *we* could say [but animals can't say], *events of consciousness* are stored within with a value tag attached to their toe, that is, to their extrospectively dead (since their time has passed) albeit introspectively wiggleable extremities that our psycho-epistemology can and does *hook* onto using the question mark from the end of its explicit and/or implicit query searches.

Which is to say, our memory capacity as such is absolutely reliable *in its ability* to attach value significance to "things" (both 1 and 2) and store them in the body *as part of the process of attaching value significance to them at the time it is so attached* to be recalled (at a) later (time)—be it recalled voluntarily with the expenditure of mental energy or involuntarily with little or no energy beyond that which is required to maintain the minimal awareness level required to stay awake.

So why do t.h.e.y want memory to be a system of thoughtballs and remembrance balls connected to brain-bones and objects as such?

The real answer to this is the short answer: because the rationalist-empiricist-reductive materialist "scientist" parts of t.h.e.y really don't think consciousness is anything.

Rather, t.h.e.y think consciousness is an ineffable substance and since their counterparts (in the world of reason worshippers) who think otherwise (consciousness is something, something as in soul is something as in as defined by the Philosophy of Objectivism NOT soul of Religion) have done great things to advance the understanding of man by man t.h.e.y had to acquiesce and give the illusion that t.h.e.y too take consciousness seriously.

But.

T.h.e.y don't.

next **MORE EVIDENCE** for the rats nest

235.236.237 [196]

Page 235 is the beginning of Chapter 12, "On Future Psychological Categories" by Jerome Kagan, who writes:

> Anyone reading the most respected psychological texts written 100 years ago would realize that accurate prediction of the future is impossible because even the most prescient prophets [good alliteration] cannot anticipate the new machines, historical conditions, and theoretical conceptions that are presently unformed. Neither Wundt, Titchener, Jung, nor Freud imagined the invention of functional magnetic resonance imaging (MRI), the microelectrodes and amplifiers that permit study of single neurons, or the influence of the cognitive sciences, which gave memory, reasoning, and concept formation a primacy over the affective phenomena that dominated inquiry at the end of the last century. Thus, a student in 2096 will probably satirize the three predictions that appear reasonable to me at the present [1996] time. The first two ideas are argued briefly because they seem obvious; the last prophecy is elaborated because it seems less apparent.[x]

As "Mind-Brain" editor R. L. Solso explained in his *Preface* to "Mind-Brain" he simply had asked author prospects to *reflect* on the past and *speculate* about

---

[196] MB p. 234, like MB p. 38, ended up being the blank back page of the end of a previous chapter. So, like before, we will advance our page count by 1 and evaluate.

the future of mind sciences. Hence, this particular author (Jerome Kagan) chose to *speculate* about the future of *Psychological Categories* and ended up being grouped by the editor into the books 3rd major category: "Psychology (Memory, Theory and Cognition) in the 21st Century". This category contains six chapters, two of which we've already commented on: J. Gay Snodgrass's and Hans J. Eysenck's.

Once again I start out here with much excitement. Compare one of Dr. Kagan's statements in the above: "…[early psychologists had not] imagined the invention of functional magnetic resonance imaging (MRI), the microelectrodes and amplifiers that permit study of single neurons, or the influence of the cognitive sciences, which gave memory, reasoning, and concept formation a *primacy over the **affective*** phenomena that dominated inquiry at the end of the last century." (emphasis mine). Compare this with the Ayn Rand-Objectivist principle: *Emotions are not tools of cognition.* "They" (the mainstream they) are finally getting it. Isn't this exciting? I think it is; maybe "pervasive" is a better word than "ubiquitous"?

Jerome Kagan received his Ph.D. in psychology from Yale University in 1954. He is a distinguished scientist in the field of Psychology. He is a recipient of the Distinguished Scientist Award of the Society for Research in Child Development. His hundreds of publications, including contributions to 12 textbooks, deal primarily with his multifaceted approach to developmental psychology. ("Mind-Brain", About the Authors, p. 329).

His interest is in Developmental Psychology. Here he is specifically interested in predicting the future of Psychological Categories in particular and so is interested in "prediction and science" in general.

His three predictions for Brain Sciences in the 21st Century are:

1. "…the invention of new procedures that rely on technical advances will permit psychologists to study the brief, private, cognitive, and emotional events that, at present, must be inferred from coarse grained overt behaviors, test performances, and self reports." (p.235)

2. "…the extraordinary influence that has been awarded to early experiences will be modulated by robust demonstrations of the influence of a child's temperament as well as the continued malleability of brain structures to experience". (p.236) and

3. "...advances in neuroscience and the longitudinal study of childhood temperaments, will be accompanied by classifications of psychological phenomena that differ from those that are currently popular. (p. 237)

I hate to be accused of reverse snobbery here but if you can untangle the meaning in prediction #2 be my guest. I can't. But then I haven't gotten my Ph.D. yet either (sarcasm intended).

Prediction #1 is directly related to the sentiment in his opening statement and reveals that Dr. Kagan *is* a *reductive materialist* and as such is dedicated to two propositions. First, that the laws of consciousness are *ultimately* reducible to the laws of physics and chemistry, specifically here, the physics and chemistry of Brain Physiology. Second, that Scientific Objectivity *excludes* Objective Introspection and *includes* only "technology" that will permit *me* to directly experience *your* introspections.[197]

For example, in his opening statement when he says "Neither Wundt, Titchener, Jung nor Freud imagined the invention of functional Magnetic resonance imaging (MRI)..." one is inclined to say, ya, so what? This statement only has meaning if you are a reductive materialist, otherwise it wouldn't make any more sense than saying Freud, et al. didn't imagine the invention of SUV"s or Personal Computers. The literalness of his 1st prediction is self-explanatory as to his view of what is objective: namely, technical advances will permit psychologists to study others private (mental) events. And by logical inference, what he does *not* consider objective: namely, those others own objective, learned expertise at introspection. His argument is *not* that most people are not good at introspection, which could be true, but that by peoples *human nature* they **can't** be good at it. Is this an example of an anti-human nature tenet? At minimum it is a *metaphysical* stance because both sides can't be true. That is, it can't be true that human nature IS capable of *objective* introspection and also true at the same time and in the same respect that human nature is NOT capable of objective introspection. In a sense, it is *obvious* that *human nature* is capable of it, the real question is: *are you?*

In the 20th century, introspection was eschewed [by some] as non-objective and hence worthless for [psychology, the] science. Dr. Kagan, in spite of himself and

---

[197] Does this mean that when two Cognitive Psychologists (call them cpA and cpB) meet and greet, that cpA says to cpB: "you're fine, how am I?" That this is the same old joke Objectivists used to say about Behaviorists is intriguing. This is curious that it STILL fits, but it fits Behaviorists *alleged* antagonists, the *Cognitive Psychologists*. Is this a coincidence or does it have more meaning? Could it mean for example, that Cognitive Science and Cognitive psychology are nothing more than Behaviorism in search of a head?

if he were to broadened his view of "technology" could end up inadvertently being correct. *Objectivism* in Philosophy and *Biocentric Psychology* in Psychology *are* emerging *new* "technologies" and they *are* going to revolutionize Psychology in the 21st Century. The main way they are going to do this is to create a *Scientific Introspection* and teach it as a skill to anyone who wants to learn it. These new 21st century men and women then, will have an Objective basis in which to exchange ideas and to repeat each others "psychological" *self-experiments*. *Self-experiments* in personal psychology that in yesterday's psychology were referred to as "experiential" and in 21st Century psychology will be referred to as …experiential. *Experiential* is to Introspective psychology what *experimentation* is to physics—that is, it is the source of organismic integration which is the source of organismic understanding. And please note the (Biocentric) use of the concept *organismic* with its implied "full body" meaning.[198] As a physical scientist I can attest to the fact that there is *no kind* of knowing that is equivalent to the knowing that is the consequence of running an experiment or two or three *on your own*. Organismic integration is the kind of integration that accompanies a *first hand* relationship to existence and this means, *experimenting on your own* with your theories and hypothesis about what's-what and what's-not. I suspect one of the reasons I responded so well to therapy is because as a Scientist-Engineer I already had *what it takes*, that is to say, I already had an *actualized* "experimental attitude" *deeply* ingrained in me.[199] So that, for example, when I read the tenet for the first time in *Biocentric Psychology* that said, "guilt subdues self assertiveness" it made sense to me so I had to *test* it out myself. At the particular (engineering) company I worked for during this time they were on their annual drive to collect for *United Way*™ and there was tons of peer pressure to *give* and to give generously and to be a person who solicits fellow employees to peer pressure them into giving also. So when my solicitor came around to my desk and asked, "Are you going to give to United Way and how much do you want automatically deducted from your weekly pay check? I said— *with all the seriousness and emphasis of an experimental scientist*—I said: No. Zero. The resultant feelings of guilt were *immediate* and the internal emotional action tendency was to abandon my "selfish" thoughts and "just contribute the goddamn money" and forget this attempt at self-assertion. I thought, wow! if this somewhat minor self-assertive behavior is difficult *for me* what about more advanced forms: e.g. quitting a job I no longer love and pursuing one I do; in this

---

[198] Or as my first wife used to say: knowing all the way down to your tippy-toes.
[199] *So did the Nazi's.* So what's yor point? Simple, testing is a virtue, but not an unconditional one.

then *I-am-in-trouble*. Seven years later I got my Masters Degree in Psychology, four years after that I quit Engineering, two years after that the State of Minnesota threatened to put me in jail because I called myself a *psychologist* in a Newsletter I sent out soliciting client-customers and even though I was *registered* with the State as an *un-licensed* mental health practitioner and only duly *licensed* ones can call themselves *psychologists*. To this day I still ask the question that no one has been able to answer satisfactorily: *by what principle do you delimit the government's ability to license production? He who licenses production controls production. Governmental control of production is fascism. Governmental control of the free market place of ideas is totalitarianism. Every person who is pro-government licensing is—at some level in their psyche—traveling on the fascist road to totalitarianism. The conclusion is inescapable: "I live in a society that is pro-totalitarian, which is to say, pro-the total state."*

So is Dr. Kagan's ideas and works going to be helpers or hinderers to the total state?

We don't yet know but lets start by looking as his first *prediction*:

> "...the invention of new procedures that rely on technical advances will permit psychologists to study the brief, private, cognitive, and emotional events that, at present, must be inferred from coarse grained overt behaviors, test performances, and self reports." (p.235)

is nothing more than a *Star Trek*™ view of 21st Century man as that of *The Borg*, who are a fictional race of creatures who are half machine/half man . If this sounds "funny" as in "weird" to you I ask you to *not* forget that the back half of the *Cognitive-Behavioral* "school" of psychology is Burrhus F...Skinner whose explicitly stated goal is to *kill* off (or if this is too strong a word for you and you need euphemisms, *to do away with*) autonomous man (who *insists* on foiling t.h.e.i.r attempts to *predict* and hence *control* human behavior).

Dr. Kagan's *third* prediction depends a great deal on *what* is currently popular:

> "...advances in neuroscience and the longitudinal study of childhood temperaments, will be accompanied by classifications of psychological phenomena that differ from those that are currently popular.".

What is currently popular is the latest version of the *Diagnostic and Statistical Manual of Mental Disorders*, or DSM-N for short, where N represents the latest revised version.[xi] The DSM talks about bi-polar mood disorders, paranoia, obsessive-compulsive disorders, schizophrenia and so on. Does Dr. Kagan's prediction mean that when temperament and the neuroscientist's electronic probes intersect in the 21st century, sparks are gonna fly. So that instead of talking about schizoids we'll be talking about spark-oids?, instead of psychotics, we'll be talking about 'short-outics? Actually, I am sorry I momentarily slipped out of my serious mode here. This is not funny and to *prove* it we have to go to pp. 102 and 103 of "Mind-Brain" even though they are not on our (approved) random list. But when we do go there we get a sense of (just) how the terminology is going to change in the 21st century when the Brain scientists studying the neurophysiology of the brain meet up with their Cognitive Psychologist colleagues at their joint conferences:

> Yet, some researchers believe that violent behavior will turn out to be physiologically determined. Raine (1993) predicts that the next generation of clinicians [that would be the 21st Century ones] and the public will "reconceptualize non-trivial recidivistic crime as a psychological disorder." (p.102-103)

This is the way "they" work (and talk). And by way of example here we can take responsibility for our involvement in t.h.e.i.r bullstuff. Since t.h.e.i.r phraseology is based on the "principle" that says scientific statements about human beings are scientific *if and only if* they are *devoid* of any and all connotations of human values we are forced, qua human beings who do possess consciousness as a primary "thing"^{200}, we are forced to re-cast their bullstuff language into common-sense language. Which, when we do this to the above it translates into: *all people who commit serious crimes over and over again are the product—not of their choices, but—of their genes* (that is, of their "psychology" which *ultimately* is their genes because psychology is really physiology and physiology is genes). Which is to say (t.h.e.y say) the criminologist-scientist Dr. Samenow is wrong. Dr. Samenow is the one (we notice) who studied the criminal mind up close and concluded that criminals are *made*—by their own *volitional* choices—not born.^{xii} Since he, Dr. Samenow, was of the *last* generation not the *next* generation in the above quote, he Dr. Samenow did not know that:

---

^{200} A "thing" whose function is to identify things and assign *value* to them. Notice how this works here, even for t.h.e.m : "they", that is their consciousness, their minds "value" phraseologies that are devoid of "values" and so t.h.e.i.r "creative" abilities produce a drivel of such poisonous sliminesses—as the statement we are here evaluating/judging in order to protect OUR sanity—that we dare not touch it, let alone handle it least its toxicity enter us directly through our skin.

"[cognitive neuroscientists of the early 21st century will] reconceptualize non-trivial recidivistic crime as a psychological disorder." Consequently, since psychology "now" means behavior "of neurons", psychological dis-order means neuron dis-order and this dis-order is caused by physiology. Since physiology is caused by genetics, ... well you get the picture: *repeat offenders can't help it, not the devil but their genes made 'em do it.*

And philosophers and clinical psychologists think people have no basis for their cynicism.[201]

Our choice, to repeat, is to go along with this and t.h.e.i.r other bullstuff or to call it bullstuff and challenge it.

Or not.

Then when the generation after the above one succeeds in creating a world safe for criminals you can choose which side you want to join: reason, egoism and freedom **or** faith, force and altruism. Which is to say, we have to remember that Dr. B. F. Skinner, the preeminent American *Behaviorist Psychologist* and the *foundation* half of the "Cognitive-Behavioral" school of psychotherapy, said in 1971 (see his book, *Beyond Freedom and Dignity*) that he was going to kill off *autonomous* man.[xiii] He may very well succeed at this in less than 114 years.

Volition—as far as the bureaucratic mind is concerned—is on the chopping block and should be eliminated on or before the year of our State, 2084.

If you are thinking that a generation is 33 years long and this won't happen in your life time note that 33 years *used* to be the case.[202] The kind of "generation" we are talking about here *is* the one fostered by our high tech inventions, especially the computer. As an ~~"old"~~ Engineer who has been around awhile I remember when the design cycle for (mainframe) computers took half a dozen years *or longer* to complete from conception to product in the market place. Now this cycle has been radically reduced. How radically *particular product's* design cycles can be reduced is a function of their old cycle's duration. Single digit development cycles, easily, have been reduced by a factor of 2; double digit ones by the same factor or even more. For example, color television existed as a technology in the late 1920's but it wasn't 'til the 1960's that it blossomed in the

---

[201] Is this cynicism t.h.e.i.r goal?

[202] At least that's what they told me when I was 12 years old in Lutheran Catechism and I told my minister I was going to figure out the age of the earth from the Bible but I didn't know what all these generations after generation of X's begetting Y's meant in terms of years. And though a "generation" of people doesn't change that much in terms of length of years, what changes is what can be designed by those people during that time period. It is in this respect that I am using the time element to predict when BIG BROTHER is going to get BIGGER.

marketplace. Today such a cycle could easily approach an order of magnitude smaller. So too with "ideas" into the *intellectual market place*. If my prediction of 3-33 year "generations" is really only 3-11 year cycles then my 2084 as a predicted year is way conservative and could very easily come to pass. But because it could only take 33 more years (or less) and since I still have 55 years more to live it'll probably affect my life too. So if you too are going to live another 40 or 50 years or so it *will* affect you too. To repeat:

Volition—as far as the bureaucratic mind is concerned—is on the chopping block and should be eliminated on or before the year of our State, 2084.

Unless you elect to do something about it. I of course think you should, but that's up to you.

Finally then, let's go back to prediction #2. I've had some time to clear my head and think about that prediction. Here is what it means:

a. experience [not volition] sculpts brains (malleability of brain structures to experience)

b. brain is mind (from the title and theme of the entire book)

c. therefore, experience [not volition] sculpts minds.

Therefore, if "we" (the bureaucrats) structure, or rather "engineer" an environment that will *control* (the individual's life) experience(s) we can (sculpt) *control* minds (that is, individuals).

But I thought Deering's *Personality Paper* dispelled the myth of *life experiences* as being the determiner of personality? Apparently he was the only one who thought so.

Maybe *you* had better re-read that paper (Chapter 17) to see what is at stake here.

I'm going to move on to the fifth random sequence on our list of 10.

257.258.259

As the title of this "Mind-Brain" Chapter (13) says: "The Goal of Theory in Experimental Psychology",[xiv] is more "stuff" about theory and experimenting and I'm guessing about *prediction* in "Science".

If I can *predict* the correct outcome of an experiment 100% of the time, then I am a scientist.

I predict that if I put a thermometer in a pan of water on my stove in my Minnesota home and heat the water up that it will start to boil at 212 degrees Fahrenheit.[203]

I do it. It does.

I do it again. It does.

I do it a third time. Again, it does.

I am a scientist.

I go to my brother-in-law's condo in Denver Colorado to repeat the experiment.

I do it. It doesn't.

I do it again. It doesn't.

I do it a 3rd time, still not so.

I am not a scientist.

I am depressed. I don't want to be a physicist anyway. I think I'll become a psychologist.

I look at the videos of myself heating water that I took during the above experimental trials.

I notice that when the thermometer in the first trial in Minnesota reached 212 degrees a smile came to my face.

I notice that when the thermometer in the second trial reached 212 degrees a smile came to my face *again*.

I notice that when the thermometer in the third trial reached 212 degrees again a smile came to my face.

I conclude the thermometer elicited, as in drew-out, my smile.

But, in Denver there were no smiles.

Notice also, the thermometer in Denver never got to 212 either.

Therefore, a 212 degree thermometer is required to illicit the smile.

The 212 degree thermometer is *reinforcing* to the smile.

Let's put this *theory* to the test.

My 12 year old daughter who also likes science was with me back in our Minnesota home and as the video shows she too smiled at the 212 mark.

She wasn't along on the Denver trip.

---

[203] As an aside notice the redundant use of the word "up" in this sentence and the corollary fact of reality's absoluteness: you can't ADD heat directly to water and *cause* its temperature to go "down". This is true 100% of the time, I predict.

Let's take her to Denver and repeat the experiment only this time lets *make*—as in *control* the experiment—lets *construct* a thermometer that *reads* 212 by using one that is offset by the difference observed on the video.

I do this experiment in Denver.

My daughter smiles.

My daughter is a child.

I do it again. She smiles again.

And I do it again. Again she smiles.

It's obvious: the "212 degree thermometer" is a reinforcer.

It elicits a smile.

I am a ~~psychologist~~ Behaviorist.

But Behaviorism is yesterday's psychology. Today's is—and more than likely tomorrow's will be—Cognitive Psychology.

I want to be a cognitive psychologist.

George Sperling, author of our current fifth random section in "Mind-Brain" is one. He graduated from Harvard with a Ph.D. and published his dissertation on "iconic memory". He didn't call his work on "information available in brief visual presentations" by this name; rather Ulric Neisser—a progenitor of *Cognitive Psychology* and a Kantian from the get-go—dubbed the content of Dr. Sperling's dissertation, "iconic memory".

Dr. Sperling spent most of his career at NYU where he continued to develop theories in visual cognition, mathematical models, and perception.

On p. 257 of **257.258.259** Dr. Sperling writes:

> Despite the apparent difference in the structure of physical and of psychological theories, it has often been suggested that there is no essential difference between them. It is simply that physicists and engineers surround themselves only with those systems they understand; therefore, their theories appear to be more potent. If physicists had to deal with naturally occurring problems, such as smashing a particular martini cocktail on the kitchen floor and predicting precisely the shapes of the broken glass and of the puddles, and the location of the olive, physicists would be as unspecific as psychologists—claiming an understanding of the general mechanisms involved but unable to generate precise predictions for the individual case.[xv]

I (*BiO Spiritualism* author) am (was) one of those "physicists and engineers" to whom Dr. Sperling refers and let me say that "we" predict that if you exceed the *elastic limit* of any material it will break, and that if you drop a martini glass on the floor the impact force—which is extremely high because the glass goes from a relatively large velocity value to zero velocity *in a very very short time*, which, because a really big number divided by a really small number yields a really really big number—is such that it *causes* the glass's elastic limit *to be exceeded* to such a degree that it breaks. "We" could give a f… less where the "individual" pieces end up. Is this what "they" mean when they talk about "individual humans"? They see us NOT as the "glass" but as the broken off pieces of glass lying around amongst the puddles? What then is the glass? The Group? The Tribe? The Society? They see us that is, not as *the* primary but as a derivative, specifically as the derivative of the primary, Group—be it Society, Tribe or some cultural Group.

I'm sure you've heard the old joke: it's not the fall that kills you but the *sudden* stop at the bottom, well the same *principle* applies to the martini glass, it's not the fall that breaks it but the sudden stop at the bottom (see Engineering Mechanics and the concept of the Impulse Force). And that if "we" (physical scientists) tried to predict the ensuing location of the broken glass and the location of the olive you could *justifiably* conclude that we'd be *as foolish* as "psychologists" who think that, "that is WHAT" *should* be predicted. To the engineering "mentality"—that is, to the *mind* that *worships* reason—life is not a broken martini glass of helter skelter fragments, puddles of booze and lone olives. Life is a *process* of self-sustaining and self-generated action and if you want to predict things about life, especially human life, then, just as in the case of glass, you had better darn well understand the *nature* of that about which you are making predictions. Glass breaks at a stress beyond a prescriptive psi (pounds per square inch) stress level, steel will break at a stress 1000 times glass's value, that's *why* when you drop your stainless steel thermos cup on your tiled kitchen floor it does *not* break: because the *resultant* impulse force-to-impact area (which is what Engineering stress is) is not *enough* to stress it beyond its breaking point.

If you are wondering if man has a breaking point the answer is, *Yes*. Man breaks at the point of impatience with those who do not respect his capacity to think, to reason, to judge, to figure things out, to identify *principles* in the *nature* of things.

Man *breaks* at the point of a gun.

Man *breaks* at the thought of his competitors getting billions and billions of tax dollars to write drivel. And then to see that drivel a demanded "product" in the alleged *free* market of ideas "marketplace".

Man *breaks* from living in a society that is only semi-free and could be freer than it is and hence better than it is.

Man breaks, but unlike martini glasses, he can put himself back together again and go out and be a human being for another day.

That is, man is *not* a martini glass.

Man has volition.

He makes choices.

We can *predict* if he chooses wrong, he will suffer the consequences (e.g. if he insists on repeatedly jumping out of that tree from a point higher up than that second big branch he will continue hurting his ankle).

We also can predict that if he chooses correctly he will reap the rewards (e.g. if as he grows older he insists on not jumping to conclusions from *one and only one* piece of evidence he will avoid the pain that can accompany unwarranted generalizations).

Man has the capacity to reason.

He makes reason based decisions.

Man has the ability to self repair.

He *can* repair the damage done to his psycho-epistemology due to years and years of religious—and/or other bullstuff—indoctrinations.

Man is a being of free will who is the *self* referred to in the statement that life is a process of *self* sustaining, *self* generated action. In man's case he generates the action required to sustain him*self*. Whether that action be automatic as given to him by nature (his homeostatic physiology) or chosen among that offered to him from geniuses (e.g., Ayn Rand's *Objectivism*, Nathaniel Branden's *Biocentric Psychology*, all the physical scientists behind my Bachelors of Aeronautical Engineering degree and so on) or simply chosen from among our own first hand observations of reality as such could sustain us *for some length of time* on a self sustaining farm.

If you are *naive* enough to think that no Ph.D.'er from Harvard would advocate that engineering scientists *should* predict the outcome locations of glass fragments from dropped glasses and if they can't they have no more claim to being scientists then do "psychologists" who can't predict with ten decimal point precision unaccompanied by super complexity the visual reaction time of human subjects then *you ... are* naive. Mystics, whether Harvard Ph.D.'ers or Shakespearean Witches, can mix issues in their pots as well as brew.

But.

Know this.

Your naiveté will not save you. It will only cause *you* to become—at best—a mixable ingredient in some one else's pot.

The issue of prediction in science is an *epistemological* issue (see weatherman example in item #2, page 40). That is, the issue is how well can a human consciousness figure out reality and predict how its chosen actions in reality will sustain and enhance its life or will cause it pain or maybe even result in its death. When I worked my way through Engineering College performing fatigue tests on titanium for the head of the Aeronautical Engineering Department to digest and give to the Air Force for their use in predicting how weight-minimized they could design aircraft that would fly and not crash I didn't assume that "prediction" was a *useless* scientific term. But then neither did I *conclude* that failure to predict omnisciently *could be used* to disqualify human consciousness in its search for truth and understanding of the world in which it exists. To repeat, prediction in science has its basis in man's life: man has a NEED to predict WHAT consequences **his** actions *might have* in existence so that he doesn't engage in the *wrong* actions: that is, the ones that cause pain and/or death. Or stated differently: *prediction has survival value.* For example, I live in Minnesota (southern not northern) and I predict that if I plant my seeds of corn in the spring I more than likely will be able to harvest corn in the fall and I also predict that if I do NOT plant the seeds I will NOT have corn to harvest in the fall. Notice that the last is more certain than the former but it is only more certain more predictable because we know that if humans don't act they can't reap the rewards of action: it's *contradictory* to think otherwise.

The fact that Dr. Sperling is frustrated over his failure to predict human behavior based on a (false) theory of humans (Behaviorism) is itself the consequent of the correct theory of human nature:

> *Wrong theory can't predict as good as right theory can.*

To think otherwise is to contend that contradictions exist.

As to Dr. Sperling's frustration level he reveals it to us himself in M-B on p. 263 when in a lucid, unobstructed moment of severe honesty he blurts out a rhetorical question to the gods above:

> What is a theoretical [Cognitive-Behavioral] psychologist to do—theorize in greater detail about less and less until he achieves perfect mastery of almost nothing at all?[xvi]

Well, to be frank: *Yes*.

And isn't it the most ironic thing you can imagine?

Isn't what?

That Dr. Sperling, in *his* moment of least *self*-confidence, has predicted—with admirable precision—the fate of anyone who chooses to become a theoretical Cognitive-Behavioral psychologist.

Are you saying that the self, qua thing as in Dr. Sperling himself, is at its best when it's the least confident?

Absolutely not, in fact I'm saying the opposite. Dr. Sperling's A. E. self lives within (as do all people's if we accept that A.lter E.go is just euphemism for *ego* for those who—developmentally speaking—*disowned* theirs at some point *in their development*) and since he has spent so much of his life inside the rigor of science he *might* be able to *instantaneously* become a better scientist by simply *flipping* his internal *hierarchy* of knowledge and values over, that is, upside down, which in Dr. Sperling's case would then make it right-side up.

But *how* does one do this?

See *BiO Spiritualism's* axiom trees in Volume II (to be written), we have to move along here or else we'll never finish.

Next is our sixth random item from Mind-Brain on our list of ten.

22.23.24

Which is Dr. Carl Sagan's and Ms. Ann Druyan's "What Thin Partitions..."[xvii] the one I had *hoped* to "hit", but to do it *twice*—see 33.34.35 below—with a random number generator almost makes me believe in Jungian synchronicity.[204]

Pages 22.23.24 could be subtitled: *Ticks 'n Moths 'n Caterpillars 'n Bees: The physical scientists royal road to understanding human consciousness.* A "consciousness" that the authors in their opening statements (three pages prior)

---

[204] But it doesn't. This is just coincidence and I am the one adding *continuity* sense to the randomly numbered, randomly sequenced page selections that we have been dealing with here from M-B and my old DOS computer's random number generator. Although I must admit it is interesting *how the flow* of these random numbers was/is such that the first number is from the beginning of the book and the last number, from the books summary so that when I get around to writing about the last number it will correspond to my need to summarize. The point here is, if coincidences were *never* interesting we'd probably *not* have a name for them.

say is not *that* much different than *that* of any living being on Earth. Or to be more precise, they said that the *partition* that divides the *cognitive* capabilities of all conscious beings (on earth) is *very* thin.

Since *very thin* to the mathematically inclined (such as Ph. D. Astronomers of the high caliber of Dr. Carl Sagan) as well as to the *practical* man-in-the-street American (such as you and me) eventually becomes zero (as in, *for all practical purposes ... etcetera)*, we can *easily* speculate that the authors' goal here is to "prove" that we humans are nothing special when it comes to consciousness.

They aren't saying that all conscious life—regardless of the *range* and *scope* of its *awareness* capabilities—is utterly amazing if looked at from a certain point of view; which it is. But rather, *what* they are saying or what "they" are attempting to say, what *they* are dying to say is that *man is nothing special*—he only thinks that he is.

The irony here is that this *argument* isn't anything special; religion has been making it for some time now.

The really peculiar, quasi-special thing about the authors' argument and line of reasoning is that it is based on many errors, one of which is an error in arithmetic. This is peculiar because one of the author's has a Ph. D. in Astronomy and is an expert in mathematics, so to make an error in arithmetic is ... not unheard of by any means, but it is kind of ... silly.

On p. 22 the authors are dealing with (and doing it pretty well too) the question, What would it be like inside the tick's brain? Specifically the author's say (after identifying that butyric acid is the chemical the tick zeros in on to drop in on its victim's skin/blood supply):

> You would know about light, butyric acid, 2, 6-dichlorophenol, the warmth of a mammal's skin, and obstacles to clamber around or over. You have no image, no picture, no vision of your surroundings; you are blind. You are also deaf. Your ability to smell is limited. You are certainly not doing much in the way of thinking. You have a very limited view of the world outside. But what you know is sufficient for your purpose.[xviii]

What becomes *extremely* important here is *what* the authors don't talk about. If there is no *significant* difference between us and ticks, consciousness wise, then the authors forgot to say that there is also a book *somewhere* in that Library (where I found the M-B book housing these two authors article) that contains a chapter written by a couple of ticks that has a part in it that goes something like this:

> Tick 1: What would it be like inside the human's brain?
> Tick 2: You would know about light and sounds and tastes and smells and sensual encounters with others as they caressed your skin and spoke understandable sounds into your ears as they tried to do you know what.
> Tick 1: What are ears?

But the author's skipped over this (assumed) fact and went on instead to the facts about moths:

> There's a thump on the window and you look up [the authors continue, speaking to me the reader, not to their brethren the ticks]. A moth has careened headlong into the transparent glass [presumably moths never fly into opaque glass, such as the frosty white light bulbs on my patio]. It had no idea the glass was there: [aside from the obvious fact it also has no idea what *idea* means either]. There have been things like moths for hundreds of millions of years, and glass windows only for thousands. Having bumped its head against the window, what does the moth do next? It bumps its head against the window again.[xix]

And so on and so forth the authors continue their writing/reasoning leading us non-moths on ... to think: *maybe we are different*?

But our hopes of finding insightful life in the "exact" sciences are crushed as quickly as they arise as these two authors try to convince us that we *should* view the bleeding obvious as suspect.

> "If we have here an insight into the mind of the moth, we might be forgiven [For what? Concluding the obvious? No,] for concluding that there isn't much mind there [but if we, qua taught by Objectivism to view *range* of awareness and *scope* of awareness as proper *yardsticks* for *measuring* consciousness, if we *observe* a fairly *low, limited* range *and* scope, then "*isn't much*" is the correct conclusion. So why

> are we being looked down on for being right?²⁰⁵] And yet can't we recognize in ourselves—and not just in those of us gripped by a pathological repetition-compulsion syndrome—circumstances in which we keep on doing the same stupid thing, despite irrefutable evidence it's getting us into trouble?"ˣˣ

Conclude the authors with the embedded rhetorical question as part 'n parcel of their (or should that be t.h.e.i.r ?) persuasion techniques. Then "they" continue on "their" merry way *without* acknowledging that moths are pathological neurotics and then ask the obvious/*logical* question: why should we base our conclusions about consciousness by studying the pathological neurosis of moths?

> "We don't always do better than moths. Even heads of state have been known to walk into glass doors [as if heads of states were some kind of superior being; President Clinton was head of state wasn't he?]. Hotels and public buildings now affix large red circles or other warning signs on these nearly invisible barriers. We too evolved in a world without plate glass. The difference between the moths and us is that only rarely do we shake ourselves off and then walk straight into the glass door again."ˣˣⁱ

Ms. Druyan and Mr. Sagan conclude this part of their argument on p. 23.

An argument to "prove" that there is no *significant* difference between me and insects—consciousness wise speaking. An argument that leaves me wondering, why do they want me to think this? Is it simply because they believe it to be so? Or is there some other—to be discovered—motive? And when they say, " … the [only] difference between the moths and us is that only *rarely* do we shake ourselves off and then walk straight into the glass door again …", I wonder if they have ever *actually* done this themselves and/or *observed* someone else doing it. I have never done this myself (not even when drunk) and I have *never* observed someone else do this (even the time an engineering friend of mine—whom I and my draftsman *predicted* before hand would do it because we almost walked into it ourselves but we *noticed* it in time and caught ourselves and stopped abruptly without spilling the coffee we had just taken from the folding table in this particular pool side area of this particular Hotel hosting this particular engineering

---

[205] Because the authors have an ulterior motive. Remember "they" said there is no *significant* difference between us and ticks and moths and other consciousness having things and so they now have to "prove" it.

symposium—who upon entering the room in his usual spaciness state walked straight into the swimming pool and who stood there knee deep in water with his suit coat and tie above the water line but who did not—and let me emphasize the not, did not, did not did not—when he got out walk back in *again*) nor have I *ever* heard of someone exhibiting such *repetitive*, stupid walking behavior.

Never.

Does this mean the authors are so superior—intelligence wise—that they get to make up "data" in their *thought* experiments and use it as if it were real data even if it isn't? Not only is it made up data but it's made up for a reason. It is made up in order to *slant* the argument towards the hypothesis they said they are out to prove. Isn't this begging the question? (Or worse: cooking the "data"?)

The tick the authors employ here is to collapse the (thin) difference between the concepts *never* and *rarely* (not to mention the *thin* difference between the correctly spelled *trick* and its misspelled *tick*, which differ ONLY by one letter). And collapsing *insignificant* differences is legitimate: if I rarely do something then for all practical, *relative* purposes I *never* do it *compared* to behaviors I always or practically always do—e.g. I almost always eat at least one meal a day but I rarely eat three square meals a day.

Moths always do what moths do and we *rarely* do what moths do … say the authors, but the truth is: Moths—*for all practical purposes*—ALWAYS do it (*repeatedly* fly into windows) but we (for all practical purposes) NEVER (repeatedly) do it. Isn't the difference between *always* and *never* a *significant* difference? Doesn't ALWAYS minus NEVER equal ALWAYS? (even *always—rarely* = almost always) so why are the mathematically astute author's asking us to accept the erroneous equation: ALWAYS minus NEVER equals THIN (ZERO), that is, equals NO significant DIFFERENCE? Symbolized, the *author's* argument becomes:

$$A - N = 0, \text{ so that}$$

$$A = N.$$

Since N(ever) = 0 it follows that A - 0 = A; it does *not* equal N. Voila! the authors "argument" *depends* on an *error* of arithmetic and so we can dismiss it as erroneous and move on.

But before we do let's deal with your objection to my conclusion by speculating that right now you are thinking I missed the point.

Sagan and Druyan (you *might* be thinking) compare the bad, stupid, *always* flying into windows *behavior* of moths to the bad, stupid, *always behavior* of an obsessive-compulsive person who repeatedly, say, washes his hands literally one hundred times a day. And just like the window "tells" the moth not to fly into it, we can tell the obsessive-compulsive person not to wash his hands so much but the moth does it anyway and so does the obsessive-compulsive hand washer. Therefore, voila (say the authors), moths and man are the same consciousness wise and differ neither in kind *nor* degree.

But what if this hypothetical obsessive-compulsive hand washer—when evaluated from within his or her own *ego* perspective—had been born and raised a Christian and so raised, *not* casually but *religiously*. That as part 'n parcel of his or her upbringing s/he had been made to feel guilty about EVERYTHING enjoyable—*even* the eyedropper drop size of enjoyment we get from washing dirty hands as we clean up before a to-be-enjoyed-even-more-pleasurably meal after a hard days work in the field or garden or yard or wherever we get our hands dirty from doing physical work.

And suppose further that this person is now a full grown and developed adult and is trying to do what Pontius Pilot did after he ok'd the crucifiction of Jesus; he—PP—washed his hands of the whole thing and declared himself free of guilt by so doing (back in biblical times it appears as if there was no separation in human action between the literal and the metaphorical).

So our hypothetical obsessive-compulsive person who throughout *even* a boring day-in-the-life cannot not get *some* shreds of enjoyment of acting in ways humans have to act in order to survive and thrive—is trying to do what PP did: wash away his sins (in the case of our hypothetical obsessive-compulsive person, wash away the *sins of pleasure*).

Now a big part of the point here isn't the literal truth of our example but the FACT that it is believable *about* a human being but *not* about moths.

So that the behavior of the obsessive-compulsive person in our example is not stupid. It may be *neurotic* to us who rarely sin sinners but neurotic—in the bejeweled psyche of the individual human being who struggles to overcome epistemological rats nests foist upon him or herself by vicious, mean, *unthinking* Christian adults—is not ALWAYS stupid; sometimes and often times it's simply, *neurotic*. And neurotic, qua human behavior, is *changeABLE.* The moths flying-into-clear-glass behavior is *not* metaphysically changeable. And *this* is a big, gigantic, SIGNIFICANT difference between us and moths ... or ticks ... or bees ...

or caterpillars... or pigeons ... or any consciousness *below* man on the *length* of range & *breadth* of scope of awareness scale.[206]

There is an unbridgeable gap—metaphysically but not epistemologically, epistemologically it's a bridgeable gap—between man and animals in the consciousness realm. This gap is called: *the ability to reason and form concepts.* Man has it, animals don't.

And it will take a lot more than a respected astronomer (who *earned* his respect IN astronomy) and his girlfriend to ERASE the difference.

If you are going to argue here that it's going to take hundreds of respected physical scientists and a few theologians with some mystic spiritualists thrown in for good measure to get the ERASURE job done then I say you are admitting something psychological-epistemological (that is, psycho-epistemological) about you, yourself.

It may not be pretty (in fact, it ain't pretty), but it is *changeable.*

In many cases all you have to do is connect the dots.

For example, if we quickly check back here to page 35 where the guru-spiritualist-mystic Deepak Chopra said in effect that the only significant difference between me and a tree is that there is no significant difference are we to *conclude* that mystics don't have a monopoly on faulty reasoning—which in this case is obliteration, which is obliterating *significant* differences *as the means* to making their argument seem sound?

What thin partitions... argues that the differences between man and animal consciousness are *thin* but in fact the *opposite* is true: the differences are so thick that they create an impenetrable barrier between man and all other known forms of conscious life. Religion called this difference man's soul and assigned all sorts of characteristics to it that *made* it more different than it was but didn't make it any more understandable; in fact religion over the long haul made it more incomprehensible.

We had to wait for *Objectivism* (in the person of Ayn Rand) to come along to explain the differences and make man's soul intelligible to man.

Unfortunately for Dr. Sagan and other reductive materialist "scientists"—who sneakily desire to replace Philosophy with Scientism—unfortunately for them *Objectivism* has been by this way so that thoughtful, reflective, insightful people can no longer *tolerate* (as well they *should not* tolerate) the *imprecision* of

---

[206] A range that includes *self* awareness and a scope of near inestimable magnitude that the teacher-astronomer Dr. Carl Sagan himself exhibits as he has shown us lay-people-students with all *his* wonderful thoughtful organizations and descriptions of the Universe of stars and Planets and Galaxies.

Scientism scientists as they try and/or *when* they try to *use* their "science" to give the man-hating premises of religion a *basis in reason*.

So what is the man-hating premise in *What thin partitions...* that science is trying to justify? It is that man is an arrogant slob because he thinks just because he has a superior form of consciousness compared to all other conscious life forms beneath him on the evolutionary scale that he *is* superior. If it weren't for religion, the tautological nature of this statement would be obvious even to physical scientists but since *religious* scientists are religionists first they can and do overlook the obvious as much as anybody else does.

The difference is that when scientists overlook it they don't just admit that they made a mistake but rather they start jumping through hoops to prove that what they thought they saw is true when in fact they simply saw wrong. And when they still refuse to see that they are wrong they start jumping through hoops within hoops within hoops (see Ptolemy's view of planetary motion for a literal example) until they get themselves (and us) so discombobulated and entangled in thinking messes that it takes the sensibilities of a stand-up comedian (or an outside Copernican astronomer) to get us out of the enmeshed entanglements we've made for ourselves (and/or let "scientists" weave for us).

These entanglements are what I am calling rat's nests. The one profiled here from *What thin partitions ...* is a good example of *more* rat's nest building and we are well advised to follow through on our analysis of it *as a type* so we can be aware of this type now and in the future and *use* our *awareness* as a self-protective weapon of *intellectual* self defense.

The particular kind of rat's nest building here is made up of strands of obliterated differences that are in fact significant and *should* never have been eliminated in the first place.

The truth is that the difference between man and animals is that consciousnesswise speaking (pun intended) this difference is really, really thick and not thin as Dr. Sagan and Ms. Duryan are advocating.

For still more evidence of rat's nest building let's consider the next (seventh) item on our random list of ten.

157.158.159

What Are Brains For? is the title on p. 157 in Michael S. Gazzaniga's Chapter 9 in the M-B book.[xxii] He starts this page with a quick answer to his own question.

Sex.

He then asks, is the distinction between what brains *do* and what they are *for* important?

And knowing what we do about the propensity of *some* scientists to obliterate *significant* differences we are hard pressed to *not* be extremely skeptical here.

In fact our automatic reaction is to answer, *Yes*, this distinction is probably not only important, but probably also critical!

But before we go off half cocked ... (maybe we should go off fully cocked?) ... that is, in this day and age, maybe we have to fully cock the hammer on our guns of intellectual self defense least we get shot in the back ... and the front ... and the sides .... by cultural messages aimed at shutting down our ego's growth and development *before* we notice that *intellectual* growth and *ego* growth go hand-in-hand.

So—hammers fully back—off we go, confident in the fact that smart people can't be ruled.

Governed by reason, *Yes*. But *ruled* by Sheep-herder wannabees, No.

Dr. Gazzaniga is an instinct theorist dressed in evolutionary determinism clothing. Or—if you don't like this judgment—he is of the "Friends, Romans, Countrymen, lend me your ears", type, "I have come to bury psychhology, not to praise it".

Or both.

Doctor Gazzaniga is a toughie among the toughies precisely because he is so smart. He is the best of the best, the cleverest of the clever.[207]

Like the rest of the toughies here he too has a Ph. D. His is in psychobiology. He is an accomplished educator and researcher in psychology and neurology and as such he (Editor-in-Chief of the *Journal of Cognitive Neuroscience*, Associate Editor of *Cerebral Cortex*, and [one who] edited *The Cognitive Neurosciences*) is " ... blazing the path for cognitive neuroscience in the 21st century.", p. 327 in M-B's *About the Authors* section we've referred to before.

He makes *one* good psychological point: *sex* (as euphemism for *pleasure*) is very very very important in human life (which is stated better by Dr. Branden's Biocentric Psychology which asserts, pleasure is a *profound* psychological need[208,xxiii]), and he (Gazzaniga) has some interesting observations about his right

---

[207] Or at least I thought so when I first worked on this selection. After working on the next, 8th, random selection (by Dr. Karl H. Pribram) I'm not so sure of this statement. As to which of these two authors is the "best" craftiest anti-psychhology "scientist" I'm not yet fully prepared to answer.

[208] With the subsumed, assumed knowledge available to everybody—even mentally retarded people—that sex is only *one*—albeit, extremely easy—*source* of pleasure for human beings. That there are other *sources* of pleasure for man is obvious but that there *might* be others of *higher*—or for sure of *longer lasting*—intensity

brain—left brain studies. However, since his observations are intended to marry psychology to brain physiology and then drop the psychology part but keep the physiology part they can't be discussed with any seriousness here.[209]

Since psychology is psychology (precisely *because* of the *kind—one* of a range & scope that includes *self*-awareness—of consciousness we have), it is *not* physiology.

Even if guys 'n gals with Ph. D.'s from America's most prestigious Colleges & Universities (with one or two thrown in here 'n there from Canada's and England's too) *want* us to think so.

In Dr. Gazzaniga's case *he* wants us to think that the neurology of the brain is the physiology that psychology is by virtue of the fact that all our instincts[210] are actually neuronal netware nests made by eons and eons worth of evolutionary "creations".

That is, Dr. Gazzaniga, qua best of the best bullstuffers, is a bit more subtle in his view of *which* non-volitional (NV) determinants *determine* human beings.[211]

---

isn't so obvious and is part of the subject matter for *BiO Spiritualism's* Book Next. To anticipate this Book consider your answer to this question: What would you pay to be in that foreplay/pre-orgastic just-on-the-cusp of orgasm state... not for minutes but for ... a day and a half!—that is, for two thousand one-hundred and sixty minutes? And to do it on your own *without* being on drugs or sex? The only answer for right now that comes to *my* mind is: a lot.
PS
If you've noticed the misspelled word in the foregoing notice also that I am leaving it in as is, as another example of: slip or slop?; not slop therefore slip. But this time I am going to call it, a *BiO Spiritualism* slip and let you speculate about all the psycho-hermeneutic meaning for Gary Deering and *his* "sense" of humor as same relates to his politically uncorrect view of retards in his yesterday psyche + *similar* kinds of views about prostitutes—or what some call: tarts. (See reference et al. TV sitcoms with scripts out of the past with their Junior High School boy's view of sex rewritten for today's "modern" women to star in.)

[209] For example, I would argue that brains are the highest *arc* in the hier-*arch*-y of our knowledge and needs and values and that as such it is a tool of consciousness to use as it *needs* to identify reality so that it—and the whole body it is an *integral* part of—*can survive*. That is, it makes more sense—AFTER studying Objectivism and Biocentric Psychology for a quarter of a century—to view brain more as a tool of consciousness rather than the other way around. This consciousness-brain "relationship" view *is* a *metaphysical* position just as is its opposite: *consciousness* is a waste-like *byproduct* of brain-in-action (just like you know *what* is to digestion-in-action). Cognitive neuroscience—in the end (pun intended)—is essentially this last, other-way-around *incorrect* view.

[210] The number of which, at most—per *Biocentric Psychology* don't forget as you read Gazzaniga—is, one: the patellar reflex (knee jerk), or *maybe* there's a couple two or three more but that's it. We are not *essentially* instinct driven creatures, we are driven by *two* fundamental, *volitional* choices: *to think or not to think* and/or *to be aware* or to not be aware of our internal world of self as well as of the external world of self as survival needs dictate.

[211] I know that back on page 144 I said I wasn't going to make NV determinants be a formal concept but if these guys 'n gals keep it up we may have to reconsider this position.

But we must note that as an evolutionary determinist he does not simply mean that evolution selects that which works because that which doesn't work is no longer around to be evaluated, but rather that evolution is ... conscious. "It" selects with a conscious purpose and in so doing we are (pre)determined by this selection process to be the hapless *instinct* ridden playthings of mother nature that we are (to which—out of self defense—we must add: speak for yourself pal).

On p. 157 our pal writes:

> The question of what brains are for is quite different from the question What do brains do? Evolution constructs [no it doesn't, it evolves, only consciousnesses can construct, e.g., man *constructs* a bridge, evolution evolves] brains that make decisions that will enhance reproductive success [no it doesn't, brains don't make decisions, man does, evolution evolves that which exists today because that which doesn't exist didn't work and the reason it didn't work is because it failed to meet existences requirements for identity and noncontradiction]. Such decision systems, however, can do many other things as well [including? Making decisions that do not *enhance* reproductive success? See Shakers, Celibate Catholic priests, and gay and lesbian people—ALL of these people do, I believe, possess organic brains?]. Frequently, psychologists and neuroscientists study what brains do, make suggestions about the atomization of the processes they study, and forget that what they are studying may be epiphenomenal.[xxiv]

By epiphenomenal he means consciousness "might be" a by-product of brain doing its (evolutionary) thing just like smoke is a byproduct of a wood log as it does its thing—burn—in my fireplace.

Attempting to leverage his undefined "evolutionary perspective" into a meaningful perspective on the bottom of p. 157 he writes:

> Many psychological models, for example, assume that information is gathered, organized, and processed in something vaguely reminiscent of a computer (i.e., a kind of associative mechanism), that such devices are universal in the brain, and that with the right environmental contingencies, perceptual [that is our *percept* forming] and

cognitive [our *concept* forming] processes can be explained.[xxv]

This is said at the end of his third paragraph before going on to his fourth where he concludes that human language is a brain embedded instinct (M-B, p. 158) and *not* a Skinnerian-Pavlovian dog-like response trained into the brain by external reality as same's influences are innately encoded via associative devices in the brain. Therefore, reasons Gazzaniga, there is a *significant* difference between what Skinnerians thought brains were *for* [stimulus-response recording devices] in relation to human language and what we *do* with them given that language is really an [automatic, beyond our control] instinct.

The attempt to stack the deck here is so blatantly obvious that the only thing that makes sense is to conclude that this guy thinks he is playing cards with blind people.

The brain is a *physical* organ, evolved by nature to do what it does just like the heart was evolved by nature to do what it does. It, the heart pumps blood, that's what it is FOR and that is what it DO. To argue that the heart used to be for pumping blood and now we can use it to pump ...air ... like the lungs do .... is ... it's .... .

I can't bring myself to say *it* (stupid) rather let me say, *it* is *analogous* to saying that the pump currently circulating the water in my swimming pool can be used in my house to replace the broken down fan behind me and to pump air around the room I currently sit in so that I can be comfortable enough to write.

It cannot. And the reason it cannot is because *man* didn't design it to do that. If he did design it to do that it would be a fan.

Which is to say, evolution evolved lungs to process air and hearts to process blood and brains to do whatever it is they do do, which per my speculation (AFTER reading and studying AR's *Introduction to Objectivist Epistemology*[xxvi] after this my "speculation") is: to automatically process all the streaming sense data from our 5 sense organs into a perception (a *perception* as defined by Objectivist epistemology, not as interchangeable substitute for *conception* as most other *non-precise* thinker-writers use it). A perception that represents our DIRECT contact with reality *as it is* and as it ought to be since it is what it ought to be by the mere FACT of being. That the brain is also the regulator of many of the body's physiological systems is also one of the things it does do therefore one of the things nature evolved it FOR.

But to argue, as Gazzaniga tries to, that what brains *do* and what they are *for* is two *different* things is wrong. To speculate that the brain does *more* than what we think it was "designed" for is one thing, but to argue it does different is wrong. For example, one of my *speculations* is that the heart muscle material is the *physical storage medium*—muscle as medium, heart as hierarchical "place"—for *our* assigned-by-us highest stored-by-our-physiology-because-they-have-to-be-stored somewhere values. This says the heart is *more* than just the physiological device that it is, but it does *not* say it—the heart—is being used by modern man for something nature did not design it for. Cave man had as much a *need* of hierarchy as does modern man. Actually to argue otherwise is to deny the immutability of *human nature* (that is, it is to confuse the metaphysical and the man-made).

Human nature is immutable. As immutable as any physical phenomenon of nature, be it electricity or gravity (or weak or strong nuclear forces).

Brains as evolved so far in nature exhibit both digital and analogue computer like functions—or rather, human beings exhibit these functions as we discover as we study and learn *more* and *more* about them as *consciousness* possessing physical organisms who have to maintain and sustain themselves in existence. To think that the brain is the predominant computer like organ (in both the digital computer and analog computer sense) is not—though it may be premature it is not at this point in our understanding of human beings—illogical to draw such an *analogy*. Brains, qua physical organ, are the automatic controllers and regulator of life's many physical functions—just like computers are used as controllers of car engine-car performance on the roadway and/or as computers are used to control and manage the many aspects of space flight—so too are brains our central computer to organize, integrate and orchestrate the myriad of physical functions required for survival. Since digital computers—not analog computers—rule the current world of computer use and development, it is the primary way in which we think about brains.

But it is not the *only* computer analogy way available to us.

Analog computers is another way. Electronic and hydraulic analog computers, for example, control and manipulate the (continuous) mathematical functions that explain electricity (in the case of electronic analog computers) and hydraulics (in the case of hydraulic analog computers).

The simplest analog computer is the bi-metallic strip thermostat in your (or your parent's old) house. In this type of thermostat two dissimilar strips of metal bonded together respond *directly* (and differently) to the temperature in the room. There is no intermediary that tells the metal HOW to respond to temperature; the metal's response is a matter of the nature of metal in general and of specific metals in particular in the case of thermostats. The bi-metallic strip responds to its surrounding temperature and then the rest of the thermostat (the *brains* of the thermostat) translates this *analogue* information into digital information and "tells" the furnace to turn on or off depending on the digital relationship of set point temperature to that of the actual temperature (if greater turn off, if less turn on, if same stay on if on or off if off) as indicated by the coil-spring driven measurement point as same is connected to the bi-metallic strip and compared to the set point.

Our brain-sense organs, we can argue, are like the (analog) bi-metallic strip when it comes to processing the data provided by our 5 sense organs as they integratedly, automatically produce *perceptions* of the world. The sense organs are *analogue* devices—as part of the senseOrgan-Brain *Analogue* Computer—evolved to respond to specific electromagnetic (in the case of eyes) phenomenon in reality or vibratory cues (in the case of ears) as same exist in reality when sounds are produced as a result of (unique) mechanical vibrations in the air caused by physical entities (chopping carrots or chopping wood) and their actions and interactions (trees falling in forests) in reality. Just as there is no *distortion* in the case of metal responding to temperature—metal does what metal does—there is no distortion of eye-brain responses to visible light (in normal not damaged by accident eyes, be it accident of nature or cars) or to mechanical vibrations in air-pressure waves as the ear-brain-consciousness-possessing-human animal LEARNS to "interpret" those air-pressure waves, that is: sounds. There can be a *big* to *large* to *great* to *vast* difference between the *subtly* with which *particular* brains (individuals) learn various sounds in regards to sounds' similarities and differences. These differences in *ability* to recognize and consciously, volitionally manipulate sounds are reflected in the individuals under comparison in their actual musical *ability*—genius in the case of Mozart—or lack thereof—in the case of me (or non-existent in the case of all life forms beneath man's range and scope of consciousness on the evolutionary scale).

In fact, if we stop and think about it, I don't think there is any phenomenon in nature that man deals with that isn't *first* dealt with via *analogue* input.

Even digital computers.

The bottom line dependence of digital computers is on the *analogue* response of transistor junctions to electrical potential: if the electrical potential is high enough the transistor junction turns "on"—that is, it *conducts* current—and if it isn't high enough it's "off"—doesn't conduct current. Transistor junctions don't distort their response to electrical voltage, they simply respond to it—that is, transistor junctions do what transistor junctions do. Man with his or her consciousness abilities simply studies and learns how to use and control and manipulate transistors "on/off" states to PRODUCE "digital" (binary) electronic computers—computers *that* actually DEPEND on analogue relationships in nature to operate and function as computers.

Man and man's brain is the same or similar in regards to his PERCEPTionS of reality: eyeballs do what eyeballs do; ears do what ears do; tongues do what tongues do; noses do what noses do and caressing hands do what caressing hands do—they caress and the brain's owner—that is, the person—"learns" to interpret these caresses as *potentially* pleasurable (in what they *ultimately* lead to, organismically speaking) or as dangerous or exciting (in what they *ultimately* lead to, man-woman relationshipwise speaking as each can sell their self short and/or long—pun not intended for men—in such relationships).

If man is computer like, then he is computer like in this *analogue* fashion that is true of ALL computer like things—including actual (digital) computers.

But man is more than any computer and just like the way in which cameras can be compared to eyes so too can computers be compared to man and vice versa. That is, as analogies they carry only so far and eventually man the model of all things great and wonderful is the thing to which all man made devices are compared—it's not, ultimately, the other way around.

That is, Man is the measure of all things. It's not, man-made objects are the measure of all things. But it's man—the maker of man-made objects—is the measure. (Again as Ayn Rand's Epistemology so thoroughly and completely explains, so see it for more on this topic)[xxvii].

As to another thing the Brain is for—beyond automatic-*infallible* integrator of sensory data into *percepts*—is that it is (we can easily speculate) the proverbial mind-over-matter *device* that mystics have been searching for since time immemorial.

And to think that it was right under their own caps all along!?!?!

Is this an example of not being able to see the forest for the trees?

Could be.

But what is it you mean here?

My *hypothesis* is that BRAIN is the mind-over-matter "device" of consciousness in addition to all the other physiological things that it is.

Oh?

Yes.

Since *consciousness* is the thing that animates animals, and animals as living—physical—organisms have *needs* that have to be met in order to survive—which ultimately means ACTING inside of existence—it follows that consciousness needs to translate its mind things into matter motion.

That is, consciousness needs a mind-over-matter "device" and voila! evolution, qua master of the form-follows-function designers (he speaketh metaphorically now) evolves a physical organ we call: Brain.

So that when *consciousness wills* the brain responds.

That is, when consciousness thinks: *I* want to wiggle the little toe on *my* left foot, ...then... *that* little ... piggy wiggles.

That a few of the little piggies next to it might wiggle also rather than just the littlest one wiggling itself is merely a matter (difference) of practice.

Everything in nature does what it is evolved to do. Brains were evolved to be consciousness' tool, that is, to be mind-over-matter devices. Which is to say, mind = consciousness ... over matter = physical body matter exclusively = brain + body's muscles + organs + all physical matter *inside the body boundaries* ... devices. Brains were also evolved to do *all* the *other* things that they do do (see the science of physiology for the most current, up-to-date shopping list of items description).

There is no separation in insentient nature between what a thing is *for* and what a thing *does*. Rather, to be precise we should say, there is no separation in insentient nature between what a thing does and what it is for: *gravity* holds matter together into units and units together in relationships that result in space as a consequent. This is what gravity *does*, this is what gravity is *for*. These terms: *does* and *for* can *only* be separated and used as Gazzaniga is trying to use them for things that pertain to *man-made* products. Dynamite was designed FOR blowing up obstacles to man's ability to efficiently produce things like roadways and/or bridges and/or tunnels. That is what dynamite is FOR. But that terrorists can strap the dynamite around their pathetic once human bodies and blow themselves up and murder other human beings at the same time *in the name* of a non-existent deity is ... *extremely* bad (soooooooooooo 'oh bad in fact it can legitimately be called *evil*) and in a very very (very) negative way *it* is a testimonial to the fact that human beings have *the power* of volition.

If they didn't they couldn't *choose* evil and become suicide-homicide bomber murderers.

But to a cognitive neuro "scientist", on the other hand, since our *behavior* (according to them) is encoded in brain physiology outside of our volitional control and our behaviors today are different than we thought they were during Skinner's reign last century and/or for that matter than there were a million years ago—that is, cave men (if we exclude the Flintstones) did *not* exhibit any knob-turning behavior but since we turn the volume up and down on our car radios—brains today are *different.*

That is, it isn't that our behavior is encoded but it is that our behavior<u>s</u> are encoded.[212]

This is why on the top of p. 158 Gazzaniga suggests he is against "... behaviorism and [the] rank empiricism ..." of yesteryear. Rank means total, complete, as in totally *exclusionary* to—in this case—any "rationalism". Yesteryear's behaviorism had an (unwritten) rule that said if anything allegedly psychological had so much as a whiff of rationalism in it it was wrong by that fact alone. Then since the government gave all the Grants to the Behaviorists, all the other follow-the-grants "scientists" [pragmatically] went along with the Behaviorists. *Now* that "others"—those with no academic ties to psychology, the college campus subject that *is* mainstream psychology's tributary—have successfully challenged and defeated Behaviorism, Dr. Gazzaniga and fellow behaviorist ex-patriot sympathizers turned cognitive neuroscientists are poised to step in and take over the field of psychology with their *brand* of cognitive "science".

But Psychology is psychology. It's not x. It's not y. It's not z. It is psychology. It's not a. It's not b. It's not c. It is psychology, which is to say:

Psychology is Psyc*hh*ology
  (It's not behavior-ism.)
  (It's not physiology.)
  (It's not philosophy.)
  (It is psychology.)
  (It's not neurology.)
  (It's not body-shape'ology.)
  (It's not bump-patterns-on-head'ology.)
  (It is psychology.)

---

[212] Note on use of underline. Except for all parts of Chapter 24 and the letters r, n, w in the word "rainbow" on page 342 where underline is used to represent red color and for all web links, the use of underline here is the only exception to the rule that underline is used exclusively to mean *blood red* as same is associated with the events of September 11th, 2001 in America. The underline use here is simply as *emphasis* of the plural behavior<u>s</u> as distinct from the singular, *behavior* and is the feeling source of my cynical nature that suggests it is only a matter of time before "they" come up with the "concept" of "behonemes" (see page 90).

(It's not Freudian.)
(It's not Jungian.)
(It's not Reichian.)
(It's not Skinnerian.)
(It is all of these and none of these, it's psychology.)
(It's not ... and so on and so forth until we get to
footnote #179...but what it is is ...)
Psychology is ... the science that

studies the attributes and characteristics that certain living organisms possess by virtue of being conscious.

And since man's distinctive form of consciousness, of mind, is his concept forming capacity this has to be given center-stage importance in the science of (human) psychology. Since man's means of survival is his ability to reason and form concepts and.... etcetera ... and so on and so forth ... see biocentric psychology for the *fullest* treatment of psychology, the science, that we have available to us to date.

Since psychology is psychology which is the science that studies the attributes and characteristics that certain living organisms possess by virtue of being conscious, human psychology studies the attributes and characteristics that human beings possess by virtue of their particular kind of consciousness. And *what* kind is that? The kind that reasons and forms concepts *by choice* or failing to so choose, defaults to animalism—i.e., by one's choice to *not* think one defaults to relying more and more on the *automatic* forms of animal consciousness and less and less on the *volitional* form of human consciousness.

Cognitive neuroscience—with the help of Government Grants to promote its *non*-volitional view of human consciousness—may very well succeed in taking over [actually I think it already has succeeded, see Chapter 15, in taking over] the field of psycowlogy, but it will not [oops, that is neither slip nor slop but an example of conscious, *volitional* choice] change the fact that psychology is the science that studies the attributes and characteristics that certain living organisms possess by virtue of being conscious.

Actually, this last paragraph as stated is incorrect. It is an inside out (possibly upside-down too) reversal. It should, rather, go like this. Bureaucratic Government via its Grants will succeed—with the *help* of Cognitive neuroscience—in taking over college campus psychology and then it will succeed [again] in *making* the definition of psychology be: the *Science of* [the] *Behavior* [of neurons and other NV things] and voila, Behaviorism will be saved!

And then the BM will be able to export her [I know that non-sexist mix-it-up-sometimes-use-him-sometimes-her writing is cumbersome but periodically I employ it just to see how it works: ... the BM will be able to export her] control to the Global world where she will be able to get income tax percentages out of the other 94% of the world's population that are equal to or maybe even higher than the 40+% of GROSS income that she now gets from some [middle and/or upper middle class and above] Americans.

Man 'o man 'o man. What will the BM be able to do with an annual income that exceeds by more than 15 times the single digit trillion dollars she now gets from the Americans? An amount—that some flat taxers say is already a ten times larger than it need be amount—from the Americans that is approaching a double digit trillion dollar bill per year. So that the BM's *potential* (to spend other people's money) is more than 100 trillion dollars per year. That's one-tenth of a ... of a ... what? I don't think I even know what comes after trillion—oh no, it isn't gazillion is it? The BM's of the One World Government are on the verge of getting an annual income of .1 gazillion dollars! Wow!

Maybe I should become a BM?

That's where the real money is.

Of course it isn't all "pure" profit, t.h.e.y do have to spend some of it on the peoples: 3 or 4% or so protecting *individual* rights to life and property from thugs foreign and domestic. And then the rest of it is left over to do lots 'n lots of other things: like research and development—specifically R & D on *How to get* an ever increasing *percentage* of a nation's (or World's) *Gross* annual income.

Since 100% is a metaphysical limit and in the United States they've gotten it over 40% so far, t.h.e.y still have room to grow.

But still, how do you do it. If you were a BM how would you do it?

If I were a [modern] BM (which thank god for Ayn Rand I am not ... but to be able to get a *piece* of the gazillion dollar pie? ... no, don't even aspire to this) I would do it by dividing the nation's populace into two groups: a 51% group and a 49% group. Then I would turn the 51% group into sheep and the 49% group into sheep herders. Then I would continue to *increase* the size of the 51% group *by decreasing the size* of the 49% group by convincing the latter that being a sheep is better than herding the poor little bastards.

And voila! Welcome to BM world.

And ... halt.

Is there no limit to yor sarcasm?

Apparently not.

Even though this is fun, enough already; we need to get back to analyzing real, live [but whether or not actually still breathing I don't know for sure nor do I need to; remember Shakespeare: ...the evil lives after] BM's.

145.146.147

These three pages are an example demonstrating that intelligence is *not* a get-out-of-jail-Free card from the *need* to check your premises.

In fact it is evidence for the conclusion that the *degree* of the need to check premises is directly related to the *degree* of intelligence: the *higher* the degree, the *bigger* the need.

And since intelligence is growable, when it does grow it does so—of necessity—over time. Hence it grows with age and as such it is not completely incorrect to substitute 'mature adult' for 'high intelligence' in the foregoing formula.

The pp. 145, 146, 147—the eighth random lot on our list of ten—are at the beginning of the second half of M-B's Chapter 8: *The Deep and Surface Structures of Memory & Conscious Learning: Toward a 21st-Century Model*, by Karl H. Pribram, M.D.[xxviii]

If you are thinking that this chapter is probably just a continuation of Dr. Snodgrass's faulty reasoning about memory as system—a system of remembrance balls and brain that is as independent of human consciousness as is eye[ball-brain]sight—you are right (see random lot #2 on our list, especially the discussion of it that starts the beginning of our current chapter.). But it isn't *just* this. Rather it is this and more.

Dr. Pribram, qua current M-B specimen under our microscopic eye, is two things: (1) an extremely intelligent human being who it just so happens (2) sold his soul to the NIH. (Where is Ernie Ford when you really need him?[213])

It's too bad that he did this and I do feel sorry for Dr. Pribram but as recipient of a *lifetime* research career award from the NIH (National Institute of Health), that is, as a *Major* Government Grantee beneficiary as Professor of Neuroscience in the departments of psychology and of psychiatry and behavioral sciences for the past 30 years at Stanford University, what else is one suppose to conclude?

---

[213] Actually—psycho-hermeneutically speaking—he's in the second half of the sentence just before this question.

That I, qua me, am simply exhibiting one of those negative qualities that my mother always told me not to exhibit when she said: "Don't take life so seriously."

Is it simply this or, per M-B p. 332 synopsis, since "... Dr. Pribram's current work involves gathering, analyzing, and reporting research results and writing reviews aimed at MAKING these results *relevant* to mind/brain issues." [emphasis mine], that since this then ... what? That the 'movers and shakers of the most prestigious Universities in America believe—hold it as a matter of principle— that they have to MAKE *reality* fit their theories rather than *make* their theories *fit* reality?

If this then, what my soul selling comment is really evidence of is of the *fact* that my nice guyness isn't completely self-purged from my own soul ... yet.

Dr. Pribram is a physiologist *not* a psychologist (and a pretty good one I suspect given his rather easy to follow discussion on M-B pp. 143 and 144 about holography and how it works to mathematically encode the light information our eye-brain system uses to see 3 dimensional objects). But to think, t.h.e.y led us to believe that *mandatory* licensing of psychology by the State would protect us from just any 'ole body—be they physiologists or astronomers or what ever — calling themselves *psychologist*.

So much for State licensing.

On p. 145, where our random selection starts, Dr. Pribram sets up to use his knowledge of holography and computers as his model for "[t]he Brain-Mind Relation". Which we, as critical readers and thinkers, have to remember is [t.h.e.i.r] euphemism for: What is the relationship [if any] between consciousness [if it exists] and brain [which does exist because we can touch it and see it when we crack open the heads and remove it from the bodies housing it]?

Which is our way of asking: is consciousness its own *axiomatic* thing as Ayn Rand's Objectivism contends or is consciousness a non-axiomatic, derived thing; derived perhaps from brain as some of the M-B authors are trying to prove. Or does it [consciousness] even exist at all and/or even if it does exist maybe it is so *unimportant* in the scheme of our pursuit of a scientific understanding of how we know things that we can dismiss it as such; as our current M-B author Dr. Pribram is trying to prove.

Well, as dangerous as it is let's live dangerously and give h.i.m the benefit of the doubt and, follow *his* proof attempts.[214]

His three part syllogism is the following.

Part I is Premise 1 (as in, All men are mortal) of his 3-part Syllogism:

Part II is Premise 2 of his 3-part Syllogism (e.g. Socrates is a man):

Part III is his Syllogism's conclusion (therefore, Socrates is mortal):

But before we can use Dr. Pribram's approach of *making* our observations fit we have to know what it is—the *specific* conclusion—to which we want our observations to fit to.

So the specific conclusion first (rough cut):

Part III is his Syllogism's conclusion:

> Therefore, consciousness is either an emergent property of the brain or consciousness does not exist or if it does it ain't worthy of scientific investigation.

Now that we have a working conclusion, let's look at our premises and finalize our conclusion.

Part I is Premise 1 of h.i.s 3-part Syllogism: P1=(Immanuel) Kant's metaphysics is correct.

> See M-B p. 146: "There is thus good evidence that a class of orders lies behind the classical level of organization we ordinarily perceive and which can be described in Euclidean and Newtonian terms and mapped in Cartesian space-time coordinates ... ."[xxix]

Class of orders that lies behind [noumenal] is, I submit, Kantian metaphysics.

---

[214] **HeIsM**ean?? Dunno. This is the first time I've used this *particular* dot word (up 'til now, they/t.h.e.y, them/t.h.e.m and their/t.h.e.i.r had been enough). I have to use it—h.i.m—in order to fit [*my* observations of *some* academicians into my theory about t.h.e.m (?)] this into *my* dot.language ... but ... what? That my earlier contention (Footnote 191, page 212) that 3rd Millennium Man's devil is in-between-the letters may have something to it? Maybe.

> Also M-B p. 147: "Dualism of mental vs. material holds only for the ordinary world of appearances —the world described in Euclidean geometry and Newtonian mechanics."[xxx]

[T]he ordinary world of appearances [phenomenon] is, I also submit, Kantian metaphysics.

Part II is Premise 2 of h.i.s 3-part Syllogism: *P2=Both Plato and Aristotle are correct.*

> See M-B p. 147 : "There is thus good evidence that a class of orders lies behind the classical level of organization we ordinarily perceive and which can be described in Euclidean and Newtonian terms and mapped in Cartesian space-time coordinates ... ."[xxxi]

[T]he classical level of organization we ordinarily perceive and which can be described in Euclidean and Newtonian terms and mapped in Cartesian space-time coordinates [i.e., our *percepts*] is, I submit, Aristotelian metaphysics and the author is implicitly acknowledging it because he knows most of us, qua the rational ones he is trying to convince, can see the logic in Aristotle [unlike in Plato which the author has to deal with explicitly because Plato is a mystic; see next].

> Also M-B p. 147: "Transformations are necessary to material and mental "instantiations"—Plato's particular appearances—of the ideal in-forms: ... ."[xxxii]

Here Dr. Pribram *explicitly* accepts that Plato's view of reality [ideal forms exist in another dimension beyond the reality we exist in in everyday life] is correct.

Part III is the Syllogism's conclusion; *C1= the following.*

> Therefore, how I, Dr. Karl H. Pribram non-judgmental scientist, MAKE sense out of all these truths is by concluding: *Therefore,* consciousness is *either* an emergent property of the brain *or* consciousness does not exist or—*most likely*—if it does exits it ain't worthy of scientific investigation *because the Plato-Kant line of Cognitive Sciences philosophy has proven that it [consciousness] isn't reliable at identifying reality and can't know.*

> For example, as I (Dr. Pribram) say on p. 146 of Mind-Brain: "At the same time, because of their *mathematical* structure defining information-processing procedures, isonomy [the name I've given to those *automatic* procedures the brain uses to *construct* our *percepts and* ultimately our *concepts* also] avoids the pitfalls of a promissory materialism [that is, who really cares if *reductive materialism* is a false principle accepted by most mainstream scientists] and, as well [avoids the pitfalls of], those of an evanescent unspecifiable mentalistic process [that is, consciousness is unknowable]."[xxxiii]

Since Objectivism has demonstrated beyond a doubt (or as I used to like to say when I was a kid and as, apparently, some Professional Objectivists *still* like to say: in spades!) that the three axioms: *Existence exists, Consciousness is conscious, and A is A* ***are*** axiomatic concepts and as such they are self evident which means they need only themselves as evidence and can only be grasped by a self and as such they have to be used in and are a part of all knowledge including the "knowledge" of those who say that if one thinks about it really really deeply he or she will discover that man really can't know because the universe in its important parts is unknowable.

More than one Objectivist writer has pointed out the obvious to us by pointing out the self-contradictory nature of the anti-knowledge types and hence t.h.e.i.r own self-canceling statements as is indicated by one question: *if the universe is unknowable how do you know this?*

T.h.e.y have never ever given a satisfactory answer to this question.[215]

Plato started the answer but just as quickly Aristotle told him/them they were wrong and should check their premises [actually it was the *ultimate* Aristotelian, Ayn Rand who told us to check our premises].

Immanuel Kant thought he had completed the answer and he probably would have been credited for so completing for some millenniums to come had it not been for the appearance *in ordinary experience* of the person / philosopher / novelist / thinker / genius Ayn Rand.

---

[215] But now [end of 20th Century, beginning of 21st) t.h.e.y think they are on the verge of doing so given that they have the power of "multiple disciplines" marching to the drum beat of *Cognitive Science.* (Since formal cognitive psychology has somewhat already abandoned the cognitive neuroscience gang, that gang has to rely more and more directly on their philosophers, Plato and Kant, and their modern day version of this [t.h.e.i.r ancestral line] as same is recast in modern day, formal *Cognitive Science*.)

It appears as if Dr. Pribram and many others in the M-B book have never heard of Ayn Rand and her philosophy of Objectivism.

That's too bad because if they had they'd not waste their precious lives attempting to prove falsehoods (granted they are BIG falsehoods, but nonetheless, falsehoods, that is lies, that is, *assertions* that that which does *not* exist, does exist. That is, t.h.e.y say: contradictions do exist).

And just as am I running out of the energy to [only] *oppose* those who oppose the Aristotle-Aquinas-Ayn line as much as t.h.e.y *propose* the Plato-Kant-Hegel line I am also "guilty" of doing here what I accuse t.h.e.m of doing: employing *deduction* as a valid tool of reason by MAKING *my* Observations fit *my* theory.

Of course this is legitimate. It is, that is *as long as* one does *not* engage in changing age-old, common sense reasoning. A reasoning that does NOT say: if the shoe *doesn't* fit, wear it. Rather ... well I'm sure—notwithstanding nonexistent memoryballs and thoughtballs—we all know, hence, can *recall* the real cliché.

So, let's halt. Backup. Revisit our claims, draw our swords, impale our enemy and move on to random lot number 9 [too bad *swords* wasn't spelled with a *c* as sounded in cinnamon because then we could call the "drawing of our cwords" (if we could switch the *c* sound back to its normal sound in time) our "*c*onclusion" words]:

Part I is Premise 1 of their/his 3-part Syllogism (e.g. All men are mortal):

Since *they*, like us, go through a reasoning process to even get to this first premise (we had to see more than *one* dead person to get here) the following is how t.h.e.y did it.

Since *philosophy*—as same is *synonymous* with Immanuel Kant's philosophy—has "proven" that we can't know and since we know we know there must be something magical about brains that allows us to know in a universe where things in principle are not knowable.

Let's see, let's engage in a *little* syllogism: premise p1: All knowledge is in a universe where knowledge is not knowable; premise p2: We know things; conclusion c1: Therefore, the brain [somehow] pumps out knowledge automatically just like the heart pumps blood and/or the lungs pump air.

That is, "we" accept Kant's metaphysical view: *the universe is unknowable*, as fact. Which, as already stated, gives us our first big **Premise 1**: [All] Immanuel Kant's *metaphysics* [I am in a universe that is unknowable] is true.

Part II is Premise 2 of the 3-part Syllogism (e.g. [All] Socrates is a man):

Plato said we humans know abstract things but we don't know what abstract means therefore it means abstractions are forms of things and these forms exist in another dimension beyond the one (reality) we live in.

Aristotle said, no. There is only *one* reality and in it we live.

Immanuel Kant (along with a goodly number of Zero A.D. Christians) said Plato is right about abstractions (being in another dimension just like heaven is in another dimension) and Aristotle is right about us living in the here and now—we so obviously do but that doesn't say what we do after we loose the ability to do.

So, since we are not geniuses (like Ayn Rand et al.) we can't challenge Plato and Aristotle and other philosophers so we'll accept they too are true.

Voila! Big **Premise 2**: [All] Plato and [All] Aristotle are correct.

Part III is the Syllogism's conclusion (Therefore, Socrates is mortal):

So since Plato, Aristotle and Kant [are dead? Har har. No, that's not the point here] are all true [but what if they aren't ALL true? ... shhhhh! don't bother me while I'm thinking] since Plato, Aristotle and Kant are all true but yet we "scientists" know we know we must do it *somehow*. How do we do it?

The brain must do it (t.h.e.y "reason"). That is, we *receive* our *concepts* (knowledge) from our brains that *somehow* process information and *automatically* pump out this knowledge (concepts) just like the heart pumps blood and/or like the lungs process and pump air.

Voila! It is our job as scientists to discover the "somehow" and communicate it to our superiors in the Government who will then give us more money to keep discovering *somehows*.

That is to say, *somehow* we have to let future BM's know that we know we humans can't know and that we will provide the BM's—for a fee—with this information that they *need* in order to keep the wool pulled over their sheep's eyes. And if the modern BM's think they don't need us anymore because they *now* know how to shear sheep on t.h.e.i.r own we simply have to ask them one question. Do you BM's know that you can milk sheep too? Or rather, do you know *how* to milk sheep? Well, we do and—for a fee—we'll show you how. And not only will we show you how but we will *prove* to you that sheep milk is 1,000 times more nutritious than milk milk and so you *should* be interested in our *somehows*. Then, in the next millennium, your BM brothers and sisters can get beyond the 40'ish percentage points [of tax confiscated wealth] that *is/has been/is* the best you guys 'n gals have been able to achieve—while still maintaining *some* semblance of *not* ruling by brute force.   You've reached the limit on the percentage of value you can shear from your sheep but that does not mean you have reached a *metaphysical* limit. That limit remember is 100%. And no we aren't advocating something as dorky as those floating-in-water creatures used in the movie, *The Minority Report*.[xxxiv]   Rather, w.e. are advocating the real thing and if you *give* us the money we'll deliver it to you on or before the centennial celebration later on this century of o.u.r hero BM portrayed in that one book by Mr. George Orwell.

But if not, then not.

33.34.35

Random lot number nine.

Finally, we are almost finished.

Note 1 on p. 33 ties in to our ticks from the earlier selection (M-B pp. 22.23.24). It is a minor tie in and serves to remind us here that on pp. 33.34.35 of M-B we are still dealing with the same authors (Sagan, Duryan) and their same Chapter: *What Thin Partitions*....

Note 2 (from M-B p. 33 also) ties in to a different part of the authors "reasoning" about what humans are really (according to them) all about. The note says: "One promising finding in artificial intelligence is the discovery that distributed data processing—many small computers working in parallel without much of a central processing unit—does very well, by some standards better than the largest and fastest lone computer. Many little minds working in tandem may be superior to one big mind working alone."[xxxv]   Which if taken by itself we could conclude that the authors are saying we little, *individual* humans are better than the big government and/or big gods, but if we did this we would be wrong. This Note 2 is attached to this line on p. 28: "Might our penchant for imagining someone inside pulling the strings of the animal marionette be a peculiarly human way of viewing the world?"[xxxvi]   Which is followed by: "Could our sense of executive control over ourselves, of pulling our own strings, be likewise illusory—at least ...."[xxxvii] And so on and so forth continue the authors, revealing their bias towards "proving" that humans are no big deal and that our feeling that we have *volitional* control over ourselves is just an illusion. I mention this last to remind us that cognitive neuroscience is not the only "science"—nor their sympathizers, the only "scientists"—that think "illusion" is a defining characteristic of man and reality. Is this an example of psychological projection on t.h.e.i.r part? Since t.h.e.y deal in illusion—so much so that we could say it is t.h.e.i.r stock and trade—they think everybody does! Hence, they conclude (?), voila! god (or nature) created man, the master illusionist who *cannot trust* his mind to *see* what it *sees*, *know* what it *knows* and *judge* a!sh%les to be—not spades, the noun, but—a!sh%les—*in spades*, the qualifier.[216]

I suppose if you have read this far you could be rooting for my nice guy to win out in the end here [pun *not* intended] and would therefore conclude here that these authors musings about philosophy—especially the question of epistemology: [as in] *What* are we?—is merely an example of *a* scientist and his girlfriend stepping outside their areas of *expertise* (his, astronomy; hers TV productions) and revealing that it is a really really very very dangerous thing to do and so one should not do it.[217] But even if you think this way, these two authors did not take your advice and so they are subject to as harsh a critique ***in your own mind*** as you can muster—or rather *should* be so critiqued *unless* you don't think the preservation of your (earthly) soul (mind) is worth it.[218]

On the bottom of p. 33 the authors start to conclude their chapter by giving the first of four views from four thinkers out of the past on the question, Are Animals Machines? The authors use Descartes for the 17th Century view, Voltaire for the 18th, Huxley the 19th and James L. and Carol G. Gould for the 20th.

They start with Descartes.

And from the selection they have chosen for Descartes I would have to conclude that his answer was/is/was: No, animals aren't machines, they are robots, but man isn't an animal per se, but rather an animal with a contradictory (rational-religious) soul.

Next, p. 34 is Voltaire's answer.

---

[216] By *a!sh%le* I mean that *opening* in the *mental fabric of the mystic's mental Universe through which bullstuff drops*. (Some call this opening the mystics inner eye—or rather, the mystics inner mouth—but I don't, I call it .... well, aynway ... oops, slip, anyway for more on this topic see this link: www.gdeering.com\ biospiritualism\BiOsLinks.htm ... AsIwasSaying link).

[217] The *it* here is to assume that your expertness in one area—Astronomy—qualifies you to be an expert in another area—Philosophy. Even though Astronomy and Philosophy both involve thinking they are *not* the same thing. Philosophy is *about* thinking as a thing and Astronomy is *applying* thinking to *specific* (Astronomical) things and presupposes you, qua scientist, qua Astronomer, know HOW to think properly (as in don't use logical fallacies as the *means* to making your points).

[218] If YOU want to use a kinder gentler approach to YOUR inner mystics you of course can but I will argue that if your life is more than one-third over AND you *do have* inner mystics, then you might not have either the time or luxury to so treat them and that a *BiO Spiritualism* driven pedantic (pedactics) might be better (faster) for you. Or not as the case could be ... in the end ... it's up to you, it's up to me, it's up to us *to decide* (and **no** action is **a** decision). As Chapter 16 here reveals, I decided in favor of the pedantic—and though it is not without risk, it is a *choice*.

His answer is, Yes and ... not only are animals machines, but so is man, or that is, he is as much a machine as are trained dogs.

Huxley next.

His last line is his answer: "We are conscious automata ..."

And finally, James L. and Carol G. Gould whose answer is their last paragraph: "It strikes us that a skeptical and dispassionate extraterrestrial ethologist studying our unendearing species might reasonably conclude that *Homo sapiens* are, for the most part, automatons with overactive and highly verbal public relations departments to apologize for and cover up our foibles."[xxxviii]

This also is the words ending Dr. Carl Sagan and Ms. Ann Druyan's Chapter, *What Thin Partitions* ... and is also a good representation of what they think too (since they *chose* it for *their* ending—that is, their "last" word on the subject for their article).

If we take-them-at-their-word then they—and t.h.e.i.r sympathizers—have absolutely no, none, nada, zero, no reason in heaven or on earth to be upset with me when I earlier referred to (Mr.) Sagan (*not* Dr. but rather, Mr. Sagan) and (Ms.) Druyan, qua *wannabe*-philosophers, as a!sh%le(philosopher)s.

The reason they can't is because my glands, that is, my *tonsils* and my *appendix* **made** me do it.[219]

---

[219] If you, qua reader, are wondering "how do I [the author] know it's *these* glands and not some others. Perhaps its my liver and stomach or my penis and pancreas, how do I know for sure?" If this then, you are *not* getting the point—here's two bucks go buy yourself a sense of humor.

Or. Looked at another way. If you, qua reader, are thinking that I am engaging in name calling here and that it's not a very academic thing to do, then make sure you remain fair about it in *your judgment* and not academically one-sided. First off, we must note, t.h.e.y *started* it. Therefore, I am just *retaliating*. They started it by calling me an unendeering homo (slip or slop? and regardless which, does it mean I'm being overly defensive?) sapien who apologizes and covers up behavior that t.h.e.y themselves don't even have the guts to admit that t.h.e.y engage in (maybe t.h.e.y are the foible-covering-up unendeering slobs they refer to in their own writings).

This constant barrage *against* the human—and by those who have every reason to be *for* the human—is not funny. Give me back my two bucks.

Or. If need be, put it towards a down payment for buying some academician you might know who needs it, a *better* sense of life.

Chapter 19: Will *Cognitive Neuroscience* become the new bureaucratic control tool of the 21ˢᵗ Century?

Give a Cognitive Neuroscientist a brain and a Government Grant to force his or her view of psychology down our throats and he/she'll inch his/her way towards making it impossible for the mind that that brain is a part of to understand the following. (Or, that is, they are your neurons and what you do with them is up to you [220].)

The following is an example of *what* I chose to do with *mine*.

The United States Government has officially endorsed *Cognitive Neuroscience* as the State's Psychology, and along with it has made "A *Call To Action*" for all "scientists" to stitch together an epistemological web *proving themselves correct*. By so doing the Government is in effect saying "... [we the government] will give you all the [grant] money you need to do this". That is, to "prove" that *Cognitive Neuroscience*—**not** *Biocentric Psychology* as guided by *Objectivism* philosophy—is the *explainer* of human psychology.

But what if *Cognitive Neuroscience* as *explainor*—we the people can and do ask—is to real psychology what a TV repair man's "description" of a television's ampere current flows and voltages and inductances and ohmic-resistance values are to "explaining" the "Mary Tyler Moore Show" during which the TV repair guy measured them. If he did this and then also took these *electrical* measurements during "Seinfeld" [or substitute any two of *your* top ten favorite TV shows] and offered us an *ampere* and *voltage* and *ohmic* "explanation" of these TV shows we would ... laugh ... really really loudly.

But the Bureaucratic Government doesn't care. Their goal isn't to explain mental health and mental illness, but rather it is to *control* and *social engineer* each and every one of us into some god-awful kind of sheepish group wondering the wilderness looking for a shepherd to lead us.

You doubt this?

---

[220] If you doubt the importance of *volition*, look at WHAT the Islamic Fundamentalist Terrorists have *chosen* to do with theirs.

On p. 57 of its document: "*Mental Health: A Report of the Surgeon General*", the United States Government writes:

> Progress in understanding depression and schizophrenia offers exciting examples of how findings from different disciplines of the mental health field have many common threads (Andreasen, N.C., 1997: Linking mind and brain in the study of mental illnesses: A project for a scientific psychopathology, *Science*, 275, 1586-1593).[i] Despite the differences in terminology and methodology, the results from different disciplines have converged to paint a vivid picture of the nature of the fundamental defects and the regions of the brain that underlie these defects. Even in the case of depression and schizophrenia, there is much to be uncovered about etiology, yet the mental health field is seen as poised "to use the power of multiple disciplines." The disciplines are urged [by who?] to link together the study of the mind and the brain in the search for understanding mental health and mental illness (Andreasen, 1997. [Oh! Andreasen is who, but why him or her get to urge? And isn't this *Government* report "urging" by citing this reference?]).
>
> This linkage [what linkage?] already has been cemented [by whom?] between cognitive psychology [the psychology of Immanuel Kant's philosophy of Kan't Know], behavioral neurology [that substitutes "behavior of neurons" for "behavior of animals" in Skinnerian, et al. Behaviorism], computer science [which views man as a super-duper Artificially Intelligent Android built by the super-duperist computer scientist in the universe—i.e. god], and neuroscience [which is physiology ... not psychology, but... physiology of the brain]. These disciplines have knit together [a rat's nest? ...] the field of "cognitive neuroscience" (Kosslyn, S. M., & Shin, L. M., 1992, The status of cognitive neuroscience, *Current Opinions in Neurobiology*, 2, 146-149)[ii]

On p. 21 this same Government Report states, "...integrative neuroscience and molecular genetics present some of the most exciting basic research opportunities in medical science." This is said on p. 21 under Number 1 of its **Action** Plan for Mental Health in the new millennium; this first course of action is:

Continue to Build the [cognitive neuro]Science Base.

This *explicit* endorsement of "cognitive neuroscience" as the integrator for Mental Health and Mental illness as same relate to The Science of Psychology is precisely that: explicit. One of the few areas in which t.h.e.y are explicit.

One wonders, why?

Why here and not everywhere?

Is it that t.h.e.y have to be explicit somewhere so that their fellow "scientists" can get the message?

Yes, because: if t.h.e.i.r fellows don't get the *message*, t.h.e.y don't get the funds.

If you (you, qua reader, not me qua yu, but you qua you) *still* believe that the linkage between the Bureaucratic Minds within the Government and their flunky scientists from the country's ivoriest ivory towers isn't real, then .... then .... then I do not know what to say ... other than ... that which follows.

Prior to the 1970's few people knew that Doctor Burrhus Frederic Skinner—the renowned American *Behaviorist* Psychologist—predicted that he *could* and *would* fill up America first—and the whole world eventually—with human beings who did not need either *freedom* or *dignity* in their everyday lives[221]. He did not say *what* he was going to use as replacement for these two fundamental needs of autonomous human beings, he simply said he was going to do away with them.[222]

Then in 1971 with the first publication of his book "*Beyond Freedom and Dignity*"—a book *openly* acknowledged to have been bought and paid for by the United States Government via the *National Institute of Mental Health* (NIMH) Grant number K6-MH-21, 775-01—Dr. Skinner told all of us *explicitly* what his plans were for *autonomous* man and how he and *his* cohorts were going to kill him off.[iii]

One cannot say, "we" did not believe him, that "we" did not take him seriously because *Beyond Freedom and Dignity* was touted as "…one of the most important happenings in 20th-century psychology…" quoting an excerpt from its own cover. The same cover that reminded us that Dr. Skinner's previous book, *Walden Two*, was a million copy best seller.

---

[221] If Dr. Burrhus F. Skinner didn't need dignity why'd he change his name to "B.F."?
[222] Actually he did say *what* he was going to replace them with but to spell it *all* out here would be anti-dramatic.

The NIMH today—a *Behaviorist [in the anti-volition, anti-freedom, anti-dignity, anti-autonomous man sense of the term] Sympathetic Institution*—is stronger now than it was in Skinner's day and it continues to grow stronger. And the scary *fact* is, it grew stronger in the shadow of one of the strongest intellectual defenses of *freedom* ever presented to the *reasoning* world.

In 1957 with the first publication of *Atlas Shrugged*, Ayn Rand said she was going to stop the *mystic, collectivist, altruistic, machine—that is, the anti-*autonomous man machine—then running the world. She said she'd do this by filling up the world with people who were *so selfish*—so *individually* selfish, *so Objectivismly* selfish—that they would *not* tolerate the likes of those who preached people didn't have *any* kind of needs of consciousness, let alone no fundamental, basic need *of consciousness* such as the *need* for freedom.

If *freedom* isn't a legitimate human need why do we *value* it so deeply?

Are we born valuing it or as we develop and grow older do we learn the *reasons* why we *should* (hence, do) value it?

The answer to this depends on how we interpret the meaning of the philosopher's assertion that human beings are born tabula rasa, that is, are born as a blank-slate. Is it as *BiO Spiritualism* interprets it—that is, as the way in which BiO Spiritualism paraphrases Biocentric Psychology: our survival *needs* are innate not learned and our to-be-developed blank slate *capacities to satisfy those needs* are programmed by us in our non-omniscient *volitional* choices as we act and re-act to the world in which we live OR is it as *Behaviorism* and all other non-need-psychology schools of thought interpret it: our blank-slate human *needs* have to be learned and hence they are *not* innate and our innate human capacities to satisfy our helter-skelter needs are programmed by the environment and/or genetics as we flailingly re-act to the world in which we have to propagate our gene pool.

The difference here is critical and it forms one cornerstone of what can be called "psycho-hermeneutics" (as in interpreting your own psychology rather than relying on someone else to do it for you) and the beginnings of a truly New Spiritualism. A *spiritualism* that cares about *precision* and being *right* (*needs* are not learned, they are discovered). A *spiritualism* that *worships* non-contradiction and cares about *truth* (learning *how* to *properly* exercise our capacities to satisfy our needs is what is learn-able). A spiritualism that starts by saying that *truth* and *falsehood* are *not* the same thing. That truth—as Aristotle said—*must be preferred*. And by implication, *the false* must be—not de-ferred, but—dis-valued. *How much* preferred and *how much* dis-valued is part of the subject matter of psycho-hermeneutics as already presented in Chapter 17 (e.g., when the skin deep Skinnerians say man has no depth—no soul/no consciousness—they are ... no right, that is, *they are wrong*).

For an example of truth vs. false consider that in Ayn Rand's *Philosophy of Objectivism freedom* is a human *need*. In *Behaviorism* it is not. Both of these positions cannot be true. In *Behaviorism*—the alleged "science" of psychology as proclaimed by the mainstream American intellectuals of the last century—not only is *freedom* not a human need, but neither is *dignity*. Contrast this with the *psychology* of the early Objectivist, Dr. Nathaniel Branden. As an Objectivist he accepts that *freedom* is a basic human need, and as a (life-centered, Biocentric) psychologist he argues so also is *dignity* [i.e. *authentic* self-esteem] a human *need*. He "preaches" that *freedom* **and** *dignity* are such *basic* human needs that without them we are not human beings. Dr. Branden's first major book on psychology: *The Psychology of Self Esteem*[iv] is totally and completely dedicated to teaching *developing* man how to become *dignified*—that is, *authentically self-valuing*—man. This book was published the same year an American explorer stepped on the moon and it is an intricate study and blueprint for man—*the explorer*—to follow as he *discovers* how to create and build his *autonomous* self out of nature's *raw* materials.

We all have the *raw* materials. As did all humans before us.

But "we" are *here and now,* so one question for us as *modern* day men and women is: Can we achieve autonomy (be self ruling in the self functions: TFAJ) *in spite* of the culture we live in?[223] That is to say, *that* is the question for those of us who *value* autonomy. For those "others" who *dis-value* autonomy...for T.H.E.M. the question is: How can I do my part to help the *Behaviorist's* and their friends kill off autonomous man? Is sending them my tax money to support their research good enough or *should* I do more?

The second question in the foregoing could very easily be one of the follow up questions that T.H.E.Y. ask themselves. But it isn't the only one *to be* asked. There are many other *better* questions that "they" could ask themselves but do not. Some of these better questions are: *what is freedom? Where does it come from? Is it guaranteed to individuals or does it depend on some kind of action on the individuals part? Is freedom valuable or is the valuing of it merely a*

---

[223] Thinking, Feeling, Acting, Judging. If we accept the BiO Spiritualism view that "culture" as a total, "whole" thing is like a "sum" of fractions and operates on the same principle: namely, before you can "*add them all up"* you have to *reduce* them to the LOWEST common denominator, then this statement is true for all who aspire to HIGHER in *any* (and all) culture(s).

conditioned—associationally "learned" in the Skinnerian-Pavlovian dog sense—response and consequently human beings can just as easily "learn" to dis-value it? For *correct* answers to these kinds of "better" questions we have to turn to the *Objectivists*, who, as a group of professional intellectuals, have become—not by default, but by *choice*—the intellectual guardians of *freedom* in America (and by default, on the planet).

One such Objectivist is Dr. Peikoff who some thirteen years after Dr. Branden wrote the definitive psychological primer on how to become *dignified* man, Dr. Peikoff published his first book "*The Ominous Parallels. The End of Freedom in America*".[v] In this book Dr. Peikoff—the intellectual heir to Ayn Rand's *Objectivism* following her unfortunate, sad death this same year—meticulously traced and identified for the whole world to see, the philosophical roots beneath and hence *the cause* of the German Nazis who *initiated* World War II and killed off *freedom* in a way never seen before. With this book Dr. Peikoff predicted that *freedom* in America was going *to die* by forces *similar* to those inhabiting the inner-conflicted ideologues—the Social Democrats—of Germany's Weimar Republic following World War I. The Social Democrats of that era thought they could integrate the nonintegrable, that is, they thought they were exempt from the *laws of consciousness* and as such that they could do the impossible. They of course didn't come out and say directly, "We think we can do the impossible", rather they "predicted" they could by *implying* they could. They implied they could *integrate* Marxism **and** Capitalism by integrating Capitalism's *methods* **into** Marxism's ideals.[vi] In essence "they" said: "Let's *promote* Marxism by *using* the Capitalists. Capitalistic man isn't very bright when it comes to [a sheep's view of] *ethics* so he should be pretty easy to control. We'll use *his* productive *superiority* to promote *our* ideology." As a result—of *trying to integrate the nonintegrable*—the (German) Weimarcians *made* themselves and their country *along with them* ineffectual obstacles to the (Nazi) thugs who eventually took over Germany.[224]

---

[224] A word of *caution* to all conscientious people who have not yet read *The Ominous Parallels* but are contemplating doing so. If you have ever wondered in your own mind how *you* may or may not have acted had *you* been a young adult living during the time of the Nazi's, this book affords you that opportunity. Dr. Peikoff, with this book, has nailed the Nazi mentality to the wall for all to see and it is a puzzlement to me why I have never seen it referred to or heard it mentioned even *once* in all the Public Television "episodes" about Nazi Germany and the Holocaust that I have watched over the past, almost 30 years now. Is it because I don't know everything and it has been mentioned and I just missed it or is there a *bureaucratic mentality* in the *public* sphere that is actively ignoring Dr. Peikoff's accomplishments? Or is this evidence of the desire for the *contradictory* on my part—on my own terms? That is, since I think "culture" is LOWEST common denominator why do I expect it to endorse the HIGHEST? Or is this evidence of me *equivocating* on LOWEST and HIGHEST? For now, I accept that the *best* possible choice here in this multiple choice

The thugs and their accomplices then, took over Germany by *predicting* that they and *their* social designers could design and produce what nobody else could: a *square circle society*. Then, these Nazi thugs and their sympathizer thugs proceeded to show the world what a *real* "square circle" looks like, and *how to* build one.

If one believed in God, which I no longer do, but if one did, it is *here* that one would stand erect, look up while throwing one's hands skyward and say: "thank god for America".

And Americans.[225]

Today is a day in the first year of the first century following all of last century's dire predictions.

And where do we stand?

In this, the first year of the first century following Dr. Skinner's prediction and efforts to destroy *autonomous* man as well as all the voluminous anti-Skinnerian by-products of numerous Ayn Rand disciple-authors—including the Herculean efforts of the still fighting Dr. Peikoff—we stand *where* freedom stands every day of its life: on the edge of the precipice of *apathy* and mental laziness. In the face of this—that is in the colloquial sense of a "in your face" attitude—the *President of the United States of America* in his year 2000 budget has authorized—unopposed in a *silence* of meekness and moral cowardice that can be heard around the world—the President has authorized Government agencies to dole out *five billion dollars* per year (to start and because of the *nature of the bureaucratic mind* to escalate every year per year thereafter) to Dr. Skinner's *followers* and *sympathizers* for them to use in putting the *final touches* on what Skinner had started—albeit not originated—and envisioned: a *totally* planned, *socially engineered* society completely devoid of *autonomous* men and women.

If you think my last sentence is excessively long, wait until you live under the kind of *engineered* society you might have to live under if the "collectivists" achieve their utopian dreams of a ruled, dictated, totally controlled "society".[226]

Along with the *irrefutable fact of the $5,000,000,000 Government Grant* to Behaviorist sympathizers it appears quite possible that three other things are just

---

question is: (a) a *bureaucratic mentality* in the public sphere *actively* ignoring all of *Objectivism's* accomplishments, with Dr. Peikoff's *Ominous Parallels* book simply being included on the "guilty by association" premise.

[225] Or if you are British, you might want to say: "...thank god for Sir Winston Leonard Spencer Churchill..."; or if you were...and so on... *freedom* lovers and *freedom* fighters know who to thank for the historical victories over tyranny—be they victories over the external kind or the internal kind.

[226] To a *true* collectivist, saying "totally controlled" and "society" in the same sentence is redundant.

as true. One, George Orwell will end up being off by no more than 100 years in his prediction made in the 1940's that "1984" would be the year *totalitarianism* takes over America.   Two: if *Objectivism* and *Biocentric Psychology* do not *explicitly* embrace each other and/or if enough of us don't *embrace* both of them—or some very close relatives thereof—for ourselves, then you, me and everybody will be double speaking "doublespeak" well before the occurrence of the Centennial celebration of "1984". A "celebration" that is being planned right now by your *wannabe* social engineers and social designer-controllers.   And three: Dr. Peikoff *succeeded* (almost single handedly albeit with a little help from his friends) in warding off a Weimarcian society in America while at the same time *inadvertently* providing the Behaviorists, *Cognitive* Psychologist-Neurologists and all *bureaucratic minds* EVERYWHERE (thanks to the Internet) a *reverse* blueprint to follow as they work to bring to fruition their "utopian" view—updated and "modernized" out of necessity—of an America ruled by a VOLUNTARY TOTALITARIANISM.

Voluntary totalitarianism is **pure** *Democracy's ultimate, inevitable, inescapable, "logical" end.*

Your success at becoming *autonomous* man is *our* only defense against it.

We can see from our observations of their illusion worship and their TV repair man "explanation" of "psychology" that the *self-contradictory* nature of such a phrase as "voluntary totalitarianism" will not and does not bother "them"—t.h.e.m, the Bureaucratic Minds and Social Engineers—in the least.   Quite frankly, *they* simply believe that "people"—that is, *you and me*—are to stupid to get it.[227]

And if the peoples start to get it?
Well…we'll just keep calling it something else.
How 'bout we call it "Behaviorism"?
Can't, they've already gotten that.
How about "Cognitive Psychology" then?
Well they 'kinda got that too because "psychology" has
become synonymous with "Behaviorism" so that
"Cognitive Behaviorism" is to *easy* to get.

---

[227] You, qua reader, think this overly dramatic? If so, you connect these three dots: •$_1$ (p. 410 of the Surgeon General's report [see References: Chapter 15, ii) with •$_2$ (HG's anti-reason, only losers use Aristotle based logic of Venn diagrams [see/read Chapter 13 in general and pp. 364, 365 specifically of Reference ii given here under Chapter 16 References]) and •$_3$ (Surgeon General's report p. 57 clarion call to action of all ivory tower types to use their "power of multiple disciplines" to *pound* [or, *urged* to link, if you prefer] the square peg 'mind' into the round hole brain [and/or vice—pun intended—versa]).©s

OK. How about "Cognitive Neuroscience"?

Ooooooooh...Grrrr-ate! That sounds great. If Donna Shalala OK's it we'll go with it and publish it on p. 57 of her first report to the nation on mental health. A report telling those same people *exactly* how she and hers will spend the billions and billions and hopefully *eventually* (in less than 65 years) **trillions** of dollars that they, the democratic peoples, freely, openly and unabashedly gift the *bureaucratic mind* in the form of excessive tax revenue out of every paycheck of every pay period of every year of their productive lives.[228]

"*Mental Health: A Report of the Surgeon General*" published in the last month of the last year of the last century of the last millennium by so many US Government agencies that it's difficult to count them all, explicitly lays it out for all of us to see. And what we can *see* is that the *bureaucratic arms* of the United States Government is pulling out all stops and is going to *enlist* and *embrace* the social engineering minded to *Socially Engineer* each and every one of us—one neuron at a time if that's what it takes—into *submission* and *subservience* to the *anti-autonomous man mentality,* whether we like it or not.

Unfortunately, *some* like it.

This mystic-collectivist-altruistic anti-autonomous man "mentality" is deeply embedded in the American "cultural mind" in a sense analogous to that which is embedded in sheep's "minds". That is, *sheep are sheepish* and if they could think and act from thoughts (which they cannot, but if they could) their "spiritual" quest would be to find a "sheepherder". Given the ever growing power of the bureaucratic mind as same is manifest in the NIMH and other Governmental agencies it appears as if our choice is being reduced to its barest essentials: Do you want to be a man (the *autonomous* kind) or a sheep. Here is one area in which religious people or more precisely "Christians" *cannot* escape the hot seat of judgment: Whose image is it that is (and at what age is it embedded), that shows Jesus as the quintessential *sheepherder* and *you* as a little sheep in his flock of sheep? It is *not* Ayn Rand's, this I *know* for *sure,* that is*, for 100%,* **absolute** *sure.*

The foregoing "vice of sheepishness" is the "danger" lurking in the mental pathways of our cultural selves and as you have witnessed here, *BiO Spiritualism* is the first book to *explicitly* advocate that what America *needs* most right now is *individuals* and especially *adult* individuals and *what* adult individuals need most

---

[228] 5 billion dollars at a growth rate of 10% per year will—by the rule of 72—double every 7.2 years, therefore, it will exceed 1 trillion dollars in 56 years. Of course if the 10% growth rate is less, it will take longer and if more, shorter.

is *The Philosophy of Objectivism* **PLUS** *The Psychology of Biocentric Psychology and* a book that shows them how to *embrace and apply* these two intellectual disciplines to help them to identify and then satisfy—with full and complete satiation—their own *true* spiritual needs.

If one believes—as the *Objectivists* do albeit not as I do but—as the (naïve?) *Objectivists* do that *Religion* is a *primitive* Philosophy then one has to believe that so too is it a primitive psychology (*thinking* lustful thoughts is the *same*—morally, psychologically, ethically, actually, practically—as acting them out in reality). Since psychology is to an important degree *applied* philosophy we can see that psychology is intimately connected to and all wrapped up in *philosophy,* which—to repeat, *some* believe—is a form of religion (or if you are an Objectivist, vice versa). Or to be more *precise*, [philosophy (to the naïve? Objectivist)] is a *form* that can *include* anything, even religion.

If this and the idea that the State is not suppose to endorse any *particular* Religion, then why—you may be wondering—the f*!@#&'h is it endorsing AND attempting to Institutionalize *Cognitive Neuroscience*?

Is it because *they* are the T.H.E.Y—the anti-Objective, the anti-reason, the anti-Ayn Rand, the anti-correct philosophy they—that are building a monument out of Kantian clay and calling it, *Cognitive Neuroscience*, the savior of us poor little wretched mentally ill people who don't know which end of the stick is up ... out of the water and hence not bent by slow moving light ... nor that *The Group* is the source of all good on earth and that since we absolutely refuse to get the message that (some) philosophers since Plato have been trying to *ram* down our throat (talk about abuse) T.H.E.Y will protect us from our self and finish building the monument. But, my real fear is, T.H.E.Y know Ayn Rand is correct and they are *afraid of her* and will do *whatever* it takes to maintain control over what they consider to be t.h.e.i.r flock, that is t.h.e.i.r *sheep,* that is *you* and *me*, that is, *for shearing*.

Is this the *ultimate* achievement for the *Bureaucratic Mind* and the *Social Engineers*: the wool they use to pull over our eyes is the same wool sheared from our own backs?!?!?!

But as Ayn Rand has told us, this is such a simple game to beat, all you have to do is: not play.

Of course this doesn't say *what* we should do as an alternative.

And do nothing is *not* an alternative.

But to do what you love *is* an alternative and is the *preferred* one.

The second choice is do what you love and can make a living at.

The third one is, do what productive work you must in order to live and set up for that day when you can do what you love.

But the goal, the motivator, the ultimate drive is to end up doing what you love. If you achieve this then you will be happy.

You will that is, if you also *worship* non-contradiction and joy.[229] These are the "given" in the tenet that says, do the productive work you love and you will be happy.

Even as I write the foregoing a part of me feels like a naive person, forget naive realist or naïve objectivist or naive anything, just plain 'ole simple naive person—says the cynical within—is one who thinks he or she can *actually* live life creatively, passionately, ... happily! Where'd they get such a notion?

Well, I got mine from *Objectivism* and *Biocentric Psychology*, where'd you get yours?

Oh!

You don't have one?

Now I *see*.

---

[229] Because then when ... you *are* happy because you *should* be happy, *you will know it*. And you will know it in the organismic sense of the term: *I see what I see and I know what I know.* I know that I *am* happy; happiness being a state of noncontradictory joy.

Chapter 20: Does *Objectivism* need *Biocentric Psychology*?

Is vice versa a tautology?

Yes. Yes.
Objectivism needs Biocentric in the same way the foundation piers and piles of the World Trade Center's Twin Towers needed their 100 plus floors above them in order to be buildings and not just foundations.

A foundation *without* floors is not a building, it's a foundation.

As to the second *Yes*, this is easy because *all* special sciences (including psychology), just like *all* people (including you and me) *need* philosophy.©º

* * *

Objectivism is the street light on your corner *illuminating* the page in your latest Action-Packed Super-Hero Comic Book that correctly depicts ...

Wait ... halt.

Before we get fully into Chapter 20 let us deal first with the "it's a dirty job but somebody has to do it" stuff.

In preparation for this manuscript I did some premise checking of my own (see Chapter 23 with its list of 35 of them) and concluded for one of them (item 9 of 35) that Biocentric Psychology is not quite as good as Objectivism because it, Biocentric, could contain perhaps two or three times as many errors as does Objectivism (which, I speculated in item 6 & 7 of 35, probably contains—at most—fewer errors than the number of things in a baker's dozen). Then—throughout the manuscript—I proceeded to be on the lookout for Objectivism's errors and I thought I had identified at least 5 of them (though most of them were/are/were a stretch).

As part of my preparation for this Chapter (20) it then became apparent to me that in order for me to be consistent I had to come up with at least ten and probably 15 (!?!?!) errors in Biocentric Psychology.

Well (Houston) we have a problem.

The most I could come up with were (maybe) four errors in Biocentric and so it follows that my previous speculation statements will remain true if and only if I can come up with at least two (solid or at least semi-solid) errors in Objectivism (on the low end of my earlier, premise-checking estimate: 2 * 2 *is* 4).

Since I do kinda have 5 Objectivism errors (though 3 of them like I said are a stretch) I will mention just the two more solid ones here and then the 4 in Biocentric Psychology also and in so doing complete my commitment [to myself] to so do this.

Objectivism's first error is the contradictory statement that Ayn Rand herself made. She made this when she said: "Objectivism is not an itself"[i] and then somewhere else where/when she said: "Objectivism is its own protector."[ii] Since a thing can't be an "it•self" and not an "it•" at the same time and in the same respect this error is easily corrected by noticing that since Objectivism IS its own protector it ALSO is an it•self (it• is *that* Formal Philosophy which protects it•self from being diluted or otherwise watered down by other not-as-objective philosophies [and amateur philosopher wannabe's—i.e., moi]—be they the formal, academic, *extrospective "publicly verifiable"* Ivory Tower ones or the informal—Marble Hearth at the base of our own, *idiosyncratic/only introspectively identifiable* ~~Blast Furnace Core~~ Giant Fire Place core—ones[230]).

Objectivism is the "thing" (the itself) that I used to reclaim my epistemological life from the garbage dumps of religion.

If this isn't an it•self I don't know what is.

Objectivism's second (and by far more serious) error is: *measurement determines the substance* of emotions, that is, if an emotion is not of a high high intensity it's not an emotion.

Though it is true that Objectivism doesn't commit this second error *directly* and much about it (it• Objectivism that is) suggests that this is Gary Deering misinterpreting Objectivism, I (Gary Deering) have to disagree. Instead I ask you to (re)consider every non-Biocentric Objectivist *definition* of emotions [prior to the beginning of the 3rd Millennium] that you've ever read in the Objectivist writings

---

[230] As an Objectivist—albeit a second tier one—I would like to think of myself as having a "blast furnace" core, but alas I do not. Since I value hearth and comfort—and always have, even as a kid I preferred shooting pool (and smoking cigarettes) and playing monopoly and/or pinochle (and smoking cigarettes) and being in where it was warm and cozy on snowy-cold wintry days (and smoking cigarettes) rather than in being out clearing the streets of snow (by hand if necessary) so the peoples could get through—so since I value hearth and comfort MORE than "real man production schedules" I have—per remembering dream images about them—a GIANT fireplace core. It might be convertible over time into a blast furnace one but as I now approach my sixth decade on earth it doesn't look like this is gonna be the case.

and/or heard at a formal Objectivism lecture and notice that they all *lack fundamentality* and they try to make up for this lack by tying emotions to CORE values as the important, essential, *fundamental* ingredient OF emotions (so in the real sense, the real Objectivist error about emotions is that their definitions *lack fundamentality* which for our purposes here—see page 1—means that all the non-Biocentric Objectivist definitions of emotions are *wrong* COMPARED to the Biocentric definition which is *right*). [231, iii]

If you conclude that an emotion has to touch your core values *before* it can be an emotion then you will be in psychhological trouble because in reality this is just an issue of measurement—the values at the core are the highest values and should and do produce emotions of the HIGHEST intensity when same are involved in our emotional reaction to events involving our *core* values directly (e.g. September 11th, 2001).

But just as we, qua human beings, have more than one need so also do we have more/are more than our core values. Consequently, when *any* of OUR values—not just the core ones—are on the line we are and necessarily do FEEL emotional—from a little bit-to a bunch-to a gargantuan amount depending on the distance from our core that any particular value is—the closer to the core the hotter (the higher), the intensity.

(And the *reason* you will be in trouble is because of a *Biocentric* identified psychological principle: *[all] emotions flow freely in both directions or they don't flow*. To which the *BiO Spiritualist* in us can add—from experience—*artificially stopped emotions are dangerous to your health*—mental health for sure and quite possibly y/our physical health also—given that emotions are pent-

---

[231] We could elaborate here if we wanted to but we won't because we will (maybe) deal with this more in the (maybe) to be written *BiO Spiritualism* Volume II book. Still we could notice here, if we wanted to, that *even* Objectivism is not beyond being snaky in its epistemological building projects (as *its* own protector we can't consider it—for obvious reasons—to be an "infallible pope" either). That is, rather than admit that Branden's definition of emotions—with its reliance on the *fundamental* fact that if an emotion isn't felt it ain't an emotion ... that is ... rather than admit that this—is right the Objectivists jump(ed) through hoops to try to account for their *lack* of fundamentality by tying emotions to CORE values only (or predominantly) so that then *even* the most repressed person could not NOT feel their "emotions" and voila, by default, *feeling* emotions becomes/became a part of their "definition(s)". My double use of present/past tense here is an attempt to notice that Dr. Binswanger in his copyrighted 2002/3rd Millennium taped lecture (see reference) on EMOTIONS has corrected—somewhat—this Objectivism error. The fact that it took 'em nearly a half a century to do it will be dealt with in Volume II via the *importance* of the time element (and its relationship to the Laplacian nature of psychological *events*) in psychological change and growth and improvement. In anticipation of this just let me say that *Biocentric* psychology with its multi-factor variance *capabilities* is the Taguchi of both real world *and* thought experiments whereas *Objectivism* with its pre World War II reliance on one-factor variance is old testing method.

up-able. Consequently, a thousand unexperienced emotions—each one individually no larger than the size of a single tear drop—can add up to a lake full of tears threatening to overflow y/our banks.)

So here too this second Objectivism error is *relatively* easy to correct. It is corrected by *relying on* and *using* the reality based, correct (*Biocentric*) definition of emotions—*an emotion is the psycho-biological form [regardless of its intensity] in which we experience our estimate of the beneficial or harmful relationship of some aspect of reality to ourself.* That is, we *should* use the (reality based) *Biocentric* definition rather than the *Objectivist's* (erroneous) desire (I speculate) to link emotions to core *only*.[232]

The "four" *Biocentric* errors that I have been able to identify are these:

1. because of synergy it is *possible* that there is such a thing as an élan vital (*literal* life energy like there is nuclear energy or solar energy)

2. reasoning is not an elitist function

3. half an equation is as good as a whole equation

4. error #4 = tbd (that is, a **ToBeDetermined error** which I *deduce* has to exist—2 * 2 doesn't = 3—even if I haven't YET found it but I think I will find it and present it in the—to be written (maybe)—*BiO Spiritualism* Book II)

Having discharged our—our as in yo~~u~~r, having discharged yor—intellectual ~~duty~~ obligation (to self) let's get back to the funner part of Chapter 20.

* * *

Objectivism is the street light on your corner *illuminating* the page in your latest Action-Packed Super-Hero Comic Book that correctly depicts the 18th Century German Philosopher Immanuel Kant—cloak and all—as the ... wait, halt, whoa, hold on.

How about some elaboration on those *Biocentric* errors?

Ok but it's gonna be short (and psycho-hermeneutic).

---

[232] Should they—the good they, the Objectivists ... that is, should they—the Master's of the Core succeed in tying emotions to C.O.R.E only then they remain in total and complete control (in-the-main introspectively though also a teeny-tiny bit extrospectively as they have a *need* to have a following of people to buy—literally and figuratively—their intellectual property).

Error #1: listen to Dr. Branden's Basic relaxation and ego strengthening procedures audio tape[iv] (*without* falling asleep) and then read Harry Binswanger's book on Teleology[v] and combine this with Dr. Branden quoting C. D. Broad (somewhere[vi]) in support of his, Dr. Branden's, view of "synergy". Synergy—per the great definer/teacher of things Dr. Branden—has to do with—is an attempt to deal with—the (felt) fact of reality that the whole thing can't always be *predicted* from a consideration of its parts only, and as such we can't always claim a priori to have knowledge of the whole. That is, the whole can be "greater than the sum of its parts" as suggested by the term "synergy" if we understand it to mean in this "can't predict" way. Contrast this with Harry B (Dr. Binswanger) who claims—essentially—that the whole is the ("predictable") sum of its parts *as long as* we recognize that the whole is the whole—which is to say, it is everything that it is including those "things" [be they things 1 and/or 2 in BiO Spiritualism speak] that we observe in the whole and then deduce: of course! given [all] these parts *this* whole *is* [logical] consequent—it doesn't have to be a priori it only has to be "makes sens(ory)e"—that is, the whole can be shown to make sense when all the (essential) facts are known and *accounted* for. The whole is not greater than the sum of its parts as the loose use of "synergy" is commonly employed, but rather the whole is the sum of its parts when parts appropriately includes both things 1 and things 2. For example, to elaborate on an earlier reference, a baked cake includes things 1—pots 'n pans and ovens and cake mix—AND things 2—the PROCESS of baking: mixing and blending and placing the mixture into and setting the *oven* at the *correct* temperature and time—say 350 °F (177 °C) for 60 minutes, NOT put the mixture into an insulated box of dry ice at -40 °F (same number for °C) for 60 days—by the one who bakes. That is, the *whole* delicious, edible, consumable chocolate cake is the *sum* of its things 1 and things 2 parts.

Biocentric Error #2: This error helped me a great deal in my personal therapy when Dr. Branden said: Thinking is not an elitist function. By so doing he "gave" me the (intellectual) weapons (I needed at the time) to fight those internal voices (religious and mother and social) that were *against* thinking—mother's = get a job *don't* go to college; religion's = *evil* fruit from the tree of *knowledge*; social = you think too much, etcetera and so on BUT it was detrimental for some-time thereafter until one sunny day in May a thousand years *after* I had gotten *all* the benefit I could out of the earlier statement that I realized the saying should *really* be:

> Thinking is *not* an elitist function, *but reasoning is.*[233]

Error #3: it's more important to praise the good than it is to damn the evil. That is, if you want to change behavior (e.g. parents changing children's behavior or enlightened self changing unenlightened self's behavior) it is better to praise good behavior than to damn bad behavior. As long as the praise is objective—matches the reality of the child's actual achievement(s)—it's ok to predominantly praise the good and minimally—if at all—punish bad behavior. Again as a—temporary—therapy device (for the self-immolating who *have* "happily" internalized the parental-religious-social job of beating the self up) this pendulum swing behavior is good advice as long as one doesn't forget to swing the pendulum back (in physics, pendulums, once started, swing themselves, but not so in psychhology—here pendulums can be started by self and/or others but they can only be swung back by self). So in the final analysis where *not faking reality* is the *real* virtue it follows that since both the good and the evil exist in reality both have to be—and hence, *should* be—dealt with.

We could argue here that the sentiment to focus only on the good, the pleasant is understandable in its appeal to our childlike innocence and that September 11<u>th</u>, 2001 was the loss of (this) innocence and that this error #3 is NOT as bad as is secular humanism's on this same topic but we won't. An error is an error but just as fire can be used to fight fire so too can an error be used to fight an error. In my personal therapy case it was good for me to *temporarily* focus (predominantly) on the good (e.g. emotions, *qua human capacity*, are good) and not [just] the bad

---

[233] Since this statement is true *twice* we could say it is true, **in spades**! In the first way it is true is this: it is true of those "elitist" *humans* who are the *only* ones in the *animal kingdom* who [metaphysically speaking] *can* reason. Then it is true the "second" time within the group of human animals in that though they *all* have the potential to reason, only those *elitist* ones who *choose* to reason 51% *or more* of the time when they are confronted with the need to reason do so *choose*. That is—as an issue of *degree*—reasoning *is* an elitist function. And so—statistically speaking—you or I or anyone can *join* the *elite* by simply *choosing* to think and reason when we should *more* times than we choose to *not* think and reason when we shouldn't. (All this with the understanding that the concept "should" derives its meaning from the *ultimate* fact that the *ultimate* value is man's life—with "value" and "life" as delineated by the *Philosophy of Objectivism*.)

(you are "selfish") because those, for example, who take it as a maxim that T.H.E.Y are entitled to *their* emotions but that YoU have to PROVE yours—in a if you can't prove them you can't USE them way—are a danger to Yor life because they plan on USING t.h.e.i.r emotions to CONTROL you (to help them with *their* ends and purposes even if such—or perhaps *especially* if such—means helping them *not* face their *pseudo* self-esteem issues). To which of course, if you know Biocentric Psychology you know it is going to reply: bullstuff! I have a *right* to enjoy my own life—that is, to the *means* to enjoying that life—that is, to *my* emotions.

But, to repeat, an error is an error. The real danger here is that one *runs the risk* of becoming a full fledged, Formal Humanist. A full fledged Humanist, a Formal Humanist is one who says we must praise the good AND NOT damn the evil. This it self is evil and must be damned. Therefore, I damn it. It's one of Biocentric Psychology's errors and is *easily* corrected by USING the Objectivist tenet: *Judge and be prepared to be judged*—the good must be praised AND the evil must be damned ... AND **I** must do it—including being as precise as is humanly possible in identifying the *objective* good to be that which is *for* life and in identifying the *objective* evil to be that which is *against* life while recognizing that life *is* a process of self sustaining self generated action.

Biocentric Psychology's Error #4, as stated, is a TBD but a ToBeDetermined with a TBC—ToBeContinued—*exercise* in The Art and Science of Thinking AND Reasoning.

NOW! back to the beginning.

* * *

Objectivism is the street light on your corner *illuminating* the page in your latest Action-Packed Super-Hero Comic Book that correctly depicts the 18th Century German Philosopher Immanuel Kant—cloak and all—as the Charles Manson of the Philosophy World.

Kantians of course will disagree and say Kant is, if not a super hero then at least, one of the good guys (just like Squeaky-what's-her-name et al. followers said of the literal Charles Manson).

If you don't count people who worship faith *and* despise reason, then *both* views of Kant cannot be treated as true—at the *same* time and in the *same* respect. The *choice* is: one of them is true or neither of them is.

Biocentric psychology is the street light on your corner *illuminating* that page in your latest Action-Packed Super-Hero Comic Book that correctly depicts the super hero to be ... *you*, that is, the *human you* in you that is *authentically, Objectivisimly* selfish.

Many humans of course will disagree and say the selfish human is not *one* of the bad guys but rather *thee* bad guy—the selfish they say *is* the super villain (just like Religion-by-any-name et al. followers of same have been saying since time immemorial).

If you don't count people who worship faith *and* despise reason, then *both* views of the selfish human cannot be treated as true—at the *same* time and in the *same* respect. The *choice* is: one of them is true or neither of them is.

Your BM Government—like a vandal with a fully loaded gun—is roaming the streets of your (epistemological) neighborhood looking for some street lights to shoot out.

Specifically, *Cognitive Neuroscience—in its role* as the BM Government's designated "integrator" and applier of the Kantian tenets embedded in *Cognitive Psychology* and *Cognitive Science*—plans on being the gun that shoots out your street lights so that the cops can't see the shenanigans that go on in the dark when they come down *your* street and *round* your corners as they carry out their patrol of your (epistemological) neighborhood.

The (epistemological) cops will protect you when they can see, but when they can't, you have only one thing to rely on.

You (and your desire to be more moral, that is, *more* Objectivismly selfish).

If you feel that epistemological crimes have been committed in *your* neighborhood and if worse: you are being blamed and/or *framed* for spiritual murder, then I suggest you call in the world's best *private detective* to help you solve the "crime(s)" and *free* yourself of all un-earned guilt.

And even, perhaps, if necessary, of some *earned* guilt too.

Yes, it is true. *Biocentric Psychology* teaches you the Art—without ever even mentioning the word—it teaches you *The Art of Self Forgiveness*.

Objectivism teaches you that *what* you (might) need to be forgiven of is: your *choice* to *succumb* to two thousand years worth of peer pressure to *worship the god(s) of self-immolation*.

Biocentric psychology teaches you that if you are a person who did so succumb then the road to recovery *starts* with *unlearning* your self-*renunciating* **T**houghts, **F**eelings and **A**ctions which are prerequisite to Judging the self *worthless* which is prerequisite to *immolating* the self.

When Ayn Rand talked about the "sin of forgiveness", she meant the sin of forgiving *others* transgressions against you, not self's. If we include her bad moments or what—by her own description—we could call her "Dominique" moments[vii], then we can say—with some degree of confidence—that Ayn Rand did *not* mean the sin of *self*-forgiveness. Quite the contrary, *Objectivism*—with *Biocentric Psychology* added in—makes possible the only kind of self-forgiveness that there is. Namely, *true, authentic* self-forgiveness that comes from—*and can only come from*—an extremely deep and profound *understanding*—what *BiO Spiritualism* calls a psycho-hermeneutic understanding—of *self*.[234]

Objectivism teaches that *context* is all important in *knowing* the external world, *therefore* so it is in *knowing thyself,* which is to say *context* is all important in knowing—whether it be in knowing the world *external* to self or in knowing the *internal* world of felt—that is, of *Biocentric psychology's* ego— self.[235]

There is one road and *one road only* to knowing the internal world of thy(ego)self. This road is called: *introspection.*

Introspection—a process of cognition directed inward—is the only road to knowing thyself and you are the only one who is capable of traveling it to the extent and degree necessary to establish an objective context for you, yourself. A context from which you can make reality based, objective judgments about the self.

---

[234] Out of fairness to *Biocentric* and *Objectivism* I should really mention here that this kind of benefit from Biocentric—self forgiveness success—is the littlest amount of benefit (we could almost call it a side benefit) that Biocentric offers to the selfless-of-spirit who have many miles to go before they are whole (humans). If you are such a spirit it would be taking away too much fun from you for me to reveal here all the benefits that you can get from Biocentric. Likewise for Objectivism: the benefits I'm mentioning here are among the least offered and since it is part of my nature to hoard things I just can't bring myself to revealing to you or otherwise giving away all the fun you can get out of Objectivism once you make the connection that it is *right*—that is, that it is the *proper* identification of the *facts* of reality as relates to properly identifying *what* human *nature* really is.

[235] The reality basis for *context* is really easy to see for one's self: simply boil water at sea level and then travel to some high elevation, e.g. Denver, Colorado and boil it there and OBSERVE that it boils at *different* temperatures in the two cases, that is, *contexts.* The *CONTEXT* that differs in our case here is the *amount of barometric pressure* and when accounted for makes it possible to answer correctly the question: At what temperature does water boil? This kind of reasoning applied to many many such examples leads the Objectivistic mind to conclude, *YES,* knowledge without omniscience *is* possible. The Plato-Kant-Hegel Philosopher lineage disagrees with this Objectivist-Aquinas-Aristotelian proposition and says that man cannot know and they simply waffle between t.h.e.i.r rationalizations as to WHY he can't. One day it's because he has a knower "device" as it were and when shown the absurdity of such a position they flip-flop over to, because he is not omniscient. Objectivism has defeated them by demonstrating that all knowledge is CONTEXTUALLY absolute and in this sense to talk of an uncertain knowledge is a self contradiction. Knowledge is absolutely true or it's not knowledge: water boils at 212 deg F (100 deg C) in my kitchen, unless I'm at a higher altitude, in which case it boils at a lower (not higher) temperature. This is knowledge. This is knowable. This is certain, and I know it and since I'm not omniscient, voila! knowledge without omniscience is possible.

OBJECTIVE judgments about the self are the building blocks of *authentic* self esteem; non-objective judgments only contribute to the continued propping up of *pseudo* self esteem and/or the knocking down of the remnants of ones *authentic* self esteem that one was able to hoard and hang on to *in spite of* a culture (be it sub or super) hell bent on destroying them. As such, non-objective judging only delays the anxiety that one must go through if one suffers from a high degree of *pseudo* self esteem, *and* desires—eventually—to undo it and replace it with *authentic* self esteem.

Authentic self esteem is a relationship between me, myself and I and "our" relationship to the external world as relates to "our" ability to survive in it *and* achieve a (BiO) *spiritual*(ism)—that is, a *happy*—life. To this extent then, *authentic* self esteem is one of the foundation piers supporting our spiritual quest for the holy grail of happiness here on this earth while we actually live and breathe.

Mental health and illness are issues in this pursuit also but we have to be very very careful and again it is necessary to repeat: we have to be extremely vigilant in that we do not confuse "value-conflicts" with "mental illness" (and vice versa).

How do we differentiate? By implementing Objectivism's advice to worship *precision* and *accuracy* when defining one's terms.

For example, *mental health*—as I've defined before per *Biocentric Psychology*—is *the unobstructed capacity for reality bound cognitive functioning and the exercise of this capacity. Mental illness is the sustained impairment of this capacity.*

In the *absence* of physical accidents and/or of *unequivocal* germ diseases and/or genetic states (that is, ones that can *only* be gotten by germs or transmitted *only* via genetics, e.g. Syphilis in the case of germs and Downs Syndrome in the case of genetics) that *cause* one a "beyond-their-control" *sustained* impairment of their *capacity* for *cognitive* contact with reality, it is *extremely* difficult for a person to *become* mentally ill.[236]

You could say, *evolution* selects AGAINST it.

A renowned and respected 20th Century psychiatrist (Thomas Sasz) and author of the book, "The Myth of Mental Illness"[viii], devoted a large portion of his life to

---

[236] I don't know for *absolute* sure if the two cited cases are the *best* cases to make my point but I assume they are *good enough* and that *you* can *get* the point by substituting—if necessary—your own known-for-sure *better* examples as means to helping you *isolate* and *differentiate* between what is, is not *within* our *volitional* control.

telling us just how difficult it is. He erred in his exuberance—as the title to his famous book suggests—on the side of caution, but, nonetheless, he did err.

It's not *impossible* to be born healthy and then *to become* mentally ill, but—to repeat—it is very, very difficult.

Your p.s. 21st Century government (if you are a modern day American or a throwback to yesterday's Russia) wants you to believe that it is an easy thing to do and/or a thing that can *happen* to you—that you can "catch" it as it were—as easily as you can get or catch a cold or some such *viral* or *germ* infection. And further: that it is just as much *outside your control* as are such infections.

Nothing could be further from the truth; unless, you are an *acculturated* modern day *globalized* "citizen of the world"—that is, one who believes (holds it as an article of faith) that *The Group* is the good, the individual the bad, "therefore" the bigger The Group (and the smaller the individual) the better. If such a case characterizes you, then you probably agree with your government and are doing all you can to help the *Bureaucratic Minds* within to institutionalize its brand of *Socially Engineered "citizen"*. A brand that *some* of us—but not all of us, *yet*—call: *Social Metaphysician.* Some of us can't afford to call it this *until* we are fully and completely back into the land of *authentic* self-esteem and since we won't be there until the end of this book we have to *wait* until then (and then ... a little bit more: until *BiO Spiritualism* Volume II to be written is written: *there*, we can and do call it that[237]).

The *bureaucratic mind* (don't forget) *is* a danger in *any* government (because it *is* a *mind* and because it has the legalized use of force on its side) and as we have already addressed here we are quite capable of handing and dealing with such mentalities (*because* we also have a *mind* and the *ability* to perfect it). We—qua individual *American* humans with the *power* of volition *living inside a relatively politically free society*—are so capable, that is. If you live somewhere else on the planet I'm not so sure as to how capable—since volition, though powerful, is neither omniscient nor omnipotent, I'm not so sure then as to how capable—the human being is at surviving such mentalities. Our concern here, qua Americans

---

[237] Unless of course it [Book 2] is never written. In this case *then* we *only* have to wait until the end of this Volume I/Book 1. Unless of course you are already there [in the land of *authentic* self-esteem] and are simply using this Book 1 to tell yourself (in essence) "...don't forget to remember..." *xyz* ... where *xyz* stands for all the *good* (for you) things that you know and have identified in your own introspective work. So, *DON'T* forget to remember ____.

who can *afford* such concern—thanks to capitalism (and let me repeat this: Thank god for capitalism!)—is more direct, personal and immediate.[238]

The high degree of difficulty in *becoming* mentally ill is *lessened* in direct proportion to the degree to which we *voluntarily* surrender our power of volition to other people, places or things.

Let me repeat this (and add the Figure below).

The *high* degree of difficulty in *becoming* mentally ill—with all exceptions as previously noted—is *lessened in direct proportion* to the degree to which we *voluntarily surrender* our power of volition to other people, places or things.

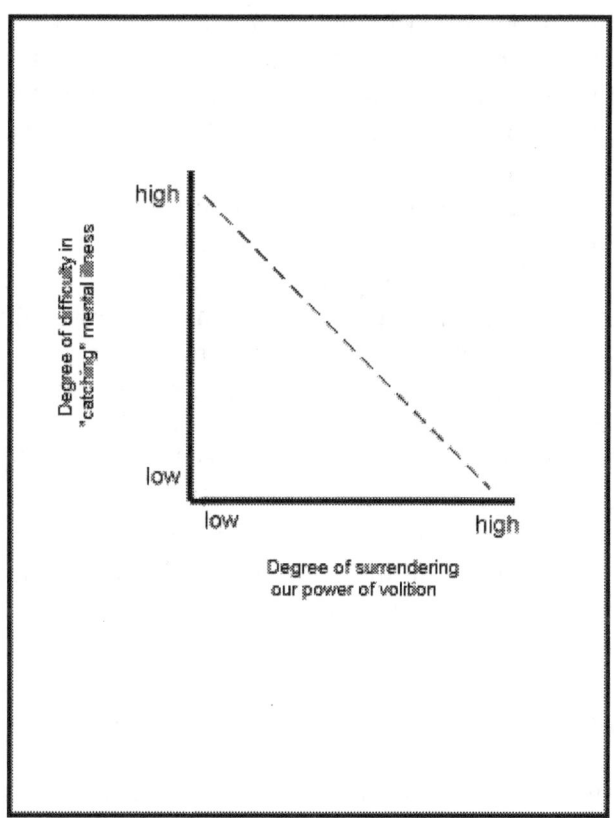

---

[238] The degree of danger exhibited by the bureaucratic mind—as same is a part of a society's government—exists in inverse proportion to the degree of political freedom in the particular society—low degree, high danger; high degree of freedom, lower danger.

We surrender it, for example, to *things* by saying, "I have *no choice*, I have to spend all this *time* maintaining the *things* I have accumulated"; completely dropping the *context* that we *chose* to accumulate them and that a proper attitude is I *own* my things, they don't own me. And that I can shed and readjust as required to get the *time* elements in my life back in line with *my* actual needs and/or changed and growing desires. And more, if I have lost this *ability* (that is, *control over my own individual life*) then I can and will seek professional help to restore it.

Going back to our ownership formula on page 8 and applying it in reverse we can say: once you cross over the 50% bridge heading in the wrong direction so that you now only retain 49% of your *volitional* (nature given or god given if you must) control *over yourself* is the extent to which you are in trouble. And if you don't correct it you will deteriorate: stagnation is not an option for humans—we either move forward or we move backward, but since life is motion we do not stand still. We move.

Psychologically one could argue I suppose that we can stay stuck for a time but the key word here is "for a time". Eventually we can't and don't stay stuck forever: eventually we become unglued and either float downstream further or we buck up and swim aggressively upstream against our own negative currents until we get back into the main river of life—where the water is calm, the sky blue and—etcetera. Which is to say, in the long run stagnation is *not* an option. And to volitionally choose *in*action as a way of life, is a choice—or *worse*, to *worship* and/or *reward* the inaction of non-production as better, superior, more moral than the *act of producing* is a choice—a choice with one and only one *kind* of consequent: negative. As to the *degree* of this *kind* it runs all the way from a little bit to a goodly amount to its ultimate: you die of starvation sitting on your ass(ets) waiting for someone else to bring you your daily bread. *Biocentric Psychology* is—in addition to being anti-ass(et) kicking, is—anti-ass(et) sitting.   This is ~~one~~ the *main* reason why the pro(foundly) ass(et)-kicking mentality of Objectivism *needs* Biocentric: because Biocentric (if it allows me to put words into its mouth) says you can't *literally* kick your own ass(ets), so stop trying. Rather, start using your psychological legs to walk the walk of an *authentically self*-valuing, *self*-assertive, *self*-enjoying-*self,* human being.

Consider:

> **mim:** are you saying the foregoing paragraph could have been titled:
> You're a(ss) is a(ss(et))?

MIM: (only if you are a writer or a wh... but, wait, halt) not point here, *rather*, consider the following.

***Objectivism* (in me):** whim worshippers are bad.
***Biocentric* (in me):** whim worshippers are under analyzers. (This from my counter to those who say of me—in *my* outer and inner dialogue—*you over analyze everything*, to which I reply: how do I know that you don't *under* analyze everything? This is to say, for me Biocentric helped me to be open to my inner dialogues, to my consciousness *processes*, to what O calls "*action* of consciousness in regards *to* content". Objectivism—in me—encouraged repression of my inner me = processes/dialogue me—*after*, that is, it convinced me that my consciousness and my soul are *one in-the-same thing*.)

OIM (Objectivism In Me): One is one's core values: You are your core values.
BIM (Biocentric In Me): I am me.

OIM: [He, she] is a second hander (with knowledge that secondhandedness is bad)
BIM: [He, she] is a social metaphysician (with same knowledge: social metaphysics is bad)
MIM: If you get a sense of superiority by a named comparison to others, don't.

OIM: Why not.
BIM: Because it creates pseudo self esteem.
MIM: Pseudo self esteem is really bad, authentically bad, no bullshit bad. If you succumb to it once and undo it you will discover that once IS enough.
mim: *Yes*, MIM means Me-In-Me.

OIM: How come (so far) O is coming up most negative in the O-B comparisons?
BIM: Because you haven't gone deep enough yet.
MIM: You mean like in the good versus the good?

mim: O is good *and* B is good and when B is better for me than O that makes O "by comparison" bad relative to B but not Bad relative to non B.

MIM: Deep enough = where definition lays, in this case somewhere in the medulla oblongata where O put it. In there it "says": a whim is an emotion the source of which I do not know and more importantly I *DON'T* WANT to know.
BIM: you mean this literally?
MIM: No. Medulla oblongata is a "sound" I like and one of the only words I remember about named parts of the brain and so I use it to mean deep in me "somewhere"—as in (as O would say)—must be somewhere but can be anywhere (until and unless … we can/do figure out exactly where; we know it's somewhere *inside* us, not *outside* us, e.g. it's not on Pluto, the planet … ~~but then it's not *in* my screwdriver either~~. Nor is it, as we will *soon* discover, in my screwdriver either.)
BIM:
OIM: No, question is: ….
NIMrod: (NotInMe/Rotting(in-me)Other'sDefinitions)

NIMROD: Your "moralizing" turns me off, it's too pedantic, it's bad, you are bad.
BIM: Do you want to make yourself *more* moral so that you can be a part of America's *emerging* 100% lfc society or not?
OIM: Do you want to make yourself more *moral* so that you can be a part of America's emerging 100% laissez-faire capitalism society or not?
MIM: *Yes*. But only *after* I've *made* myself capable of answering the following question in the affirmative: Do I want to be happy and/or happier?
OIM: All whims are bad so since whims are emotions all emotions are bad.
BIM: How come you mad this mistake?
MIM: Is this a brandian slip?
OIM: COuld be.
BIM: Typo or O slip?
MIM: Halt.

mim: Pun intended?
MIM: Apparently not.
mim: You sure? Your typing ability is pretty fast but your subconscious is faster.
MIM: What pun?

OIM: Point?
BIM: Point?
MIM: Owning objectivism and biocentric psychology is a bitch.
OIM: Bitch? That's a stup—
BIM: Halt.
MIM: By bitch, I mean, it's a really really hard, difficult thing to do but I honestly feel, believe, think it is the best, smartest thing I've ever done in my life.
mim: My methods are my methods and they did work.

OIM: Therefore, you SHOULD be happy, are you?
BIM: In the end it was all about you, qua *individual* yu, we "knew" it even if you didn't.
mim: Yes. I "knew" it too.
MIM: The end.
mim: The beginning.
MIM: Halt.
mim: ToBeContinued.
MIM: Stop. Go on to something else.
mim: OK. Is the first line here with the word, "you're" instead of "your" slip or slOp?
MIM: Neither, it's correct usage: *You* ARE a is a.

So, which way *we* move is up to us since we as individuals posses the *power* of volition, which is to say it *resides* in us and based on everything we know at this point in the state of our knowledge it *only* resides in humans and no other (known) form. It does not reside in rocks or stones or insects or non-human animals of any kind in the known Universe and it for sure does not reside—as a *unitary* thing—in Groups. *Volition is a power the seat of which is located inside the individual human being.*

Yes, volition is a *power* and if we loose it or it is diminished in us—without concern for the moment as to the *how*—to a significant degree then we can *feel* mentally ill but to conclude that we *are* mentally ill—*without a fight*—is abnegating the throne of our human spirit. And if you do do this, make no mistake about it; there are plenty of *social engineers* and *government bureaucrats* around who will more than gladly confirm your erroneous self-diagnosis. In fact, *some* will even *help you make it.*

Psyc*hh*ological mental illness—in contradistinction to the previously mentioned unequivocal germ disease and/or genetic and/or physical accident caused *organic* mental illnesses—is the wages of self-sins for self's who refuse to take full and complete, 100% responsibility for their *own* life *and* happiness. That is, of sins *by* the self, *against* the self. And if you want to call this "illness"—which I don't think you should, but if you must—then call it what it is: "value-illness". Somewhere in your life and by some yet to be discovered means perhaps, *you* have *internalized* the *wrong* values and you have to discover—just like everybody else does—*what* the *right* values are and then proceed to *make* them your own (and/or to *acknowledge* that your *right* values—the ones that do match reality—are right, that is, *good*).

This is what it means to say: *man is a being of self made soul.*

If you fail at identifying, pursuing and acknowledging the right values then you *will* have sinned against yourself. But with one important difference between you and those traditional *usurpers* of spiritual values—i.e., between the *faith* worshipping religionists—and the *rational-spiritual* you. The rational you is *quite* capable of *self* improvement which entails *self-forgiveness* and striving for and achieving *authentic* self-valuing.

The *faith* worshipping you is the soul reason why Ayn Rand had to stand by the deathbed of your mind and tell you the ... one ... *secret* word ... that *was* destroying your life.[239]

As we note in Chapter 23, no one is coming to save us, to take care of us, we have to do it ourselves. *How* we do it is still up to us. Whether we seek and find **competent** psychhological help is up to us or whether we try it alone is up to us, but that we *must do it* is not up to us—nature has already sealed our fate in this regard. Our *choice* is to *accept* or *reject* the metaphysical fact of *self-responsibility*.

In today's (first years of the new millennium) America and its cultural worship of pseudo self esteem and the "virtues" of self-*ir*responsibility this line has to be repeated no fewer than 10 times in order for it to sink in.

Our *choice* is to *accept* or *reject* the metaphysical fact of *self-responsibility*.
Our *choice* is to *accept* or reject the metaphysical fact of self-responsibility.
Our *choice* is to accept or *reject* the metaphysical fact of self-responsibility.
Our *choice* is to accept or reject the metaphysical *fact* of self-responsibility.

---

[239] A purely personal example. I would like to say here that the use of *soul* for *sole* was a Brandian slip but since I chose it consciously I can't, but I suppose I could call it a Brandian step.

Our *choice* is to accept or reject the *metaphysical* fact of *self-responsibility*.
Our choice is to accept or reject the metaphysical fact of self-responsibility.
~~Our *choice* is to~~ I *accept* ~~or *reject*~~ the metaphysical fact of *self-responsibility*.
~~Our *choice* is to *accept* or~~ I *reject* the metaphysical fact of *self-responsibility*.
Our *choice* is to *accept* or *reject* the metaphysical fact of *self-responsibility*.

By nature we are self-responsible whether we accept it or not and in this sense, self-responsibility is not a choice, it is a fact.[240]

In the final analysis—that is, from within the *ego* perspective within ourselves—psychological mental illness or "value illness" (if you must but to repeat I think "value-conflict" a much much much much—and let me say it one more time—much better view) *includes* the sins of others against the *reality* needs of our selfish selfs. The only *justifiable* exception to holding self responsible for self is when those *others* actually, *physically* abused the self *as the means* to getting that self to act *against* his or her own *reality* based *metaphysical-epistemological-ethical* benefit.[241] This does *not* include when parents use *mild* physical force—e.g. spanking them for going into the street—to save the child's *life*—that is, the child's *ultimate* value—from being run over and *ended* by a car. Children—we must remember are born *tabula rasa* which among other things means they—do not *yet* understand the mechanics of momentum and in this context must be spanked—if necessary—to keep them from going into the street where they could be maimed or killed by a car or truck or any such fast moving vehicle coming down your street. When a big, heavy object collides with a little lighter one it isn't the big one that flies off into the wild blue yonder, it is the little, lighter one. The mechanical engineering equation governing this is: $m_i v_i$ before collision = $m_i v_i$ after collision (m is mass, v is velocity, the product $m_i v_i$ is momentum and the equality is the principle of the conservation of momentum: momentum is conserved across an event, that is, total momentum—does not change, it is transferred—is the same at the end of the event as it was in the beginning. The subscript *i* stands for all individual masses—and their respective velocities—involved in the event.)

A new born and developing self cannot—by *any* stretch of the imagination—be expected to know and understand a College level course in Mechanical

---

[240] So that the "need" to repeat the sentence one more time is left up to the reader.
[241] There is some sense in which the *threat* of physical force to the *child-mind* can be treated in the same way as *actual* physical force used against a fully developed *adult* mind but the *precision* required to properly deal with this idea is beyond the scope of the current book and so we will deal with it in a later one.

Engineering, nor can they be *expected* to know the implications of such an engineering equation on the physical body.[242]

Adults, however, are expected to know this *fact* (not necessarily its equation for Engineers which is the Engineer's way of evaluating the *fact of momentum*) and to *use* this *objective* knowledge for the *survival*—that is, *selfish*—benefit of their *moral* charges (that is, their children).

No self is born with innate knowledge of what's good for it and what's not. The self has to discover and learn these things, including learning that these things are *not* arbitrary. When an 18 wheeler Big Rig truck hits your dainty little two-seater convertible it is not "arbitrary" that the convertible is squashed and the truck dented rather than the other way around. If it were the other way around *once and awhile* THEN you could conclude "things" are arbitrary.

But as a fellow human being I know that you have no *reality* basis for worshipping the arbitrary.[243] To so worship is a *choice,* a *choice* that *your* volitional self can make and/or *has* made.

The self we are talking about here is the *same* one that came out of the womb a fully functioning *physiological* body-self hell bent by nature's unfolding forces on becoming an *autonomous* physical, psychological and spiritual *self* ASAP.

If you are not that much different than me then nature unfolded and developed your *rudimentary* ego-self within a year or two of *your* birth and you have been struggling ever since to actualize a happy, joyous life for you, yourself … and … it—*it*, qua embryonic *I*, that is.

An ego-self that *probably* didn't get (and/or didn't want) a heck of a lot of epistemological help from its culture and/or subculture in its struggles to achieve that glorious of glories: *autonomy* of body, mind and spirit.

An *autonomy,* that is, that is the *only* path to happiness.

If happiness is your purpose then *autonomy* is your friend.

If *autonomy* is your friend then a "mother please I'd rather do it myself" attitude—*properly managed*—is your *best* friend.

And if in this regards you have *lost* your best friend and want him or her back then *Biocentric Psychology* affords you a means to self-reconciliation.

---

[242] A simpler explanation here would be to relate this—by analogy—to inoculations: give the body a little bit of the disease as means to preventing it from catching the full disease. That is, substitute a little pain—spanking—for big pain—body mangled and mashed by an automobile. However, such an analogy does not offer a means to differentiate between cars-running-over-bodies and religion doing it.

[243] As a degreed Aeronautical-Mechanical Engineer with a quarter of a century's worth of experience in conducting engineering tests and experiments in reality I know this in spades!

Not everybody lost their best friend in this way but for those of us who did, Biocentric—*with Objectivism as guide*—is the road, the path, the way, the method, the process to reconciliation.

Since Objectivism teaches that the mind leads and the emotions follow we can't say Objectivism *needs* Biocentric because Biocentric re-introduced emotions into O(IM), even though it did.

Since Objectivism teaches that *emotions are not tools of cognition*—which they are *not*—we can't say it's because Biocentric helps us understand that saying what emotions are not, isn't the same as saying what they are.

And Objectivists—of all people—know this better than most because Objectivism teaches that *except* in the rarest of terms *definitions* state what a thing is, it—a *proper* definition—does not state what a thing is not.[244]

For example, one such *legitimate* exception is: a bachelor is a man who is NOT married.[245] But: *emotions are not tools of cognition* is not one such exception. This is easy to see when we look at the *correct* (Biocentric) definition of emotions: *emotions are the psycho-biological form in which we experience our estimate of the beneficial or harmful relationship of some aspect of reality to ourself.*[ix]

Emotions—according to Ayn Rand—*are the means by which we enjoy life.*[x]

This is *true* of emotions but it is still not a *definition* of emotions. (It is a description.)

If emotions are the means to enjoying life—which is easy to agree with—and happiness *is* non-contradictory joy, then *without* emotions there is no *means* (to joy) and without joy (means) there is no happiness. Is no happiness, that is, just as much as and *perhaps* more so than there is no happiness without non-contradiction. Which is to say, *self-consistency* can be used in place of *non-contradiction* [to create a *pseudo* happiness] but *joy has no substitute*. Consequently, true happiness remains a two dimensional—not one dimensional—problem to be solved.[246]

---

[244] And for good reason. For example, a banana is not a car; which we notice is *true* but not of much value, unless you are a Californian who has just opened a store specializing in the sale of bananas and you want to advertise yourself by driving around in a car shaped like a banana. But the car is still not a banana and a banana is still not a car and we still haven't defined WHAT a banana is but merely said one thing out of a universe of things it is not and if we insist on saying what it is not we will run out of life before we delineate and exhaust the vast number of things that a banana is not. A banana is not a screwdriver.

[245] Or perhaps we should say: "is neither married nor *narried*". See reference at end of paragraph for more.

[246] In the end it is actually a three dimensional problem: 1) we have to understand the meaning of—including the absoluteness of—non-contradiction, 2) we have to understand the meaning of joy and 3) we have to integrate our understanding of both and *apply* this integration to our own personal life.

Objectivism is the solution to the non-contradictory part of happiness, but not the joy part and depending on one's *idiosyncratic* approach to joy, [idiosyncratic] ObjectivIsM can be a hindrance.[247]

Since *Objectivism* teaches that all *whims* are bad and that by whim they mean an *emotion* the source of which its possessor does not know and—most importantly—does not *want* to know,[xi] I cannot conclude for you that Biocentric helps us understand that even though *all whims are emotions* it does not follow that all emotions are whims, even though *Biocentric* does so help us.[248]

And to my knowledge since *Objectivism* was the first to say that the moral and the practical *are the same thing* and that mind and body are an *integration* we can't say it's because *Biocentric* said this first because it did not and besides, to my knowledge no one is saying that it did.

And, also, to my knowledge even though *Objectivism* says repression is not good for you, this is way too abstract for those of us who were (are) repressed (as badly as *was* DJ) and thereby runs the risk of remaining on the shelf of the intellectualizer's closet rather than being brought into the full view of Biocentric's down-and-dirty challenge to face *the possibility* that you can be repressed and not know it. Albeit, with quotes around "know".

And yes, because it smacks of mysticism it is risky to so "reason", but so is life—risky and maybe that is why we have emotions: to *help* us *manage* the risks.

Emotions are *not* tools of cognition, but they *are* tools of survival—as clues.

Emotions as tools are clues and vice versa: as clues are tools.

At least they are for the *developing* human within, and though neither Objectivism nor Biocentric said this maybe it can help us understand that Objectivism did not mean reason and emotion in its paraphrased (Christian) parable about render unto Caesar the things that are Caesar's and unto god the things that are god's. But rather—it must be emphasized—Objectivism was referring to *reason* (god) vs. *faith* (Caesars) when it replied "...in our philosophy there is no room for Caesars"[xii]. And maybe Biocentric had to do something to

---

[247] If you are a stronger than me Objectivist and are saying here you would never ever in a million billion gazillion years succumb to the non-Objectivist conclusion that since *all whims are emotions all emotions are whims* then I as one who ~~came dangerously close to~~ so conclud~~ing~~ed, commend you. I commend you honestly and sincerely and do not mean it here either sarcastically or derisively, but sincerely: congratulations and I must add, don't take your goodness for granted; you are good. *Honor* it.

[248] Actually it's just plain 'ole logic that helps us: Even though *All men are mortal*, it does *not* follow that *All mortals are men*. Voila! Even though *All whims are emotions*, it does not follow that *All emotions are whims*. That I personally made this logical error and needed Biocentric to help me see it may say something negative about me, but ... I yam what I yam and thank god for Biocentric AND Objectivism with their help in *discovering* errors and *correcting* them.

disconnect somewhat the linkage it helped form between faith and emotion that resulted in disparaging emotions beyond reason, which is to say, beyond that which sane men can call "reasonable" [and hope to remain sane]. Since Christianity and Western Philosophy have shared the same bed (or if not this, then for sure the same bedroom) for a decades worth of centuries it is dangerous for us who succumbed to religion's wily ways to accept (prematurely) the Ayn Rand claim that religion is a primitive philosophy. What if it isn't? What if it is more a primitive *spiritualism* which, as a "thing" [spiritualism] is the ***integration*** of Philosophy and Psychology in the individual soul. In my personal experience, religion—as I've suggested earlier—is a diabolical creed designed by Architects of Haunted Houses. And as such, Religion—qua dilapidated crack house for "drug" runner/*faith* pushers—makes the *epistemological structure* that the modern day BM Cognitive-Neuroscientist Architects are *trying* to build look like some kind of rat's habitat by comparison.

Faith *is* bad, emotion is like reason: good.

Reason *is* good, emotion *is* good, faith is bad, evasion is worse.

Objectivism, in its need to be ruthless—given that it came to power *in spite* of two thousand years of religious bullstuff—can cause the unwary (such as myself at one point in my development) to conclude: emotions are not good. This conclusion is a wrong one to draw and is another reason why Objectivism needs Biocentric Psychology. Biocentric psychology tells us that emotions are good and shows us how to *use our reason* to *personally* cash in on this fact.

Faith and evasion are bad, reason and emotion are good.

Faith and evasion are a married couple, not faith and emotion. Emotion is married to reason and just as marriages can go bad they can go good too. They also can be corrected from bad to good if need be.

Faith at best is perverted reason; at its worse it is a void, a vacuum, the negation of reason, of reason the capacity. Faith—qua capacity—is perverted reason and emotion—qua capacity—is the first casualty in the war between *reason-in-faith* and *faith-in-reason* as same is waged inside *developing* man.

Reason and emotion each are human *capacities* and as such are good. As such each is also pervert-able and once perverted require psyhhology to un-pervert.

All human capacities are pervertable and since humans have volition they can pervert their own capacities. But it still depends on *why* are they perverting them (e.g. is it for "perceived" *survival* reasons or for "love" of perversion "reasons") before one can *conclude* about others and/or self that one is pervert*ed*, which is to say, not all perversions are ~~perverted~~ perverse.[249]

Some can be *neurotic*.

Modern day (Biocentric) psychology is quite capable of solving most—if not yet all, for sure most—*neurotic* problems. Those who like to think otherwise (the ones who usually disparage psychology by pointing to Freud and all his errors) do so for a whole variety of reasons, but the fact remains: *modern* day (Biocentric) psychology can cure most psychological ills.

But what it can't cure are philosophical ills, these have to be cured by me, myself and I (or in your case, by you, yourself and ... your yu).

Both *Objectivism* and *Biocentric* support the view that treating emotions as tools of cognition is wrong.

Objectivism says it is a choice to do this and it is a choice that *reason* worshippers *should* not make.

Biocentric says treating emotions as tools of cognition is a default position. It is the *practical* consequence, contends Biocentric, of the error of choosing *faith* over *reason* as the valid way to validate knowledge: if you [do] accept ideas without evidence you *eventually* are forced to say, *feels right*, therefore, is right.[250]

So that people who have a history of treating emotions as tools of cognition now face a new danger: treating emotions as if they are *as-bad-as* faith.

Dr. Branden—the moralist that he is—sensed this (potential problem) and devoted many years of study, reflection and teaching that emotions are not bad, but are good. He taught that the "trick" is to understand them and *use* them for your own *selfish* benefit and *enjoyment* of life which is what nature intended them to be used for in addition to **protecting** you when you were young and developing and had not the means (that is, your *fully* developed *conceptual* capacity) to even understand philosophy (this last about the *protecting* value of emotions for *developing* man is a BiO Spiritualism—not Biocentric—iObservation [i as in iNTROSPECTION]).

---

[249] For "love" of perversion examples see the Nazis in Peikoff's *Ominous Parallels*, Reference xv this chapter.

[250] Unless you are a short, stocky, balding guy on one of those two TV shows "measured" by our TV repairman. In this case you might say, feels right *therefore* is wrong and vice versa and if you are going through therapy to help yourself *change*, this could be—temporarily—good counsel. But only temporarily, because in the long run right or wrong determinations are the providence of reason; emotions are the form in which *you* experience *your* personal, idiosyncratic right and wrong rights and wrongs.

Objectivism needs Biocentric to keep it—Objectivism—from making the mistake that Biocentric's neo-Objectivist founder made when he was a pre-neo-objectivist and suggested real strongly that since faith defaults—pragmatically as pragmatics must do—to emotions, emotions are *as* bad *as* faith. This is not true. Faith is bad, emotions are good and they—faith and emotions—are not the same *exact* thing.

Making emotions be tools of cognition can be reached by two—not just one, but two—roads: by default on the primary responsibility to develop your reasoning ability or two, by explicit, conscious, volitional choice.

If you made the "choice" by default you may have an easier time of undoing your wrong "choice" than one who made this choice by choice (or vice versa—pun intended). But the *need* to undo and correct this *incorrect* choice is independent of the form of your error.

If we wanted to we could transform this into a principle: the *need* to undo and correct erroneous choices is independent of the form of those choices. Whether they occur by default or direct action does not affect the need to self-correct on the mind (soul) building level of our being.

Both *Objectivism* AND *Biocentric Psychology* help us to correct ourselves at this soul/mind building level of our being.[251]

To this extent then and from our own personal, idiosyncratic, SELFISH perspective we can observe, hence we can conclude, hence we *should* conclude four things: 1) Objectivism is good; 2) Biocentric psychology is good; 3) Objectivism is a tool; 4) Biocentric psychology is a tool.

They are both tools *for us* to *use* to become the happy spiritualists this book says we are capable of becoming.

Biocentric Psychology needs Objectivism for the same reason we all need it: because of its *correct* view of concepts which it has laid out for us in "Introduction to Objectivist Epistemology".☺s

In order to get proper instruction in this you need to go to the source.

But eventually you have to write out (or make *explicit* in some form) *your* understanding of it as I am writing out mine (making explicit) here. If my understanding helps you to better understand Objectivist Epistemology (Whose

---

[251] An analogy here may help to illuminate what I mean. In today's world of computer domination one can hardly not notice the many computer books about computer programming languages that have titles like: [Programming language name] in 21 days, e.g. *Perl in 21 days*; *Visual Basic in 21 days*; *C/C++ in 21 days*; and so on. My statement here about Objectivism PLUS Biocentric psychology being *good* programming tools for human souls means my book here could have been titled: *O/O++ in 21 years* (if, that is, one views *Biocentric* as iterative *Objectivism*).

answer to the question, *Can I know*? is: *Yes*, and how! knowledge without omniscience is possible and *Objectivist Epistemology* shows us how it is) and/or to be motivated to learn it, then great. But, to repeat, the following "exercise" is primarily for me and is case study material to show you what eventually you have to do in order to make Objectivist Epistemology your own personal possession.

*   *   *

Will Objectivism be able to de-fang evil?

Only time will tell. It is of course my *wish* that the answer to this question is *Yes*! but as "we" used to say when I was 10 years old: *wish in one hand and sh...stuff in the other and see which one fills up the fastest.*

(modified) Street smarts, remember.

But, for the "adult", *conceptual* elaboration of this "view" read Dr. Leonard Peikoff's intellectual article titled: "The Analytic-Synthetic Dichotomy"[xiii]. It explains all-the-way-to-the-core what is really at stake and going on here and if you don't go all the way to-the-core, your 10 year old (male) "metaphysics" will not be enough to save you.[252, xiv]

As example consider: when I was in the 10th grade in High School (after living for 5 years inside a 10 year old boys' metaphysics) my science teacher—not liking my "natural", albeit waning, albeit struggling self-confidence in the belief that knowledge is possible—asked me mockingly: "...if no one is in the woods and a tree falls, is there a sound?". To which I said, *yes* of course there is. But his and the classes laughter—as they said, if no one's there *how do you know?*—caused me my continuing sense of self doubt about my ability to deal with "philosophical" questions and so I started to think: who can *really* know ... anything ... anyway. Then later that same (kind of) week five years earlier my playground friend near the swings asked me to *prove* to him that the color I saw and called "blue" was the same, exact, identical color that he called "blue". I of course couldn't do it. And yes, there was a sense of, if I can't prove it then I can't claim to know ... anything.

---

[252] For a fairly good, competent, artistic *concretization* of 10 year old boy's metaphysics see the movie, *Waterworld*—especially the scene of the children on the rustiest of rust bucket boats with equipment that *still* operates *perfectly* even after *not* being maintained for, what, a thousand years (not to mention, a thousand years of exposure to a salty sea water environment). So that for a 10 year old that IS being taken care of by nature it is "logical" to answer: No, to the metaphysical question: *Do I live in a universe where I need to MAINTAIN my values?* But for adults who are no longer being taken care of by nature or anyone or thingelse, the answer is: *Yes* I do. Is this why Objectivism, in the person of Ayn Rand defines *value* as: something *we* act to gain and/or **keep**? (emphasis mine).

At the time I didn't know what an *ostensive* definition was nor did I know that it was Immanuel Kant, the German Philosopher from the 18th Century, looking out at me from behind the eyes of my 10th grade teacher (let alone that t.h.e.y had already wormed their way(s) into my 9 year old[!] friend). It took a genius and some dozen years or so to save my sorry ass(ets) when she said: Kant is easy to figure out ['ya that's easy for *you* to say] once you reduce his whole argument to its essence. When you do that you observe that Kant's "argument" is: we humans can't see *because* we have eyes, can't hear *because* we have ears and all the way to: we can't *sense* the world *because* we have *world sensors*.

Oh my God! I spent years trying to figure Kant out and finally gave up and went full speed, head-first into Engineering.

Thank God for Ayn Rand.

But since there are no gods—plural or singular—Ayn Rand mistakenly concluded that religion—as an intellectual force—is dead and that it died with the Renaissance. ®o3(?)

Her error was—I believe two-fold—she confused religion with the Judeo-Christian versions of it and she was *too* compassionate.

As such and as I said previously, Ayn Rand, the founder of the *Philosophy of Objectivism* and staunch defender of religion stretched the meaning of human compassion beyond its elastic limit when she declared: *religion is a primitive philosophy*.

It is not. It is a thief.

Religion stole my life.

And I am not going to let it get off so easily.

Which is to say, the need for spiritual self-defense has gotten more not less in the wake of P.S. 21st Century and my *prediction* is it's going to get even more than this because the BM can now see (having been shown the way by *Islam's* Ivory Towers—that is, by the Ayatollahs of the Islamic world) *how* to *fuse* the *soul* of Attila and the *soul* of the Witch doctor into the body of *one* "person" and give him or herself the remote control switch—complete with on/off switch, volume control, channel selector and detonator button—to run the resultant "body politic" at his and hers—the BM's—bidding.

Ayn Rand gave us the tools to combat all of this by giving us the tools for spiritual self-defense in a world where Attila and the Witch Doctor were two *separate*, independently recognizable, concretizeable foes but Tomorrow Man, Third Millennium Man, faces a new, "integrated" foe: Fundamentalist Religion "Man".

Fundamentalist Religion "Man" is another reason why Objectivism needs Biocentric.

Ayn Rand in her own words said—and hence the Professional Objectivists now believe—that religion is a primitive philosophy. I keep telling them it isn't. Religion is a thief. It stole my life so I know. Granted, Biocentic Psychology gave my life back to me but this fact alone is not enough to convince other Objectivists of the *importance* of Biocentric and that they should re-adopt it and fold it back into Objectivism proper. (Or not ... as the case may be. As in it is OK to keep them separate for the purposes of study and understanding.)

Spiritual self-defense is as good as and as moral as bodily self-defense and just as difficult, if not more difficult, to learn how to do. Learning how to do it starts with *accepting* that it must be done in order to protect ourselves from (the new*)* totalitarian BM mentalities.

And though it is probably true that *no kind* of totalitarianism will work *forever,* it does not logically follow from this that *no kind* cannot work *long enough* to not devour *some* individual lives. The devouring of one individual life—*if that life is yours*—is as bad as it needs to get for *t.h.e.m.* to achieve *t.h.e.i.r.* goal (as far as you are concerned).

So, it is my hope that in reading and *thinking* about *BiO Spiritualism* you will find many useful insights for *you yourself* to use to take back and/or to keep your *spirituality*, your *psychology* and your *morality*—the three things you need most—to defend yourself against the new *voluntary totalitarianism* threatening to take over our country and our lives. This *voluntary* totalitarianism *is* the new totalitarianism that the *21st Century Group* hopes beyond hope will (finally) work and provide T.H.E.M. with what they have been searching for ever since Plato walked on the planet: an *unlimited* and *unending* supply of empty headed *human bodies* to feed on.

Islamic fundamentalism has found the bodies and is feeding on them as I write. One could even say that Islamic fundamentalism has "succeeded" where the Plato-Kantian line failed. One could, but would one need more before so concluding?

More than what?

Suicide-Homicide Bombers!?!? Talk about cannon fodder!!!

Actually, the correct answer here is probably: *Yes. Yes* you even need more than this. After all it took a great deal to explain the forces behind the Nazi's (see Dr. Peikoff's *Ominous Parallels* book[xv]) so it will take just as much to explain the religious forces behind the Militant Islamists. It would take an evaluation of their full philosophy—that is, their metaphysics, epistemology and ethics—to render an objective understanding of how this particular version of evil works.[253]

But for me to succeed fully in my taking (spiritualism) back efforts I do not have to understand Militant Islamists beyond that which I can observe in the suicide-homicide bombers. This alone is enough: any person who would willing blow up their one, irreplaceable, unrepeatable life for the sake of an ideal beyond the selfish self—that is, for a non-selfish self ideal—is ... dead.

Dead is not the same as alive. Dead is bad. Alive is good.

So is success: success is good.

So, when *you* along with me *succeed* in our taking-back and maintaining efforts, my book will be a success—at minimum—for two people.

no longer (5/24/02)

Two at a time—for <u>now</u>—is^ good enough for me.[254]

* * *

If the foregoing sounds overly dramatic to you then *you tell me* what the following several "observations"—when taken as a WHOLE—mean. {With "our" Chapter 5 & Chapter 17 psycho-hermeneutic "analysis" technique/editorializing comments in braces} and the "observations", that is, non-editorial comments as all other text.

1. [The philosophers] Plato-Kant-Hegel *are* the intellectual builders of Auschwitz. Dr. Leonard Peikoff, *Ominous Parallels - The End of Freedom in America* [xvi]

2. Figure 2 is a triangular schematization [p. 11, Rychlak[xvii]] of what we would like to call the Kantian model, which also could be considered a Platonic model: there we see the advocacy of the idea that we humans [*thinkingwise*] go from the most abstract to the least abstract with a degree of complexity best described as *pure* chaotic rather than the way

---

[253] For example, why do Christians tend to *implode* when they finally self destruct but Islamists *ex-plode*?

[254] Since t..h.e.y.—the Mystics of Muscle Islamic fundamentalists—keep reminding us that there is *potentially* 1.2 billion of "them", it is more scary **now** (10/12/01) then it was when I first started this manuscript (2/12/00). But as any rational person can readily calculate: since there is almost 6 billion people on the planet and only a billion or so of them, they are actually in reality outnumbered 5 to 1. Alls I can say to this is, thank (those non-existent supreme beings called) god, there is still time for REASON to triumph.

[Figure 1 preceding p. 10] John Locke says: we build from the least abstract to the most abstract, building complexity on top of simpler as we go.[xviii]

3. While [Immanuel] Kant did not publish empirical results of any kind and his writing on these [how the human mind works] topics is *notorious* for its difficulty, his *thinking* has *left its mark* on most *theoretical* writings in **cognitive science** today. (Gardner, p.59, emphasis mine)[xix]

4. There can be no doubt that all our knowledge begins with experience. (Immanuel Kant)[xx] {Apparently Kantian's do know something.}

5. Although, chronologically, man's consciousness develops in three stages: the stage of sensations, the perceptual, the conceptual—epistemologically, the base of all of man's knowledge is the *perceptual* stage. (Ayn Rand, *Introduction Objectivist Epistemology*[xxi].) {Is this true or false? And if there is no "empirical" evidence to support this claim, aren't you—with all *your* (actual) introspective skills and abilities—the empirical evidence?}

6. *But* though all our knowledge begins with experience [back to Kant now], it does *not* follow that it *all* **arises** out of experience {as *testified* to by those who *scold* Doubting Thomas's??? and/or as *opposed* to those who say it does—e.g. see John Locke in item #2 here who says all our knowledge literally RISES on top of experience as we build complexity on top of simpler as we go}. For it may well be that even our empirical knowledge is made up of what we receive through impressions and of what our own faculty of knowledge (sensible impressions serving *merely* as the occasion) *supplies* from itself.[xxii] {IKYPU[255], *emphasis* mine, plus a question we should ask about Kant's use of the concept "impressions". If I hold a piece of wax—say a candle— in my right hand and curl the fingers of my left hand into a fist and press my ring into the candle is the "impression" my ring leaves in the candle objective or does the candle *supply* something from itself to distort the impression of my ring? There are only two ways you can answer yes to this question. One is if you define *distort* to mean *lack* of highly distinct edges. Two, you will

---

[255] Pronounced as it looks: icky-pu. It stands for the idea that just as Objectivism is an Upgrade to Aristotelianism so is Kantianism an Upgrade to Platonism, voila! IKYPU ... **I**mmanuel**K**ant**Y**our**P**hilosophy**U**pgrade ... **Your**'s as in t.h.e.i.r.'s.

erroneously answer the question yes if you have already succumbed to Kant and his notions of "pure" reason that teaches there is only one exception to the rule we can't know and that exception is when it comes to knowing this rule, then we can know that we can't know. Because *Objectivists* know that contradictions do not exist they have no problem rejecting *this*—as well as any—contradiction. If however, you—the non Objective in you that is—accept the notion that contradictions exist then you in essence are *making* your "candle" so soft, limp and impotent that it won't be able to *hold* the impression of anything, let alone *distort* them.©oseeDr.HarryBinswangerTape (xxiii)}

7. Ayn Rand, drawing an analogy between "knowing" and "seeing" says that Kant's *pure* "reasoning" is this: the "reason" we can't see is **because** we have eyes[xxiv]. {And this is not a tongue-in-cheek comment: Kant means it! *And so do his followers and admirers.* Ayn Rand and Objectivism—as decoder ring for order on a page in that Action-Packed Super-Hero Comic Book referred to in the beginning to this Chapter—helps us decode *this* and *other* mind-*destroying* messages in Kantianism.}

8. Discriminated awareness begins on the level of precepts [not sensations]. (Ayn Rand[xxv])

9. In Gibson's view [1950, 1966, 1979, {going back to Howard Gardner's writing on Cognitive Science[xxvi] and to present an Ayn Randian *type* view—a Gibsonian view—that didn't come directly from Ayn Rand … in Gibson's view} organisms are so constituted, and live in a world so constituted, that they will readily gain the information they need to survive and to thrive {notice the appeal to *reason*—my comment here, not HG's—as same relates to the *commonsense* idea of *survival* as being critically *important* to humans}. Thus, when one detects the third dimension, the relevant spatial information is simply presented in the light, without one's having to infer distances or to correlate information from eye and hand; there is no need for the kinds of *unconscious inference* which scientists from Helmholtz on have proposed. {If you are an Objectivist sympathizer, notice how close to the truth Gibson is here and also that he dates from the 1950's. Ayn Rand's *Introduction to Objectivist Epistemology* was first published in the mid-60's.}

10. Howard Gardner again[xxvii]: In the light of *today's* psychology, this [Gibson's view] is certainly a radical perspective. Indeed, a reader of this

book {present company excluded of course—again my, not HG's comment} might well ask why, in this *cognitively* oriented age, anyone would take it seriously. I [HG, qua Kantian sympathizer] think there are three reasons explaining this: one, Gibson is a clever SOB; two, Gibson has a set of interlocking concepts he developed {*interlocking* as in *hierarchical* complexity on top of simpler as opposed to the chaotic, non-interlocking randomness of complexity on top of *notorious* incomprehensibility per Kant's view?!?[256]} and thirdly, Gibson's persuasiveness comes from the simplicity of his point of view. {Why is simplicity a *disqualifying* element? Is it because IKYPU's worship chaos, randomness and the chaotic as an *end in itself?*}

11. {*An example of T.H.E.I.R. "reasoning" after they have abandoned what nature gave them.* [For the following go through and read only the words in **bold** and then go back through and read everything, remembering that this is Cognitive Science's big-gun attack "against direct perception" as part 'n parcel of its view that we humans do NOT *perceive* the world DIRECTLY but rather, INDIRECTLY with the *nature* of this "indirection" to be figured out by Cognitive Scientists[xxviii]]}. **But many other aspects of perception simply do not lend themselves to direct registration and interpretation. The raw intensity array which constitutes the first image** {*first* as in baby's first, or as in first image upon opening my eyes to let in the image? If this last then this whole discussion is begging the question, therefore it must be the first, which is what? If not after a few hours of birth than within a few days at absolute maximum} **is unmanageably vast:** {For man made computers but not for nature made ones. It is unmanageably vast *only* for AI designers who have to come up with the algorithms needed by their robots to "see" the world, but humans see the world automatically... *perceptually* ... and flawlessly ... and *yes*, a stick partly submerged in water and partly out that looks bent but isn't is a flawless perception: this is the way a stick-in-water looks. It would be flawed if and only if sometimes it looked bent and sometimes it looked straight, but of course it doesn't: it ALWAYS, *flawlessly* looks bent.} **the only feasible first step is to replace the intensity array by a *representation*** {if you are trying to "prove"—as the

---

[256] And I was worried that I wouldn't be able to find evidence outside of Objectivism pointing to Kant as the in situ rat's nest.

Cognitive Scientists are trying to do here—that conscious experience is *not* direct but is indirect, then relying on *representationalism* as describing the situation is circular} **of the significant intensity changes in the image, as Marr and his colleagues have done in positing the primal sketch.** { 'kinda like the way, I suppose, in which images are transferred over the Internet via slow modems to your computer screen, first they are vague renderings with *minimal* visual information then they are filled in with *more* visual information so as to be clearly identifiable ... but halt! This is the way I experienced my first *conscious* subconscious visual image, but I didn't and don't conclude that the *process* is the same. Maybe our perceptual process is to build on top of this first streaming image with more streaming image and use the first *as basis* to make the next more clear while at the same time *not contradicting the first.* Notwithstanding checksums, this is NOT the way the Internet does it, there the feed comes from a completed picture to begin with and is simply *metered* as to how much of the image is transmitted, the brain is more dynamic than this, its rudimentary first picture is minimal and then minimally more to get clarity but clarity to a maximal point using minimal information, no more no less than is required to get clarity, that is, recognition, that is: *identification.*}. **Moreover, other aspects of perception—for example, the perception of motion** {notice, NOT of that which moves, but of *pure* motion like the "kind" that that stand up comedian Dr. Peikoff pejoratively-humorously referred to in one of his taped logic lectures: "There's jumping in the next room. What's jumping? Nothing's jumping, there's just jumping."}—**simply do not occur in a direct way** {circular "reasoning"—t.h.e.y are trying to prove that we do *not* directly perceive the world but rather *indirectly* via some brainball(s) mechanisms that ultimately make Kant's nonsense make sense} **but, rather, involve the devising of structural descriptions on which perceptual mechanisms can then operate.** {that is, this is *what* "we" as designers-of-artificially-intelligent-robots *would have to do*: we would have to create programming code that the robot could "hang" jumping-as-object on (see Computer programming languages C/C++ and OOP=Object Oriented Programming which treat *everything* as an object ... that is—we speculate—as thing 1).}. **And *by the time*** {i.e.? if not a few days old, then within weeks or for sure months of birth} **one is dealing with object recognition** {e.g. "jumping" is object? ... in other room???} **one has encountered a process that is *mediated* by prior knowledge** {i would hope so and i wonder isn't this then an *interlocking* type of thing? And at *this* age-stage is my little i still yet to be capitalized?} **and by "beliefs" through and through** {*yes*, i knew the thousands of truths in Objectivism by age 3 months, i just hadn't developed the ability to print yet so i couldn't write them out...hey, *I want some royalties*} **and can in no way be accomplished "directly" by detectors.** {Who said they could? Is this an example of (academic) lying? Ayn Rand said our "direct" connection with reality is via *perceptions* which is the combination/*integration* of detector (eyeballs, ears, etc.) and a brain-nervous system that *automatically* integrates what the detectors detect. So, *what* cannot be detected *directly* by detectors *is* everything that detectors do not detect. But—and this is the big BUT—this does *not* include the things that they *do* detect. To include these is *absurd*. As absurd as is this:

> ... since my thermometer detects temperature the temperature it detects is not detected. Rather, the liquid mercury *infers* the temperature—or in modern day, scientific jargon parlance, the temperature in-forms the mercury—and the mercury expands or contracts as it "knows" the temperature—or some physicist—wants it to.

And further, *what* detectors are "t.h.e.y" talking about: the ones I use to detect their printed words on the page? Or the "ones" I use to identify and *figure out* their meaning, for example, not my eyeball but my memoryball and/or my thoughtball? These last two are NOT detectors and suggesting that they are by failing to differentiate between them is —at best—false}.

12. {Back to Ayn Rand.} A *percept* is a group of sensations automatically retained and integrated by the brain of a *living* organism. It is in the form of percepts that man grasps the evidence of his senses and apprehends reality. When we speak of "direct perception" or "direct awareness," we mean the perceptual level. Percepts, not sensations, are the given, the self-evident. The knowledge of sensations as components of percepts is not direct, it is acquired by man much later: it is a scientific, *conceptual* discovery.

13. {To me personally the last 5 sentences in the foregoing (#12) are the five most important sentences Ayn Rand ever wrote.}

14. Howard Gardner p. 313. There is a big difference between seeing *x* and seeing *x as y*, and what is *central* to COGNITIVE PSYCHOLOGY [emphasis mine] is the ability to see something as an entity—a rock as a tool or [a rock as] a weapon or [a rock as] a stool rather than just a [Kantian] blob.

15. The error (me speaking now) {in the foregoing #14 may or may not be innocent. The error is in "t.h.e.i.r" use of the word "entity". By it [entity] they DO NOT mean as the first developmental sequence that a child goes through as he or she grows and develops and *learns how to use* his or her nature-given faculty of awareness. (As Ayn Rand means when she talks about *entity-identity-unit* in her *Introduction to Objectivist Epistemology* as the sequence in which—develop-mentally—the child proceeds to take in reality.[xxix] For example: entity=rock; identity=round, hard, not edible; unit=*this* particular rock and *that* rock over there versus these squishy, edible, round things hanging from those trees over there.) The real BIG difference, HG and Kantianism notwithstanding, is in seeing a rock *as a rock* and not *confusing* it with the *head of a Cognitive Scientist* simply because *both* are round and hard. The ability to USE a rock as a hammer or stool or club is preceded by the ability to "see" the rock as a *hard* thing, that is *as a rock* (we think of a rock as rock-hard and a coconut as also hard but not as hard and so we "see" that the former can be used to crack the latter and not vice versa). This process of "figuring out" what a rock can, cannot be used for is a different issue. It falls under what Ayn Rand calls the *range* and *scope* of consciousness which are the two *yardsticks* we use to *measure* consciousness*es* from their lowest expression in amoeba as "aware" enough of their environment so as to be able to move through it, to the highest level as expressed in man that can read **and** understand what I have just written here (including *making* the *judgment* that my sentence is too long}.

16. {Back to Ayn Rand.} The building-block of man's knowledge is the concept of an "*existent"* —of something that exists, be it a thing [thing 1?]; an attribute or an action [thing 2?] {"everything" is some-thing to human consciousness, BiO Spiritualism's 4th Principle}. Since it (existent) is a concept, man cannot grasp it *explicitly* until he has reached

the *conceptual* stage. But it is implicit in every percept (to perceive a thing is to perceive that it exists) and man grasps it implicitly on the perceptual level—i.e., he grasps the constituents of the concept "existent," the data which are later to be integrated by that concept. It is this implicit knowledge that permits his consciousness to develop further.[xxx]

{To develop further, that is, if (and now we return to normal writing} *that* consciousness does *not* fall into the hands of those who want to destroy it.

If it does, and it is young, then, if it survives, it will have to undo the destruction when it gets old enough and wise enough to know that it has suffered (some) destruction and it has to elect (choose, voluntarily, volitionally) to DO something about it—psychhologically, epistemologically speaking.

If on the other hand it doesn't fall into the hands of those who want to destroy it, but rather want to nurture it, then it has more normal developmental issues to deal with.

They, that is, *the foregoing 16 points* then taken as a WHOLE mean that *philosophy* is our most important (intellectual) commodity without which we are f*!@#&'ed.

I hate to be so almost blunt here but the way I figure it is, somebody better f*!@#&g be before—not after—but *before* the *Bureaucratic Mind* and its soldiers of fortune—the Social Engineers—put the finishing touches on their creation of non-autonomous *sheepish* man.

And who [pray tell] are the most anti autonomous-man advocates?

The Behavioral Psychologists.

As Social Engineering types the Behaviorists are the *most* anti-autonomous man advocates and are people who think that rat mazes will unlock the secrets of *human* nature.

Since Dr. Branden, qua Professional Psychologist looking in on mainstream psychology, has dissected and laid bare the *irrationality* at the core of the Behaviorist's thinking they have been kicked out of "psychology" by their own kind and replaced with a new crop of rat maze advocates. This new crop says, "Of course rat mazes can't unlock the secrets of human nature, everybody knows that but what most don't know yet is that what it really requires is: a rat's nest.

Epistemologically speaking.

In the *Mind and Brain Sciences of the 21st Century* book we got many different statements from many (allegedly) different types of psychology thinkers. From *behaviorists* and *cognitive psychologist* sympathizers, for example, we got the view that somehow these two disagree with each other and that cognitive psychology is pro-consciousness in a sense that is as important as is *Objectivism* and *Biocentric* pro-consciousness.

Nothing *could be* further from the truth (pun—and sarcasm—intended).

So let us now conclude our evaluation of *Mind and Brain Sciences in the 21st Century* by completing the 10th and final item on our random list of ten from that book.

306.307.308

Mind-Brain's Chapter 16 (*Mind Sciences and the 21st Century*) by Robert L. Solso is a summary of all 19 authors' 16 Chapters with Foreword and includes our 10 randomly selected sections of three pages each. M-B pp. 306,307,308 *specifically* summarize Richard F. Thompson, Carl Sagan and Ann Druyan, Endel Tulving, Michael Posner and Daniel Levitin, Karl Pribram, and Bernard Baars.

Since R.L. Solso is the editor of this book and is the one who solicited the various authors to predict what they think will be the important elements in psychology in the 21st Century one would not expect him to criticize their respective answers and he does not do so (nor should he). Rather, he writes glaring approval synopsis of each authors position on their particular answer to his solicitation to predict the future of psychology in the 21st Century (though if you "listen" to his tone—as you read it for the very first time—you can tell which ones he really likes and which ones he's just being kind to). Consequently, these three pages are filled with the same anti-human nature tenets as we found for the particular authors mentioned here that we also covered before so rather than rehash this we go directly to our summary.

In summary (psycho-hermeneutically first; listing of anti-human-nature tenets second):

Richard F. Thompson: Friends, Romans, Countrymen, lend me your blankouts, I have come to revive behaviorism not bury it (page 136 here).

Carl Sagan and Ann Druyan (pages 232, 258 here): Scientism, qua philosophy, is the best philosophy and if it wasn't for us Scientists and our propensity to purposefully misname things (e.g. Heisenberg's *uncertainty* "principle", *imaginary* numbers, *Chaos* "theory" and so on) professional religionists and other mystics would not have the ingredients required to create paper (mâché) tigers.

Endel Tulving, not covered directly by us, but indirectly through **Dr. Snodgrass** whose anti-human nature thing is: my magic act, like all magician's magic acts, are actually not acts, but real. We really do do the magic, its not illusion, its not trickery, but we really really do cut the person in half.

Michael Posner and Daniel Levitin—see footnote #184, page 208 here for the psycho-hermeneutic evaluation of their position, while noticing that—their anti-human nature thing is their assertion: consciousness is a derivative *not* a primary (*not an axiomatic primary* as Objectivism asserts and demonstrates to be the case).

Karl Pribram (page 251 here): science doesn't *check* premises, it *accepts* them and then MAKES sense out of their implications, that is, it makes sense out of the conclusions that follow. Whether those conclusions' premises are true or false doesn't matter to real scientists. If somebody tells a scientist that all dogs are cats and that mippy **is** a cat, then the scientist rightly, scientifically *can*, *does* and *should* (per KP) conclude: mippy is a dog.

Bernard Baars—along with the following—not covered directly by our random list of 10: Alan Gevins, Ernest R. Hilgard, Neal E. Miller, Henry L. Roediger III, Edward E. Smith, and Robert L. Solso—though we can consider **R. L. Solso** (editor of M-B) to be covered by association as already stated and actually by this summary chapter in M-B that he wrote.

Since my goal was to show how the authors on our original list of ten were advocates for the anti-human nature positions in science and since we've covered some of our authors above (as indicated by the **names-in-bold**), allow me to summarize the remaining ones below.

Psycho-hermeneutic summary continued:

Hans J. Eysenck (page 143 here) is: a mystic dressed in a scientist's white lab coat.

Michael S. Gazzaniga (page 239 here) is: an instinct theorist dressed in evolutionary determinism clothing; man does *not* have volition in *any* sense, so for sure not in the sense philosophy (Objectivism) asserts he does.

Jerome Kagan (page 219 here): if you can't accurately count the number of raindrops that are falling, you can't really say for sure whether or not it is raining. Therefore, the science of meteorology will be greatly improved in the future when they invent rain-drop-counting machines. (And *when* such machines are invented I—JK—*predict* we humans will *finally* be able to conclude *with* certainty that the fact that our head and clothes are drenched after standing outside in the open is proof that it is—maybe—raining out.)

George Sperling (page 226 here): reductive materialist par excellence, but a reluctant one, an accidental tourist, an I hate it but I don't know what else to do about it (in his own words):

> *What is a theoretical [Cognitive-Behavioral] psychologist to do—theorize in greater detail about less and less until he achieves perfect mastery of almost nothing at all?*

And finally then, the anti-human nature tenet(s) of each are what?

They are as follows:

Richard F. Thompson
Man does *not* have a volitional, efficacious, causative consciousness because consciousness either does not exist or if it does it is a derivative not primary thing.

Carl Sagan
In my role as a Scientism Scientist it is my job to prove that the religious doctrine of original sin **is** correct.

Ann Druyan
Girl friends of scientists are scientists too.

That is, if guilt-by-association is wrong then so too is praise-by-association. That is, Carl Sagan **is** a praise-worthy *astronomer*.

Karl Pribram
Man doesn't (really) need epistemology.

Hans J. Eysenck
Man doesn't (really) need ethics (in ALL areas of his endeavors).

Michael S. Gazzaniga
Man does not have volition.

Jerome Kagan
Man cannot (really) know.

George Sperling
Man cannot trust his reasoning capacity to arrive at truth.

And finally:

Robert L. Solso

Scientists, qua human beings who study subjects *intensely*, are good *because* they are scientists; which is to say *proper* reasoning is not objective it is circular.

And finally the Grant count.

How many of the 16 Chapters of Mind-Brain (see yor curiosity on page 136 here) were directly funded and/or subsidized by Government Grant money?

Ans: 4.

That is, 25% which *isn't* as many as I originally thought it was going to be.

Consequently, I have to conclude that the 19 authors of M-B are not as BM'ish as I originally thought but are just plane 'ole scientists who don't know anything (worthwhile) about psy*chh*ology.

Part IV:

On the *Art* and *Science* of *Becoming*.

Can you be your own Psychotherapist?
And get the world's best client in return?

When I told the above idea to a(nother) soon to be ex-friend of mine he said:
"You know what *they* say about lawyers who defend themselves?"
Even though I knew the correct answer, I replied: "What?"
He said: Such lawyers are said to have '…a fool for a client…'.
Me: no comment.
He: Maybe in the cases you are advocating here the same will be said about those who will want to be their own therapist. Maybe it will be true that those who want to try and manage their own therapy will have a dufus, a dunce, a fool for a client?
Me: Either that or *maybe* it highlights one of the main differences between lawyers and psychhotherapists.
He:

Chapter 21: *The Ninth Principle: Reality rules*

Ask not, what can *you* do for Reality? but rather, what can *Reality* do for you?

Reality's 1st rule is: *contradictions do not exist*.
Reality demonstrates this to us by: *not having any*.
Reality's second rule is: *self **really** matters*.
Reality demonstrates *this* to us by: *evolving* man—the rationally *selfish* animal—him or her *self*.
Since *Objectivism* is the only philosophy to drill home these points, once you *get Objectivism* then your answer to the question; What can *Reality* do for me? can be rephrased into: What can *Objectivism* do for me?
One of the things it can do (for those of us who need/ed it) is answered in the following.
It can be your *guide* in any psychotherapy you *choose* to go through and *succeed* at.
Any?
Yes, any.
Then *after* your successful therapy you can say: No one's mental health can exceed the *degree of caring* exhibited by his or her *own* therapist.
Metaphysically, no one has the *potential* to *care* about you as much as you do.
No one.
Not even God?
Especially not God.
God—ultimately—cares only about God stuff (e.g., how to keep the universe from winding down and collapsing into nothingness, and stuff like that, which is to say he/she/it/they/them are *too busy* to care about you as much as you *need*).
What about religion?
Unless yu can tell me of a religion without God, I'd say we've already answered that.
What about Philosophy, especially the Philosophy of *Objectivism*?

Still no. Since Objectivism is the *selfishness* philosophy it cares more—in the long run—about "itself" than about you.

So are you saying that Objectivism, a *modern* philosophy, is no different than religion (a *primitive* philosophy) so therefore, Objectivism is a religion?

Absolutely, god-awfully NOT. *Objectivism* is not a religion. *Objectivism* is *better* than religion. *Objectivism* is part of what religion has been trying to be for thousands of years but has failed at it. Religion has failed because it hitched its wagon to the star of *faith* while at the same time attempting to **kill** *reason* at every conceivable opportunity. *Objectivism* was the first to say, NO! STOP! HALT! You've got it all f... screwed up, you've got it all topsy-turvy upside down, inside-out, REVERSED! *Reason* is man's crowning glory NOT faith. *Faith* is for thugs and laggards and wannabe controllers of the human *productive* spirit. Reason is for men—real men. Real men desire to be as reasoning capable as they can achieve. Wimps and babies-in-adult-human bodies want faith, desire faith, worship faith and T.H.E.Y. don't dare let you have your reason because if they do you will be there to remind them that they *are* wimps and adult babies.

(No it is not my intent here to create another "syndrome"; one called *adult babies of reasoning parents*. As a speculative psychological theoretician I don't see my job as most do. That is, I do *not* see my job to be one who "creates" psychological syndromes for the geneticists to discover genetic causes for and/or for drug companies to discover new drug "cures" for. But I can easily *imagine* my religious enemies—and/or the reductive materialists—*trying* to do this at sometime during this 21st Century.)

Religionist Mentality Therapist (wondering why this particular client before him has a red cross-hairs drawn on their forehead right between their eyes)**:** Are you an adult baby of a reasoning parent or parents?

Client: Yes I yam! (Stops to cry.)

RMT (handing **C** a tissue or two with look of sincere concern)**:** I feel sorry for you. It is too bad your fat—was it your mother or your father that was the reasoning parent?

C: In my case I got a double dose! It was both of those evil bastards!

RMT: Let's not overreact now. Your parents thought they were acting in your best interest. You can't blame them that they succumbed to reasons tantalizing *voice*. They aren't the first to do so and they won't be the last. Reason is a scourge on the face of the earth and it has to be eradicated, but it will take time.

The church is patient—patience in fact is The Church's most salient characteristic and its middle name—The (patient) Church has been working on eradicating reason for eons and it will continue to do so, so don't *you* fret.

C: I ain't fretting you dumb SOB, I'm mad as hell and I ain't gonna take it any more.

RMT (without any sense of self whatsoever, turns the other cheek): I know you're upset right now and I understand that and since I am the *adult* here I will let you rant ... a little bit. But I should warn you that if you get out of hand I will call in my alter-ego and he won't be so nice. So, just a warning, be careful.

C: Are you muther f*!@#&g threatening me you little c*!@#*!@%r!

RMTAE, reaches into his coat pocket and pulls out a 357 Magnum with a barrel as long as his d..., arm and squeezes off one round that ends up entering C's head dead center on that red magic marker cross-hairs somebody else drew there.

RMT/A.E.: I don't threaten.

> *Human nature* predates *Objectivism*.
> *Objectivism* predates *Biocentric psychology*.
> *Biocentric psychology* predates the *today* me.
>
> However, I predate the today me too, that is to say, my psycho-philosophical development started the day my *tabula rasa* mind slowly but surely started recording in **my** being, photographic impressions of **my** father's face. Based on dream awarenesses I had during my therapy *intense* years—that is during the years 1976 to 1986—I estimate this tabula rasa "psychological non-existent me" *transition*-to-the *starting point* psychological me, to be at or about the time I was six months old. Or if not this then at *whatever* age it was that I was able to pull myself up and stand on my own two psychological feet by holding on to my father's knees and studying his face as he sat on the family couch. In particular I observed myself making photographic impressions of his (moving) mouth and *only* his mouth as he sat there. Since at that age I had no independent concept of the concept *what* I can't say *what* he was doing: be it watching TV[257], listening to the radio or talking to someone else in the room. All I know is I was *tunnelly* focused on the *shape* and *movements* of his mouth (therefore, he must've been

---

[257] Though this can't be so because we didn't get our first TV until I was 6 *years* old, which was in 1951.

talking).²⁵⁸ At the age I am now, *mimicry* as-early-learning process seems to be the word that best describes *what* I was engaged in at the time. And yes, this is part of my *learning* and *developmental* psychology theory that we will return to in more detail in a later work (maybe).²⁵⁹

For now.

Mimicry—monkey see, monkey do—and *imprinting*—why do you think kids have *such* a hard time separating from their custodial parents—are the two *forms of learning* (or I should say the *initial* forms of learning) for the newly born human being to use—for better or for worse—between the ages of zero and 5. This is not one of *BiO Spiritualism's* Nine Principles, but for now it is one of its *working hypothesis.*

My *preliminary* "philosophical" development *ended* when I was 5 years old, which is to say it ended on *that* day *during* that year when I realized that I was responsible for my own *sense* of life and that I was responsible even though it was a burden I had wished at the time not to have had to have born so early. But, being aware that my *imprinted* father was not going to father me in a way I needed, I *accepted* the responsibility, albeit fearfully, to father *my-self* (see footnotes 111 and 112 on page 114).

All human beings do this. Their individual differences are simply in the age at which they do it or rather start it. My high school English teacher notwithstanding—once begun half done—starting is not the same as completing

---

[258] Is this ability to tunnelly focus our senses an innate ability or a developmental fact? When my youngest daughter was 4 years old and we were out to Chucky Cheese for pizza one night she said to me do you hear that dum-dum-tee-dum sound? Hear what? I nearly yelled, the dbA sound level in the room from all the clanging racket "musical" sounds going on was almost unbearable. The cliché, can't hear myself think was quite applicable. Anyway she asked again and persisted she wanted to know "where" that sound was. So I started looking around the restaurant and low and behold I finally found it. Up near the ceiling on a ledge about 30 feet from our table was a mechanized animal character (I think it was a teddy bear that looked like a monkey or vice versa) stepping on a pedal and with every step step step there was a corresponding dum-dum-dum on the drum he was "playing". I was absolutely amazed as to how she could separate that one sound out of the what seemed to me to be a thousand sounds in the room. Now of course I think she was not able to integrate all the sounds since her sensory development was still dealing with individual senses; just as I as an adult couldn't dis-integrate all the sounds in the room until I *chose* to focus on and isolate just one of them.

[259] And to anticipate where this maybe work is headed consider the iObservation that since my ~~father~~ ... since my old man felt sorry for himself to the point of being pathetic about it and I also went thru this phase did I also mimic it via the musculature structure my dad would have for sure had on his face (and quite possibly *whole body language*) so that since he REFLECTED in his body his essence I MIRRORED it in my (developmental) life by mimicking him without making the proper SELFISH modifications early enough in life to have benefited more than I have now that I made them LATER in life ... and etcetera and so on and so forth ... to be determined (maybe) and especially to find those guy(s) research on facial expressions as manifestations of inner psychological states and ... halt. TBC/TBD (maybe).

so people also differ in the age at which they achieve complete and total separation from parents and along with it accept the metaphysical fact of self-responsibility[260, 1]. For example, I started at age 5 (or 4) and some one else may not have started until 8 or ~~80~~ 18.[261] I finished on one bright sunny morning in Chicago 1986 at age 41[262]. Others who started early enough maybe could have finished by age 14 or so or if not this early then for sure earlier than age 41.[263]

This beginning and ending individuation process is an awareness from my therapy intense years and is not a *BiO Spiritualism* principle but one of its working hypothesis. I do not have (yet) any such awarenesses as to *when* my philosophical *development* **began**, but I *suspect* it was at or very soon after I was born: I have some vague recollections of having "geometric" dreams from a very very very early age where I experienced a "conflict" between the vision of

---

[260] Most if not all psychologists agree with the human need to separate and differentiate from their parents—with parent understood to mean, one or ones who performs the parenting functions of providing for the child's early survival needs that the child is not capable of providing for him or herself—that they have a name for the process. It is called, *individuation*. I passed into the 50% individuation/separation-from-my father-zone when I was 14 years old. I remember it clearly. The scene setting was similar to that one in the Tracy and Hepburn movie *Desk Set* where Tracy was leaving Hepburn's apartment and then he came right back in pretending to be drunk and he proceeded to act out being drunk and funny. The scene for me, visually, is just like this but the characters differ. It was the time when my old man came home drunk and proceeded to act just like Tracy in that scene—except of course, it wasn't acting, but it was funny. Or rather *to me* at the time (and for the *first* time after having been in many of these "scenes") it was funny and so funny in fact that I laughed *at* him (not *with* him, but **at** him) and so hard in fact that I actually did buckle over and roll on the floor. I don't remember all the details of his antics but I do remember myself having this humongous, gigantic feeling of I AM NOT HIM ... HE IS NOT ME. And I laughed and laughed and laughed. And, *Yes*, it was super duper cathartic (maybe the Bible is wrong, maybe parents have to *earn* being honored in ALL aspects of honor). Six years later—while in college, during one of our bee…whatever, six years later I moved into the 75 percentile zone of psychological separation and for the final-100% got-the-separation/individuation-job-done see main text sentence and footnote after next for details.

[261] I was going to say 80 here but then I realized this isn't an advertisement for toys: anyone who has not *started* this process by age 28 is in trouble, big trouble and will have to *work* overtime to correct for it.

[262] Yes, it was during one of Branden's weekend intensives held there at the time. It wasn't in the intensive per se but it a café nearby during a conversation over lunch that I was having with one of the female participants. As we talked—yes there was a mutual attraction that did not go any where—but as we talked I had a sense of "Reuben" (my father or old man as we kids used to call *them*) being in-the-sinews of my being (as in, **reuben-in-me**). The sense was as if I were sitting on bleachers at a ball game and he was running around down below them trying to direct my behavior: **rim**: "Don't say the wrong thing here. **mim**: This girl is sexy. **rim**: Though, she probably won't like you anyway...." The adult me "iObserved" these "goings on" with super excited interest and I proceeded to have my *second* best time ever of all times I ever had at one of Dr. Branden's intensive. For the *best of the best* see the first time and its consequences as replayed through the car rental episode vignette given in Chapter 24.

[263] Some of course never finish the process and go to their grave totally and completely puzzled about life: what's it all about??? is the last "look" on way too many peoples face. According to my developmental theory, the first look is: write life's story here upon my blank face.

something that *looked* thick but *felt* thin. My thick-thin period of development lasted—I'm guessing here—about a month, maybe less. It represents (SWAGerly speaking) the *initialization of meaning* of sensory data to the yet to be formed self (in fact one could argue that the "felt thin" is initial *ego*, which is—among other things—*that* which feels). It is the starting point of the feeling we can all relate to when some one says: "Man is the measure of all things.".[264, ii]

Since it was almost 30 years later before I *consciously* experienced my self experiencing "what the eye sees" at the brain inlet of streaming sensory data (what I refer to as consciously seeing my first subconscious image), I tend to agree with the Cognitive **Therapy** (not to be confused with Cognitive Psychology) theorizers who say that "shape" and "color" are two *fundamental* streams that the **brain** deals with.[iii] (Ignoring for the moment that black and white is *more* fundamental than color. For example, my oldest daughter didn't see the color in our color TV when we first got it three months *before* her fourth birthday even though she did see it on that very same TV set later one morning during a *Scooby-Doo* episode a few months *following* that birthday, or as she put it: *when did we get color TV?*)

So, as I was saying, it was a Saturday afternoon. One of those lazy, *not* hazy but crystal-clear, jumping-into-a-pile of raked leaves, autumn Saturdays in the Midwest and I was in my (second) ascetically furnished, post separation, pre-legal divorce apartment. I had one of those cushions from that time period (middle '70's) that looked like a midget chair without any legs. That is, it was a stout, pillowy small chair-back with stout, pillowy chair arms but no legs. This one was made of red corduroy and stuffed with something soft but solid enough to hold the quadriplegic chair shape. I sat on the floor with it as a back rest up against the wall separating my dining room from the living room I currently was in. As I looked at the opposite apartment-white wall that should have had a couch on it but didn't I slumped into sleep as I tried to practice my "ego strengthening and relaxation" procedures. As my journal records, I had some minor dreams and then a very profound *if only I could figure this one out* "dream". In front of me was a very large WHITE KEY floating in space surrounded by a very misty red threaded substance, this substance was like a thick, stringy but not sticky cotton candy of the type sold at County Fairs and Carnivals—except this cotton candy was very very deeply-like-you-never-saw-before *redder* and *brighter* and **thicker**

---

[264] In the Ayn Rand sense of there is only one universe (existence) for us *to* measure, not in the Protagoras sense of multiple universes "created" by us measurers.

than any **red** you've ever seen. Then, *Key* I thought, *big white key,* what's the *key*? Surely if I figure this one out I will know the secrets of the Universe.

Since the eyeball lets in the light and defines the context—the literal field of view in this case—and we know that the eyeball is connected to the brain (via the optic nerve) it is *logical* to conclude that the brain is what processed the eyeball *collected* electromagnetic data (light). And the process in my first hand experience here was like that of adjusting the focus on a microscope. Out of focus, or rather at the lowest (hypnopompic in this case) level of focus there was shape (key shape in this case) and there was stringy color (red and white only in this case). Once "key" was "recognized" as the shape, focus started to go to "what's the key?", something's key, to instant awake without moving a muscle, to Oh! Notice! … but don't move one single muscle first … red corduroy edges and how they form key like edges on the white wall … no depth perception … full awake now full "integrated" view and full context: my apartment living room, me resting my head on corduroy pillow's left arm with SINGLE (LEFT) EYE OPEN staring at distant white wall, view fully is what it is. It is me in my living room with my left eye peering out of my head resting on a *red* corduroy pillow—with the bridge of my nose forming the right boundary of the visual field— staring at the distant *white* wall. The visual context went through multiple levels of identification as I became more and more conscious, that is, more and more awake until its final end state of fully aware of all the sensory data and of me, myself and I fully awake.

The **red** stringy material was from the **red** corduroy and the white from the opposite white wall in my apartment. The key was formed by the edges of the corduroy and the ridge of my nose as it flows up my face to my left eye socket and eyebrow and on around taking in as much as I want with my rollable eye. In the case at hand though, the eye was not rolling but perfectly dead-still looking straight out of the socket. The focal point of the eye took in the streaming red and white color and key-shape data. The mystical, ghostliness of the whole event left a lasting impression and had I not had the wherewithal to pay *sharp* attention to my *context* upon full awakening I probably would have assigned some "mystical" meaning to this one particular event. And by mystical I don't mean "reasoned interpretation" of the event but rather by mystical I mean *superficial*, not very deeply thought about but easiest as in what first comes to mind "explanation".

So, do I think genetics determines human psychology?

Whoa partner. Where'd this come from???

It came from *everywhere* as in it is *always* there as an issue. As an issue, that is, for psychological man—psychologically *developing* man. Either we are "determined" by our *volitional* choices as Ayn Rand's Objectivism contends or *we are not*, as everyone else contends.

So, we have to answer *fundamental* questions ourselves: Do I think genetics determines human psychology?

No and Yes. Yes at the *automatic* level of forming *perceptions*—but this isn't psychology, it's *physiology*. So, No, not at the level that counts; that is, the *conceptual* level. Here, I *determine* me and you determine you.

Do I believe in environmental determinism as the Behaviorists and their born-again offspring, the Cognitive Neuroscientists do? No, I believe me determines I and I *determines* me when we are talking about *determines* in a meaningful way, which *means* my life, my joy, my abilities, my achievements, my happiness, my every-thing (1 and 2 wise) that *counts*.

I and me, grammatically are—after all—two ways of saying the same thing.[265]

I am me.

Therefore, **you** are *you*.

Since I was determined by me, you were determined by you and we can put to rest right here and now any *pretense* that we were determined—*meaningfully* determined, where it counts determined—by forces outside our self's self.

If as counter argument you are going to say my *genetic endowment* is what *caused* me to be born a *human baby* rather than an *oak tree sapling* and hence I am "determined" by my genes, then make sure this is the *exact* same thing you mean *each 'n every* time you *think* it. Because if it is, then I have no problem with it, because it is not what "they" mean when T.H.E.Y. use the concept: *genetically determined*. By "genetically" determined they mean by forces outside your control—as far outside your control, that is, as is the physical phenomenon of gravity and electricity—and they mean this in spite of them telling you it's not *precisely* what they mean. We established many pages back that what "they" mean by "precision" is not what "we" mean. When we say "precise" we mean, *precisely clear, clear enough to be understandABLE*. They mean *muddy*. To them "muddy water" is better than "clear water". Their "reasoning" is this:

1. muddy waters appear deep
2. deep is good

---

[265] As Dr. Peikoff has already pointed out for us to consider...NOW I know what Ayn Rand means when she says human beings have two legitimate things to offer each other: trade and KNOWLEDGE.

3. voila! Muddy is good.

That Human beings are beings of self-made consciousness (souls) can be used by us as a (working) hypothesis.

And the hypothesis accepting "I" that I refer to here is the one that got its first full shot at life between the ages of 0 and 9 after fully developing its PER(as in pre)ceptual abilities between the ages of 0 and 5 and then its rudimentary *conceptual* ability between [0 and] 2½ and 10 and its first taste of *fully* applied abilities between the ages of [0 and] 7½ and 20—with all the trial(run)s and tribulations associated with the first and second decades of life on earth for the selfish individual taken as givens.

As well as all the other nine or ten or N multi-year cycles one has gone through since.

As to how many cycles—whatever their duration—we have to go through before we become full human-adults is a matter of *individual* life.

Using 9 as my basis I am *proud* to report that it only took me 4 to 5 cycles before I *finally* got it right.

Now I am concerned primarily with what am I going to do with the rest of my life now that I'm all grown up and a *real* human being?

Write non-fiction books and tell fictional stories and continue *trying* to beat the horses as well as continue trying to discover—not the best trade route to the orient, but rather—the best trade route—that is the best path—to the top of my *own* mountain.

No doubt, *true* spiritualism is this path.

And as I've already stated (page 7): *true* spiritualism is the *process* of **making** one's self the sole, prideful owner of a worthy and efficacious consciousness. A consciousness that is worthy of happiness *because* it is competent at producing it.

And as I am asserting herein, *BiO Spiritualism* is the **best** (known to me at this point in my development) *spiritualism*.

BiO Spiritualism takes *as a given* all the tenets of *Objectivism* and all the tenets of *Biocentric Psychology* and **applies** them *mutatis mutantis* to the self as self seeks to maintain itself as a living, breathing, happy individual *in the world*.

Spiritualism in this sense is pre and post operative: as *process* it goes on throughout our life from birth-to-death and it generally is something we become more and more interested in (and aware of) the older we get because we realize that life is finite and if we hope to *achieve* happiness in it we had better darn well know what we are doing and if we have failed to find it on our own we can turn to the professional therapists for help:

C: If you don't threaten, then what do you call what just happened.

RMT/AE: *Epistemological death* to *eidetic* personalities that don't—in justice—*deserve* to live on. Especially the **C**(onventional Social Metaphysical) ones.

Chapter 22: As Client check your Spiritualism premises

I am Alpha and Omega, who are yu?

That's exactly who I thought you were: Alpha and Omega. The first and the last. The beginning and the end.

At least this is *who* my first *big* book tried to tell me God was when I was but 9 years old and could finally read good enough on my own to *take on* by first *big* book.

At *that* time of course I didn't know what the word *spiritualism* meant, let alone that it had anything to do with *epistemology*.

By the time, some 5 years later, I had succeeded in reading the same big— King James version of *The Holy Bible*—book from beginning-to-end for the second (and final) time, I was a firm believer that Alpha & Omega, First & Last, Beginning & End AND God were One and in-the-same thing.

How I "knew" this I did not *know* anymore than I knew *how* I wiggled my fingers whenever I wanted to; I just "did it-knew it-did it" *somehow*.[266]

At *that* time of course I still didn't know what the word *epistemology* meant, let alone that it had something to do with *happiness*.

It wouldn't dawn on me until some 40 plus years later (that is, until two seconds ago) that if one were to substitute modern day philosophy's concept of *Existence* (it exists) for religionist's view of *God* (God is) and rewrite the Bible with this substitution, one would end up at least *a thousand miles* closer to the *true* truth than the Bible as is, is. But since *The Holy Bible* suggests that its heaven is outside of *Existence*—a place that does not exist—the as is Bible's distance from the truth has to be measured in cosmological units (c.u.). Since c.u.'s are many parsecs and a parsec is hundreds of thousands of astronomical units (a.u.) and one a.u. almost equals a hundred million miles, one and only one *certain* conclusion jumps out at us:

---

[266] The brain is the how? Maybe. Maybe if, we assert that *form* does follow *function* so that the brain is nothing more than the metaphysical organ—the *form*—that follows the *function* of mind-over-its-own-matter (he said, holding up has right hand and wiggling his fingers like they were little dancing snakes standing on their tail moving to the beat of a *volitional* consciousness).

a thousand miles ain't much.

Existence—as the modern day Philosophy of *Objectivism* has demonstrated—is the sought after Alpha & Omega, First & Last, Beginning & End.

That is, *Existence exists.*

And what's even more esthetically pleasing to me is: I *know* it.

I see what I see and I know what I know and vice versa: I know what I know and I see what I see.

* * *

Spiritualism—as the *process* of *making* one's self happy—exists in the interface between Art and Science. Consequently I, as the 21st Century's first *BiO Spiritualist* write at the interface between Fiction—the *art* of showing things as they *should* be—and Non-Fiction—the *scienc*e of showing things as they *are*.

BiO Spiritualism in the end is the integration of (the Philosophy of) *Objectivism* and (the Psychology of) *Biocentric Psychology* in the soul of one individual.

Me.

If you want it to be so in your soul too, then you will have to do something *in reality* similar to and/or analogous to what I am doing here (as well as, *have done* to get *to here*).

And just exactly what is it that I am doing here and how might you benefit from it?

I am letting you watch me show myself the *end* of my personal journey *of self-acceptance* through the *process* of *self-transformation* as I understand it from the nature driven and nature protected first 9 years of life through the next 9 years of struggling to find a *rational* universe to the next 9 where I *refused* to give up the struggle and through the next 9 after that when I made it half way through therapy and then after that when I woke up one morning $2/3^{rd}$'s of the way into the next 9 years completely and totally *free*—and I mean *completely* and *totally* free—of my deeply held belief in god and my neurotic dependence on *faith* as a self-accepted legitimate tool of mind. I mark this day as my entry point into *adulthood*. Granted I was 42 years old, but I too have always been a late bloomer.

This *freedom-from-faith* day is the day I completed nature's psychological development task of going from programmed (by human nature's two programming forces: *fear*—of being unfit for life—and *love*—of efficacy) to *volitional* self regulation (my I *choosing* to value efficacy and worth). This means, among other things, it is the day I could no longer say: "the devil made me do it", or "*god* gets credit for all my good, I get the *blame* for everything else" and so on, which is to say, it is the day I accepted full and complete responsibility for everything I *think*, everything I *feel*, everything I *say* and everything I *do*.

To me this day is my *moral* birth-day—my *adult* moral birth-day.

Since there are no gods and never has been any, *morality* lives (and dies) inside the individual *souls* of individual human beings. (For more on the fundamental nature of reality and man's place in it—that is, metaphysics—see the *Objectivist* concept of axiomatic concepts, that is, of primary, self-evident concepts, especially the first axiomatic concept: E*xistence exists.*)

Individual souls in the foregoing includes your individual soul, my individual soul and everyone's individual soul which—as a universal—in *Objectivism* and *Biocentric Psychology* is known as and is called: *consciousness*.

Soul is consciousness, consciousness is soul.

Your consciousness, your soul is a "thing". A thing that is *not* separateable from your body but is an *integral* part of your body in a way analogous to cream-in-coffee: an inseparable union and an irreversible—speaking **strictly** metaphorically—chemical combination made by existence's—speaking **strictly** anthropomorphically—best chemist: the one we call, *nature*.

Your consciousness has the capability of throwing your mind-body unit into a beaker in the *laboratory of your mind* and boiling off the mind to study the body or to boil off the body to study the mind, but if you try either literally in reality the result is death to the organism.

Mind and body do not exist in reality *apart* from each other and they can only "exist" separately in the fashion just mentioned: as an *abstraction* inside human consciousnesses' capacity *to abstract*.

For examples in "reality" of mind without body (that is, in "an awareness state" that is *closer* to awake then it is to that of a deep sleep/dream state) see "out-of-body" experiences reported by self and/or others and notice that they always (seem to) occur (for the first time at least) under *extreme* pain. Be it extreme *physical* pain as may occur in a car accident victim waiting for and/or undergoing an operation to repair a seriously damaged body, or extreme *psychological* pain—extreme anxiety for example—as may occur in one going through a really severe crisis of self-esteem. Man's tolerance for pain—be it physical and/or psychological—has an upper limit and when that limit is reached consciousness attempts to withdraw from the "place" where the pain is experienced—i.e., the body—but since it can't literally do so, it does it the only way it can: by retreating into the human abstracting capacity. To the extent to which "it" can fully retreat is the extent to which the one in whom the retreating is being done *experiences* an "out-of-body" sensation.[267]

For examples of body-without-mind look at a corpse which *is* dead and decaying now that the mind has died first.[268]

Why does the mind die first? Because life *is* a *process* of self-sustaining, self-generated action and since the self doing the *generating* and the *sustaining* is the mind, is consciousness, death means the end of self—which is that *which* generates, that *which* sustains; that which we call consciousness. A self, such as me my-self or you your-self are *particular* instances of consciousness, specifically *particular* instances of *human* consciousness (which of course doesn't exist except as particular instances). *Human* consciousness is different than non-human *animal* consciousness as is *measured* by the *Objectivist* identified *yardsticks* for measuring consciousnesses: *range* and *scope* of awareness. Hence, we humans know that animal consciousness is different than insect consciousness because we can *observe* that a dog's range and scope of awareness is more than an ant's (that's why dogs make better pets than ants). Similarly, we can and do *observe* that an insect's range and scope of awareness is more than an amoeba's (that's why ant farms sell better than amoeba farms). (See *Objectivism* for more, especially their observation that *consciousness is conscious* is another axiomatic, self-evident primary.)

Mind and body—a union as inseparable as is green from grass—are an anchor in reality for the concept of "integration". Mind and body *are* integrated.

Consciousness is the "mind" that is "integrated" into every sinew of the body.

---

[267] The body? ... metaphysically speaking, is the *place* inside the Universe *where* pleasure and pain are experienced.

[268] Or study modern day, contemporary psychology's non-theoretical, theoretical base called: *Behaviorism* (yes, this *is* sarcastic which is also something I am "working" on; that is, as you have already discovered in an earlier chapter I also am pedantic and I'm working on that too—that is, working to *change* both, but until and unless... well, for now *this* is who I [y]am ... and the change has started.) . Or, look at those people who are so numb to life that they refer to themselves as: numb. No, wait...halt. This last is not correct. Since feelings are "in-the-body" and numb is an absence of feeling, numbness is a(nother) example of mind without body. So Body-without-mind, an "out-of-mind" experience would have to be one where one feels like a robot, an automaton, a non-thinking zombie roaming around the world not knowing *where* one is, metaphysically speaking. A zombie driven by subconscious forces it has no (conscious) clue about whatsoever because it does not think... specifically, does not think consciousness is a thing-like-thing in that it has *needs*. And in general does not think thinking is a virtue and if and when carried to the *ultimate* end in a particular person, qua zombie, who thinks *thinking is a vice*, we arrive at a real-life example of what is known—in horror fiction—as: the living dead, which is to say: an out-of-mind experience (which *might* be to say: Jeffery Dahmer).

Integration therefore—psychologically, morally, spiritually—is good, moral, spiritual.

Consciousness (as BiO Spiritualism speculation) *is a full body experience* and *only* a full body experience, which means—among other things—that when the soul "travels" it does so within the confines of the body. It can travel from the top of your head to the interface between the soles of your feet and the ground you are standing on (test this yourself right now by pausing and being aware of the soles of your feet) and from the tip of your left middle finger to the tip of your right middle finger and *all points in-between* but it *cannot* and does *not* "travel" the quarter of a million miles required to get to our moon or the quarter of a million astronomical units (4.3 light years) to our nearest star α Centauri *without* bringing the body along. And a mystics *wish* and claim that it does is not proof that it does. All sensible logic says it doesn't, *therefore*—every single, individual, *faith*-based/faith-*dominated* psycho-epistemology (without exception) in the Universe notwithstanding—it does not.

That you *need* to integrate and manage all your values and knowledge—as opposed to dis-integrate and mismanage them as mystics would have you do—is not up to you, but *what* you *attempt* to integrate is.

So, you can start (or continue) your *spiritual* journey here—but in the end—the *integration* of *Objectivism*, qua the *correct* philosophy, and *Biocentric Psychology*, qua the *correct* psychology, in your own *individual* soul is up to you. The only thing you have to remember is: no one—not me or you nor anyone—can integrate the non-integrate-able.

I wish you well in your future spiritual quests and depending on which *one* of the following 10 *exhaustive* categories you currently fit into, I offer an associated *prediction* which you *might* be able to use as an *action plan* for your *spiritual* self's benefit. That is, if you are:

...

But wait.

First, just for fun, write down your answers (*be sure to write them down*, anywhere will suffice) to two questions *before* you read the categories.

1. Are you FOR Objectivism, AGAINST Objectivism or NEUTRAL to it?
2. Are you FOR Biocentric Psychology, AGAINST it or NEUTRAL to it?

OK. Good.

Here then are my predictions.

If you are:

1. FOR Objectivism *and* FOR Biocentric Psychology, then look forward to a passionate life.

2. FOR Objectivism *and* AGAINST Biocentric Psychology, then look forward to a mutedly happy life.

3. AGAINST Objectivism *and* FOR Biocentric Psychology ... look forward to a screwy life.

4. AGAINST Objectivism *and* AGAINST Biocentric Psychology ... look forward to a scary life.

5. NEUTRAL to Objectivism *and* NEUTRAL to Biocentric Psychology ... if you read EEWBAR (EverythingEverWritenByAynRand) and read and listen to EEWATBNB (EverythingEverWrittenAndTapedByNathanielBranden) you will not remain neutral.

6. NEUTRAL to Objectivism *and* FOR Biocentric Psychology ... look forward to discovering Objectivism

7. NEUTRAL to Objectivism *and* AGAINST Biocentric Psychology ... look forward to a puzzling life.

8. FOR Objectivism *and* NEUTRAL to Biocentric Psychology ... look forward to discovering Biocentric Psychology

9. AGAINST Objectivism *and* NEUTRAL to Biocentric Psychology ... look forward to a puzzling life.

10. OBLIVIOUS to BOTH ... read EEWBAR and read and listen to EEWATBNB, which is to say ... look forward to discovering *Objectivism* AND *Biocentric Psychology*.

Since *Objectivism*, the formal philosophy, is a How To primer in the Art and Science of How To be a *selfish* human being and since *Biocentric Psychology*, the scientific psychology, is a How To primer in the Art and Science of How To get and keep *authentic* self esteem, after *you* successfully integrate these two in your own soul you will become a *selfish* person who *feels* really really good about him or herself *because* you now have what it takes to become and/or remain happy for the *rest of your life*.

After this, *your* (sacred) happiness—or its absence—cannot be accredited to anyone other than you.

Good luck

Chapter 23: As *Therapist* check your life premises

Every man (woman and child over the age of 12) *is* an island.

If you are more than 12 years old, then there is a *secret* you can be let in on.
That *secret* is this: *there is no one coming to save you.*
You have to save yourself.
Fortunately, *the way*, to saving yourself, is *given* to you by nature. It is called, *learning*.
You have to *learn* how to save yourself by learning, how to learn.
After you complete *learning how to learn* over the next few years of your *development* you will then face the first step in learning how to save yourself. This step is to learn the answer to the question: *what* is it I need saving from?
If you are just barely older than 12 and the adults you trust are telling you that the answer to the *what* question is: from yourself, my advice is: *find different adults to trust*.
If you are rarely able to remember when you *were* 12 years old, you probably know and have known for sometime that the answer to the *what* question is: *evil*.
But regardless of your age—be you young, old or middle—one thing you may not know but *should* know is: evil is *not* a metaphysical force.[269] That is, it is not a *presence* but an *absence*. *Evil is the absence of the good.* Evil is *what* you need to be saved from and the *only* way to do it is to do it yourself. And the *proper* way to do it is: figure out *what* **is** true and good and important and then be *for* these every day *in* your every-day life.
For example, for me right now, *my* every-day life is devoted specifically to writing about *BiO Spiritualism. A*s relates to my specific purpose for this to develop the idea of a totally and completely New Spiritualism, **not** New Age, but *New Dawn* as in the *Dawn of the Age of Moral Individualism*—I take the following to be *true* and *good* and *important.* Which is to say, respectively, I am

---

[269] Here now—in the destroyed shadows of New York City's Twin Towers—we notice that evil is in fact a man-made force and it can be pretty persistent, consistent but still not as consistent, persistent, unchangeable as is nature. So, even though September 11th happened it doesn't make evil a metaphysical force, but it does underscore the fact that: "Box cutters don't murder, non-hypocrite practitioners of religion do."

Check your (life) premises 331

a person who ... is (and/or wants to continue being) *for* these things *cognitively, normatively, and esthetically* every day of the week:[270]

1. We are born tabula rasa. This means, among other things, that I am not born knowing that Washington DC is the capital of the United States. Nor am I, among other things, born *knowing* that apples are good for you. (Nor that Islamic Fundamentalism, qua religious fundamentalism, is *more* primitive and hence more dangerous than 21st Century Christianity and is *more* to such a degree that we can now conclude *ostensibly*—by pointing at the destructive events on September 11th, 2001 as they unfolded in the Eastern half of the United States of America and say—that *faith* without *reason* leads to evil.)

2. The senses are valid. This means, among other things, that when I *hear* myself sing *I hear what I hear and I know what I know* and I know I had better not ever—if avoiding embarrassment is my goal—voluntarily stand up and sing in public.

3. The Good is that which *is* **for** life. This means *actual* life here on earth— or the moon or mars or wherever whenever such becomes possible—as one lives it.

4. The Evil is that which *is* **against** *rational* life. (As the destructive events in America on September 11th, 2001 have demonstrated, in spades!)

5. If you want to *believe* that I am taking item 2 on *faith*, I challenge you to refer to page 318 herein for the example of my own direct, *first hand* experience dealing with streaming sensory data *at the inlet to the perceptual level* of consciousness. Of course this experience is not required in order to accept the *validity* of the senses. But what is required is *intellectual honesty*. If one says out loud and/or writes: "the senses are not valid" and then one chooses *not* to ask: "by which sense modality do I *hear* the claim?" or "which sense modality do I use to *read* the claim?", then one should be suspicious of ones intellectual motives. Are those motives to *prefer*—hence seek— truth, or to allow oneself to feel safe and secure in the thought—sarcastically expressed: "Oh, NOW! I know why nothing makes sense to me, *because* the senses are *not* valid. Whew, wow, thank god for creating a Universe built on the principle of

---

[270] Wants to, that is, *in spite of* heavy cultural pressures to abandon them.

contradiction: that is, that A is not-A, existence does not exist and neither does my faculty of awareness."

6. *Objectivism*, the philosophy, *exists* and is good and at most contains fewer errors than the number of things in a baker's dozen (see Chapter 20).

7. Restating number 6 so as to emphasize it: *Objectivism*, the philosophy, is good and at most contains fewer than a dozen or so errors. (This statement is made in part out of deference to Ayn Rand. She is the one who pointed out that not only are we humans not gods but nobody is and since consciousness does not exist apart from body, the *no-body is god* observation includes all *possible* speculations about god or gods. This obviously then includes Ayn Rand herself and if there were no, none, nada, zero errors in her *Philosophy of Objectivism* this would make her omniscient, which—as we all deductively know—can't be. Granted, to say Objectivism must have some errors is not to say WHAT those errors are. See Chapter 20 for—some of—the *what*).

8. *Reason* **is** better than *faith*. The war over this issue has been waged, fought and *won* by the Philosophy of *Objectivism*. Go there to immerse yourself in those battles and if *after* you do, you come out *pro*-faith and *anti*-reason, then ... wait awhile and try again.

9. *Biocentric Psychology* (of Dr. Nathaniel Branden) exists and is good and may contain two or three times as many errors as *Objectivism* does, but the nature and number of these errors is so manageable compared to the rats nest of errors in any other "School of Psychology" that we can almost use it as an example of the meaning of *manageable*. For example by contrast: by *un-manageable* I mean: I challenge you to *make* sense out of and use for your own objectivismly selfish *benefit* any "School of Psychology" other than *Biocentric* Psychology and succeed—that is, MAKE yourself *authentically* happy—at it *without* using Objectivism to *conceptualize* your experiences.

10. Evil is the *absence* of the good. If, for every error in *Objectivism* there are a thousand or a million or more truths and for all other non-Objectivist/non-Aristotelian philosophies the reverse is true—for every truth there are a thousand or more errors—how can anybody doubly and negatively conclude that since *Objectivism* has—at most, a *handful* of

errors—that it is *not* good and its "competitors"—by comparison—are *not* those (epistemologically) *paved roads to hell* we hear so much about?

11. Unless you are Adolph Hitler and/or some other such ilk historical figure: e.g. the (initially) no-name Middle Eastern pilots who *voluntarily* highjacked and crashed Passenger filled commercial planes into American soil and buildings—killing American civilians *as their goal*—and/or unless you are a *true* Nazi mentality as same has been identified by Dr. Peikoff in his *Ominous Parallels* book,[i] you can *only* asymptotically approach a *perfect* reversal—inside your own soul—of the *proper* definitions of good and evil as given in numbers 3 and 4 above and still exist and be alive as a being who is for the "good" and against the "evil". A "good" and "evil" which have to be put in quotes here at the bottom of the asymptote because they are in danger of crisscrossing their content. Once crisscrossed—it is my personal speculation—evil goes from an *absence* to a *presence*. At this point a question arises that I can't answer and the best I can do is to *warn you* to *never* put yourself into a position where you have to face answering it *individually*. That question is this: *Can evil—once crossed over into—redeem itself?*

12. If you cross over the asymptotic line into evil, you do so *voluntarily* and once done the only vocation left open to you will be that of murderer. *True* evil has no other occupation. Or at absolute minimum, it seeks and desires no other career.

13. *Existence exists, Consciousness is conscious, A is A.*

14. Once learned and accepted for the self-evident primaries that they are, the three *Objectivism axiomatic concepts* given in number 13 can be—*but should not be*—but can be—*but should not be*—taken for granted.

15. Individuals *should* have *shoulds*. (If you need to *initiate* yourself into the art and science of *non-contradictory identification,* then state this statement about "shoulds" in the negative and then try and *make* sense out of it. You can *state* the nonsensical—*One should not have any shoulds*—but you cannot—and neither can anyone else—*make* sense out of the nonsensical. All such attempts *eventually* make the maker nonsensical, which is to say, not-sane, which in its *most* severe form is to say, in-sane. The insane are those who—either through choice or through an *accident* of nature—have "mastered" the art of "integrating" the non-integrate-

able. Most people—developmentally speaking—when over-pressured by their culture and/or subculture to "integrate" the nonintegrable opt for *compartmentalization* rather than insanity.[271])

16. Consciousness exists on a continuum and is a big faculty/capacity. How big, nobody yet knows for sure. Speculation puts it to be bigger than a house and smaller than the Universe itself. Some say not much smaller but that is pure speculation at this point in our knowledge and I am content for now to accept that *Consciousness is conscious,* it exists on a continuum and its main job is *identification*. (as identified and delineated so far by the *Professional* Objectivists—see their writings[ii])

17. *Existence is identity, Consciousness is identification.* (More good, typical, *excellent Objectivism* discoveries).

18. When an individual consciousness explicitly *identifies* itself *for the first time* as a thing, specifically as a thing called consciousness, it is a moment of personal *rhapsody* for that consciousness and is the equivalent of saying consciousness has discovered soul, which is itself, which is to say, consciousness has discovered itself, which is to say: *I have met the friend and he is I.* That is—using myself as an example—*my* consciousness is *my* soul and my *soul* is my *consciousness* and the first time I discovered this in my own *personal* way, circa 1975, it was a rapturous moment for me. And since *your* consciousness is *your* soul and your *soul* your *consciousness,* I assume this same experience—if you haven't already experienced it—eagerly awaits you around some corner in your own future growth. And this kind of *self* discovery rhapsody should not—and let me repeat this: should not, should not, should not—be *confused* with the "self" reports of religious people when they give testimonials to their religious "epiphonies". These "epiphonies" are just that, *epi-phony* experiences that are really consciousness *taking care of* mind. A specific, concrete, individually *structured* mind, that is, that has finally *buckled* under the weight of a 100%, *pure* faith-based epistemology. Rather than let it completely collapse, consciousness does

---

[271] Mental *compartments* are "places" where we put our mistakes. Places where we put our mistakes *until* some future date when we will have the ability to correct them. If we never develop/grow our abilities then our compartments fill up with bullstuff and so do we and we end up in psychhological trouble because of it. Some of us—as noted earlier—become fatheads because of this stuffing and others of us just plain 'ole slugs. Emptying our compartments then becomes a psychological problem for us to solve. Whether or not we solve it is up to our *choice*.

something and even though I personally went a long ways down that erroneous faith-as-tool-of-mind *path*, I never experienced what religionists claim to experience in their "religious experience" *testimonials*. But, having been to the edge and looked over the *faith abyss,* I—as one who dared go there—get to *speculate*—as *reward* for bravery—about *what* the alleged religious experience means—assuming of course that religious people are being *honest* in their self reports and as such they mean *something*. And so here is my *speculation*. Consciousness *simulates* the feeling of rhapsody for the buckled mind rather than having it go insane—or worse, *amoral*—and this in turn *allows* the *human being* within to go on living a *simulated* life as a human being by *substituting* man-made *self-consistency* where nature had intended *non-contradiction* to rule. Metaphorically speaking, the life force is *not* weak and is one reason Philosophy counsels us to: *check our premises*. And then re-check them. And then, check them again. The other reason is, we are not gods with the power to know and do *all*, but humans with the power to *reason* all (that comes within our purview) *choose* a lot (out of lots 'n lots of choices and optional ways of thinking and being that confront us) and *do* many things (among the *tremendous* quantity of options an *unobstructed* consciousness affords us.)

19. We are not gods, but if we are anything we are one heck of a robust design when it comes to *living the human life* and getting as much out of it as we can. (And I use "design" here in its metaphorical sense, not, and let me repeat, not its religious-mystic sense of a "designer" of nature. See number 13 and read and study *Objectivism* to understand *that* existence is *eternal* and does not require a *causal* explanation: *Existence exists*.)

20. There is no god, so *obviously* Jesus cannot be his son. (Nor can *any* religion's claim about some human being's *special* relationship with god be true. And by "any" I mean it in its *exhaustive* sense of: any and all, as in no, none, nada, zero, zip, no exceptions.)

21. Either, *Religion is a primitive philosophy* as claimed by *Objectivism* OR the statement itself is *one* of *Objectivism's* errors referred to in number 6. And if it is one, then it can serve as *evidence* that Ayn Rand, by uttering it, stretched the meaning of human compassion beyond its elastic limit.[272]

---

[272] I suppose one could argue that by *primitive* Ayn Rand meant savage not seminal. If this, then ... well, we'll see ... time will tell.

I personally experienced Ayn Rand—in the way her writings *spoke to me*—as having *more* compassion in her little finger, than all the alleged compassion in all the Lutheran minsiters on the planet—be they the sum total of the current ones or a summation including *both* the quick and the dead ones.

> A side note here to the use of the misspelled word**, minsiters** for **ministers:** Freud does not have a monopoly on Freudian slips, I call my "Freudian slips" *Brandian slips* because I almost *always* know where they are coming from. For example, here as I was about to correct the "misspelling" I became aware that I was thinking: *sinister ministers.* I find this absolutely amazing that my subconscious mind can point this out to me and *draw my attention* to it by simply reversing two letters in a word! Wow! what an *efficient* consciousness and (English) language we humans have!!! And oh, let me not forget to say: *sinister ministers* are *not* our friends. (And whether or not other languages are *as* efficient as is English I don't know because I don't know any other language(s) as *intimately* as I know English).

22. *BiO Spiritualism*, qua (applied) science, is *reductive*—not reductive materialism, but rather, reductive—*realityism*.

23. There are basically two kinds of people in the world: those who want to *control reality* and those who want to *control those* who *do* control reality. (And <u>now</u> [do] we have to add [a third kind: e.g.] those who want to murder both of the first two kinds[?] Or are these an endpoint type of the second kind? And if they are the true t.h.e.y , is the Bureaucratic Mind the other endpoint? And is this just a restatement of Attila and the Witch doctor? Or worse yet, Osama bin Laden's henchmen and all like minded Islamic fundamentalists represent the "successful" fusing of Attila and the Witchdoctor?)

24. In the *absence of physical force,* which one of the ~~two~~ ~~three~~ ~~two~~ three types *you* become is totally and completely up to you.

25. The first kind I call *Metaphysical Metaphysicians* and the second kind, *Social Metaphysicians* (see the science of *Biocentric Psychology* for the

meaning of *Social Metaphysics and Social Metaphysicians*)[273]. But I do not belabor the point when it comes to my view of others, which is to say I do not make the *classical* mistake of using psychological "labels" to make oneself *feel* superior to others by a *comparison-to-others* standard based on categories—real or artificial ones—that come pre-packaged with instructions *encouraging* one to *evade* one's own *strengths* and instead treat ones psyche as if it were a bag turned inside out. That is, by turning our human personality inside-out metaphysically and saying it is determined by forces outside its control. For examples of these latter kinds see Chapter 17. For more discussion about Metaphysical Metaphysicians and Social Metaphysicians—including use of Hero and Villain as endpoints—see BiO Spiritualism Volume II (to be written). Rather, I strive to use these labels and I recommend others use them in the same way: *only* as "labels" for internal, eidetic personalities—be they formed or forming—or what some call sub-selves or *introspectively* whatever we relate to as *profile* senses-of-ourselves. We can and should only use these labels to *describe* others if we are truly, that is *factually*, beyond the negative gravitational pull of *pseudo* self-esteem. Which is to say: if in reality we value ourselves *highly* because of our *actual, rational* achievements independent of what others say and/or do in regards to those achievements (and/or in regards to their own achievements independent of us), then we can be said to possess *authentic* self esteem.

26. *Authentic* self-esteem is good. Really, really good.

27. One of the *rewards* of achieving *authentic* self esteem is the *freedom* to judge others as basically *good* or *bad* and/or evil in their *particularized approach* to life and happiness and, to repeat, in the absence of achieving *authentic* self esteem for ourselves it is too dangerous to do this kind of judging, yet this *kind of judging* is *exactly* what is required for us to *define* ourselves *individually* and to end up in life getting what we want.

28. We can fail in life in basically one of two ways: either in not getting what we want or in not wanting what we get. Success requires both: that we

---

[273] Even though these lead to a two (x-y) axis classification scheme (in *BiO Spiritualism*) with a lowest level within Social Metaphysicians called Villains, I will have to revisit this issue in future writings. And I am speculating here that in so doing, it will require me to add a Third Axis—one called evil DOERS—which will deal with the psychhological factors that separate those who ACT OUT in reality from those others with the same or similar ideas who do not. (Z-axis Killers??? Ummmmm, sounds like the title for a good, old-fashioned murder mystery.)

get what we want *and* we want what we get. <u>(And now we must also add that: WHAT we want matches [that is, must match] the REALITY of our human nature needs for survival and since suicide is the opposite of survival no one can rationally argue that humans have a "need" to commit suicide; be it suicide-homicide bombing of self and others or any other kind of suicide. *Needs* relate to life and survival; *need* frustration to death and destruction and anyone who "succeeds" in *reversing* this metaphysical relationship inside their own soul *will* become a monster. If fundamentalist Islam has proven anything for sure, it is that *monsters* are *made,* not born.)</u>

29. One of lives hardest challenges is for us to decide what we do want. The issue of success or failure presupposes two things: that we *want* and that we *know* what we want. In the *absence* of wanting and/or knowing, success is a metaphysical impossibility and failure is practically a force of nature.

30. For example, right now as I write this book (3:33am, 5/14/01) I am (re)defining successful life for me myself to be one where I make a living through being a writer and a N*ew Dawn Spiritualist* [i.e., 21st Century psych(h)ologist] and not necessarily in this order and if I can't achieve this then I will have failed (again). And until and unless I can feel as if failure is not an option *in regards to this specific goal* I will stay stuck and be unsettled in my life. Based on my own first hand knowledge about myself that I've acquired through many many years of hard work mastering the *art of* knowing myself—not in the religious sense of "know thyself"...to be original evil, but in the *human* sense of *know thyself—introspectively*: I know (what I know and I see what I see, I know for example) that I *will* get this feeling but I don't know right now *all* the steps in HOW I do it or WHEN it will happen, but to repeat I know it WILL happen because I have started the PROCESS (a *process* that has—*in the past—resulted* in this feeling).[274]

31. Success in life leads to happiness and failure to misery. When we do succeed and are happy, this is great and good and wonderful and motivates us to strive for more and better life and this too is good.

---

[274] 3/12/2004: Still don't have it, still working on manuscript. (…). 5/25/4: (99% done with manuscript) working on my next project to make my first million, so sorta don't care totally and completely whether I make it by this (and other) book(s) or *that* (non-book) project.

Failure and misery on the other hand *is* depressing and not good, but since life is *conditional* this outcome now and then is possible and we have to learn *how* to deal with it. The best way to deal with failure is to make sure that when we do have successes that we *praise* ourselves for them. *Self-praise*, that is *pride*, is the *best* anti-depressant known to man. Which is to say, we *should* PRAISE the good in ourselves because more than likely we are going to need it and therefore we *should* also *praise* it in others because if we ever have to face *serious* failure we can look to those praise-worthy others as *evidence* that success is *possible*.

32. *Introspectively* we know whether or not we are happy and to what extent or degree. On *some* level of the consciousness continuum we "know" this even if we *claim* we don't. False claims about our actual happiness usually are the product of psychological repression, though not exclusively—they also can be the product of lying. But since it is *possible* to be repressed and not know it we have to be very careful— very, very careful—about concluding that we are lying if we say we are happy and it turns out we are not and/or we say we are unhappy and it turns out we are not. Lying means we know the truth and *choose* to tell ourselves and/or others the opposite or negated version *because our ego can't tolerate the truth*. Repression on the other hand means we don't know the truth but *pretend* we do and *assert* the pretense with a *simulated* confidence that we temporarily borrow from *authentic* certainty.

33. *Introspection* is good and is a learned skill and is as Ayn Rand defines it: *a process of cognition directed inward*.

34. For me, qua individual human being, there is *no higher moral authority* than the judgment of my own mind. The same is true of you, qua individual human being. So, if you say, "god or some such higher consciousness *other than your self* is your *moral* authority", you are exercising the judgment of your own mind whether you acknowledge it or not. And when *you* steal a pack of cigarettes (a purely personal example here from my own *childhood* and applying what I said in number 25 to my own eidetic "y‍o‍u") and say *the devil made "y‍o‍u" do it*, **I** can no longer do and say the same thing. If **I** steal a pack, I have to say: Gary Deering *did* it and it was a *wrong* thing to do and I *will* think about it and I *will* do better in my future actions. "Yu" now have—thanks to yor false gods and

devils—the *illusion of a moral sanction* to continue in yor bad behaviors but Gary Deering does not. So **I** wonder:

35. *Whose* moral code is better?

Or should that be, *which?*

* * *

Author's Note to next and final Chapter:

Chapter 24 was originally written as an *eBook* and sold online (Booklocker.com, 2000). Nine copies were sold and the book withdrawn by me for personal reasons. These have been rectified and the original modified and reproduced here as Chapter 24. It is interesting that this material seems to fit so perfectly here as the major component of this last and final Part (IV)—especially since it was among the first, chronologically, to be written.

Chapter 24 is a Case Study of one and is best used if read *sequentially* from start to finish for all 60 some pages (though skimming and scanning over as ***your own personal interest*** dictates is OK too). As a *Case Study* the names have been changed to protect the *innocent*, except that any resemblance between the invented name Joshua Deer and the author is not coincidental.

Also when the Chapter is re-read in the ways suggested in SECTION TWO of the Chapter—and each time you do it you will experience it as more and more helpful—it should also be done *in sequence*.

After about the 3rd or 4th read—with each being done *f a s t e r and f a s t e r and faster*—you probably will have exhausted all the benefit you can get out of the Chapter and will be ready to move on to something else.

You will have exhausted *all* of the benefit, that is, that you *personally* can get out of reading this kind of case study IF you pay *specific* attention to the *tone* of *your* internal voice. This "voice" (and its tone)—for better or for worse—is the voice of your *actual* Sense-of-Life. Granted, my writing as author has a tone—be it sarcastic or angry or humorous or joyous or happy or back 'n forth and so on and so forth, but as my writing has a tone—so does *your* reading. Therefore, for your personal benefit pay *special* attention to where my writing is toneless but your reading isn't or where yours is more emphatic or less emphatic than mine. An "emphasis" driven *perhaps* by such parental messages as:"…don't make mountains out of molehills" or the religious "corrected" version:"…do make molehills out of mountains ".

These "inner voices" are invaluable sources of *introspective* information for us and our goal is to observe and control "them" rather than be controlled by t.h.e.m. (pun intended).

In preparation for reading this last chapter AND during the reading of it I ask you to keep the 3 P's of BiO Spiritualism—*Philosophy, Psychology and the Personal*—firmly in mind:

Philosophy is white OR black, *Psychology* is white AND black, and spiritualism is the color of your *Personal* r̲ai̲n̲bo̲w̲.

Chapter 24: *When the Lexus smashes into the Olive Tree, then what?*

(How to GROW out of your problems and into your life. And protect and promote your own mental health in-the-process)

Joshua Deer [275]

Learn How to [({Think})]red

Thinking is the process of using YOUR mind, Joshua, to figure things out. *Things* are everything that exists, be they entities (including ourselves), attributes of, or relationships between and figure out means *identifying* the truth about these things. Truth means **making** our conclusions about them **match reality.** Reality is the text book of life; a text book that is like the teacher's copy: it has the answers in the back of the book. We just have to figure out how to compare its answers to our answers and *how to* adjust our answers as required to get ever more perfect matches. But before we do *any* adjusting we have to remember that it is a *two part book* and we have to know for absolute sure which part we are in—that is, we have to *learn* which part we are in and then take cognizance of it when we do the tweaking to *make* our answers match reality.

Learn How to [(*Feel*)]green

Feelings are the physiological part of emotions, Joshua, and emotions are automatic value calculations performed in the brain and experienced in the body outside of the brain which we can choose to express or not express to the outside

---

[275] See Author's note on previous page before reading this final Chapter. Also note that due to the excessive expense of printing colors in current (2/10/2005) *book* printing technology the color red in this chapter 24 which was intended to be used for "thinking" as a "thing" has been replaced with [({underlined word})], as has "feeling" as a green "thing" been replaced with [(*italicized word*)] and action/acting as a blue thing with [regular word]. When a single word has three or more letters colored—which produces a rainbow colored word when color coding is used—uses only the underline, *italics* and regular letter to communicate color. Any use of parenthesis alone without brackets and braces is just standard usage for parenthesis.

world. That is, we can choose to express them or not to express them if ... if we have not mistakenly convinced ourselves that we can bring our emotions into or out of existence by an act of will. We cannot. Emotions are. We have to think to figure out what they tell us about ourselves, Joshua, and we have to do it after, not before, but AFTER we have **experienced** them. Experienced emotions are like experimental test results. You (the scientist you, whether professional or amateur) would not think for one split-second that you could evaluate experimental results BEFORE you ran the experiment. Emotions, Joshua, are your own personal laboratory in that two part world of people and things and your place in it. Learn how to conduct your own experiments and interpret their results and if not yet, to eventually become adult enough to take responsibility for planning, developing and conducting your own research projects into the nature of YOUR life. That is, generate your own theories and/or use those of your favorite theoreticians, test them out in reality and look at the emotional responses of your results and then adjust your theories and re-test as required to get an ever increasing better match between yourself and reality. Man is a being of self made soul, Joshua, and like ALL things man-made that actually work in reality—they work BECAUSE man MADE them work—so too does man himself "work" in reality: because he makes himself work. How well, is the subject matter of individual lives. Man is a being of self made soul, which is to say, a being of self made efficacy and worth: made so by theorizing, testing, evaluating, re-testing, re-theorizing, re-evaluating and re-adjusting himself to be better and better—that is, happier and happier—as a consequence of every "test" *sequence*.

Learn How to [Act]blue

Acting is the means by which we sustain and own our material selves, experience ourselves as moral beings and discover new and improved ways to improve our mental and physical health so that we can live longer, healthier, happier lives. Which is our purpose for existing: to get *as much of* this *good* thing called happy life as *we* are *capable* of getting. That is, life *is* an end in itself.

Joshua DO IT

[({Think})]ᵣₑd

When someone says to you Joshua, "absence makes the heart grow fonder" [({think})]. [({Think})] if that's so, why do *they* also say, "out of sight out of mind"? Which is to say, look for the contradictory, you only need [({one})] contradiction to legitimately *invalidate* and reject wrong ideas. Even Einstein said this, "it takes only ONE negative experiment", he said, "to prove me wrong". You do need more than one *non-contradictory* piece of evidence, however, to [({validate})] correct ideas and [({prove})] yourself [({right})]. But these *more* are *possible* and are also the product of do-it thinking, that is Joshua, of do-it-YOURSELF-thinking.

[(*Feel*)]green

If you've ever been an emotionally [({repre})][ssed] guy (or gal) in group therapy you know that this is easier said then done. That is, when someone says to you, just do it: [tell] the group what you are [(*feeling*)] right now, and you panic at the thought and [({think})], but I don't [(*feel*)] a goddamn thing right now and I usually don't, except sometimes... sometimes I [(*feel*)] scared, like when it's going to be my turn to speak, hey, maybe I'm scared. That's it, just [do-it]: [(*I'm scared*)].

[Act]blue

[Act] doesn't mean like you are in the movies and they click the two wood pieces together and say "action" and then you proceed to [act out] according to a script written for you by others that you have voluntarily agreed to act out. Acting here means according to a script you've written yourself...for yourself... so to speak. After you've spent sometime [({thinking})] about yourself and your needs as a *rational* human being and after you've experienced yourself as a [(*feeling*)], emotionally self-accepting human being then it's time to be [act-out] assertive. For example Joshua, you've been a Minnesota (USA) nice guy for so long that it's beginning to not make sense anymore and to not make sense in an eerie sort of way and some California car rental agent tries to tell you AFTER your week is up and you are returning the car you've been using to get back and forth to your *first ever* group therapy intensive that the cost of the rental car is the *more* expensive of the two ways of calculating it and *not* the cheapest like "they" told you when you *started* the rent-now pay later agreement a week before. If this then... *allow* the pent-up anger loose from your center chest area and as you [(*feel*)] it unwind as if it were a Mark Twain depth-sounding rope with "nots" tied at equal intervals along its entire length with that whole length wrapped tautly around a gigantic fishing reel embedded in your chest [({<u>THINK</u>})]: *this guy hooked the wrong fish.* And then proceed to [act out] years worth of *unexpressed* anger by telling the agent in effect, no way hoe-zay, I'll pay the cheaper fucking rate as I was told a week ago, you ain't gonna pull this s... on me you m..... f....., who the f... ... et cetera, et cetera, et cetera and other "choice" phrases that the unreeling rope "nots" *will hook* and pull out of you if *you* just *allow* it to happen and don't get in the way. Then, when you get all done, don't light up a cigarette rather say to the other person who *tried* to take advantage of you: hey, don't take it personally.

And walk away. DO NOT FEEL GUILTY. [And notice] [({<u>how bright</u>})] the sunshine [(*seems*)] today... even if it is midnight and you've got less than one hour to catch the red eye flight back home to Minnesota.

Granted Joshua you probably will feel a little bit crazy and want to [conclude] that *if this is crazy I want crazy* but [({<u>THINK</u>})]: maybe NOT [(*feeling*)] YOUR emotions... NOT [experiencing] your emotions... NOT <u>b</u>eing your emotions...EVER.. is WHAT is crazy. *Your* emotions Joshua tell *you* what *you* Joshua actually think of life's events—for better or for worse—they reveal *your* actualness, an actualness that *you* must know before *you* can [do] anything about it.

[(*Felt*)] emotions are *data for the mind*, *expressed* emotions are *more* data for the mind.

Emotions "force" us to act *only after* we have denied them their "right to exist"...so to speak. Though the real *right* here is our right to have and express our own emotions as we see fit...and of course *to bear responsibility* for the consequences. Emotions have a compelling nature because that is one of their functions: to compel, to propel us into action to sustain our lives. Putting aside *for the moment* emotional responses *of the kind* we get to an oncoming MAC truck that is about to hit us head on, the compelling nature of emotions in the fully developed, rational, well integrated, *adult* human being is like that of a *loving parent*: they [(*po*)][i][(*nt*)] us in **a** direction, they do not push us unless we "need" pushing nor do they pull us unless we "need" pulling. The *uncontrollable* pushing and shoving and pulling and twisting comes about only because we've tried to deny that emotions exist and have a *proper* (identifiable) function in our life. But that function is *not* as a replacement for thinking. Emotions point and they at times point with a strong, assertive do-this-or-else sense. Sometimes we need to follow that sense and sometimes we don't. It's up to our [({reason})] to decide. If we decide, for example as you did Joshua, that our need to be guiltlessly self-assertive is *more important* than taking care of the feelings of others then it is our choice and we take responsibility for it. For example, we can even decide to run an experiment to *test* the (alleged psychology) assertion that says: "guilt subdues self assertion", by doing something like this. You are at work and a self proclaimed do-gooder comes around to get you to donate money out of your weekly pay check to the *United Way*™ because you *should*. You are *aware* that the bulk of your motivation *to donate* is driven by a desire *to avoid guilt* so you say **this** to the volunteer soliciting *your* money: **NO**. No, I am not contributing anything. When the volunteer stands there with a look that suggests he's auditioning for a role in the movie "Dumb and Dumber" and you notice the pressure welling up inside of you to [(feel)] guilty and along with it a desire to say, "oh, OK here I'll contribute ...", re<u>si</u>st it like the **plague** and [({know})] you will not die from guilt feelings alone. Then the next day ask yourself if you *now* have any *first hand* experience to validate the (alleged) psychological principle that says, "guilt subdues self-assertiveness". But hey, don't take my word for it, rather *[({<u>run your OWN experiments</u>})]*, [(*evaluate your OWN results*)], [*draw your OWN conclusions*] ... <u>a</u>nd <u>w</u>rite [your] <u>o</u>wn <u>t</u>est <u>rep</u>or<u>t</u>s.

But remember to [({<u>think</u>})] about each and every aspect, to [(*feel*)] what things do mean to you and to [act] so that <u>you</u> are the true <u>bene*fici*ary</u> of those actions.

For example, when "they" say, if god had wanted us (men) to [cry] he would have given us tear ducts, [({<u>THINK</u>})]: he did give us tear ducts.

Or when they say, if god had wanted us to get angry he'd given us the CAPACITY to BE ANGER, [({<u>THINK</u>})] (and notice): not to [get] *angry* but to [BE] anger. And whether you believe in god or not isn't the relevant point here: we humans have the [(*CAPACITY*)] to feel and whether it is a product of god's doing or nature's does not change the *fact* that you have the [(*capacity*)]. I don't [({<u>think</u>})] either god or nature is wasteful, you have many capacities, learn how to use each and every one of them to satisfy YOUR needs.

Of course Joshua, you and we have to know FIRST what those needs are. To discover [({that})] [read] [({this})]:

The Psychology of Self-Esteem, by Dr. Nathaniel Branden,

available at:

http://www.amazon.com/exec/obidos/ASIN/0840211090/ref=nosim/garysvennsvennan

and/or

this:

Atlas Shrugged, by Ayn Rand

available at:

http://www.amazon.com/exec/obidos/ASIN/0451191145/ref=nosim/garysvennsvennan

and/or

if you are looking to start exploring your *own* inner world and desire to get started for **$FREE$**, then peruse *Gary's Venns* at gdeering.com and use it as your own personal thinking-board device as you continue improving your own ability to be your own psychological mirror. Or (or rather, and/or) find and go to a therapist in your own area who is interested in *your* GROWTH and development towards becoming and being autonomous, objectively *selfish* man. Or—if you want and *can afford* the best then—click here:

http://www.nathanielbranden.net [276]

---

[276] Try not to get sucked into the "fights" between Professional Objectivism and Dr. Branden. They have a history that goes back half a century. Rather go to my web site and after you enter for **$FREE$** as GUEST click left on the **PSYCHOLOGY VENN**, then right on **Raise** and read my introductory remarks about their "differences". Take from them what YOU need to learn how to get and maintain authentic self-esteem and to be objectively selfish so that you can achieve and maintain a happy life. Since the selfishness philosophers are new to the "game" of taking responsibility for the moral development of the world—a task, for better or for worse, that has been handled by religion since time immemorial—they, the new guys, are necessarily going to be a bit skittish...wouldn't you be if such was your job? Granted, they are trying to get you (us) to take full and complete responsibility for our own moral growth and development but since they are doing it against a background of super entrenched altruism as a moral ideal they have to do a tremendous amount of persuading and in so doing they are saying they know what is best for mankind. Again, this is a tremendous responsibility to assume and so if they fight amongst themselves a little bit is anyone really surprised? I'm

Otherwise, to repeat, visit my web site and explore it for **$FREE$** as Guest. Click here:

>http://www.gdeering.com/

Then choose/click on *Gary's Venns.*

---

not, so I repeat: see my web site to help you PUT YOURSELF FIRST, even ahead of the "battles" between Objectivism and Biocentric.

Joshua BE IT

The Future

Of

[({<u>**Thinking**</u>})]

&

[(*Feeling*)]

&

[**A**cting]

Joshua

… but first…

About the Case Study's Participant:

Joshua Deer

Joshua's Ego
(i.e. that changeless
constant within)
AND Self Image

Joshua'
(i.e. the not
ageless whole)
AND Your Image

"Joshua" has a Masters Degree in Counseling Psychology from the College of St. Thomas, St. Paul, Minnesota, USA.

He also has a Bachelor of Science degree in Engineering from MIT (University of **M**innesota's **I**nstitute of **T**echnology) and he worked as a research scientist and test engineer for more than 20 years. He started this career in 1968 (see photo at left) as a test engineer working for the General Electric Company testing satellites and satellite components for the Apollo Space Program. He ended this career in 1990 after two decades of doing basic research on and designing, developing, building and bringing to market (for a multi-billion dollar Fortune 500 company that *allowed* itself to be bought out by an inferior member on the same list) a super advanced (for its day and age, though the hand typed-punch-carding was on the wall: numbered-days) *super charged, liquid cooled, dual sized* mainframe computer: one that was *expandable* to super-computer size. A thousand or more were eventually sold to customers throughout the world and generated a few billion dollars worth of revenue for the company. For the company Joshua had wanted to quit 10 years earlier but did not because he felt a sense of loyalty and responsibility to them. A sense of loyalty and responsibility that he managed to fully and completely discharge during his last ten years in their employ.

After that he got bored and quit.

Today, in addition to being a freelance writer and aspiring author, Joshua provides individual counseling/spiritual advice on line:

http://www.gdeering.com/

Prior to this he ran an in-office counseling service under the name STI (**S**elfishness **T**raining **I**nstitute) for the mildly neurotic who wanted something better out of life and who were *eager* to put in the time and effort to get it and who were—consequently—really fun, exciting, extremely hard working (psychology wise) people to work with. He inactivated this service after the State of Minnesota threatened to send him to jail for calling himself a "psychologist" in one of his newsletters when he wasn't *licensed* to do so (to call himself a psychologist that is, not to write a newsletter and mail it out to solicit customer-clients). Fortunately for Joshua—and I mean this here very seriously, *fortunately* for Joshua—he had received a medium sized—ultimately forgiven—loan from a rich relative (his now favorite brother-in-law and mini hero who lives in California) so he could drop his psychology interest and be the "money man" behind him and his—Real Estate sales, production home building experienced—second wife, Nicole, as they jointly decided *they* could become millionaires (yippee, Skippy!!) by starting and running their own General Contractor-Residential Home Building Construction Company.

The plan was for then Vice President of Marketing and Sales Nicole and her production partner Hank to leave the national builder they worked for and to run the new home building business and for Joshua to be—as he was more than *content* to be—the behind the scenes "money" man, 6 class-hours-trained accountant and all-about-town computer guru who would take care of all their company computer needs—be it software and/or hardware. **Mistake #1** was made right out of the chute, but they were too young and energetic to see...no, to believe it: Nicole had said we really need $500,000 *minimum* to do this right but Joshua said 'naw, this $150,000 loan of mine will be enough, *we can do it*, plus I have about twenty grand worth of life savings from my Engineering career that can be used *if necessary*. It was in the first part, of the last decade, of the last century, of the *second* millennium—i.e. 1990—that Joshua Deer began **Lesson #1** in learning the meaning of "naiveté". He was 45 years old. But he is and always has been a late bloomer.

As to the meaning of "if necessary", that came so f*!@%$g fast Joshua didn't even have time to learn it.

In the fall of the first year of the *third* millennium (i.e. last week) Joshua and second wife Nicole filed bankruptcy and their past 10 years reads like a soap opera.[277]

After quadrupling their business in three years and then doubling that a year latter, Hank—the Head of Production and co-owner partner along with Nicole—died of a vicious skin cancer *without* key man insurance but *with* a determination to beat it—two years prior it had gone into remission. A year before that, one of Hank's five sons—Ben—killed himself—*at* Hank's home, *using* Hank's 357 magnum revolver, master bedroom wing-back chair and one bullet. Joshua took the call at work from Hank's distraught wife and located Hank out in the field and told him to get home... immediately.

Because Joshua had an engineering background and had already been sucked into Customer Service [278] through a rash of roof leaks resulting from sub subcontractor work that was less than fine quality workmanship, **mistake #3** was being born during Hank's illness: ***Joshua started to assume responsibility for Production****—this ended here*:

---

[277] For Joshua it reads like a soap opera that is and this is another reason why names had to be changed. For "Hank" and his family I'm sure it is more like a *Greek Tragedy* but Joshua is not "qualified" to speak for their *evaluations of events*. Such is their **responsibility** and the matter-material of their own individual and collective selfish lives.

[278] This is another FIRST accomplishment for Mr. Joshua Deer. Because of his nepotistic-romantic relationship with his second wife Nicole—who is, remember, President -Owner of the Company—he "got" to be the Manager, the Leader, the Head of *Customer Service* and set up all the computer data bases and systems to deal with and keep the many many home-owner customers happy. That is, in the history of self advancement through male-female relationships Joshua (for anybody who has ever had to work in customer service can appreciate) is the first man on the planet to *sleep his way to the bottom*.

Gary = Joshua home from the quarry

After Hank died Joshua took some how-to-pass-the-exam cram courses and then took and passed the states *mandatory* testing and got the Builder's *License* (jesus, f*!@%$g ca-rist, *what* is the state going to *license* next?) that *permitted* the now 100% owned by his wife's building company to keep building. (I hate to deviate so far from the main thought here, but I better hurry up and write faster before the State requires *writers* to be licensed along with everybody else, and don't laugh UNLESS *you* can tell me by WHAT *principle* YOU or anybody else in this American culture of the year 2000 is going to stop "them" from eventually doing this...can you name it? I say you **cannot** because culturally no such principle exists today. For more on this see my upcoming book: *BiO Spiritualism. Body, Mind and Spirit - Man's Means, Nature's End.* That is, assuming I get *it* finished and distributed *before* the State requires mandatory testing and *licensing* of all writers. And *unlike* that contemporary wimp

American actor Bal-baby who threatens to leave the country every time one of *his* favorite *bureaucrats* doesn't do well in the polls, I *will* leave (a self promise *made* public so I can't evade it... well, so that it's *harder* to evade) if "they" [make] licensing of writers a mandatory requirement in America, USA.[279])

If serious physical illness has a psychological stress component and if not grieving is psychologically stressful then I'm surprised Hank lived as long as he did. As part of the watching-over-the-body process prior to the burial of his son—i.e., during the wake—they cremated Ben. On the day after the cremation Hank said to me, "...this morning they handed me my son in a box...". The ocean of tears—having been outlawed by Hank's generation of men—were invisible to the naked eye and like I said, Hank died a year later.

Whether or not a year after that can be considered **Mistake #4** for the *aspiring* millionaires is unknown—and somewhat "academic" because I believe the cliché is, "three strikes and you're out", is it not? In 1996—a mere 6 years after producing their first years worth of *six* homes and a mere year and a half after their peak *production* of nearly 70 homes per year they still thought they could pull it off and either save the company or at least get some of their life's savings and sweat equity back out of the business. (**Mistake #1A**—that is, the year the Feds said Joshua's accounting practices of trying to compensate for inadequate capitalization were invalid and the company owes the Government somewhere between 50 and a hundred thousand dollars—was discovered, fortunately, during the one and only time the company made a profit and during the third time in as many years that the company was audited by the government. Hence, the company was able to come up with enough money to pay off the Feds and "happily" it was "only" $71,000. And it's a *so what* and a *who cares*, who needs money *for growth* anyway, the government's "need" of a *surplus* is much much more important—that is, **Mistake #1A,** being a self generated off-shoot, sub-mistake won't even be counted as a deserving-of-its-own-number mistake.)

Joshua let his Builder license with the state of Minnesota (USA) expire this year (2000) and he decided to go back to pursuing his life time triplet twin treats of *philosophy-psychology, math-science* and *thinking-writing* with the new desire to become a published writer.

His experience with "growth" is considerable because—say some—he is *obsessed* with growth and the *reason* for this obsession—say those *same* some—

---

[279] Though I must admit it's a scary thought because, where would I go?

is because Joshua is and always has been physically short for his age: 55 years, 67 inches (height) . But to this Joshua can self-assuredly say: **nonsense,** and then just as assuredly add: he's obsessed with growth BECAUSE *stagnation is not an option*. The government bureaucrat-sheepherders **know** this and it is time—as far as Joshua is concerned—for the citizenry-sheep (which he *sometimes* counts himself among) to learn it too AND use it for their own SELFISH benefit.

Voila! *How to GROW yourself out of your problems and into your life.*

Number One thing is: [take] responsibility for yourself and develop a life affirming attitude and in those moments when life threatens to get you down, cry and rant and rave and kick and scream and grieve and do *whatever* it takes short of *physically* hurting yourself and/or others to get your pro-life attitude back and in full and completely functioning form. And THINK: reason is pro-life, *initiated* physical force—and let me repeat this, initiated, initiated, *initiated* physical force—is anti-rational-life, so how can the two go together? If *you* think they can, **you** <u>are</u> **wrong,** THINK AGAIN, and if you need help click here:

http://www.amazon.com/exec/obidos/ASIN/0672527251/ref=nosim/garysvennsvennan

and read p. 80 in Chapter 7: "Faith and Force: The Destroyers of the Modern World."

and/or

http://www.amazon.com/exec/obidos/ASIN/0453003699/ref=nosim/garysvennsvennan

and read p. 17 in Chapter 1: "The Objectivist Ethics"

and/or

for $FREE$ click and read:

http://www.gdeering.com/ . . . *Gary's Venns*

enter as **Guest**, click left: **un-published LTE's** then click right: **Killer Kids**

Tip #1: if you are the *kind of person* who has *problems to be solved* and your *first* impulse is to always give others the benefit of the doubt, then [change] it. *Start* by giving yourself the benefit of the doubt and then *Think* it in your thoughts... *Feel* it in your person... *Act* it out in the world (if you need to act it out in your mind first, that's okay). For example, when someone bumps into you DO NOT say "excuse me". Either [wait]... for the bumpor to say something apologetic or do this: [☹] ... or both and move on.

Tip #1A: if you are the kind of person who has problems to be solved and your first impulse is to never give others the benefit of the doubt, then [change] it. Start by *observing* your interactions with others and noticing your half of those relationships. For example, when *you* bump into someone else, say "excuse me". Then ask yourself, "why is this the first time in my life I made a correct observation about myself? Is this because I'm too self-centeredly aware or because I have not developed enough mental capacity to ALSO be *aware* of the world around me?". Then for now, accept your answer and *Think about it* in your thoughts... *Feel* it in your person... *Act* it out in the world (if you need to act it out in your mind first, that's okay) and do this: [☺] ... and move on.

Aside from this the rest of it is easy. Read on to discover the rest of the HOW TO's in the *How to do it* tradition of America—still the best country on the planet.

By now it is probably a cliché but if it isn't it for sure is an old saying in *Biocentric Psychology*: "There is nothing wrong with having problems, it's what *you* [do] about them where *right* or *wrong* enters in.".

Biocentric Psychology—though a very, very young science—has other cliché and truism possibilities languishing among its many volumes and words of wisdom. Consider:

- Emotions are not *right* or *wrong* because these concepts do not apply to emotions
- Guilt subdues self-assertiveness
- An unexamined emotion is like an unopened letter
- Reason and emotion are suppose to operate in harmony
- The mind leads and the emotions follow
- Emotions are not tools of cognition (this one belongs to the *Philosophy of Objectivism*) and it is a valid comment *about* emotions
- Faith worship, de facto, defaults to emotionalism as a tool of cognition: that is, *feels right <u>therefore</u> is right* is the *only* reality option

left to those who believe *faith* is superior to reason and who practice *what* they preach
- Emotions are not tools of cognition but then neither are they bananas (this one is *BiO Spiritualism's* - that is, mine) and is given to emphasize the importance—the life and death importance—of forming and making *proper* definitions which, to my knowledge, only the *Objectivists* know HOW TO do ... and How to teach it to the rest of us
- Emotions are a barometer of what's for us or against us
- Emotions are easily *definable* as 6 ideas comprised of 25 concepts and once *you* grasp the definition you
will be well on the road
to being able to [tell]
the
difference between
a [({thought})] and an [(*emotion*)] **inside your own being**.

This book will help you to that end and when you master the ability to do this you will be well on your way to *growing* out of any and all of your personal life problems—what some call *psychological problems*. (But which I can't because I do not have a *license* to call them that.)

And remember, there's nothing wrong with **having** problems it's what *you* [**do**] about them where *right* or *wrong* enters in.

If you choose to *evade* them, that's an example of **wrong.**

If you choose to *do* something about them in action, that's an example of **right.**

Another Biocentric cliché candidate is: "...everything you do counts...".

Everything.

Including letting the United States Government Bureaucrats define mental illness for you as being undefinable.

According to the United State's Surgeon General, mental illness is *not* definable but since "they" the government bureaucrats want to be treated as serious thinkers "they" will stoop to defining it. Their "definition" is this:

> Mental illness is the term that refers…to all diagnosable … health conditions that are … characterized by alterations in

thinking, mood, or behavior associated with distress and/or impaired functioning.[280]

According to *reality* the *proper* definition of mental illness is:

Mental illness is the sustained *impairment* of your human capacity for *unobstructed* cognitive contact with reality.[281]

Notice that the second—correct—definition does not say **how** the impairment is achieved and/or maintained. It could be "voluntarily" [done] by the individual (the most likely) or "involuntarily" achieved, either by another: e.g. some brutish person who uses actual physical force to control you or "involuntarily" by some force of nature, be it disease or car accident or some such accident rendering you incapable of *volitionally* exercising your capacity for cognitive contact with reality in an unobstructed fashion.

Unobstructed is not an either/or phenomenon but exists in degrees. Like consciousness itself, it exists on a *continuum*.

People usually know (I know I do sometimes) that they don't want to know more about their self problems and may want to *evade* them.

[Don't] do it.

People generally can find another, a significant other, who will help them maintain a *pseudo* self-esteem if they in turn do the same "favor" for their partner.

Don't do it.

Rather, THINK. *Authentic* self-esteem is good, *inauthentic* or what can be called *pseudo* self-esteem is bad.

If you value the *good*—the *life serving* good—and eschew the bad—the *life negating* bad—then *you* will be able to act so as to be the *beneficiary* of your own actions. This in and of itself is a *life serving good*.

To explore this issue to its fullest, click and read this:

---

[280] Department of Health and Human Services, *Mental Health: A Report of the Surgeon General* (Washington DC, U.S. Government Printing Office, 1999), p. 5.

[281] Derived from Nathaniel Branden, The Psychology of Self Esteem (New York, Nash Publishing, 1969), p.101, PB: Mental health is the unobstructed capacity for reality-bound cognitive functioning—and the exercise of this capacity. Mental illness is the sustained impairment of this capacity.

The Psychology of Self-Esteem, by Dr. Nathaniel Branden,

available at:

http://www.amazon.com/exec/obidos/ASIN/0840211090/ref=nosim/garysvennsvennan

and/or

to explore it part way for **$FREE$** click and read:

http://www.gdeering.com/ . . . *Gary's Venns*

enter as **Guest**, click left: **PSYCHOLOGY** then click right: **rAIsE**™

Briefly here: *authentic* self-esteem is only possible to the objectively selfish. Consequently, *pseudo* self-esteem, that is *inauthentic* self-esteem, *false* self-esteem, *phony* self-esteem is that *alleged* "self-esteem" that we attempt to "derive" from actions that do **not** contradict the view that says "helping others satisfy their needs is *more* important than helping yourself satisfy your needs and if you help others *ahead of yourself* you will be a good person and will have *authentic* self-esteem as a result". This last myth—behind the one where *adults* tell you that god is a real existent—can be considered the 2nd Biggest Lie.

THINK about it. And to *understand* what's at stake even deeper still, click and read this:

Atlas Shrugged, by Ayn Rand

available at:

http://www.amazon.com/exec/obidos/ASIN/0451191145/ref=nosim/garysvennsvennan

and/or

for **$FREE$** click and read:

http://www.gdeering.com/ . . . *Gary's Venns*

enter as **Guest**, click left: **PHILOSOPHY** then click right:

STI and follow the screen prompts.

Life is a problem to be solved and if *you* were god *what* would you do? Create humans and then give them a *consciousness* that is the very meaning of "problem solver" **or** give them a *consciousness* that distorts and obstructs reality?

THINK.

Your problems are simply that: problems. You have the worlds best *problem solving* "computer" right between your shoulders and it even includes your shoulders...and your feet and your legs and ... everything about you that IS you. ALL you have to do is LEARN How To...use it. For that click and read this:

http://www.amazon.com/exec/obidos/ASIN/0452010306/ref=nosim/garysvennsvennan

> (I have no for $FREE$ alternatives here other than perhaps check it = *Introduction to Objectivist Epistemology*, by Ayn Rand, out in the Library.)

Man, qua human being, is a self programmer.

Are you a human being?

All *philosophies*—including the primitive ones we call religions—are *programming languages* for the human "computer". This "computer" this "being" this "spirit" this **mind** consists of a brain AND a body. You are the programmer whether you like it or not. Nature does not give you another choice in this matter. You can be the active programmer of your own "computer" or the passive user of others programming. The choice is yours.

Remember, everything *you* [do] counts.

E̲v̲e̲r̲y̲t̲h̲i̲n̲g̲.

[Do] it right, y̲ou reap the rewards, [do] it wrong **you** suffer the consequences.

Such is nature's *justice*.

If you define *wrong to be right* and *right to be wrong* nature will not let you get away with it.

Neither will nature prevent you from *pretending* that *wrong* is *right* and *right* is *wrong* or whatever, who cares, who has to care, I sure don't.

For example, when you say to yourself, what'd 'ya mean contradictions don't exist, if a contradiction is something I hold in my brain or in my person as a clash between ideas then CONTRADICTIONS exist *because* they exist in me and your premise, that they don't exist is bull shit and false and voila, I don't have to listen to you anymore.

To which that other internalized voice will say, or can say if *you* have *developed* it enough (in *BiO Spiritualism* we call the <u>process</u> that we are engaged in here: going *way up* to come back down), it can and will say**:** **halt**. The *contradictions-do-not-exist* metaphysical primary means that when you discover a contradiction (including your [(*feelings*)] something *might not* be right) it is your [({<u>mind's</u>})] *evidence* that something is amiss, it could be *you*, or it could be *you*, these are really the only two "choices" available. It is NEVER reality, it can be our interpretation of reality to be sure but it is never reality per se: *reality is an absolute*. **But,** and this is a big but, **BUT** here is where that **two** part nature of our text book of reality comes in. Remember I said you had to know which part of the "book" you are in? This means we have to ask ourselves: are we in the *man-made* part of reality or the *metaphysical* part independent of the man-made? This distinction is *critical,* so critical in fact that you must (as in, you *should)* click here and read this to *fully* and *completely* understand the issue:

http://www.amazon.com/exec/obidos/ASIN/0672527251/ref=nosim/garysvennsvennan

p. 28, Chapter 3 :"The Metaphysical Versus the Man Made" by Ayn Rand

        and (not and/or but both\and):

http://www.amazon.com/exec/obidos/ASIN/0452010306/ref=nosim/garysvennsvennan

p. 88, *The Analytic-Synthetic Dichotomy* by Dr. Leonard Peikoff.

> (Again, I have no for **$FREE$** alternative here other than perhaps check them out in the Library.)

To continue our example here, in this case "your" assertion that *contradictions in your head are examples of contradictions that exist* is itself an example of an "apparent" contradiction or what in *BiO Spiritualism* we call: an "apparent" contradiction". That is, I don't yet have a name for it. For now we can use the colloquial term, *paradox.* The paradox **is** your [(*clue*)]. The "contradiction" HERE is *not* that you hold contradictory ideas BUT that*: you* [({<u>think</u>})] *you can* [do] *it with impunity.* **That's <u>the</u> contradiction.**

Now that *you've* identified the contradiction, the *real* contradiction, you can come back down (from the higher reaches of your *reasoning* and *abstracting* abilities).

You cannot hold contradictory ideas with impunity (no one can). And if you have everybody in the country telling you that you can, you still can't. If you refuse to take responsibility for the *proper* development of your own capacities, those capacities will not work to automatically give you a happy life independent of *your* contradictions. If you end up with a miserable life it will be your own fault (up to the limits set by the fact that it can't be 100% your own fault **Until and unless...** you live in a society that is 100% laissez-faire, free market capitalism[282]). As an American, since we are pretty free, your failure to achieve happiness is *more than likely* your own fault. This is more true today than it has ever been in the history of mankind. When human beings didn't know where their next meal was coming from, to think about the joys of living may have been more difficult than now. But now that we KNOW our next meal is coming from Capitalism and what a meal that is there is much less [({reason})] *to doubt* the *possibility* of human happiness. Of human happiness as being the purpose, goal and meaning of life and a very achievable goal at that ...today...in America. That is, the goal *to be happy* here in my one and only life. **This** is my purpose in life.

Granted, *I need* the right philosophy—*Objectivism*—to *guide* me.

Granted, I *need* the right psychology—*Biocentric*—to *help* me undo my past mistakes and to help keep me on the straight and wide.

Granted, I *need* the right ethics—*Objectivism*—to *guide* my choices, to help me answer the question: *How should **I** act?*

Granted, I *need* the right ... *sense* of life—*heroic benevolence*—to *motivate* me to climb the mountain of *growth* and achievement and to obtain authentic self-esteem and pride and to fall in like with...rea*s*on[283].

Rea*s*on—as the **TFA** ~~colored~~ color-simulated visual here suggests—is the *only* reliable source for a truly multi-colored all-for-one and one-for-all so*ci*ety.

---

[282] Unfortunately for us capitalism worshipers, the pseudo self-esteem builders—that is, those who want to institutionalize pseudo self-esteem—have a vested interest AGAINST a 100% laissez-faire capitalistic society. If you think this is an attempt by me to "politicize" pseudo self-esteem, then I will argue that you are not looking deep enough. You need to dig deeper into your own psyche and self-understanding. *For help* with this see the remaining pages of this book and the previous 23 Chapters.

[283] For definitions and discussions of the reason-faith problem click here: reason: p. 407; faith: p. 158: *The Ayn Rand Lexicon*, edited by Dr. Harry Binswanger and available at:: http://www.amazon.com/exec/obidos/ASIN/0452010519/ref=nosim/garysvennsvennan .

For example: if you *believe in god*, re*a*son "says" you are wrong, but re*a*son also "says" you have a *right to be wrong* and nobody but nobody has a right to *physically force* you to be right.

This is the *way* re*a*son works.

Contrast this with the way **faith** "works". If you do *not* believe in god, **faith** "says" *you* are wrong, but **faith** also "says" *we* have a right to beat you up until you agree with us and nobody but nobody has a right to stop us from beating you up: gods will be done.

So it's extremely important to [({THINK})].

As it is also important to experience our [(*FEELINGS*)].

And to [ACT] on our measured judgment.

[({THINK})] first.

YOU Learn It

Learn How to [({Think})]

Pick up any good book on the science of logic or click and read this: http://www.amazon.com/exec/obidos/ASIN/0070466491/ref=nosim/garysvennsvennan[284]

to discover that thinking is a learnable skill.

All you have to do is to learn HOW TO reason. That is, how to draw *valid* AND *true* conclusions and how NOT to succumb to all the deductive and inductive *fallacies*. But rather to learn HOW TO use the laws of deduction and induction to properly identify the **facts** of reality and use them for the betterment and survival of your own life.

Learning how to think properly is a life long joy and one place to start (if you haven't already) is with understanding the *hypothetical* statement. Then when someone says, "heez got his p's and q's all mixed up" you will know what they mean.

The hypothetical form is this:

>If p then q.

>e.g.

>If (p)I'm alive then (q)I'm breathing

>I'm not breathing—therefore—I'm not alive.

And your discomfort here—not your tiredness, if any, because that *can be* a sign of repression, but your discomfort, if some—with the last "conclusion" can serve as [(*evidence*)] to [({consider})] this further.[285]

---

[284] Dr. Leonard Peikoff, perhaps the world's best living philosopher as well as the preeminent Objectivist philosopher, recommends Engineers and/or "engineering mentalities" (of which I was one when I took his taped Logic course back in the '70's-'80's) that they do not allow themselves to get sucked into (my words) the symbolic language aspects of formal logic, rather focus on the *concepts* and *forms* and *fallacies*. This is excellent advice (in the referenced logic book = *Schaum's Outline Series: Logic*, this means you can and probably should ignore the material on *The Predicate Calculus*).

[285] What I mean here by using your feeling of discomfort as a lead, as evidence and motivation to look deeper is analogous to the sense of relying on your "ear" to determine grammatical construction when you write:

The *hypothetical* argument has four forms that can be evaluated for validity. As it turns out two of these are VALID FORMS and two aren't. The four are:

If p then q.
q
——therefore——
p   FORM 1

If p then q.
Not q
——therefore——
Not p   FORM 2

If p then q.
p
——therefore——
q   FORM 3

If p then q.
Not p
——therefore——
Not q   FORM 4

If we use a known-to-be-true statement to test these four forms we can easily conclude which ones are invalid reasoning forms.

If fire then oxygen.[286]

---

e.g., "Bob and me went to the store" ...doesn't "sound" right, "Bob and I went to the store" does because when I drop Bob and say, "I went to the store" that *is* right compared to "Me went to the store.". And obviously just as your "ear" isn't infallible, neither are your discomfiting feelings, that is why we say your feelings are clues—they point—and should be used as such; *ultimately* the truth is figured out by REASON.

[286] In my (earlier) copy of the referenced *Schaum's series Logic* book (copyright 1988, Chapter 3: "The Propositional Calculus", p. 40) the authors use this particular hypothetical as an example for saying that statements that are of the "p 'only if' q" *type* are the same as "p then q" *type*. That is: "There is fire *only if* there is oxygen" means "If there's fire then there's oxygen" or simply, *If fire, then oxygen*. I think a good way to use these really solidly true, easy to understand statements is as I have used it: *as a test* to check out a logical form to see if its form is valid. To me this is like having the answer in the back of the book, or what we "engineers" used to call (and I suppose they probably still do call it), *a sanity check* on the outcome of complex calculations or it's like the *reliability* that comes from counting on your fingers when doing addition or subtraction. *If fire then oxygen* is all you have to remember, then use it to determine if a particular form is valid, you don't have to memorize all the different forms.

Then with p = fire, q = oxygen we proceed to evaluate:

FORM 1:

If p then q.	If fire then oxygen
q	oxygen
——therefore——	——therefore——
p	fire

This is clearly not *always* the case so, voila, FORM 1 is invalid.

This means that (after you experience it leading to false conclusions for more than just this one case) FORM 1 is invalid ALWAYS without exception.

Consider next, FORM 2.

If p then q.	If fire then oxygen
Not q	Not oxygen
——therefore——	——therefore——
Not p	Not fire

This clearly is *always* the case so, voila, FORM 2 is valid.

This is the "form" of our first hypothetical also, lets test it.

If I'm alive, I'm breathing.	If p then q
I'm not breathing.	Not q
——therefore——	——therefore——
I'm not alive.	Not p

FORM 3

And voila! Example number 2 is also.... wait, halt!

This IS false, right now as I write this I can hold my breath for long enough to classify it as not breathing, yet I live!

Since the basic hypothetical—i.e., If I'm alive, I'm breathing—violates the known *truth* and can be demonstrated to NOT CONTRADICT known valid Logical Forms it must be false and/or improperly stated.

Here's Lesson #1: remember I said if you detect a contradiction you have two "choices"; either there is something wrong with you, or there is something wrong with you. Reality per se, is NEVER wrong. Since we can *observe* ourselves holding our breath and still be alive (reality) it is obvious that the "reasoning" is false. So what is wrong?

The answer is: precision, or more precisely: *im*precision.

The original hypothesis is to loosely stated and does not properly, precisely integrate the observable facts. It should be something more like this:

If I'm alive, then I'm not holding my breath for more than 115 minutes at a time.

Then, p = "I'm alive" and
  q = "I'm not holding my breath for more than 115 minutes"

and revisiting form 2 we have:

	I		I'm not holding my
If p then q.	**IF** am	**THEN**	breath for more
	alive		than 115 minutes

Not q   Not {I'm not holding my breath for more than 115 minutes}
               =I am NOT breathing for 116 minutes
——therefore—— ————therefore————————
Not p   Not alive

This clearly is *always* the case so, voila, FORM 2 is—still—valid. (And NOTICE, *valid* along with a *true reality matching* premise PRODUCES valid AND true CONCLUSION. You can count on it.)

Next Form 3.

If p then q.   If fire then oxygen
p   fire
——therefore—   ————therefore————
q   oxygen

This clearly is *always* the case so, voila, FORM 3 is valid.

And finally Form 4.

If p then q.   If fire then oxygen
 Not p   Not fire
——therefore—   ————therefore————
 Not q   Not oxygen

This clearly is NOT *always* the case so, voila, FORM 4 is **in**valid.

Studying and learning these and other logical *forms*—e.g., *either-or*, *either* he is alive *or* he is dead—is analogous to learning *basic* addition and subtraction and multiplication and division *facts* in arithmetic and math: you *need* them to be good at math. Similarly you *need* logical reasoning basics to be good at thinking. Once you make the basics part of your knowledge and understanding then you can deal with much more sophisticated "logic" just as you could deal with much more sophisticated "math", be it algebra or linear differential equations AFTER you had the "basics".

For example, if it is true that guilt subdues self assertiveness and I am not very assertive then *maybe* guilt—feelings of—have something to do with it.

IF (guilt subdues self-assertiveness) THEN (maybe I can become *more* assertive which is something I *value* if I [challenge] my feelings of guilt when they arise in everyday settings).

(As an aside here for those of you who are familiar with literal computer programming, notice the "nested" **if** statements in the foregoing: the explicit *and* implicit! Human reasoning we can grant **is** involved and complex but by the same token we have to grant that human's have the CAPACITY to deal with it. That capacity is: *consciousness.* Consciousness as a faculty and a power is the blessing and the curse. If mis-used BY YOU it's a curse, if properly used BY YOU, it's a blessing —blessing as in a *good for you* "gift" of nature. Or of your parents, depending on how fundamental you want to be.)

So the above *hypothetical* about guilt and self-assertiveness *could be* or *could not be* true. I say lets test it out a few times. OK, here comes Jack the do-gooder to get me to give away some of *my* money each and every week, month in and month out and ....

Test number 1 "worked". I felt so much pressure-to-act from guilty feelings over the threat of being evaluated as bad by my fellow humans for NOT contributing that I almost fainted. But I didn't contribute and to this day I still don't. And in those times when I do (e.g. sometimes I donate no longer useful to me household things to local charities) I am sure—beyond doubt sure—that I do it NOT from guilt but from I want to because I HATE wasting things and/or I want the tax deduction. Both, truly selfish benefits. (IF we lived in a truly 100% laissez-faire capitalistic system the tax deduction would not be there but the dis-value of wasting things would be.)

Test number 2 also worked as did tests number 3 through 101...that is, *today* it is *obvious* to me that *guilt subdues self assertiveness*. IF you doubt it I *challenge* you non-assertive types to run your own tests *in reality* and if during that time you run across those who tell you that you can *label* your guilt producing shoulds "musterbations" I invite you to STOP. THINK. First off, who says masturbation is bad (Christians do I believe) and secondly if you ACCEPT the bad connotation about "shoulds" by what means do you NOT eventually conclude: I should not have any shoulds? If you happen to be one of those who has already succumbed to their "reasoning" here, then my advice is "go up to come back down". "I *should* not have any *shoulds*?" is contradictory. **Contradictions do not exist**, *therefore* there is something wrong with this statement and/or those making it. (**Notice,** I did **not** say there is something wrong with you—unless you are the person making the statement—because this is that Part of that *reality text book* we call the *man-made*. The man-made, once made is real, but not *unchangeable* as is the law of gravity , which is the *metaphysical-unchangeable reality* part of the text book of us deciding to jump off the top of our ten story apartment building—a man-made choice—because we took drugs that made us feel we could fly...like a bird. We can't, that's a fact—a metaphysical fact—learned the hard way by some. Though, such *high flyers* probably died before they could actually *integrate* and learn their *test results* on "flying". 'Alls I can say here is thank that non-existent god I was an Aeronautical Engineering student during the 1960's where I *learned* the flying equation: $p_1v_1=p_2v_2$ that when applied to the *right* airfoil shape creates lift—a shape that does **not** include man's arms and/or body—... as well as I learned the *dangers* of ingesting *anything* that is *calculated* to *dull* your *consciousness.*[287] However, please note, my beer drinking escapades in or out of college—unbeknownst to me at the time—were "calculated" to "enhance" my consciousness via *un-blocking* my *obstructed* view of reality inculcated in me through my *religious* training (granted, I allowed it, but that's a different story). Though it "worked" at the time, in the long run learning *Objectivism* and *Biocentric* "worked" *better*. Now when I get drunk—which is "only" once a year on my Mexico vacations—it is usually to help me *evade* the fact that I'm NOT a good dancer and then I dance and have fun *in spite of myself.* (Thing I haven't been able to *figure out yet*, however, is *sometimes* I have a hangover and *sometimes* I don't. And yes, it is on my TTD list to sign up for and take dancing lessons.)

---

[287] It was to be some years before I would learn of the analogous dangers that accompany the "swallowing" of bad ideas.

So, what is wrong with "them" is easy to figure out here: "they" are sloppy thinkers; "they" do not care about *precision* and in fact "they" think precision is bad. At least bad when it comes to the need to THINK *precisely* and to form precise *concepts* (notice that the word itself is precise: it consists of a **p** first, not any *other* a-z letter, then an **r** second, not any *other* a-z letter, then an **e** third, not any *other* a-z letter, and so on... **c+i+s+e** which adds up to: **precise**. PRECISE is precise.)

You can be like "them"—imprecise—or you can be like me or if you are *more* precise than me then I can be like you or stay at my *own level of precision* because I'm a 101 years old and I'll probably only live to be a 109. That is, RELEVANCE is ALWAYS relevant and IRRELEVANCE is NEVER relevant. (This last is for those who erroneously say, NEVER say NEVER. Oops, for you sharpies out there who can *go way up* faster than I can I made a mistake, it should be: IRRELEVANCE is *never* RELEVANCE.)

You SHOULD have *shoulds*. *Shoulds* that is, that are FOR your life. That is, you *should* have principles—moral standards—that you live by and then *when* you *violate* one of them you SHOULD feel guilty. Guilt here has *survival value*: if you didn't feel guilty you would have no way of knowing that self-destruction was just up ahead around the next corner.[288]

Voila! Since I *should* feel guilty when I violate **a** standard I *do* feel guilty when I violate **a** standard, hence I better by god have standards that are indeed FOR life because if they are AGAINST life then my feelings, my emotions will not be able to save me. Will not because my emotions are dedicated to IMPLEMENTING the programming that I have established for my own human computer. That human "computer" that is, that is known as: me, myself and I.

But, *what if* I don't know HOW to experience WHAT life means TO ME?

Learn How to [(Feel)]

Feeling means *experiencing* your emotions *in your body*. Some of the alternatives to *feeling your emotions in your body* is to repress them, to intellectualize about them, to project them on to others and any other "creative" ways you can think of so as to NOT experience them (e.g., you are a man, rather

---

[288] This is so "neat" I can hardly stand it. Sometimes I "wished" there was a god so that I could thank him or her or it for "designing" us humans to be such fantastic creatures: don't you just love it?!?.

you are a male and in the presence of others—say watching a sad movie on TV—and you experience a *desire* to cry but you'd be embarrassed so instead you grab a hunk of flesh from the left side of your love handles and pinch it—hard—and it helps you to NOT cry).

So the process of learning how to feel, how to e-mote (e-mote.com?[289]), how to feel your feelings is just that: a process.

If you are an emotional repressor I think you should go into therapy with a professional therapist and work on de-repressing and feeling your feelings.[290]

Repression is a really big deal and I don't think man's knowledge has advanced far enough yet to allow him to un-learn repression without [action], that is by (just) [({thinking})] about it only without [doing] it and the best place to [do it] in the modern world is inside a therapist's office ...or beating up pillows in your own house with a tennis racket is okay too I suppose... or screaming and yelling in your car is okay, though this is dangerous or can be depending on how far back from the land of the repressed you have come and on what the population density is of the city in which you drive.

So **Tip #1** *here* is: To learn how to express your emotions, learn how to allow yourself to feel them first then as you are feeling them express them [in action] to those you are with. That is, BE your emotions. If you are angry, BE anger. If you are sad, BE sad. If you are fearful, BE afraid. If you are soft and loving, BE soft and loving.[291]

If you are noticing a lack of enthusiasm here on my part it is because emotions are the most difficult letter of the TFA How To advice I am writing about here. That is, the most difficult part for me.

But this being said, *difficult* does *not* mean impossible.

---

[289] Is the impulse-to-humor another "tool" for not feeling?
[290] Though this in and of itself is not enough, but rather a first step. If you need help with step 2 use me, click here and explore for **$FREE$**: http://www.gdeering.com/
[291] This "soft and loving" one can be the hardest to do BECAUSE sometimes or often times when you are in this mood you are overly accepting and tolerant of others opinions, even if those opinions are stupid. Stupid is NOT good. For example, based on what modern day philosophy knows, *altruism as an ethical ideal is bad for you*, really bad for you. Consequently, those who say it is *good for you* are stupid. And please notice: stupid—that is, possessing lots of "knowledge" that **is** false—is better than morally corrupt (choosing that which you know to be bad for you BECAUSE IT IS BAD). So the "trick" is to say to yourself, THINKING is thinking and FEELING is feeling and never shall their respective functions be interchanged. Never.

An emotion is the psychosomatic form in which man experiences his estimate of the beneficial or harmful relationship of some aspect of reality to himself. (Branden, *The Psychology of Self-Esteem*, Nash Publishing, New York, 1969, p. 69.)

Recasting this we get, emotions are the *psychosomatic* form in which we experience our estimate of the beneficial or harmful relationship of some aspect of reality to ourself.

And so for Joshua and *you* (and all of us) it becomes: *My* emotions are the *psychosomatic* form in which *I* experience *my* estimate of the beneficial or harmful relationship of some aspect of reality to *me myself and I*.

Both the word count = concept count = 25 (does, that is, for those who have achieved an owner's amount [see page 8] of integration for more than 12 hours out of every day and/or for more than 4,383 hours out of every year. If not, then *me, myself* and *I* are dissimilar enough for enough moments out of every day [or year] to count not as one but as 3 thing 2's) and the idea count = 6 are retained in each *re-cast* definition (in *BiO Spiritualism* we call this *re-casting* process: applying principles to you, yourself). And though it wouldn't necessarily be disastrous to use more or fewer words in the re-casts, it could be if you used more or fewer ideas. The six ideas are:

1. Does *psychosomatic* mean: *felt in the body, generated in the mind?*
2. Can an *emotion* be an emotion, *if and only if* it is psychosomatic?
3. Can Joshua's *estimate* be incorrect as well as correct? (That is, is Joshua fallible?)
4. Are there subjective *beneficials* and subjective *harmfuls* that are *not* objective and can Joshua's ideas about what is, is not *objective* be incorrect as well as correct? (That is, is Joshua *not* Omniscient?)
5. Does *some* aspect of reality mean *any* aspect? (Assume indifference is a legitimate intensity level, one equal for all practical purposes to zero.)
6. Does Joshua's view of *himself*—e.g. as a being like Socrates, that is a *mortal* being who can miscalculate: *assign* a zero to what *should* be a positive or negative value and/or vice versa—affect his emotions (or lack thereof)?

(Answers: If you answered yes to all of the above, you are correct. If not and/or you are interested in more, see the teleömeter in *BiO Spiritualism* Volume II—to be written.)[292]

For our purposes here it is just as well we use the Branden "poetic" definition of emotions: *emotions are your barometer of what's for you or against you and to what degree.*

As an ex-admirer of those good 'ole boys —'either yer fur me or yer agin me'—I can sink my teeth into this one.

Joshua's emotions are HIS barometer of what is FOR him or AGAINST him (as *he* sees it, including both his incorrect AND correct "sights") AND TO WHAT DEGREE.

---

[292] IF

(you are going to argue that there are really 7 ideas in the *emotions* definition, not 6 but 7—the 7th one being, "Does word-order have significance?"—and use as "proof" of your observation that in #3 and #4 of the 6 ideas, Joshua says *incorrect* first and *correct* second rather than the other way around—which 5 years ago would have been the case—and that this has revelatory power ABOUT Joshua)

THEN

(I will simply say that this—being an issue of *psycho-hermeneutics*—is way way, way beyond our scope right here and if you are interested in it see example of it in Chapter 17).

AND

I will also say, revisit ideas here (keyword, *complex*) on pages 89, 90 et al. and page 366, footnote 286 concerning the *complexity* of us humans and our ability to deal with it

(AND THEN I will ADD: *compare* this *human* complexity and *human* capacity to deal with it to that of a *literal* computer and then ask yourself this question: *On what f*!@%$g planet do those computer scientists live who think that literal computers are or can be more than human beings?).*

Planet Zero, I say.

The potential clichés surrounding this "poetry" are starting to well up inside of me (qua 20th Century American male groping for his dropped glasses on the floor of the 21st Century):

- "they" expect you to be a weather man without instruments
- "they" expect you to predict the weather without the use of instruments
- "they" say anger is bad
- "they" say hate is bad
- "they" say only cry-babies cry
- "they" say real men deny their emotions
- "they" say ... wait a minute, these aren't clichés born of the poetic definition but they do pose an interesting question:

Who's they?

IN THIS CASE I'd say "they" is me. I started to (re)learn HOW TO experience my emotions in my body and express them to the outside world on November 24th, 1974 but because of the nature of emotions: *they are **way too** personal*, I am **not** going to go into that here. Rather, if you are really interested then click and read the following:

http://www.gdeering.com/ click through *Gary's Venns*

to *The Joshua File* on the **PSYCHOLOGY VENN** and read it.

The best advice I can give on Learning *How to Feel* is that which I have given:

1. Read AND study Branden
2. go to your own therapist and work on expressing and experiencing or vice versa your own emotions and
3. DO IT on your own on a day-in and day-out basis.
4. EVERYDAY ... until you master it. After that you can be more selective in your "expressions".

Other psychological theoreticians have views of what they think emotions are but only Branden's properly integrates the facts of reality as to WHAT emotions really ARE.

Now that we KNOW HOW TO think and feel, next we have to:

Learn How to [Act]

How should I act?

For the *correct* answer, click and read:

http://www.amazon.com/exec/obidos/ASIN/0451163931/ref=nosim/garysvennsvennan
especially Chapter 1: "The Objectivist Ethics" by Ayn Rand.

[Acting] means self-assertion. To say, Learning HOW TO act is equivalent to saying, Learn HOW TO be self-assertive.

First prerequisite here is, be a self.

Secondly, *value* self-assertion.

Thirdly, value selfishness, objective selfishness or what some call rational egoism but be careful and make no mistake about it: rational egoism means selfishness. Do not allow yourself to *pretend* otherwise.

Then start by [doing].

LOOK for opportunities to be self-assertive.

But wait, halt.

First you have to know what is a self?

A self is that which acts AND thinks AND feels AND judges AND reflects on what he or she has done, thought, felt and judged.

Contrast this with the definition of "ego". Ego is that within us that thinks and feels and acts. It's not WHAT it thinks nor WHAT it feels nor WHAT acts it performs, it is—to repeat—THAT within that does the thinking, feeling acting.

Ego is capacity, *self* is capacity exercised.

Self is ego plus judgment summed into action.

Since the "self" subsumes the "ego" it is not possible to have an ego bigger than self because all attempts to do this end at the boundary of self, consequently ego can be as big as self, but to repeat not bigger.

According to *Biocentric Psychology*, ego is the subjective sense of self and self is ~~the extrospective integrated sense of self~~ ... ~~the integrated objective sense of ego~~

~~plus judgements~~ ... halt. I do not know how to "encapsulate", as in "nutshell" WHAT Biocentric Psychology thinks self is, other than to say I doubt it would disagree with Ayn Rand's "definition", which is as given on p. 441 of *The Ayn Rand Lexicon.*[i]

> A man's self is his mind—the faculty that perceives reality, forms judgments, chooses values.

IF all this is true THEN the human psyche is ____ by nature. At... ...halt. Stop.

{This ...*process*... is one of the reasons why I love that one *particular* set of *triplet twin treats* that I said I really liked—that is, of *thinking-writing*—because often times *during the process of writing* I discover new things for myself. Here I have discovered not only a new thing *for me* but quite *possibly—maybe—*a new thing for the **www** (*w*hole*w*ide*w*orld) or *at minimum* a *new way of looking* at something that could prove to be invaluable for my readers and clients. But before I can conclude this I have to spend some (considerable more) time thinking about it. Consequently, I plan to keep it under wraps until I've had enough time to think about it and develop it further and *then* I'll present it in some upcoming book.}

Granted, the self subsumes the ego but for the purposes of study and understanding, which is WHAT reflection requires, we can abstract an internal sense of self and call it ego and think of the WHOLE us as THE SELF.

If you've ever had a dream where you had a sense of someone looking over your shoulder at your life events then you have experienced *first hand* THE SELF as MONITOR-OBSERVER of your thoughts, feelings and actions.

If you've ever had that sense that you are being watched and you are not double-oh-seven then you have a first hand knowledge about THE SELF as contrasted with a corresponding first hand sense of "ego", or THAT which is being watched: watcher and watchee.[293]

In the end of course it's all *integrated* into one gigantic functioning whole and this whole is called... Joshua Deer himself, or John Doe his self, or Betty Doe herself or Your Name yourself.

---

[293] When my youngest daughter was about 6 years old she asked me, "what's ego?". We continued on our walk a couple of steps and I was at a complete and total loss until finally I said (with raised, loud voice): "WHAT are YOU asking me?!?, is something wrong with you, DON'T you know that!" There was a pause as she hung her head... and I said: "that" *inside of you now* that feels hurt and like crying ***is*** the ego. She, herself, burst into tears and said, "I get it".

Integration is the key word here.

Integration is good.

Strive for *integration* and *as you achieve it* you will be *growing* beyond your problems and into your life. Or depending on your own individual circumstances and as the case maybe: into "**a**" life.

You DO IT

[({Think})]

[({ Re-read this book and be-aware of your thoughts. ALL of them. The contrary ones, the affirming ones, the confusing ones, the ricochet ones—that is the ones where your mind veers off rather than think about what you are reading and the issues at hand.

Being aware of *your* self and *your* mind and thoughts is step one in thinking about the self and self's life. For example, as you practice the art of introspective monitoring ask yourself questions like: why did MY mind *choose* to think ...that...or this?

DO IT.

NOW.

(Or later today is okay too if you can't do it right now, but make sure it is *today*.)

PS

And as you do this, make sure you also notice WHAT it is you are doing. You are practicing *The Art of Self Awareness* and in-the-process *valuing* self-awareness as a psychological value and then striving to own it as your own personal virtue. As you develop this virtue take it with you into all parts of your life and notice the growth that accompanies its use. And I don't mean this in the abstract only but rather in its particulars, that is, WHEN you do experience something positive for yourself MAKE NOTE OF IT

and use it as a bridge to the next one and the next one and ... so on, to higher and higher ledges in pursuit of your own personal peaks. })]

[(*Feel*)]

[(Re-read this book and be-aware of your emotions. ALL of them. The contrary ones, the affirming ones, the confusing ones, the ricochet ones—that is the ones where your mind veers off rather than allowing you to feel what it is you actually do feel about what you are reading and the issues at hand.

Being aware of your self and your mind and your feelings is step two in thinking about the self and self's life. For example, as you practice the art of introspective monitoring ask yourself questions like: "am I feeling my emotions in my body or am I up in my head"? "Do I think that since all whims are emotions all emotions are whims and since whims are bad so too are emotions?"(that is, do I "automatically" think illogically, that is, in logically invalid forms?). And when you do make a distinction between this is a feeling and [({that})] is a thought, remember the feeling and [({the})] [({thought})] and leverage them to ever higher and higher and more and more such differentiations.

DO IT.

NOW.

(Or later today is okay too if you can't do it right now, but make sure it is today.)

PS
And as you do this, make sure you also notice WHAT it is you are doing. You are practicing The Art of Self Acceptance and in-the-process valuing self-acceptance as a psychological value and then striving to own it as your own personal virtue. As you develop this virtue take it with you into all parts of your life and notice the growth that accompanies its use. And I don't mean this in the abstract only but rather in its particulars, that is, WHEN you do

experience something positive for yourself MAKE NOTE OF IT and use it as a bridge to the next one and the next one and ... so on, to higher and higher ledges in pursuit of your own personal peaks.)]

[Act]

[Re-read this book and be-aware of your action tendencies. ALL of them. The contrary ones, the affirming ones, the confusing ones, the ricochet ones—that is the ones where *your* mind veers off rather than [({think})] about what you *are* reading and the issues at hand and then [(*feeling*)] their meaning *to* you and then you doing something about them.

Being aware of *your* self and *your* mind's chosen actions is step three in [({thinking})] about the self and self's life. For example, as you practice the art of introspective monitoring ask yourself questions like: "am I making action choices to avoid guilt or to seek joy and happiness"? "Do I define joy to be the *absence* of pain? Is joy and happiness forbidden to me BECAUSE of my chosen philosophy or is it—not only permissible but—the *goal* of my freely, volitionally chosen philosophy? If it is true that nature abhors a vacuum, does it follow that my *capacity* [(*to feel*)] will be filled with something and it might as well be *joy*...because if it isn't, *suffering* will fill the void? (Or worse: the void or as some call it, that hollow feeling in my chest or stomach or wherever in your body you experience THE VOID will collapse under cultural forces to be ... a zombie, an automaton, a non-thinker, a person who can produce "10,000 tons of coal" but not ONE measly ounce of true joy and happiness)?

If *the void* is in you contact your local therapist and start filling it today ... with joy and happiness.

DO IT.

NOW.

(Or later today is okay too if you can't do it right now, but make sure it is *today*.)

PS
And as you do this, make sure you also notice WHAT it is you are doing. You are practicing *The Art of Self Assertion* and in-the-process *valuing* self-assertion as a psychological value and then striving to own it as your own personal virtue. As you develop this virtue take it with you into all parts of your life and notice the growth that accompanies its use. And I don't mean this in the abstract only but rather in its particulars, that is, WHEN you do experience something positive for yourself MAKE NOTE OF IT and use it as a bridge to the next one and the next one and ... so on, to higher and higher ledges in pursuit of your own personal peaks.]

PPS
Take responsibility for yourself, USE your therapist don't end up saying "oh I went to therapy once and they didn't help me." If that is true, CHANGE therapists and go again...and again... and ... DO whatever it takes to have and live a happy life. This is your only ONE.

FPS
A*n*d *the*n *NOTICE tha*t a*s yo*u *d*o A*O*A (all of the above) you will be practicing and learning *T*he *A*r*t* *a*nd *V*i*rt*ue *o*f Se*l*f R*e*spo*n*s*i*bi*l*i*t*y.

You BE IT

The Future

Of

[({<u>**T**hinking</u>})]

&

[(*F*eeling)]

&

[**A**cting]

is...

...up to you.

With the existence of objectivism AND biocentric psychology no one in the USA...halt... restart.

With the EXISTENCE of *Objectivism* AND *Biocentric Psychology* AND the World Wide Web no one on the planet—save the statistically *few* who have *legitimate* birth defects and/or those who have suffered sad, unfortunate, *tragic* physical accidents and/or those born into totalitarian, dictatorial brutish countries—*but no one else* has a right to claim that the *tools*, the "technology" does not exist to help them successfully solve any and all psychological problems and to achieve and maintain forever their own mental health and well being. The BIG Three—*Objectivism, Biocentric Psychology*, the World Wide Web—EXIST, they are there to be used and your choice is to *use* them or to *reject* them by *not* using them.

Mental "illness" is not a new phenomenon discovered by modern day *bureaucrats*. Neither is mental health. And as *Biocentric Psychology* properly defines it :

> *Mental health is the unobstructed capacity for reality bound cognitive functioning and the exercise of this capacity. Mental illness is the sustained impairment of this capacity.* (Branden, *The Psychology of Self-Esteem*, Nash Publishing, 1969, p. 101, pbk.)

Since you are one of those who cannot claim they do not have, or had once but now due to forces beyond their control no longer have their "god given" (i.e. human nature given) *power of volition*, you cannot claim to have an "incurable" mental illness. The concept of an "incurable" mental illness—in this context—is a myth.

In this book I used myself ... as a "case study" and though I am 55 years of age and economically bankrupt I **am** (as in *I know what I know and I see what I see*) happier today than I was yesterday and I am *not* unhappy like I *was* 25 years ago.[294]

---

[294] For the proper definition of happiness click here: p. 198: *The Ayn Rand Lexicon*, edited by Dr. Harry Binswanger and available at::
http://www.amazon.com/exec/obidos/ASIN/0452010519/ref=nosim/garysvennsvennan
or to explore for **$FREE$** click here and read second post script (P.P.S) at the end of the STI Letter:
http://www.gdeering.com/ *Gary's Venns* enter for **$FREE$** as Guest, click left on the **PHILOSOPHY**

In an era before the Internet I used *Objectivism* and *Biocentric Psychology* (and some other "psycho-therapies" also) to help me solve *my* psychological problems—among which the most formidable one was, repression—and the only thing the Internet adds to the equation is that it makes *Objectivism* and *Biocentric Psychology* available not just to those fortunate Americans—who seem to get everything—but to the **W**hole **W**ide **W**orld.

As to the economic bankruptcy "dialogue" in my mind? I say this:

SM1.**Joshua.1**: "Well Mr. smarty pants, if you're so great why are you bankrupt?"
    Joshua.2: "Granted, I'm ECONOMICALLY bankrupt but it's like PeeWee Herman said—rather, *reversing* his suggestion and labeling it *the PeeWee Herman defense, we* can say**:** "that's what I am what are you, I'd rather be economically bankrupt than epistemologically corrupt."
    Joshua III: "We have got to go higher. TBC."
    Joshua II: "What does SM mean?"
    Joshua III: " I said, ToBeContinued."

VENN then right on the **STI VENN** and follow screen prompts to get to the end of STI "letter". Sorry, but if you don't know the answers to the three gate-keeper questions there you will have to figure them out yourself. When you get through all three you can then read to or scroll down to P.P.S.

Epilogue

Joshua II: "Still, I have one final question: *In a nutshell*, what does it mean to:

out of your problems?"

Joshua III: "OK, but this is it. It means:

G_{et}R_{eal}O_rW_{ilt}.

AFTERWORD

Objectivism for Christians:

Religious un-CONversion and other flip-flopping techniques for getting your psyche back in-line with reality *without* deep-sixing your mental health (or vice versa).

But first, here's my theory on evolution.

This "theory" is based on the observation of all those dead end branches you see in the evolutionist's evolutionary *tree* as they trace the development of modern man—the most complex of living organisms—from his humbler beginnings (roots) in the simpler life forms and/or in the *remaining* to be discovered [Reichian bions[i] notwithstanding] *transitional* inorganic-to-organic forms (pre-seeds, if such is really required).

Actually this theory is not "my" theory but rather one devised by Honk Honk LaRue.

He says that "they" (whoever they are, he said without really saying *who* they were) that *they* discovered a human like body buried at the end of each and every one of those dead-end branches.

Imagine, Honk Honk says, if you will that you are watching a Public Television documentary on evolution and they flash up on the screen a schematic of man's evolutionary Tree—replete with main trunk, roots and branches but no leaves. This schematic is like a white stick-tree on a black background but with fat multiple branches that fan out from the main fatter trunk. The main trunk connects modern man at the top to the primordial seed at the bottom, beneath the roots of the simple celled bacterium et al. organisms. Then envision, Honk Honk says, that at the end of many of the outcropping branches where they dead end there is an outline of a dead-ended humanoid (an outline not unlike a homicide investigators chalk outline of a dead body on a street or sidewalk).

Well says LaRue what happened was a group of enterprising archeologists found those chalked outlines drawn on the floor in some remote, ancient cave in France and they excavated beneath them and discovered the corpses of the dead-enders. Then they took these mummified corpses into the lab and did a modern day forensic analysis on them. And by forensic Honk Honk says he means as full and as complete a forensic analysis that modern day science can perform: from a Quantum analysis of the mummified blood-to-DNA analysis of hair follicles-to-a Quantum Bio-Physics analysis of the micro meat slices of each mummified brain of each mummified corpse.

After comparing *all* the results from *all* the dead-enders to results from many many autopsies of modern day men and women they discovered *one and only one* difference between them and so, says Honk Honk, *it* has to be the reason those other humanoids dead ended (evolutionarily speaking wise) and we didn't.

Well, what is the *it* I asked?

Oh, says Honk Honk, those dead-ender other guys didn't have, a *sense* of humor.

Does this mean, I asked, that this *is* our 6th sense and so somewhere in our brain we have a humor ball?

The End

Afterword

Oops. What about Christians for Objectivism?

They had better hurry up and make the final unCONversions in their own souls before it's too late.

Too late for what?

For the political system known as <u>Militant Islam</u> to defeat (<u>read, kill</u>) the political system known as 100% laissez-faire capitalism and in the process thrust the entire planet—and not just a continent or two *this* time, but the entire planet earth—backwards into another dark ages.

And when the entire human race is being forced by brutes to worship the primitive—as in worship it or die—who will survive long enough to emerge as a savior?

Since there wasn't a first Jesus—a Jesus qua *son* of (non-existent) god(s) that is—how can there be a second?

Unless, maybe, perhaps, unless ... *if you think about it* ... *maybe* the question for my next book should be:

Is Ayn Rand God's second son?

As *sequel* to this book, you of course already know the *correct* answer (on *three* counts). But what you don't know yet is: how do you prove it?[295]

---

[295] That is, how do you prove that the sequel to *Yes* is *No* and not *Yes 2*?

REFERENCES
(some with notes and elaborations)

Part I

[i] Branden, Barbara. *Language and Definitions*. Lecture delivered by author. Guilford, CT: Jeffrey Norton Publishers, Inc., 1967, 1986. Audio-Forum Audiocassette #707.

Chapter 1

[i] Woolf, Henry Bosley, Editor-in-Chief, and others. *Webster's New Collegiate Dictionary.* Springfield: G. & C. Merriam Company, 1976. All references herein to 'dictionary definition' or 'the dictionary' or 'my dictionary' refer to this dictionary.

[ii] Rand, Ayn. "THIS IS JOHN GALT SPEAKING", Part III, Chapter VII in *Atlas Shrugged.* New York: Random House, 1957, page 1022, (hc).

[iii] *The Ayn Rand Lexicon: Objectivism from A to Z.* Edited by Harry Binswanger. New York: New American Library, 1986, start with the letter *H* on page 198 (soft cover edition) which starts with the word *Happiness*.

Chapter 2

[i] Rand, Ayn. *Atlas Shrugged.* New York: Random House, 1957, page 731, (hc).

[ii] Rand, Ayn. *The Virtue of Selfishness*. New York: New American Library, 1961-1964, p. 13.

[iii] The source of this "second" part: *and/or earlier formed sensory based integrations*; of the definition of reason—**Reason** is the faculty that identifies and integrates the material provided by man's senses and/or earlier formed sensory based integrations—is either Dr. Branden or Dr. Peikoff (I think). I've been unable to find it so as to formally document it (I think it is in one of Dr. Peikoff's taped lectures from the '70's but I'm not certain). The point (to me and "us" as aspiring "BiO Spiritualists") is that this second part is/has been/is an important part of dealing with reason because we don't usually deal with reason as a thing until long after we already have within us a large amount of conceptual-

ideational-conceptual "material". (And so this second part is especially helpful when debating with reason's enemies within & without. That is, when debating with the Professional and/or Neo-Professional Christians and their eidetic counterparts as "they" are expert at stealing concepts, dropping context, mixing issues and a whole host of other epistemological sins against the ego—which ultimately is against the self.)

Also this affords me the opportunity to apologize for my appalling lack of an anti-laziness attitude in the realm of "research" and documenting **all** the "things" I've learned from others. It's just that sometimes it's such a boring thing to do that I just can't do it so I end up doing it the best I can which is-s/b*-is ok since Objectivism is really not an *invention* as much as it is a *discovery* of the *facts of reality* and as such the *ultimate* "documentation" is *reality it self*.

    * s/b is shorthand for *should be*

[iv] Branden, Nathaniel. *The Psychology of Self-Esteem*. Toronto: Bantam Books, Inc., by arrangement with Nash Publishing Corporation, 1969, paperback, 239.

[v] ibid.

Chapter 4

[i] Chopra, Deepak. *The Seven Spiritual Laws of Success*. San Rafael, CA: Amber-Allen and New World Library, 1994.

Chapter 5

[i] Woolf, Henry Bosley, Editor-in-Chief, and others. *Webster's New Collegiate Dictionary*. Springfield: G. & C. Merriam Company, 1976.

[ii] Chopra, Deepak. *The Seven Spiritual Laws of Success*. San Rafael, CA: Amber-Allen and New World Library, 1994.

[iii] Zukav, Gary. *Soul Stories*. New York: Simon & Schuster, 2000, 15-16.

[iv] This is from a Q & A in some Objectivist publication from the 70's or 80's. I can't find which one it is right now so I have to use/rely/default to the fashion of endnote i and vi in Chapter 20 and let it be as a documentation loose end to be tied up eventually (by me, in some future publication of mine). Assuming I have

a future and don't die prematurely, that is, before my 109th birthday (which as of today's—2/20/06—second-half-of-my-life writing leaves me 49 years to so tie).

[v] Branden, Nathaniel. *The Psychology of Self-Esteem.* Toronto: Bantam Books, Inc., by arrangement with Nash Publishing Corporation, 1969, paperback, 3-4.

[vi] Samenow, Stanton E. *Inside the Criminal Mind.* New York: Times Books division of Random House, 1984.

[vii] Dino De Laurentiis Presents, 1975. *3 Days of the Condor.* 118 min. Hollywood, CA: Paramount Pictures, 1991, videocassette.

Chapter 6

[i] Rand, Ayn. "THIS IS JOHN GALT SPEAKING", Part III, Chapter VII in *Atlas Shrugged.* New York: Random House, 1957, page 1022, (hc).

[ii] Branden, Nathaniel. *The Psychology of Self-Esteem.* Toronto: Bantam Books, Inc., by arrangement with Nash Publishing Corporation, 1969, paperback, 99.

[iii] Rand, Ayn. "The Psycho-Epistemology of Art", Chapter 1 in *The Romantic Manifesto: A Philosophy of Literature.* New York: Signet, 1975, 18.

Note: Dr. Branden's formal definition of Psycho-epistemology dates to 1969 and the Ayn Rand one to 1975. However, according to *The Ayn Rand Lexicon* page 392 (see reference i here in Chapter 20) this Ayn Rand formal "definition of Psycho-Epistemology" was in the 1969 edition of *The Romantic Manifesto.* Since it wasn't in the earlier article—"Check Your Premises/The Psycho-Epistemology of Art" in *The Objectivist Newsletter*, Volume 4, Number 4, April 1965 the 1969 date will serve as the earliest date I could find. And even though this isn't a big deal to me, it's a little deal because I use it on my website in a gatekeeper question readers need to get through in order to continue on in the website. Since today is March 13, 2006 and that website gatekeeper question was generated last century I wanted to use this opportunity to discuss it a little bit more (but to repeat, its not that big 'ah deal so this is all I'm going to say about it here and now.)

Chapter 7

[i] These are taken from pp. 221 through 232 of xyz (see reference vi Chapter 20– this is like that, I lost two not-properly-backed-up hard drives during the writing

of this book and this reference was on one of them and I can't remember it and I can't find it right now but hope to in the future, so for now the best I can do is): In order, they are quotes from: Alexander Solzhenitsyn, Chinese proverb, Kim Hubbard, James Oppenheim, Frater Achad, Epictetus, Helen Keller, Joseph Addison, Elinor MacDonald, Mme. De La Fayette, John S. Mill, Gerald Jampolsky, Andrew Carnegie, Charles Montesquieu.

[ii] Rand, Ayn. "THIS IS JOHN GALT SPEAKING", Part III, Chapter VII in *Atlas Shrugged*. New York: Random House, 1957, page 1022, (hc).

Chapter 8

[i] Wehr, M. Russell, and James A. Richards, Jr. *Physics of the Atom.* Reading, Massachusetts: Addison-Wesley Publishing Company, Inc., 1960, 133 – 131.

Chapter 10

[i] Shermer, Michael. "The Shamans of Scientism." *Scientific American*, June 2002, 35.

Chapter 11

[i] Rand, Ayn. *We the Living.* New York: Signet/New American Library, 1959, authorized paperback reprint of Random House, Inc. hardcover, 1936.

[ii] Rand, Ayn. *The Fountainhead.* New York: The Bobbs-Merrill Company, 1943.

[iii] Rand, Ayn. *Atlas Shrugged.* New York: Random House, 1957.

[iv] Rand, Ayn. "Faith and Force: The Destroyers of the Modern World", Chapter 7 in *Philosophy: Who Needs It.* New York: The Bobbs-Merrill Company, Inc, 1982.

[v] Rand, Ayn. *For the new Intellectual.* New York: Signet Books (Ninth Printing is an authorized reprint of a hardcover edition published by Random House, Inc.) published by The New American Library, Inc., 1961, page 14.

[vi] http://www.thedenverchannel.com/news/4151804/detail.html
TheDenverChannel.com
"Some People Push Back:" On the Justice of Roosting Chickens
Essay By Ward Churchill . N.p., n.d.

This POSTED ONLINE Article was read and "digested" by me on 3/15/2005, that is, here is what this "essay" means (to a BiO Spiritualist).

Since *he* (Professor Ward Churchill) is saying in this essay that a country's *adult* citizens (such as, for example in this essay, he says of the American citizens in New York's Twin Towers on the morning of September 11th, 2001) are (were) legitimate *military* **targets***, he is saying that we American's would be *justified* in killing absolutely every *adult* person in the Middle East *because* they are all *adult* citizens of the Middle East that *invaded* and *attacked* us on September 11th, 2001. (The homogeneity of the Islam religion in the Middle East and its conscious, moral, *actual*, de facto influence on its politics makes the borders of its "individual" countries artificial and tactical.) Or, if this is extrapolating Professor Churchill's *hypothesis* too far then *in the least* he is saying we would be justified in killing every *adult* citizen in Saudi Arabia. Since the *Philosophy of Objectivism* has identified *and* made us aware of the philosophical *principle* that says: *morality stops at the point of a gun*, this Churchill guy cannot/**must not** be listened too. There *is* such a thing as *helpless* victims among adults and *some*—probably *most*—adult citizens in *dictatorships* come under this heading.

Since dictatorships are the cause of war$^{☺o}$, if there were no dictatorships there would be no wars.

Many countries on Planet Earth today *are* dictatorships but the United States of America is *not* one of them.

So to argue as University of Colorado's "ethics" Professor Ward Churchill does that dictatorships (such as those of the Middle East) are justified in *initiating* force against non-dictatorships just-as-much-as non-dictatorships are justified in *retaliating* and self-defending is to prove finally, formally and once-and-for-all that the *Public* School System in the United States of America *has to* be replaced—from *top* to bottom—with a *Private* system.

Those who *advocate* otherwise are (potentially) as thuggy as thugs get and as such will only succeed in the future in producing more thugs and eventually the *ultimate* thug. *The ultimate thug is an Attila-Witchdoctor fused into one.* (And though it is true that in the race to produce these t.h.e.m the Islamic Middle East has won hands down, it doesn't mean that aspiring BM's elsewhere on the planet will stop in t.h.e.i.r endeavors to create their own versions of ultimate thugs.)

But to repeat, *The ultimate thug is an Attila-Witchdoctor fused into one.* One body and soul that is, but one with *two* mouths—one mouth *dedicated* to *forcibly* confiscating the time and money of a Country's *individuals* and the other mouth dedicated to *justifying* the confiscation. {Or is this the "definition" of a BM? Now this *is* getting confusing: as archetypes, what are the boundaries between the Attila, Witchdoctors and BM's? Are there boundaries? When I was a Christian (or at least a Christian sympathizer) The Church took it as a matter of pride (the hypocrite types did that is, even though it was implicit pride, they still took it as a matter of pride) that The Church was "above" (any country's) Politics. Now (as an a-theist sympathizer) whenever I get the sense (from Talk-Radio et al. Mass Media/"Banner" instrument-tools)[**] that The Church is *thinking of dropping this tradition* it is indeed a scary iObservation/thought and my warning in footnote 99 on page 105 gets (or *should* get) another red-flag.}

---

[*] This being the case, it would be logical to conclude that Professor Churchill would see those adult citizens of other countries who were *also* killed in the WTC by the Middle East attack, he would see them as: collateral damage.

[**] For "Banner" reference see *Newspaper-By-Same-Name* in Ayn Rand novel given in Reference ii above.

[vii] Steiner, Andy. "CLA scholars unlocked: The life of a public intellectual". In *CLA Today*, Volume 3, Number 2, Published by the University of Minnesota, College of Liberal Arts, Minneapolis, MN, Spring 2000, 4.

Later note: I discovered *The Public Intellectual* with his/her commitment *and* devotion to "the public good" via the reference cited—that is, I discovered "t,h,e,m" in the year 2000. Today (7/6/2005)—that is, the month I plan to finally, formally submit my manuscript to be published—I did a Google on "Public Intellectual" and got more than 48 million hits !?!?!?!?!? So much for my earlier thoughts that I was on to something unique. So allow me here to summarize my position that I will (maybe) explore in Book 2. That position is this: The Public Intellectual as a thing (2) separate from the Professional Intellectual will emerge in this the new, 3rd Millennium World as a new, "Born Again" Public Intellectual and as such will spear-head a new attack on individualism—only this time it will be an orchestrated, *Global* Attach. Oops ... slip or slop? To be explored in more detail (maybe) in Volume II.

And as such—in some sense—Life does go on. But as individuals who live and breathe NOW we *can* and *will* and *must* do battle with the BM and his cohorts—regardless of what they name themselves, and/or *rename* themselves as the case usually is. (For one example of the latter, see the *Creationists* redefining/renaming themselves as/the "Intelligent Design Advocates".)

[viii] Rand, Ayn. *For the new Intellectual*. New York: Signet Books (Ninth Printing is an authorized reprint of a hardcover edition published by Random House, Inc.) published by The New American Library, Inc., 1961, page 32.

[ix] Usha Lee McFarling (Los Angeles Times), "Forever Freud", *St. Paul Pioneer Press*, 17 May 2000.

[x] Merto-Goldwyn-Mayer ; George Pal production ; directed by George Pal ; screenplay by David Duncan. *The Time Machine*. 151 min. Burbank, CA : Turner Entertainment : Warner Home Video, 2001, videocassette release of the 1960 motion picture.

Chapter 12

[i] Lions Gate Films presents a View Askew production, *Dogma*. 128 min. Culver City, CA : Columbia TriStar Home Video, 2000, videocassette. Originally released as motion picture in 1999 starring Ben Affleck and Matt Damon; writer & director Kevin Smith; producer Scott Mosier.

[ii] Universal Pictures & Beacon Pictures presents, *End of days*. 123 min. Universal City, CA : Universal, 2000, videocassette. Originally released as a motion picture in 1999 starring Arnold Schwarzenegger; produced by Armyan Bernstein, Bill Borden; written by Andrew W. Marlowe; directed by Peter Hyams.

[iii] Branden, Nathaniel. *The Psychology of Self-Esteem*. Toronto: Bantam Books, Inc., by arrangement with Nash Publishing Corporation, 1969, paperback, 202.

Chapter 14

[i] Woolf, Henry Bosley, Editor-in-Chief, and others. *Webster's New Collegiate Dictionary*. Springfield: G. & C. Merriam Company, 1976.

Chapter 15

[i] Budget of The United States Government, FY 2000, Appendix. OnLine: http://www.gpoaccess.gov/usbudget/index.html . FY 2000/ Department of Health and Human Services, except Social Security ... hhs.pdf.

Note: NIMH and SAMSA directly are budgeted over $3 billion in this Fiscal Year 2000 budget and by the time you add in all the possible parts from all the National Institutes of This (e.g. Alcohol Abuse and Alcoholism) 'n That (Drug Abuse) et al as well as for other non-directly related things but important to the business of Mental Health nonetheless, e.g., Buildings and Facilities, the $5 billion estimate for "all things" Mental Health is probably low.

[ii] Department of Health and Human Services, *Mental Health: A Report of the Surgeon General* (Washington DC, U.S. Government Printing Office, 1999), 5.

[iii] Locke, Edwin A, *Is Contemporary Psychology an enemy of the People?*, © 1998 Edwin A. Locke, audiocassette (P) 1999 Second Renaissance Books.

[iv] ibid.

[v] ibid., p. 4.

[vi] Three references:

(a) *1984*. Orwell, George, Originally published: *Nineteen eighty-four*, 1949. San Diego : Harcourt Brace Jovanovich, [1984], 1977.

(b) *Anthem*. Rand, Ayn, Originally published: New York : Dutton, 1995. New York : Plume, 50th Anniversary edition, 1999. Also includes a facsimile of the original English ed., published in 1938, with Rand's editorial changes for the American ed. in her own hand.

(c) *Fahrenheit 451*. Bradbury, Ray, 1953. New York: Ballantine Books, 43rd Printing August 1976.

[vii] Branden, Nathaniel. *The Psychology of Self-Esteem*. Toronto: Bantam Books, Inc., by arrangement with Nash Publishing Corporation, 1969, paperback, 101.

[viii] I just (4/1/5) relistened to this tape and "discovered" that my recall of this tape's content from a couple of decades back when I first listened to it wasn't exactly perfect: Ms. Branden talked about 5 *rules* of definitions which it just so

happens translates into the 8 *criteria* we've been using here. I still like thinking about definitions in terms of the 8 criteria so we will continue to use these for now.

For formal reference here see Part I, i.

Chapter 16

[i] Solso, Robert L., editor. *Mind and Brain Sciences in the 21st Century.* Cambridge: The MIT Press, 1999 pbk.

[ii] Gardner, Howard. *The Mind's New Science. A History of the Cognitive Revolution.* With a new epilogue by the author: "Cognitive Science After 1984." Basic Books, A *Division of* Harper Collins *Publishers*, 1985, 1987, 366.

[iii] Solso, Robert L., editor. *Mind and Brain Sciences in the 21st Century.* Cambridge: The MIT Press, 1999 pbk., 325-339.

[iv] Warner Bros. Presents, *Contact*. 150 min. Burbank, CA: Warner Home Video, 1997, videocassette. Based on the novel by Carl Sagan.

[v] Thompson, Richard F. Chapter 3: "Will the Mind Become the Brain in the 21st Century?", 39. In *Mind and Brain Sciences in the 21st Century*, edited by Robert L. Solso. Cambridge: The MIT Press, 1999 pbk.

[vi] ibid., 40.

[vii] ibid.

[viii] Rand, Ayn. *Introduction to Objectivist Epistemology.* New York: New American Library, 1966. Chapter 1 and p.31 **range** as standard of measurement for differentiating one type of consciousness from another and p.41, **scope** as means of more precisely measuring some psychological phenomenon.

> **Note For Me For Book2:** *Range* and *scope* as Ayn Rand uses these terms are to philosophy (and ultimately to psy*ch*hology) what [length, mass, time and temperature] = means of differentiating (say, atoms from basketballs) ... and [rulers/yardsticks/metersticks/wavelengths of light; weighing machines/scales/balances; stopwatches/metronomes/atomic clocks; and thermometers/thermocouples] = means of *more precisely* measuring (say, the millionths or billionths of a meter for atom

diameters vs. the many inches for diameters of basketballs) ... are to the natural sciences/physics/chemistry/etc (and ultimately, Engineers who use/*apply* these sciences).

So that in anticipation of a direction in which we might head and include in book 2, consider the following question and its (unsupported) answer (for now):
What is the distance—inside consciousness—between a <u>state</u> of repression and its corresponding or related <u>un-repressed</u> state?
Ans: 864,000 clicks.
(For some more on this until and unless book 2 is written, refer to footnote number 195 herein.)

[ix] Branden, Nathaniel. *The Psychology of Self-Esteem*. Toronto: Bantam Books, Inc., by arrangement with Nash Publishing Corporation, 1969, paperback, 31.

[x] Thompson, Richard F. Chapter 3: "Will the Mind Become the Brain in the 21st Century?", 40. In *Mind and Brain Sciences in the 21st Century*, edited by Robert L. Solso. Cambridge: The MIT Press, 1999 pbk..

[xi] ibid.

[xii] Rand, Ayn. *Philosophy: Who Needs It*. New York: The Bobbs-Merrill Company, Inc., 1982, 3.

[xiii] Peikoff, Leonard. *The Ominous Parallels. End of Freedom in America*. New York: Stein and Day, 1982, 14.

[xiv] Branden, Nathaniel. *The Psychology of Self-Esteem*. Toronto: Bantam Books, Inc., by arrangement with Nash Publishing Corporation, 1969, paperback, 36,37.

[xv] Thompson, Richard F. Chapter 3: "Will the Mind Become the Brain in the 21st Century?", 41. In *Mind and Brain Sciences in the 21st Century*, edited by Robert L. Solso. Cambridge: The MIT Press, 1999 pbk.

[xvi] Branden, Nathaniel. *The Psychology of Self-Esteem*. Toronto: Bantam Books, Inc., by arrangement with Nash Publishing Corporation, 1969, paperback, 36.

[xvii] Snodgrass, Gay. Chapter 11, "The Memory Trainers", 209. In *Mind and Brain Sciences in the 21st Century*, edited by Robert L. Solso. Cambridge: The MIT Press, 1999 pbk.

[xviii] Eysenck, Hans J. Chapter 15, "The Future of Psychology", 277, 293. In *Mind and Brain Sciences in the 21st Century*, edited by Robert L. Solso. Cambridge: The MIT Press, 1999 pbk.

[xix] Lindzey, Gardner; Calvin S. Hall, and Richard F. Thompson. *Psychology,* 2nd edition. New York: Worth Publishers, Inc., 1975, 1978, page 4.

[xx] Rychlak, Joseph F. Introduction to Personality and Psychotherapy. A theory-Construction Approach. Boston: Houghton Mifflin Company, 1973.

[xxi] ibid., 209.

Chapter 17

[i] Sarason, Irwin G. *Abnormal Psychology*, Second Edition. Englewood Cliffs, N.J.: Prentice-Hall, Inc., 1976, 1972.

[ii] Neel, Ann. *Theories of Psychology: A Handbook*. New York: Schenkman Publishing Company, John Wiley & Sons, 1977.

[iii] Liebert, Robert M., and Michael D. Spiegler. Personality. Strategies and Issues, Third edition. Homewood, Illinois: The Dorsey Press, 1978.

[iv] Lindzey, Gardner; Calvin S. Hall, and Richard F. Thompson. *Psychology,* 2nd edition. New York: Worth Publishers, Inc., 1975, 1978, 695-700.

[v] Eysenck, Hans J. Chapter 15, "The Future of Psychology", 284, 285. In *Mind and Brain Sciences in the 21st Century*, edited by Robert L. Solso. Cambridge: The MIT Press, 1999 pbk.

[vi] ibid., 272.

[vii] *The World Book Encyclopedia*, 1980 ed., s.v. "inquisition", "torquemada, tomás de".

[viii] Branden, Nathaniel. *The Psychology of Self-Esteem*. Toronto: Bantam Books, Inc., by arrangement with Nash Publishing Corporation, 1969, paperback, 68, 69.

[ix] ibid.

[x] Rand, Ayn. *Introduction to Objectivist Epistemology*. New York: The Objectivist, Inc., Fourth Printing, 1973, 73.

[xi] Peikoff, Leonard. *The Ominous Parallels. End of Freedom in America.* New York: Stein and Day, 1982.

[xii] James Randi, see him online at http:// www.randi.org and in particular his *An Encyclopedia of Claims, Frauds, and Hoaxes of the Occult and Supernatural* online at: http:/ / www. randi.org/encyclopedia/

[xiii] Eysenck, Hans J. and Sarjent, Carl. *Explaining the Unexplained, Mysteries of the paranormal.* London : PRION ; Garden City Park, NY : Avery Pub. Group [distributor], 1993, paperback, Preface, 6.

Chapter 18

[i] Branden, Nathaniel. *The Psychology of Self-Esteem.* Toronto: Bantam Books, Inc., by arrangement with Nash Publishing Corporation, 1969, paperback, 3-4.

[ii] Efron, Robert. "Biology without consciousness—And its Consequences". In *The Objectivist*, Volume 7, Number 2 edited by Ayn Rand and Nathaniel Branden. New York: The Objectivist, Inc., February 1968, 6.

[iii] Snodgrass, Gay. Chapter 11, "The Memory Trainers", 209. In *Mind and Brain Sciences in the 21st Century*, edited by Robert L. Solso. Cambridge: The MIT Press, 1999 pbk.

[iv] Rand, Ayn. *Introduction to Objectivist Epistemology.* New York: The Objectivist, Inc., Fourth Printing, 1973, 11.

[v] Efron, Robert. "Biology without consciousness—And its Consequences (Part III)". In *The Objectivist*, Volume 7, Number 4 edited by Ayn Rand and Nathaniel Branden. New York: The Objectivist, Inc., April 1968, 9.

[vi] ibid.

[vii] ibid.

[viii] Peikoff, Leonard. *Objectivism:The Philosophy of Ayn Rand,* Chapter 2—Sense Perception And Volition. New York: Penguin Group, First Printing, December 1991, 52.

The "how" cannot be used to negate the "what," or the "what" the "how"—not if one understands that A is A and that consciousness is consciousness.

[ix] Branden, Nathaniel. *The Psychology of Self-Esteem.* Toronto: Bantam Books, Inc., 4th Printing, March 1972, paperback, Back Cover.

[x] Kagan, Jerome. Chapter 12 "On Future Psychological Categories", 235. In *Mind and Brain Sciences in the 21st Century*, edited by Robert L. Solso. Cambridge: The MIT Press, 1999 pbk.

[xi] As of this day, 2/13/06 the latest version of DSM-N is IV: *Diagnostic and Statistical Manual of Mental Disorders - Fourth Edition (DSM-IV)*, published by the American Psychiatric Association, Washington D.C., 1994, the main diagnostic reference of Mental Health professionals in the United States of America.

[xii] Samenow, Stanton E. *Inside the Criminal Mind.* New York: Times Books division of Random House, 1984.

[xiii] Skinner, B.F. *Beyond Freedom and Dignity.* Toronto/New York: Bantam/Vintage Books/Knopf, 1971 pbk. Front cover to page 1, page 1 through page 215, from page 215 through Back cover—excluding page just before back cover advertising Bantam Book Catalog. Except for this exception the *entire* book is an *assault* on *autonomous* man—an assault with one and only one goal: kill off autonomous man.

[xiv] Sperling, George. Chapter 13 "The Goal of Theory in Experimental Psychology", 253. In *Mind and Brain Sciences in the 21st Century*, edited by Robert L. Solso. Cambridge: The MIT Press, 1999 pbk.

[xv] ibid., 257.

[xvi] ibid., 263.

[xvii] Sagan, Carl, and Ann Druyan. Chapter 2 "What Thin Partitions ... ", 19. In *Mind and Brain Sciences in the 21st Century*, edited by Robert L. Solso. Cambridge: The MIT Press, 1999 pbk.

[xviii] ibid., 22.

[xix] ibid.

[xx] ibid., 23.

[xxi] ibid.

[xxii] Gazzaniga, Michael S. Chapter 9 "What are Brains For?", 157. In *Mind and Brain Sciences in the 21st Century*, edited by Robert L. Solso. Cambridge: The MIT Press, 1999 pbk.

[xxiii] For some examples of first decade, 3rd Millennium (re) tarts see HBO sitcom, *Sex in the City* [is this slip or slop ... or ... a hearing problem, this is the way I've always heard the audio references to this... the correct title is, *Sex and the city...*], any episode, HBO Presents, 2003'ish ±, Hollywood, CA, HBO Studios Santa Monica Blvd. And also

Note: least I be misunderstood here and labeled a prude (though at my fiftiessomething age then and my sixtiessomething age now, being a prude isn't that big a deal) let me tell you (very quickly) about the verbal exchange that used to occur between me and my male friends who thought me a whuse back then for being a stay-at-home husband (see Footnote #81, p. 94).

THEY: Your'e a whuse.
ME: My wife and I—after having been through some really serious psychhological retraining—have simply reversed roles.
THEY: How so?
ME: Well, I now see her as a money-making-machine and she see's me as a sex object.
They, **always** followed this with one of three responses: laughter and/or envy.
But, they also *never* questioned *why* they *have to* use Viagra and me not.

[xxiv] Gazzaniga, Michael S. Chapter 9 "What are Brains For?", 157. In *Mind and Brain Sciences in the 21st Century*, edited by Robert L. Solso. Cambridge: The MIT Press, 1999 pbk.

[xxv] ibid.

[xxvi] Rand, Ayn. *Introduction to Objectivist Epistemology*, expanded second edition Edited by Harry Binswanger and Leonard Peikoff. New York: Meridian, April 1990.

[xxvii] ibid.

[xxviii] Pribram, Karl. Chapter 8: "The Deep and Surface Structures of Memory & Conscious Learning: Toward a 21st-Century Model". In *Mind and Brain Sciences in the 21st Century*, edited by Robert L. Solso. Cambridge: The MIT Press, 1999 pbk.

[xxix] ibid., 146.

[xxx] ibid., 147.

[xxxi] ibid.

[xxxii] ibid.

[xxxiii] ibid., 146.

[xxxiv] DreamWorks Pictures and Twentieth Century Fox present, *The Minority Report*, 146 min. DreamWorks Home Entertainment : Distributed by Twentieth Century Fox Film Corp., c2002, videocassette.

[xxxv] Sagan, Carl, and Ann Druyan. Chapter 2 "What Thin Partitions ... ", 33. In *Mind and Brain Sciences in the 21st Century*, edited by Robert L. Solso. Cambridge: The MIT Press, 1999 pbk.

[xxxvi] ibid., 28.

[xxxvii] ibid.

[xxxviii] ibid., 37.

Chapter 19

[i] Department of Health and Human Services, *Mental Health: A Report of the Surgeon General* (Washington DC, U.S. Government Printing Office, 1999), 57.

[ii] ibid.

[iii] Skinner, B.F. *Beyond Freedom and Dignity.* Toronto/New York: Bantam/Vintage Books/Knopf, 1971 pbk., 216/Acknowledgments.

[iv] Branden, Nathaniel. *The Psychology of Self-Esteem*. Toronto: Bantam Books, Inc., by arrangement with Nash Publishing Corporation, 1969, paperback.

[v] Peikoff, Leonard. *The Ominous Parallels. End of Freedom in America.* New York: Stein and Day, 1982.

[vi] ibid., 148.

References   409

Chapter 20

[i] ... ~~redo:~~ not, OK as is and here it is ... though I paid ninety bucks for the Objectivism search CD [*The Objectivism Research CD-ROM, The Philosophy of Ayn Rand,* Published by Oliver Computing, LLC, Indianapolis, Indiana, April 2004, Rev. 7.] I could not find this reference (and though my tone here sounds negative on the CD I am not, rather I am *quite the contrary*, the CD is a heck of a thing to have and it works very well and I like it (the fact that I bought this CD *expecting* to find this particular reference but didn't is ... ? ... it's... what? ... tough luck?...my own fault? ... what? ... it's ... yor usual crybabyness and fear of saying, I know what I know ... AR said this somewhere and I know it, the fact that I can't find the source right now is ... too bad). I like the CD so much in fact I wished "they" [the good they] had everything AR ever said or wrote on CD because THEN I'd be able to find where she said/wrote what I am here [et elsewhere] saying and/or believe she said. So ... I guess ... until and unless ... I can officially document the source for this "claim" I will have to conclude that this is an example of an Objectivism-In-Me "problem" and look forward to *BiO Spiritualism* Volume Next where I might be able to fill in that which is undocumented here in *BiO Spiritualism* Volume Here/Now (see *vi* below also and *vii* too).

[ii] ibid.

[iii] Binswanger, Harry, *Emotions*, 3-tape set, CB72D, Ayn Rand Bookstore c/o The Ayn Rand Institute, Irvine, CA, 2002, audiocassettes.

[iv] Branden, Nathaniel. *Basic Relaxation and Ego-Strengthening Program.* Los Angeles: The Biocentric Institute Inc., 1973. Audiocassette.

[v] Binswanger, Harry. *The Biological Basis of Teleological Concepts.* Edited version of doctoral dissertation written from 1969-1973. Los Angeles: The Ayn Rand Institute Press, 1976.

[vi] Deering, Gary. " 'The (his subconscious) Book of Somewhere' ". Shoreview and St. Paul: Recall & Remember, 2005, page N_1 (with N = actual source TBD and presented in Book II). Whether or not it was C. D. Broad I'm not 100% sure, but I am 100% sure it was relying on *some* philosopher to make his point.

[vii] ibid., p. N_2, with N as previously. Somewhere I read or heard it said that Ayn Rand had said "...Dominique was me [AR] on a bad day ...", but I can't find the

source right now. If I am wrong on this point and Ayn Rand meant to include self-forgiveness in her advice giving then we can thank our lucky stars *even more* for Biocentric Psychology, which does *not* promote such bad advice.

[viii] Szasz, Thomas S. *The Myth of Mental Illness*. New York: Harper and Row, 1974.

[ix] Branden, Nathaniel. *The Psychology of Self-Esteem*. Toronto: Bantam Books, Inc., by arrangement with Nash Publishing Corporation, 1969, paperback, 68, 69.

> **Notes**: Using "bachelor" as the *means* to demonstrating that an *exception* to the *definition-should-be-positive-not negative* "rule of definitions" in epistemology, causes ~~m(y)/our~~ ones mind—in this the first decade of the 3rd Millennium—to go off on a tangent ... of sorts.
>
> A tangent here (in Chapter 20) that we can (appropriately) exploit in order to show *a* (that is, *one*, that is, moi's) "BiO Spiritualist's" approach to solving "problems"—in this case a "social" problem.
>
> One big social issue of our time is whether or not "we" should allow "gays" to marry. That is, whether or not "we" should allow them to enter into a moral-legal contract sanctioned by the group (society) at large.
>
> I, qua heterosexual male, like to think that since "we" invented marriage (probably circa the same time Jung's cavemen invented the wheel) we get to keep the term and the new people to the table have to—or *should* have to—use a *different* term. So why not the next one in line (alphabetically speaking), that is, they should refer to their moral-legal union as a, "narriage" with *narriage* having all the legal rights and privileges currently granted to marriage.
>
> This "sounds" ok to me except for one factor—the slippery-slope factor, which can and does go like this: if "we" allow *narriages* does it then follow that those who will eventually want to marry their pets (this inevitability is as predictable as rain given that pet insurance is a new thing now and so over the ensuing decades its premiums will rise to such a level that these people will want to marry their pets and include them in their work coverage) "should" be able to do so and all we have to do is call these "marriages", *not* marriages, *nor* narriages but rather, oarriages

and then ad infinitum—parriages, qarriages, rarriages, etcetera and so on—until the concept "zarriage" is devoid of any meaning.

Well if we were animals who couldn't think in principles the slippery-slope factor would be a legitimate concern.

But we are not. We are animals who *can* think in principles and the principle, or at least a lead here to the principle, is coming up with a proper—that is, reality based—definition of marriage.

A *marriage* is a voluntary moral-legal union between two *volition* possessing beings who have not—for reasons beyond their control—lost their individual power of volition.

This then solves the slippery-slope problem (animals below man do NOT have volition) and *points* to a solution to the marriage vs. narriage problem.

But it does not yet solve it because we don't know for sure whether volition is the most fundamental, essential ingredient or whether volition AND sex of partners is/are? (For example, if everybody had been gay and narried since Jung's cavemen days, we probably wouldn't even be here now to discuss it as an issue—evolution would automatically deselect those who do not engage in sex with the opposite sex and produce offspring as a byproduct. However, since BiO Spiritualists are a-theists we can't rely on the Pope's (Pope's as symbol for "The Church's") argument that *procreation* is the *only* moral justification for sex and so are still not able to end this discussion, which is to say ....)

Since there is not enough space here to develop this theme fully, I plan to deal with it in future writings and let what I have written here so far stand as a two edged sword. First edge is as introduction to the problem of "marriage vs. narriage" and second edge is as a kind of demonstration of the way ones thinking *can be* affected by ones choice to say YES! to BOTH Objectivism AND Biocentric Psychology.

They *are* the greatest.

Don't 'ya just love 'em?!?!?!?!?!

[x] Rand, Ayn. *Playboy's Interview with Ayn Rand.* New York: The Intellectual Activist, 1964, p. 6.

[xi] Rand, Ayn. *The Virtue of Selfishness.* New York: New American Library, 1961-1964, p. 3.

[xii] Rand, Ayn. "THE FACE WITHOUT PAIN OR FEAR OF GUILT," Part II, Chapter IX in *Atlas Shrugged.* New York: Random House, 1957, page 636, (hc).

[xiii] Peikoff, Leonard. "The Analytic-Synthetic Dichotomy", 1967. Included essay, 119-164, in Rand, Ayn, *Introduction to Objectivist Epistemology.* New York: New American Library, First Mentor Printing, April 1979.

[xiv] Universal Pictures and Lawrence Gordon present a Gordon Company/Davis Entertainment Company/Licht/Mueller Film Corp. production, a Kevin Reynolds film, *Waterworld.* 136 min. Universal City, CA : MCA Universal Home Video, 1996, videocassette.

[xv] Peikoff, Leonard. *The Ominous Parallels. End of Freedom in America.* New York: Stein and Day, 1982.

[xvi] ibid., 37.

[xvii] Rychlak, Joseph F. Introduction to Personality and Psychotherapy. A theory-Construction Approach. Boston: Houghton Mifflin Company, 1973. 11.

[xviii] ibid., 10.

[xix] Gardner, Howard. *The Mind's New Science. A History of the Cognitive Revolution.* With a new epilogue by the author: "Cognitive Science After 1984." Basic Books, A *Division of* Harper Collins *Publishers*, 1985, 1987, 59.

[xx] Alston, William P., and Richard B. Brandt, , eds. 1978. *The Problems of Philosophy.* Boston: Allyn and Bacon, Inc., 625.

[xxi] Rand, Ayn. *Introduction to Objectivist Epistemology.* New York: The Objectivist, Inc., Fourth Printing, 1973, 11.

[xxii] Alston, William P., and Richard B. Brandt, , eds. 1978. *The Problems of Philosophy.* Boston: Allyn and Bacon, Inc., 625, 626.

[xxiii] See (hear) Dr. Binswanger's candle example in: Binswanger, Harry. *Consciousness and Identification,* copyrighted 1989 H. Binswanger, Audiocassette Lecture #1, Tape 1 of Lectures 1 through 3 on six Cassette tapes.

[xxiv] Rand, Ayn. *For the new Intellectual.* New York: Signet Books (Ninth Printing is an authorized reprint of a hardcover edition published by Random House, Inc.) published by The New American Library, Inc., 1961, page 32.

[xxv] Rand, Ayn. *Introduction to Objectivist Epistemology.* New York: The Objectivist, Inc., Fourth Printing, 1973, 11.

[xxvi] Gardner, Howard. *The Mind's New Science. A History of the Cognitive Revolution.* With a new epilogue by the author: "Cognitive Science After 1984." Basic Books, A *Division of* Harper Collins *Publishers*, 1985, 1987, 308.

[xxvii] ibid., 310.

[xxviii] ibid., 311.

[xxix] Rand, Ayn. *Introduction to Objectivist Epistemology.* New York: The Objectivist, Inc., Fourth Printing, 1973, 12.

[xxx] ibid., 11.

Chapter 21

[i] Twentieth Century Fox Presents, *Desk Set*. 103 minutes, Color, 1990. Videocassette. Originally released as a motion picture in 1957 starring Spencer Tracy and Katharine Hepburn; Screenplay by Phoebe and Henry Ephron, based on the play by William Marchant; produced by Henry Ephron, directed by Walter Lang.

[ii] Rand, Ayn. *Introduction to Objectivist Epistemology.* New York: The Objectivist, Inc., July 1966, Volume 5 of 6, Number 7 of 12, p. 5.

[iii] The side point I was going to highlight here was that *Cognitive Therapy*, a la Aaron T. Beck, has some good to it but *Cognitive Psychology*, a la Ulric Neisser, Robert L. Solso, et al., does not and so one should not confuse the two and especially one should not conclude that Cognitive Therapy is applied Cognitive Psychology. It is not. But since this side point is just that—an aside—I will not deal with it here beyond this but may revisit it in future works. Another point to notice is that *based on my own personal experience* "shape" and "color" *are* two fundamental streams that the brain deals with—that is see the example I give on this same page about my first "subconscious image".

Chapter 23

[i] Peikoff, Leonard. *The Ominous Parallels. End of Freedom in America.* New York: Stein and Day, 1982.

[ii] www.aynrand.org

Chapter 24

[i] *The Ayn Rand Lexicon: Objectivism from A to Z.* Edited by Harry Binswanger. New York: New American Library, 1986.

Afterword

[i] Reich, Wilhelm. *Wilhelm Reich Selected Writings. An Introduction to Orgonomy.* New York: Farrar, Straus and Giroux, 1951-1973. First Printing, 1973, page xix.

www.ingramcontent.com/pod-product-compliance
Lightning Source LLC
Chambersburg PA
CBHW080533300426
44111CB00017B/2699